W9-BDV-068

This Book Comes With Lots of
FREE Online Resources

Nolo's award-winning website has a page dedicated just to this book. Here you can:

KEEP UP TO DATE. When there are important changes to the information in this book, we'll post updates.

GET DISCOUNTS ON NOLO PRODUCTS. Get discounts on hundreds of books, forms, and software.

READ BLOGS. Get the latest info from Nolo authors' blogs.

LISTEN TO PODCASTS. Listen to authors discuss timely issues on topics that interest you.

WATCH VIDEOS. Get a quick introduction to a legal topic with our short videos.

And that's not all.
Nolo.com contains thousands of articles on everyday legal and business issues, plus a plain-English law dictionary, all written by Nolo experts and available for free. You'll also find more useful **books, software, online apps, downloadable forms,** plus a **lawyer directory.**

Get updates and more at
www.nolo.com/back-of-book/PEND.html

☒☒ NOLO # The Trusted Name
(but don't take our word for it)

"In Nolo you can trust."
THE NEW YORK TIMES

"Nolo is always there in a jam as the nation's premier publisher of do-it-yourself legal books."
NEWSWEEK

"Nolo publications… guide people simply through the how, when, where and why of the law."
THE WASHINGTON POST

"[Nolo's] … material is developed by experienced attorneys who have a knack for making complicated material accessible."
LIBRARY JOURNAL

"When it comes to self-help legal stuff, nobody does a better job than Nolo…"
USA TODAY

"The most prominent U.S. publisher of self-help legal aids."
TIME MAGAZINE

"Nolo is a pioneer in both consumer and business self-help books and software."
LOS ANGELES TIMES

7th Edition

Patent Pending in 24 Hours

WITHDRAWN

Attorneys Richard Stim & David Pressman

SEVENTH EDITION	JANUARY 2016
Editor	RICHARD STIM
Illustrations	SASHA STIM-VOGEL
Book Design	TERRI HEARSH
Proofreading	SUSAN CARLSON GREENE
Index	JULIE SHAWVAN
Printing	BANG PRINTING

Stim, Richard, author.
  Patent pending in 24 hours / by Attorneys Richard Stim & David Pressman. -- Seventh edition.
      pages cm
  Includes index.
  ISBN 978-1-4133-2201-9 (pbk.) -- ISBN 978-1-4133-2202-6 (ebook)
  1. Patent practice--United States--Popular works. I. Pressman, David, 1937- author. II. Title. III. Title: Patent pending in twenty-four hours.
  KF3120.Z9S75 2015
  346.7304'86--dc23

                              2015023490

This book covers only United States law, unless it specifically states otherwise.

Please note

We believe accurate, plain-English legal information should help you solve many of your own legal problems. But this text is not a substitute for personalized advice from a knowledgeable lawyer. If you want the help of a trained professional—and we'll always point out situations in which we think that's a good idea—consult an attorney licensed to practice in your state.

Dedication

Thanks to David Pressman and Susan Putney.

R.S.

I thank Rich Stim and the other staff at Nolo and my clients for their good work and helpful suggestions in making this book a reality.

D.P.

About the Authors

Richard Stim is an attorney specializing in intellectual property. He is the author of several other intellectual property books including *Getting Permission: How to License & Clear Copyrighted Materials Online & Off* (Nolo); *Music Law: How to Run Your Band's Business* (Nolo); and *Profit From Your Idea: How to Make Smart Licensing Deals* (Nolo). He writes the *Dear Rich* blog (http://dearrichblog.com) where he answers questions regarding intellectual property.

David Pressman has had over 40 years' experience in the patent profession, as a patent examiner for the U.S. Patent Office, as a patent attorney for Philco-Ford Corp., Elco Corp., and Varian Associates, as a columnist for *EDN Magazine* and Entrepreneur.com, and as an instructor at San Francisco State University. He contributed the Patent, Trademark, and Copyright entries to the *World Book Encyclopedia*. He's also an inventor, with two patents issued. When not writing, dabbling in electronics, programming, inventing, or playing his trumpet, he practices as a patent lawyer in San Francisco. Originally from Philadelphia, he has a B.S. in Electrical Engineering from Pennsylvania State University. He spent his first year in law school at the University of Pennsylvania and completed his second and third years at George Washington University, where he served on the Law Review and received a Juris Doctor degree. He is also active in the general semantics and vegetarian movements. His mother, Mildred Phillips, is also a writer, having composed lyrics for numerous published songs, including Bill Haley's "Mambo Rock."

Table of Contents

Appendixes

The Provisional Patent Application

"You don't get up in the morning and say I'm going to invent something. It doesn't work like that. What might happen is you might trip over the carpet. And you think to yourself, 'I'll go and nail the carpet down.' And as you walk into your workshop, you think, 'I haven't finished paying for the carpet yet so I can't put nails through it. So, suppose I screw to the edge of the deck, a piece of plastic that would hold the carpet down. Then it could look neat and stop me from tripping over the carpet.' That's how an invention comes about."

—Trevor Bayliss (inventor of the Freeplay radio), interview on "The Todd Mundt Show," NPR, February 8, 2001

Congratulations—you invented something! So what's next? If you're like most inventors, your first concern is to make sure nobody can steal your great idea.

There used to be only two foolproof ways to lock in a claim of invention ownership. One way was to build and test the invention and to keep a solid record of the inventing process (usually accomplished with a properly witnessed and dated notebook). Unfortunately, building and testing an invention, unless it's very simple, is beyond the capability and budget of most inventors.

The second method for claiming ownership was to get a patent. A patent gives you the right to prevent others from making, using, or selling your invention for a limited period of time. But this protection comes at a price: You can expect to spend anywhere from $5,000 to $10,000 or more to file a patent application through an attorney. And because fewer than 3% of all patented inventions ever make any money, you might never see a return on your investment. This puts some inventors in a bind: If they don't file for a patent right away, someone else might steal their idea. But if they file too soon, they risk spending money on legal protection for an invention that may not be commercial.

Wouldn't it be great if there was an inexpensive way to establish an official claim to your invention before filing for a patent—so you could figure out whether your invention would turn a profit before you pay to protect it? Well, there is—the provisional patent application.

In this chapter, we'll explain the benefits—and the disadvantages—of filing a provisional patent application. To give you an idea of what a provisional patent application looks like, we've also included two examples in the last section of this chapter, one based on William Lear's car radio, and the other based on Louis Pasteur's process for improving beer and ale (later to be known as "pasteurization").

After reading this book, you may decide that the provisional patent application is not for you. You may determine that your invention lacks commercial potential or is not patentable. Regardless of whether you ultimately file a provisional patent application, this book will help you see your invention in a wider context—in relation to patent law, licensing opportunities, and other inventions within your field—rather than just as an isolated creation on your workbench.

How a Provisional Patent Application Works

In 1995, President Clinton signed a law that allowed inventors to file a provisional patent application. This process offers an effective, fast, and cheap way to safeguard your place in line at the United States Patent and Trademark Office (USPTO) for up to one year until you file a regular patent application.

A provisional patent application (sometimes referred to as a PPA) consists of text and drawings that describe how to make and use your invention. It's a short document—often five to ten pages—written in plain English, with none of the arcane language used in regular patent applications. In fact, if you've written a technical article that accurately describes how to make and use your invention, you can submit that as part of your application. You do not need to hire a draftsperson to prepare formal drawings; you can furnish informal drawings as long as they—in conjunction with your written statement—show how to make and use your invention. You can either send your description, drawings, a return postcard, and a cover sheet and fee transmittal form to the USPTO by USPS Express Mail (along with the fee—$130 for small entities or $65 for micro entities—discussed later),

> The first home computer—the 1975 Altair—didn't have a monitor and had toggle switches instead of a keyboard and mouse.

or you can transmit the materials electronically with a credit card charge authorization (as we'll explain in Chapter 6). Once this is done, you have established an effective filing date for your invention and you can use the term "patent pending" on your invention—at least for 12 months from the filing date.

A PPA will *not*, by itself, get you a patent. In order to patent your invention and obtain some of the benefits listed above, you must file a regular patent application—a more complex document—and the application must be approved by the USPTO. The provisional patent application is a simple, inexpensive strategy for preserving your rights while you decide whether to file for a regular patent. But if you want that patent, you will have to file a regular application within a year after you file your provisional application.

What If You Don't File Your Regular Application on Time?

You won't automatically lose patent rights if you fail to file a regular patent application within a year after you file the provisional application. But you will lose the benefits we describe in this chapter—for example, the earlier filing date and the right to claim "patent pending" status. Under the first-to-file patent law, effective March 16, 2013, if you file a regular patent application for an invention whose provisional patent application has "expired," you will not be entitled to the benefit of the filing date of the PPA. If the invention has been publicly disclosed or offered for sale, this will prevent you from filing a regular patent application *after* the public disclosure or offer for sale, unless the disclosure or offer for sale was made by you or someone acting for you and it was made less than one year before the filing date of the regular patent application. However, as a general rule, it's best to avoid any disclosure prior to the filing date.

RESOURCE

Patent It Yourself. Some readers may find it helpful to use David Pressman and Thomas J. Tuytschaevers' *Patent It Yourself* (Nolo) as a companion resource while using this book to prepare their provisional patent applications.

Federal Circuit Requires Clarity in Provisional Patent Applications

In 2002, the Court of Appeals for the Federal Circuit (CAFC)—the federal appeals court that specializes in patent cases—issued an important ruling involving provisional patent applications. The case, *New Railhead Mfg. Co. v. Vermeer Mfg. Co. & Earth Tool Co.*, App. No. 02-1028 (7/30/02), involved two patents: one for a drill bit for horizontal directional drilling of rock formations and the other for a method of horizontal directional drilling. Both patents claimed the filing date of a provisional patent application. The lawsuit occurred when New Railhead Manufacturing, the company that owned the patents, pursued a company it believed was infringing.

At the heart of both patents was an invention in which a drill bit was angled with respect to its housing (known as a "sonde housing") and operated at a specific heel-to-toe ratio. The CAFC ruled that the underlying provisional patent application failed to adequately describe the angled structure of the drill bits, and therefore, the company that filed the patents could not get the benefit of the provisional filing date.

The court wrote, "The provisional [patent application] never states that the drill bit is angled with respect to the sonde housing, does not mention or describe the toe or the heel, and does not mention or define the heel-toe ratio." Unfortunately, New Railhead Manufacturing had made offers for sale prior to filing its provisional applications and as a result of the one-year-sale rule, both patents were invalidated.

The *New Railhead* case reinforces the principles described in this chapter: If you want the benefit of the provisional filing date for a later patent, your provisional application must describe the invention in such full, clear, concise, and exact terms as to enable any person skilled in the art to make and use it. If you leave out an element of your invention, fail to explain all of the operating elements, or if your later patent application adds new matter, you won't be credited with the earlier filing date. If, after preparing your provisional patent application, you are in doubt as to whether it meets the legal requirements, seek the advice of a patent professional. Information about locating an attorney can be found in Appendix E.

Some Patent Basics

In case you're not familiar with patent law, here are a few basics that will help you understand the material in this chapter. (We discuss patent law in more detail in Chapter 2.)

The USPTO issues three types of patents—utility patents, plant patents, and design patents. Utility patents protect what we commonly think of as "inventions." When we use the term "patents" in this book, we are always talking about utility patents, unless otherwise noted.

An invention can be virtually anything that's functional. Utility patents protect a broad range of inventions: mechanical devices, medical procedures, chemical formulas, methods of doing business, software programs, animal and plant life, and improvements on past inventions.

Your invention must be new. The USPTO grants patents for new (or "novel") inventions only. Your invention isn't new if someone previously invented it, patented it, or wrote about it prior to your filing date. There is an exception, however, if you (the inventor) or anyone who obtained the subject matter from you made certain disclosures of the claimed invention within a limited one-year grace period prior to filing.

A patent is a "license to sue." If you get a patent, you can stop others from making, selling, or using your invention for 17 to 18 years. Think of your patent as a "hunting license"—one that gives you the right to sue infringers for damages and other legal remedies.

Advantages of Filing a Provisional Patent Application

Filing a provisional patent application confers a number of benefits:

- You can take up to a year to assess whether your invention will sell before committing to the higher cost of filing and prosecuting (the official term for "pursuing") a regular application for a patent.
- You can use the "Patent Pending" notice to deter others from copying your invention.

- You establish an official U.S. patent application filing date for the invention.
- Your application is preserved in confidence.
- The expiration date of your patent will effectively be extended, if the USPTO later approves your application.

We discuss each of these benefits in detail in the sections that follow.

Assess the Commercial Potential of Your Invention Before Filing for a Patent

Alexander Graham Bell almost didn't get the patent for the telephone. On the day that he filed his patent application, a rival inventor, Elisha Gray, filed for the same invention. Historians attribute Bell's victory at the USPTO to several factors (see Appendix A), the most important of which was that Gray never bothered to fight for the patent. Gray, a businessman, didn't believe that the telephone had any commercial potential and filed his patent documents as an afterthought. He believed (as did his business partners and attorneys) that the telephone was a novelty not worth pursuing.

Gray and his attorneys were wrong about the commercial potential of the telephone (as was Western Union, which turned down an opportunity to buy Bell's patent for $100,000). Two years later, when the patent's value became clear, Western Union backed Gray in an unsuccessful lawsuit to terminate the Bell patent.

But it's unfair to judge Gray harshly in hindsight. Determining the commercial potential of an invention can be difficult—sometimes even impossible—until you've actually tried to sell it.

Considering that fewer than 3% of all patents ever make money, the vast majority of inventors probably shouldn't bother with the time and expense of filing a patent application. Unfortunately, there's no accurate way to predict whether any invention will fall into that lucky 3%. What if the invention is a commercial success but no patent protects it from being stolen by others? Inventors dutifully prepare and file patent applications as insurance against this possibility.

> **Dr. Frederick Banting,** who patented a method of controlling diabetes through insulin injections, was very concerned about who took credit for his invention. He tackled one associate who took credit, knocking his head against the floor. He rewarded another by giving him half of his Nobel Prize money.

Once you file the provisional patent application, you will have almost a year to assess the commercial potential of your invention before you have to prepare a patent application. That should be enough time to make a preliminary assessment about commercial potential. If everybody you've shown it to says "no thanks" and backs away from you slowly, there's probably no reason to bother filing a regular patent application.

Watch Out for Scam Artists

The Dallas Morning News included the following statement in an article:

"Many young companies don't have the money now to seek out a permanent patent—which can cost $10,000 to $15,000 per application—and are asking Mr. Klinger to help them get a one-year patent. Provisional patents cost less than $1,000 to file."

Oops! As you know by now, the provisional patent application does not, by itself, get you a patent; it merely provides a placeholder or a record of your invention that you can rely on—at least for 12 months—to support a regular patent application.

But misconceptions about provisional patent applications reappear with such frequency—even in newspapers—that a lot of inventors believe them. It's no wonder that scam invention promotion companies can prey on unknowing inventors by claiming that a provisional application will get you patent rights. The USPTO website (www.uspto.gov) and the Federal Trade Commission website (www.ftc.gov) both offer tips on how to avoid disreputable invention promotion companies.

Use a "Patent Pending" Notice to Warn Potential Thieves

There's a certain cachet to labeling your invention "patent pending" or "patent applied for." Putting those words on the bottom of your invention or in an advertisement sends a message that you've filed an official claim on the invention. This marking often deters manufacturers from stealing your invention—they do not want to pay for creating tooling or molds to produce the invention if they know you may get a patent for it.

In Alexander Graham Bell's day, the only way you could claim patent pending status was to pay an attorney to prepare and file a regular patent application or file one yourself. Nowadays, you can use the label once you have filed a provisional patent application. (Using the terms patent pending or patent applied for without filing an application is a criminal offense.)

> James Murray Spangler was an asthmatic janitor who invented the vacuum cleaner to protect his lungs while cleaning rugs.

Keep in mind that marking your invention patent pending doesn't give you any patent rights. You cannot stop anyone from copying, selling, or using your invention during this period. Patent rights do not kick in until after your regular patent application is approved. The label simply lets the world know that you have staked a patent claim and are waiting for the patent to issue. As we explain in "Preserve Your Application in Confidence," below, under certain circumstances—if you file a regular patent application that is published by the USPTO before the patent is granted—you may be able to sue for damages during part of the pendency period.

Establish an Official U.S. Patent Application Filing Date for Your Invention

Filing a provisional patent application gives you an official patent filing date. Under the current patent system (as of March 16, 2013) the United States rewards the inventor who is first to file (FTF) with a patent. In other words, the inventor with the earliest official filing date wins the patent.

The filing date is also important for another reason. If your patent later issues, it becomes part of the prior art against which other patent applications are judged. The date your invention becomes prior art (known as the "102(e) date" because it references 35 U.S.C. § 102(e) of the patent law) is the date you filed your provisional patent application. Other inventors who try to patent the same invention must prove that they invented their creation before the 102(e) date of your invention.

> **EXAMPLE:** Bob files a provisional patent application on April 1, 2014. He then waits a year and files his regular patent application on March 1, 2015. The USPTO later issues him a patent. Sam invents a mobile telephone switching system identical to Bob's invention but he doesn't file until April 10, 2014.

Bob's provisional patent application will be considered prior art and can be used to block Sam's application.

Preserve Your Application in Confidence

If you're like most inventors, you have a secretive streak. And that makes sense—after all, if word got out about your invention, somebody else might claim rights or instigate a dispute at the USPTO. Because of this, most inventors won't disclose anything about their inventions, except under the terms of a signed nondisclosure agreement. (We provide suggestions for a nondisclosure agreement in Appendix B to this book.)

The basic bicycle design devised in the 1880s by J.K. Starley—two wheels of equal size with a crank mechanism in between—has stayed the same for over a century.

The provisional patent application guards your secrecy while preserving your rights at the USPTO. Nobody at the USPTO will read your provisional patent application unless you file a regular application within 12 months and you need to rely on the date of your PPA because a dispute arises with another inventor as to your rights (or the PTO cited a reference against your patent application that has an effective date earlier than your regular patent application but not earlier than your PPA). Otherwise, the PTO will never even read your PPA and it will sit safely tucked away in the PTO's files.

Please, Mr. Postman

According to inventors' lore, you can prove the date of your invention by describing your invention and mailing a copy of the description to yourself—that is, by certified or registered mail. Supposedly, the postmark on the sealed envelope proves your date of invention. Our advice—*Fuggedaboudit!* The courts and the USPTO refuse to accept such so-called "post office patents" as evidence of patent priority. In addition, the date of invention became largely irrelevant after March 16, 2013, when the United States adopted a first-to-file patent system.

If you file a regular patent application, the USPTO will treat that application with secrecy for the first 18 months of the examining process. Approximately 18 months after you file your regular patent application, the USPTO will publish your application (unless you requested nonpublication at the time you filed). Publication can be a good thing. It paves the way for you to sue later (after you get your patent) for infringements that occurred after the patent is published. On the other hand, it can be a bad thing if your secrets are released, but your patent isn't granted.

Extend the Expiration Date of Any Patent That Later Issues

Your patent expires 20 years after the date you file your regular patent application. However, you don't get 20 years of patent rights. Because the USPTO takes approximately 12 to 36 (or more) months to complete the examination and because you don't get any rights until the patent actually issues, most patent owners will have only 17 to 18 years of patent rights. That's unfortunate because many inventions enjoy their best commercial returns during the final years of their patents.

Formica was so named because it was created as a substitute "for mica," an expensive natural substance used in electrical insulation.

Filing a provisional patent application can stop the clock for at least a year on patent examination. Your 20-year term starts from the date you file your regular patent application, not your provisional patent application. So your patent rights, if the patent issues, end one year later than they would have if you filed a regular patent application instead of a provisional.

> **EXAMPLE:** Loren files a regular patent application on March 1, 2014. If her application is approved, the patent will expire on March 1, 2034. If Loren files a provisional patent application for her invention on March 1, 2014 and then waits a year to file her regular patent application, the resulting patent will expire on March 1, 2035.

Advantages for Foreign Applicants

Inventors living outside the United States can also benefit from filing a provisional patent application. Here's why:

- Unlike a regular patent application (that must be filed in English), a provisional patent application can be filed in any language.
- Like their U.S. counterparts, the foreign inventor can obtain the earliest possible prior-art date—the date against which competing patent applications will be judged.
- If the foreign inventor files the provisional patent application and the home country patent application at the same time, the foreign inventor—like the U.S. inventor—can preserve ownership rights in the United States and extend the life of the U.S. patent, as discussed in the previous section.

Potential Disadvantages of Filing a Provisional Application

After reading about all of the advantages we've described, you're probably ready to sharpen your pencil and get down to work on your provisional patent application. But before you do, there are some potential drawbacks you should be aware of.

Inaccuracy Will Undo Your Protection

If your provisional application fails to explain how to make and use your invention in "full, clear, concise, and exact" terms, you can't count on it for any of the purposes described in this chapter—for example, an early filing date, proof of invention, or constructive reduction to practice. Leaving out an element of your invention or failing to explain all of the operating elements could be fatal inaccuracies. Other inaccuracies include using faulty supporting data or drawings that don't match the written description. Deliberate inaccuracies will also destroy your patent hopes—for example, if you are not the true inventor or you filed even though you knew the invention did not qualify for a patent.

Modifications Require a New Provisional Application

If you modify the manner in which your invention operates or add any new technical information that was not in the provisional application (known as "new matter"), you cannot rely on the date of the provisional patent application for such new matter. You can file a new provisional application that reflects these changes. Adding, subtracting, or modifying parts, or changing the structure or operation of the parts would all qualify as modifications. You will not be able to rely on your provisional patent application date for these new developments.

You Must File Foreign Patent Applications Within a Year

You must file patent applications in any country in which you seek protection within one year of your provisional patent application's filing date. If you fail to file for foreign patent protection within one year of that date, you will lose any right to obtain the benefit of your provisional patent application's filing date in foreign countries.

If you miss the one-year deadline, you can still file in foreign countries—provided you have not sold, publicly used, or published your invention before the foreign filing date. This could be a problem if, during the period between your U.S. and foreign filing, someone else filed for a similar invention. Since the United States accounts for one-quarter to one-third of all sales for most patented inventions, many inventors are not interested in pursuing foreign patent rights. However, if you think that a foreign manufacturer may want licensing rights, it's generally a good idea to preserve your foreign patent rights. We discuss foreign patents in more detail in Chapter 6.

Preparing Your Provisional Patent Application

Believe it or not, you really can get your provisional patent application on file within 24 hours, as promised in the title of this book. But your overriding concern should not be speed; it should be accuracy. How fast you prepare and file your provisional patent application will depend on your knowledge of patent law, your familiarity with inventions similar to yours, and your ability to accurately describe your invention.

In order to properly prepare a provisional patent application, you will have to:

- learn some patent law basics
- learn about the prior art associated with your invention, and
- accurately describe how to make and use your invention.

That's a tall order and we've only got about 23 hours left, so we'd better get started. But before we do, here are examples of provisional patent applications for two historic inventions. We made these up to give you a sense of what a provisional application should look like.

Drinking Beer and Listening to the Car Radio: Two Provisional Patent Applications

If you like drinking beer or listening to the car radio, you can thank Louis Pasteur and William H. Lear. There were no provisional patent applications available when these men created their inventions—both Pasteur and Lear filed regular patent applications to preserve their rights. In order to give you an idea of how simple it can be to draft a provisional patent application, we have reduced these two patents to provisional applications. The full text of each patent is included in Appendix A so that you can compare these with the real patents. We've included the original patent drawings with each provisional patent application but, as we explain in Chapter 4, you can furnish less-formal drawings. You will find more examples of provisional applications of famous (and not-so-famous) inventions in Appendix A.

Louis Pasteur

Pasteur's Improvement to Making Beer (Pasteurization)

Background: Prior to Louis Pasteur's invention, the production of beer was hindered because the boiled extract or seasoned hop (known as "the wort") was exposed to air. That exposure affected the quality and amount of beer produced as well as the stability of the beer—that is, how fast it spoiled.

Pasteur discovered that by preventing exposure to air, a larger quantity and better quality of beer could be produced. Pasteur's process—later known as pasteurization—partially sterilized the beer and subsequently was used to sterilize liquids such as milk and orange juice, as well as cheese. His improvement in Brewing Beer and Ale was patented in France in 1871 and in the United States in January 1873.

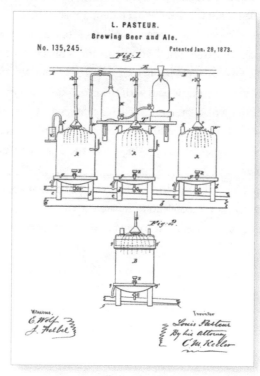

Illustration 1

USPTO Cautions Regarding Provisional Patent Applications

Note that the USPTO has published the following cautions regarding provisional patent applications:

- Provisional patent applications are not examined on their merits.
- The date of a provisional patent application cannot be claimed if a regular patent application has not been filed within one year.
- A provisional patent application cannot claim the benefit of an earlier application (foreign or domestic).
- The disclosure of a provisional patent application must be clear and complete enough so that an ordinary person skilled in the field of the invention can make and use the invention.
- All contributors to the inventive subject matter of the provisional patent application must be named in the provisional patent application.
- The regular patent application must name at least one inventor who was named in the provisional patent application.
- In order for a regular patent application to claim the date of the provisional patent application, the provisional patent application must be filed with the proper fee and must be complete.
- If the basic fee is not paid with the provisional patent application, the fees can be paid later, but the PTO charges a penalty fee.
- Provisional patent applications are not available for designs.
- No subject matter can be added once the provisional patent application is filed.
- No patent will result from the provisional patent application unless a regular patent application is filed within a year or the provisional patent application itself is converted to a regular patent application.

A Provisional Patent Application for "Pasteurization"

I discovered a better way to brew beer and ale. My process prevents the wort (the boiled extract of malt or material seasoned with malt or other qualifying ingredient seasoned with hops) from exposure to air. The result—compared to existing methods of beer production—is the production of a larger quantity of beer as well as a beer that is more aromatic and less likely to deteriorate in transit or storage.

I accomplish this by expelling the air from the boiled wort while it is confined in a closed vessel (or vessels).

The attached drawing helps to explain my invention. Three casks AAA (Fig. 1), made of iron, wood, or other suitable materials, are supported on stands below a water pipe E. The water pipe has branches, each with a valve, and at the end of each branch, a flexible hose and spray nozzle P. On another stand T is an apparatus MM that generates carbonic-acid gas. The carbonic gas is supplied to the casks and is released from the casks at the escape tubes x which extend into cups or chambers v from which the gas can be collected by a gasometer.

The wort is prepared in the usual manner and while boiling hot is placed in a cask. Carbonic-acid gas is conveyed into the cask for the purpose of expelling air. There must be a thorough penetration of carbonic-acid gas into the liquid to expel all contained air.

Then, the water pipe sprays the cask to cool it. A trough c is placed below the casks to collect the water. As the temperature is reduced to about 20 to 23 degrees Celsius (68–73 degrees Fahrenheit), the yeast or fermenting material is added to induce fermentation. After first fermentation, the beer can be sent through the valves R into casks or barrels for future use.

The beer does not have to be removed and fermentation can be completed in the cask. But in this case, a small quantity of air may be drawn into the cask to speed fermentation. The air drawn into the tube should be filtered through cotton or passed through a hot tube to kill or extract any germs that it may contain. The apparatus shown is adapted for making small quantities of beer but the capacity may be varied quite easily.

William Lear

Lear's Car Radio

Background: If you like to listen to music in your car, you can thank William Lear who, with his friend Elmer Wavering, coinvented the first car radio in 1930. Unable to afford a booth fee to show their product at an automotive trade show, Lear and Wavering parked outside the convention center, played their radio and took orders in the parking lot. Lear's company sold the radio device under the trademark *Motorola*—combining "motor" and Victrola—and it was an instant hit. But for Lear, that was only the beginning—he went on to invent the eight-track tape format and navigation aids for aircraft. He later founded Lear, Inc., the supplier of the Lear jet.

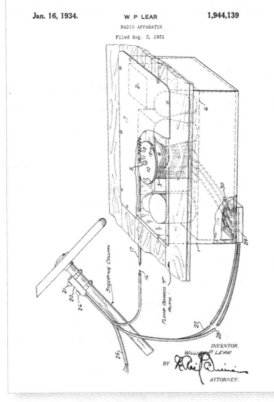

Illustration 2

A Provisional Patent Application for Radio Apparatus

I have invented a new radio receiver that is portable and can be used in automobiles and other similar vehicles. It can be operated by a remote control that can be located within easy reach of the operator.

In automobiles, considerable vibration and jerking occurs. In the usual radio there are variable condensers or capacitors. These are usually mounted so that their axis is horizontal during normal operation. Such condensers are particularly sensitive to the vibration and jerking, resulting in a change of adjustment.

I have determined that this can be eliminated by disposing the gang condenser so that its shaft is in a vertical position. This will enable practically all the jars and bumps to be taken up by the bearings of the condenser and eliminate or reduce any tendency to throw the condenser out of adjustment.

Also, the vertical position enables the remote control apparatus to be streamlined. Practically all of the remote controls used on such sets make use of a flexible cable, which must be connected to the condenser's shaft. The vertical mounting makes it possible to minimize the number of sharp bends and turns in this cable.

Also, when the radio is mounted in the vehicle, it must be protected from water, sand and other elements to which anything suspended underneath an automobile is exposed. To provide such protection, I provide a container, preferably metallic, for shielding purposes. I permanently fasten the container to the automobile, preferably hanging it from the bottom of the floorboards. I mount the radio as a unit on a chassis in this container. This makes it easy to replace the vacuum tubes and service the radio.

The set is energized from any suitable source of potential, usually the storage battery of the automobile and a separate battery for the plate supply of the radio's vacuum tubes. Various connections between these sources of potential and the set must be made through the radio's protecting casing. If an ordinary cable is passed through the casing, repeated removals of the set from its container will result in sufficient clearance between the cables and the container wall to admit water, sand or other undesirable elements. In order to avoid this, I preferably provide a detachable connection, one part permanently fastened to the casing and the other part permanently fastened to the chassis. This detachable connection may consist of any suitable plug and socket arrangement, having as many terminals as may be found desirable. With such a detachable connection, the complete chassis may be removed and replaced as often as desired, without endangering the protection afforded by the casing.

The drawing shows a radio set embodying the above concepts and mounted in an automobile.

Suspended underneath the automobile's floorboards, through a suitable aperture, is a metal casing 1. It contains the radio receiving set 2. This set includes the usual elements, such as rf transformers, vacuum tubes, tube sockets, and the like. It also includes a tuning element, a gang condenser 3. The gang condenser has a rotor 4, rigidly mounted on a shaft 5. The entire radio is mounted on a chassis 6 and can be removed as a unit from casing 1 upon the removal of cover 7.

The condenser is mounted so that its rotor shaft 5 is vertical when the set is installed in the automobile.

To operate condenser 3, a pulley 10 is rigidly fastened to the upper portion of its rotor shaft 5. Pulley 10 has a pin 11, to which is anchored one end of a coil spring 12. The other end of the coil spring is anchored to a fixed portion of the set, so that there will be a tendency for the condenser to assume a position of either minimum or maximum capacity. I have shown it in the maximum position.

Pulley 10 is also provided with an anchor block on its edge. One end of a cable 16 is anchored to the anchor block. This cable is positioned in a groove 17 in the periphery of pulley 10 and extends out through the side of casing 1. Cable 16 is in a sheath 17, and the entire assembly leads to a control unit 20, here mounted on the steering column of the car. The control unit has a control knob 21 for moving cable 16 lengthwise. By actuating knob 21, the driver may adjust rotor 4 in any desired position with respect to the fixed plates of condenser 3.

To energize the set, suitable connections are made to current supplies—the automobile storage battery and a separate battery for the plates or anodes of the vacuum tubes.

A cable 25 leads to a combined volume control and switch 26 of control unit 20. From the control unit a pair of cables 27 and 28 lead to a socket 29, rigidly fastened in the bottom of casing 1. Socket 29 is tightly sealed in casing 1 so that no water or dirt can enter the casing. A cooperating plug 30 is mounted on chassis 6 so as to mate with socket member 29 when the chassis is in the normal position in the casing.

Various wires from plug 30 go to the several pieces of apparatus in the radio. When the radio chassis is removed from casing 1, plug 30 is automatically withdrawn from socket 29. Chassis 6 is rigidly mounted in casing 1 by suitable hardware (not shown).

If you're diligent and follow the instructions in this book, you will be able to file a provisional patent application within 24 hours. Of course, as singer James Brown might add, *"Sayin' it and doin' it are such a different thing."*

To see if someone could actually accomplish the filing within 24 hours, we asked an inventor to time himself as he went through the paces. Our inventor, an experienced toy designer, has licensed many toys in his 30-year career but had never prepared or filed a provisional or regular patent application. At the end of each chapter, we'll discuss any problems he encountered.

The Invention

The subject of our time trial is a method of simulating tears in a doll (that we'll call *Baby Tears)* using LEDs (light emitting diodes). Our inventor is not claiming rights to any electrical or LED technology related to Baby Tears, only to the new use of the LED technology within a "crying" doll.

Initial Problems

The first issue for our inventor is whether to permit the publication of his invention in this book. Once published, it becomes "prior art" (see "Establish an Official U.S. Patent Application Filing Date for Your Invention" in this chapter). Our inventor would then have one year to file a provisional patent application; otherwise all patent rights would be lost. In addition, if the book were published before the provisional patent application was filed, our inventor would lose the ability to file for foreign patents. (For more on foreign rights, see Chapter 6.)

> Though patented in 1938, the first commercial electric photocopiers were not sold until 1958.

Another issue is that once the invention is published, our inventor can no longer protect it as a trade secret. As a result, he can't claim the advantage of secrecy within the toy industry. Competing inventors and toy companies could read about the idea, possibly before it comes to market. (For more on trade secrecy, see Appendix B.)

Our inventor is willing to assume the loss of trade secret rights, risk the loss of foreign patent rights, and assume the obligations to file the provisional patent application within one year. (As we'll see, these prior-art risks became a nonissue as our inventor filed several months before this book was first published.)

Time Spent on Chapter 1
45 minutes

Time Remaining
23 hours 15 minutes

So far, our inventor has spent 45 minutes reading this chapter and considering issues about trade secrecy and publication. Okay, there are only 23 hours and 15 minutes left!

Get Updates and More at This Book's Companion Page

When there are important changes to the information in this book, we'll post updates at

www.nolo.com/back-of-book/PEND.html

You will also find other helpful information at this page including interviews with *Patent It Yourself* author David Pressman.

Deciding Whether to File a Provisional Application:
The Seven Hurdles

"We start our projects by asking if there is a really important problem—medical or environmental—and do we think we have an insight as to how to solve such a problem. We then figure what it would cost to do, the risks involved and then whether we would be able to put it in production and make money....Invariably, if you start with 'It's a really big problem' and 'We have a really good idea!' by definition people will be willing to pay a fair price to have this new invention."

—**Dean Kamen, inventor of the portable insulin pump, surgical stent, and Segway human transporter. (Interview with Ira Flatow, "Science Friday," January 25, 2002.)**

Consider these statistics: Only about half of the patent applications submitted each year result in a patent and fewer than 3% of those ever make money. In other words, of the approximately 250,000 patents granted each year, 242,500 of them will gather dust, not profit. For those who use an attorney, the average patent application costs anywhere from $5,000 to $10,000 or more to prepare—which means that inventors are wasting somewhere in the neighborhood of a billion dollars each year patenting inventions that will never sell. Ouch!

Why waste time and money patenting inventions that won't sell? Because most inventors (and their employers) see patents as insurance. Their thinking goes like this—since you can't always predict what will sell, your safest bet is to get legal protection for everything that appears to have a chance. Patent lawyers encourage this with the maxim "Patent early and patent often." Unfortunately, not every invention is patentable and not every patented invention is commercial (that is, can be sold at a profit). There's no reason to file a provisional patent application for an invention that will never acquire a patent or earn money.

So, how can you predict whether your invention will be among the 50% of patent applications approved and among the 3% of patented inventions that become commercially successful? Ask yourself these seven questions—and file a provisional patent application only if your answer to all of them is "yes."

1. Is it commercial?
2. Did you invent it?
3. Do you own it?
4. Is it useful?
5. Does it fit in one of the patent "classes"?
6. Is it novel?
7. Is it something that is not obvious to other inventors?

An invention that can clear each of these hurdles is more likely to earn you some money and be patentable. But some of these hurdles will be more difficult than others to surmount. To help you figure out how your invention will fare, we provide you with information regarding patent law and direct you to some methods that have proven reliable for assessing an invention's financial success (see below, "Should You Bypass a PPA and Go Straight to a Regular Patent Application?"). Generally, you should file a provisional patent application if you perceive any chance for commercial success and your invention falls in one of the statutory patent classes. Then, during the 12 months before you have to file a regular patent application, you can investigate the commercial potential further. You can never predict with 100% certainty whether you will make money, but you can make a decent forecast during those 12 months. If things look bleak, don't bother filing the regular patent application.

Should You Bypass a PPA and Go Straight to a Regular Patent Application?

There can be disadvantages to filing a PPA, particularly if the PPA is not detailed enough. In addition, some inventors feel that a year is not enough time to properly assess the value of an invention while others are concerned about the need to file foreign applications. For these and other reasons—more disadvantages are provided in Chapter 1—some attorneys recommend filing a PPA only if there is an imminent filing deadline, you don't have enough money or time to prepare a regular patent application, or you need to lock in an early date in a quick and relatively cheap way.

Even if you can't acquire a patent, other forms of legal protection—including copyright, design patent, trade secret, or trademark law—may protect your idea. You will find a brief explanation of each of these concepts in the appendixes at the end of this book.

Parker Brothers initially rejected Charles Darrow's game of "Monopoly." The company thought it had 52 fundamental flaws and took too long to play. Darrow later became the first game inventor to earn a million dollars.

Hurdle #1: Is It Commercial?

Turning a discovery or creative idea into a product that can be sold (known as "product development") is a long process. For example, ten years passed between the date Stephanie Kwolek discovered aramid fiber and the date Dow Chemical first used it in Kevlar fiber bullet-resistant vests.

As we explained in Chapter 1, one of the primary benefits of filing a provisional patent application is to obtain time to assess the commercial potential of your invention before you file a regular patent application. If you do it right, you can accumulate up to 12 months of sales information before filing your regular application. (You must file a regular patent application within one year after you file the provisional patent application.)

> CAUTION
> **If you want foreign patent rights, you can't wait 12 months.** See "International Rules to Remember" in Chapter 6.

Although the USPTO usually won't consider your invention's commercial potential in deciding whether to issue a patent, you should consider it very carefully when you decide whether to file a provisional or regular patent application. If you're like most inventors, you're convinced that your invention has commercial potential. But keep in mind that many other inventors—including the creators of the fingertip toothbrush (5,875,513), the nose wiper (4,536,889), and the three-legged pantyhose (5,713,081)—all felt the same way. All of these inventions received patents—but you'll have a hard time finding them in your local Wal-Mart.

Although there is no foolproof method of determining your invention's commercial potential, there are a few ways to figure your odds of success.

Consider Factors That Affect Profitability

In *Patent It Yourself* (Nolo), by David Pressman, you'll find a list of 55 positive and negative factors that can help you determine whether your invention has commercial potential—in other words, whether someone will be interested in licensing or buying your invention.

Among the factors to consider are:

- Cost: How much will the parts cost? How much will assembling the parts cost? How much will the packaging cost?
- Competition: Are opposing products firmly entrenched? Is there a niche in the market just waiting to be filled by your invention?
- Ease of use: How easy is it to obtain results from your invention?
- Demand: How many people are really going to want your creation? As to this factor, you may wish to do your own research on the reactions of family and friends, as described below.

Additional factors were developed in the 1970s by the University of Oregon's Innovation Center. The center came up with a number of questions you can consider in trying to figure out the commercial value of your invention including:

- Will there be legal problems commercializing your invention?
- Are there safety issues (for example, a potential for consumer injuries) that may scare away investors or licensees?

> Disc brakes were not widely used on cars until 50 years after they were patented.

- Will your invention have a positive or negative effect on the environment—and how will this affect the commercial potential?
- Will your invention have a positive or negative effect on society—and how will this affect the commercial potential?
- Who will buy your invention?
- Will your invention's usefulness diminish over time?
- How long does it take to learn how to use your invention?
- Will your product be distinctive? Will it stand out in the marketplace?
- Will your product provide a valuable service?
- How sturdy is your invention? Will it require frequent maintenance?

- What is the likelihood of new competitors appearing once your invention is commercialized?
- How practical is it to produce your invention for sale?
- Will the demand for your invention die off?
- Will consumers find that your invention is compatible with their needs or lifestyles?
- What does marketing research tell you about the demand for your product?
- How can your invention reach consumers? What methods of distribution are available and what will they cost?
- What do you perceive as your invention's primary function? Will consumers have the same perception?
- What competition exists for your product now?
- Have you any way of estimating the potential sales?
- In what stage of development is your invention?
- What type of start-up expenses do you anticipate in order to manufacture the device?
- What do consumer trends indicate about the demand for your invention?
- Is there a potential to expand your invention into a line of products?
- Is there a need for your invention?
- What type of promotion will be needed to sell your invention?
- Does your invention's appearance add to its commercial appeal?
- Is your invention affordable to the relevant market?
- What forms of legal protection are available for your invention?
- How long will it take to receive a payback on your invention?
- What is the margin between the cost and sales price?
- Is your invention dependent on or related to another device or product?
- Is further research and development necessary before you sell the invention?

It may be difficult for you to answer these questions, particularly at the beginning of the invention process. And the importance of each factor will vary, depending on your field and the purpose of your invention. However, if it becomes obvious when you look at all of these factors together that the brilliance of your invention may pale under commercial scrutiny, it's time to reconsider your options. For example, an invention that has fluctuating demand, an unfeasible production system, and a slow payback period will be difficult to successfully commercialize.

Keeping Your Invention a Secret

You'll want to keep your invention a secret until you decide whether to patent or market it. Filing a provisional patent application won't reveal your invention—no one at the USPTO will even examine it. But if you file a regular patent application, your invention will be disclosed to the public within 18 months of that filing unless, at the time you file, you file a Nonpublication Request that indicates you will not be seeking foreign patent rights. (In order to conform our patent laws to the rest of the world, U.S. inventors must permit their invention to be published within 18 months after filing if they want foreign patent rights.) If you obtain a patent, your secrecy will be lost because the patent will be published by the USPTO. If you elect to file a Nonpublication Request and the USPTO rejects your patent application, your invention will remain a secret.

The Bag of Parts Analysis

A successful toy representative explained that the first thing he does when considering a prospective toy idea is to isolate the parts and imagine those parts in a bag. How much would this bag of parts cost? He then multiplies the cost of parts by five to get an idea of the retail price (referred to as the "price point"). Finally, he compares the potential retail price with the competition. If the price point is above the range of competing toy items, the rep will not handle the toy. No matter how brilliant the toy idea, the rep believes that it will be too difficult to convince companies and stores to handle an item that is not priced competitively.

Test the Waters Yourself

One of the simplest methods of determining marketability is to conduct your own personal market research. Conducting such a market survey can help you figure out whether potential consumers will have any interest in the device.

Neon lights do not have to contain neon gas. Other gases can be used to create different colors.

This type of research requires some preparation. You will need to come up with a presentation that explains or demonstrates what your invention does. If you don't have a prototype, you'll need to find some way to show or describe your creation so that the viewers (start with family and friends) can evaluate it. You will also need to ask the right questions. For example: Would you buy it? What is the most you would pay? This process will give you good practice for preparing and making presentations to potential partners or investors.

Because your presentation might require you to disclose information that should be maintained as a trade secret, you may need to take precautions. Rather than have each guest sign a nondisclosure agreement (an unfriendly method of getting opinions), you can ask evaluators to sign a "log and comment" book or a page in your inventor's notebook that says:

The undersigned have seen and understood Joan Smith's confidential invention known as [*insert the name of your invention—for example, "the Purple Plunger"*] on the dates indicated below, have made the following comments on the invention, and agree to maintain the invention in confidence.

_____   _____
Signature   Date

_____   _____
Signature   Date

Although this is not as protective as a disclosure agreement, it both puts an evaluator on notice that the invention is confidential and provides valuable feedback.

! CAUTION

Testing your idea on friends or family. Using friends or family for opinions can create uncomfortable situations. They may be hesitant to tell you the truth—and if they manage to overcome their reluctance, you may be offended or hurt by their comments. Here are three tips to help deal with this issue:

- Avoid taking criticism personally.
- Do not interrupt or argue when an evaluator makes criticisms.
- Test your idea on people whose opinions you trust.

Get an Expert Opinion

Although the opinions of a focus group can be helpful, they may not be sufficient to tell you whether your invention will sell. Perhaps your testers are not the intended consumers of the item or perhaps they lack the proper industry perspective to determine potential success. In this situation, you may need an expert opinion.

Who counts as an expert? Generally, anyone involved in a product's chain of distribution is an expert of sorts, from inventor to manufacturer to supplier to distributor to salesperson to consumer. If you have an auto accessories product, for example, you might solicit the opinion of a mechanic, a driver, the owner of an accessories store, or a gas station attendant. Being an expert doesn't require a college education or a fancy title—what you really want is someone with experience, knowledge, or expertise in the appropriate marketplace.

Local inventor groups may provide expert evaluations or lead you to organizations that assess marketability. Some companies provide objective evaluations, often for a fee. Keep in mind that you will usually need a prototype (or some model or mock-up) of your invention in order to obtain an expert evaluation.

Inventions That Lack Commercial Potential

Trying to market a new product is like gambling—and, as in any game of chance, you have to know when to quit. This may be the most difficult decision for an inventor to face. You must temper the high hopes that come with the excitement of inventing and try to take a realistic view of the future. Remember, this invention only embodies one product of your creative ability. If you were able to create this invention, there is more intellectual property in your brain waiting to be mined. Don't be discouraged! Sometimes, it's possible to improve your idea later to make it more commercial—for example, it wasn't until many years after inventing his clever spring and bracket contraption that inventor George Carwadine realized that his device could be the arm of an adjustable lamp (commonly found in offices and homes today). Or you may come up with an entirely new invention that has a better chance of commercial success.

If at First You Don't Succeed

Dr. Martin Sturman invented a "safe" hypodermic needle that would protect health care workers from accidental needle pricks, but health care companies rejected his design. After this rejection, he teamed with Maurice Kanbar and two other inventors to improve his invention. Before beginning the redesign, they surveyed nurses (who as a profession, experienced 46% of all such accidental injuries). They learned that they had to change the invention so it could be "safed" with one hand (Sturman's original design required two hands), preferably with one finger, without requiring the user to look away from the patient. Also, nurses wanted to hear or feel a "click" to let them know that it was locked. With this research, the team returned to the design table and created their innovative needle protector, which was promptly licensed by Becton, Dickinson, and Company, the largest manufacturer of health care safety products.

Hurdle #2: Did You Invent It?

This may not seem like much of a challenge for most inventors. But you can only obtain a patent if *you*—not your uncle or a coworker, a subordinate, or someone who offers the invention to you—invented something. So, if your late uncle is the person who really thought up and perfected the invention, you're not entitled to the patent (although your late uncle's estate can file for it).

EXAMPLE: Genentech (a biotech company) claimed that its scientists invented a genetically engineered human growth hormone product, Protropin hGH. The University of California claimed that its scientists invented the same product. Genentech's claims crumbled when a former UC scientist admitted that he sneaked into his old lab one New Year's Eve, took DNA material, and passed it on to a Genentech scientist. What was the price tag on this "who invented it" dispute? Genentech had to shell out $200 million to UC—and millions more in attorneys' fees.

If there are multiple inventors, each inventor must be named in the provisional patent application. And if you want to claim the benefit of the provisional application filing date, your regular patent application must have one inventor in common with the inventors named in the provisional application. If you accidentally fail to list an inventor, you can correct that error later. But if you intentionally exclude an inventor on a provisional or regular patent application, the USPTO or a court can render the patent worthless. For example, a couple of years ago, the inventors of three biotech patents lost their rights when a court determined that two inventors had been intentionally left off the applications. (*PerSeptive Biosystems Inc. v. Pharmacia Biotech Inc.*, 56 U.S.P.Q.2d (BNA) 1001 (CAFC 2000).)

> After assisting Bell in his invention of the telephone, Mr. Watson enjoyed careers as a shipbuilder, geologist, and Shakespearean actor.

How do you tell if someone else is a coinventor? That can get tricky. A coinventor is anyone who makes a contribution to at least one novel and nonobvious concept that makes the invention patentable. In patent drafting terms, the coinventor must contribute something substantial to at least one of the patent claims.

Alexander Graham Bell

Determining whether a contribution is substantial can be tough. For instance, if one person came up with the concept for the invention and hired someone to build a prototype and test it, the second person is not a coinventor. On the other hand, if a prototype builder came up with valuable contributions and at least one of these contributions found its way into a patent claim, both people should be named as coinventors on the patent application. For example, James Drake thought of the idea of adding a sail to a surfboard. However, he developed many other ideas with Hoyle Schweitzer, a businessman who liked to surf. The final result of the collaboration was the sailboard—a mast attached to a surfboard with a universal joint and a boom for the rider to hang on to. Both men are listed on the patent as coinventors.

What Are Patent Claims?

A patent grants you the right to stop others from making, selling, using, importing, or offering your invention for sale during the term of the patent. The extent of your rights—that is, what you can stop others from doing—depends primarily upon the scope of your patent claims. These claims, which you make as part of your regular patent application, establish the boundaries of your invention in the same way that a deed establishes the boundaries of real property. For example, Alexander Graham Bell's claims for the telephone were very broad—they allowed him to stop others from using a variety of methods of transmitting the human voice over wire. Courts interpret other patents—for example, Amazon.com's one-click business method patent—very narrowly.

Drafting patent claims requires special writing techniques and knowledge of patent terms. Many inventors rely on the expertise of a patent attorney in drafting this crucial patent language. You can find examples of patent claims in Appendix A of this book. Each patent contains a section near the end that starts with the language "I claim" or "We claim" and includes a numbered list. In Chapter 3, we explain how to decipher this claims language.

If you work with other inventors on your invention, you should reach an agreement establishing each inventor's respective rights. (In Appendix B, we explain how to prepare a sample joint ownership agreement for inventions.)

To back up your ownership rights (and to deflect others who may claim rights), you should document the important steps you took to develop your invention in an inventor's notebook (also known as a lab notebook—see "Creating Your Inventor's Notebook," below). Two witnesses—people who understand what you are doing—should sign and date each page of the notebook. The USPTO and the courts generally accept properly witnessed notebooks as corroborating evidence of an inventor's conception, reduction to practice, and inventorship.

Creating Your Inventor's Notebook

Your notebook will serve as the diary of your invention. Include everything relevant to the invention process, such as correspondence, photographs, receipts for invention purchases, test results, theories, descriptions, procedures and comments about other inventions, and sketches.

It's easy to create your own inventor's notebook—simply copy the format in the sample page we've provided in Appendix D. You can also purchase lab notebooks through Eureka Lab Book, Inc. (www.eurekalabbook.com) or Scientific Notebook Company (www.snco.com).

Hurdle #3: Do You Own It?

In David Mamet's play *The Water Engine*, an inventor finds the Holy Grail when he creates an engine that can run on water. Soon, however, an unethical patent attorney tries to get the rights, arguing that the inventor's employer owns the invention. The battle becomes heated and the inventor is killed—but not before destroying his invention and hiding the documents showing how he made it.

Battles over real-life patent ownership often become heated, but they are usually decided by legal rules, rather than violence. Generally, you will have to transfer rights in your invention to your employer if any of the following are true:

- You signed an employment agreement that includes provisions requiring you to give up all rights in advance of creating an invention (commonly referred to as preinvention assignments).
- You were hired specifically for the purpose of creating an invention.
- Your employer acquires a "shop right."

RESOURCE

Employee inventions are covered in more detail in *Profit From Your Idea*, by Richard Stim (Nolo).

Preassignment Agreements

Approximately 100 years ago, Earl Dickson combined pieces of surgical tape with gauze to create the first adhesive strip bandage. His invention was intended to help his wife, who suffered burns and cuts while working in the kitchen. Mr. Dickson's employer, the Johnson & Johnson Company, acquired the patent to this invention because Dickson made it during his employment and it was related to the employer's existing business. Johnson & Johnson soon became the leading manufacturer of these bandages, which it sold under the "Band-Aid" trademark.

The Rolex watch company did not enjoy great financial success until debuting its self-winding invention in 1930.

If you are employed, review your employment agreement (if you have one) to determine the circumstances under which the business can claim ownership of employee-created inventions. If your agreement is like Earl Dickson's or those of thousands of other engineers, scientists, programmers, chemists, and other innovators, it probably contains a preassignment provision giving your employer ownership of all inventions that are:

- made during your term of employment
- related to the employer's existing or contemplated business
- made on the employer's time—that is, the time for which the employee is paid—or using the employer's facilities or materials, or
- made as a result of activity within the scope of the employee's duties.

The rationale behind these preassignment agreements is clear—employers want all of the benefits of their employees' company-related creativity. For employees, the agreements often create confusion—for example, who owns an invention that's marginally related to employment but created on an employee's time? Unfortunately, legal cases are filled with disputes over employee-created inventions. And unfortunately for employees, this case law, combined with an employer's financial clout, gives employers a strong advantage in these disputes.

Preassignment agreements usually obligate you to disclose your inventions to your employer so the employer can determine if they're assignable. Disclosing an invention simply requires you to report the invention; it does not necessarily mean that you will have to give up your rights. The final determination of who owns an invention depends on the terms of the employment agreement and the law of the state where the employee/inventor works.

> **Although invented in 1914, the zip fastener (or zipper as it was later known) was not widely used in clothing until ten years later.**

Eight states— California, Delaware, Illinois, Kansas, Minnesota, North Carolina, Utah, and Washington—require that the employer furnish a copy of the law on preinvention assignments to new employees. Regardless of what your employment agreement says, an employer in these states cannot claim ownership of your invention if it:

- is created with your own resources
- does not result from work you performed for your employer, and
- does not relate to the employer's business.

Employed to Invent

Even if you don't have an employment agreement, your employer owns your invention if you were hired to be an inventor—that is, your primary job responsibility is to solve a specific technical problem. This is known as the "employed to invent" principle. In one case, for example, an engineer who had no written employment agreement with his employer was chosen to be the chief engineer on a project to devise a process of welding a "leading edge" for turbine engines. Even though there was no preinvention assignment, a court held that the company owned the patent rights because the engineer was hired for the express purpose of creating the process. (*Teets v. Chromalloy Gas Turbine Corp.*, 83 F.3d 403 (Fed. Cir. 1996).)

Shop Rights

In the two situations described above (written employment agreements and the employed-to-invent rule), the employer becomes the owner of all patent rights. However, the employer can also acquire a more limited right, known as a "shop right," to use these innovations. If your employer has a shop right, you can still file a patent and claim patent ownership, but your employer has the legal right to use the invention without paying you.

A shop right can occur only if the inventor uses the employer's resources (materials, supplies, or time) to create an invention. Other circumstances may be relevant, but use of employer resources is the most important criterion. Therefore, you don't need to worry about shop rights unless you created the invention on the employer's time or using the employer's resources. The shop right attaches automatically. Shop right disputes are not uncommon and sometimes end up in court.

> The Dutch electronics firm, Philips, did not patent the audio cassette invention because it wanted the device to be adopted as an audio standard throughout the world.

Hurdle #4: Is It Useful?

Even though Shakespeare, Picasso, and Mozart were geniuses, their creations would not meet the standards of the USPTO. Lovely though your creation may be, you can only obtain a patent if your work is useful. Under our patent laws, aesthetic works—though they entertain, instruct, or amuse us—are not considered useful.

Assuming that your invention does something—that is, it produces a result or makes a product—you should have little difficulty establishing usefulness. On those rare occasions when the USPTO rejects an invention for being "not useful," it relies on commonsense reasons—for example, a drug is not safe to use, the invention causes a nuclear explosion, or the purpose of the invention is illegal.

> **EXAMPLE:** The USPTO rejects Bob's brilliant invention for counterfeiting one-hundred-dollar bills as lacking "usefulness." Unless Bob can demonstrate some alternative legal use of the invention, the USPTO's rejection will stand and he will not obtain a patent.

How Do You Separate Form From Function?

Intellectual property laws—the laws that grant rights to artists, inventors, and other creative types—separate innovations into those that are functional and those that are not. Utility patents and trade secret law provide limited monopolies on functional creations; design patents cover aesthetic or ornamental creations; and copyrights cover aesthetic and other creations of authors and the like. How can you determine whether your creation (or a feature of it) is functional or aesthetic? Ask the question: "Does this make the product work better or is it done primarily for looks?"

For example, the Gibson Guitar company may claim a utility patent in the electronics of its electric guitars, but not in the unique V-shape of its Flying Vee Guitar. The shape is primarily for looks, not function. On the other hand, a uniquely shaped hook used on a hanger may be primarily functional—even if it also looks good—if it prevents the hanger from snagging on clothing.

If you have created some fabulous ornamentation for your invention, you may be eligible for a design patent that protects the ornamentation or for a copyright. However, you can file a valid provisional patent application only for an invention that falls in one of the classes associated with utility patents, not for a design. We discuss the various forms of intellectual property protection in Appendix B.

Hurdle #5: Does It Fit in One of the Patent Classes?

To be eligible for a utility patent, an invention must fall within one of five classes defined by statute. If you have a functional innovation (see Hurdle #4), you probably won't have any problem demonstrating that your invention fits within one—and maybe two—classes. Even if you have difficulty classifying your invention, patent examiners liberally construe this requirement and may even assist you in making the final determination. The five classes are:

- processes and methods
- machines
- articles of manufacture
- compositions of matter, and
- new uses of any of the foregoing.

Note: We made "new uses" a separate class of invention since these are treated separately and since the "Definitions" statute (35 USC 100(b)) states that "process" or "method" includes a new use.

Processes and Methods

The USPTO defines processes and methods (the two terms are synonymous in patent law) as one or more steps for doing or making something. For example, the patent for pasteurization (see Chapter 1) is a process and method patent because it describes the steps required to remove bacteria in liquids. If you've perfected a process for doing something useful—for example, a software process or a method of doing business—you fulfill this requirement. Some famous examples of patentable processes are George Washington Carver's method for making paints and stains, Patsy Sherman and Samuel Smith's process for treating carpets (commonly known by the trademark, Scotchgard), and Leo Baekeland's method for creating plastic products.

The Xerox 914—the first push-button plain paper copier introduced in 1960—was called by *Fortune* magazine, "the most successful product ever marketed in America."

Machines

The USPTO defines machines as devices or things that accomplish a result by the interaction of parts. For example, the Zamboni Ice Rink Resurfacing Machine travels across ice rinks with spinning blades and ice conveyors, shaving and smoothing the surface. An electrical circuit or a software program can be a patentable machine if it involves the interaction of devices or parts that create a useful result.

Articles of Manufacture

The USPTO reserves the articles of manufacture category for objects that accomplish a result without movable parts (such as a pencil or a garden rake) or objects with movable parts that are incidental (such as a safety pin or folding chair). Examples include Sarah Boone's invention of the ironing board, which enabled users to press clothing, and John Rand's collapsible tube design, which led the way for dispensing toothpaste and glues. The machine and manufacture categories overlap—for example, devices such as mechanical pencils, cigarette lighters, and electronic circuits might fall into both categories.

> The Center for Energy and Climate Solutions determined in 2000 that the Internet saved 1.5 billion square feet in retail space and 2 billion square feet of office space and reduced the amount of greenhouse gases emitted into the atmosphere by 35 million metric tons.

Compositions of Matter

The USPTO classifies chemical combinations or combinations of other materials that produce a result as compositions. A familiar example is Roy Plunkett's invention of PTFE (polytetrafluroethylene), sold under the trademark Teflon. Except for genes, naturally occurring substances cannot be patented, but combinations or extracts of natural materials may qualify— for example, Felix Hoffman's life-saving invention of aspirin. Also, naturally occurring things that require extended effort to discover and isolate, such as genes, can be patented. In 1980, the Supreme Court ruled that living organisms (such as human-made animals or plants) could receive patent protection as compositions.

New Uses—The "5th" Class of Patents

You may create a novel use for an existing invention—like the inventor who figured out a method of removing prairie dogs from their homes using a powerful vacuum. Although a patent statute categorizes new uses in the "process" category, the PTO and patent experts treat new uses as a separate patent class. Note that if you get a patent on a new use and the underlying invention is covered by a process, composition, article, or machine patent, you may not be able to make, sell, or use your new use unless you have authorization (in the form of a "license") from the patent owner.

How Would You Characterize This One?

Using the invention in Jack DeLorean's Patent 6,142,320 (see Illustration 1), you can store several rakes, brooms, hoes, and other long-handled tools in one safe place. On first sight it appears to be clearly an article of manufacture, since it's basically an object with no movable parts—a bar or arm that is fastened across the walls which join to form a corner of a room. However, the PTO initially rejected it as lacking novelty since bars or arms were old. Then, when it was claimed as a new-use process (a method for storing items), the PTO allowed it. This was done because the method by which the old arm is used is new. The title of the patent, "Method of Storing Elongated Implements Between Corner Sidewalls, a Holding Member and a Floor," says it all.

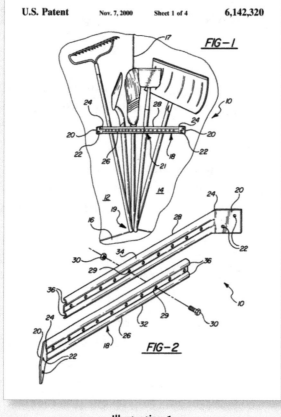

Illustration 1

Hurdle #6: Is It New?

In Chapter 1, we explained that your invention must differ from previous inventions or existing knowledge to qualify for a patent. The USPTO refers to existing inventions and knowledge as prior art. If your invention differs physically or operationally in some way from the prior art, you have made it over this hurdle (but not necessarily over the obviousness hurdle, as we will show).

> **EXAMPLE:** In 1951, Edwin Land patented instant photography. The product that used this process—the Polaroid camera—introduced this novel concept to people who were used to waiting weeks for developed pictures. Using Mr. Land's invention, a photograph would appear fully developed within minutes. Subsequent instant camera and instant film patents obtained by the Polaroid company in the early 1970s were used later to prevent the Kodak company from manufacturing and selling Kodak's version of an instant camera.

Prior art includes:

- anything in public use or on sale in the world before the filing date of the patent application
- prior patents that issued before the filing date of the patent application
- prior publications dated before the filing date of the patent application
- anything that was publicly known or used by others before the filing date of the patent application
- anything that was made or built by another person before the filing date of the patent application, or
- U.S. patents that have a filing date prior to the filing date of the patent application. The effective date of a patent that is based on a provisional patent application is the date the provisional is filed.

There is one exception to the rule that anything publicly known before your filing date is prior art: Any disclosure that came from you, the inventor, and was not made over a year before the filing date is not considered prior art to you but it is prior art to anyone else.

(For information on searching for prior art, read Chapter 3.)

Hurdle #7: Is It Obvious?

Today, we consider packaged bandages with peel-off adhesive-covering strips (sold under the trademark, Band-Aids) to be obvious. At the turn of the century, however, nobody had considered or created prepackaged gauze adhesive bandages. Many of the inventions mentioned in this chapter (for example, the safety pin and the ironing board) seem obvious, now. This is one of the paradoxes of truly great inventions—once created, they seem obvious.

All inventions must meet a requirement of nonobviousness. To figure out whether your invention meets this test, you have to consider whether people working in the field would consider the invention obvious or whether the invention has any new and unexpected results. Albert Szent-Gyorgy, who discovered Vitamin C, summed up this hurdle when he said, "Discovery consists of seeing what everybody has seen and thinking what nobody has thought."

Stephanie Kwolek's Persistence: How to Create a Nonobvious Composition

Stephanie Kwolek

In 1964, while working for DuPont, Stephanie Kwolek was part of a team attempting to improve tire strength. One day she accidentally dissolved a polymer, and the result was unlike any other solution seen in the laboratory. She thought she was onto something unique, but a supervisor told her it wasn't even worth spinning (a processing method that turns the liquid substance into fibers). After Kwolek pleaded to spin the substance, her supervisor finally relented. The result was a flexible yet strong aramid fiber that was to become known as the trademarked product, Kevlar. The composition was not obvious to those in the field—as demonstrated by the attitude of Kwolek's supervisor. As a result of her persistence, she came up with a nonobvious invention and because Kevlar is used to make bulletproof vests, she has also saved countless lives.

Your invention is most likely to meet the "nonobviousness" test if it produces new and unexpected results. If your invention's new and unexpected results are not clear-cut, it may be considered nonobvious if any of the following is true:

- It has enjoyed commercial success.
- There has been a need in the industry for the invention.
- Others have tried but failed to achieve the same result.
- The inventor did what others said could not be done.
- Others have copied the invention.
- The invention has been praised by others in the field.

RESOURCE

Many of the subjects of this chapter—for example, drafting patent claims, determining commercial potential, and assessing patentability—are discussed in detail in David Pressman's *Patent It Yourself* (Nolo) and the patent resources provided in the appendixes to this book.

Time Spent on Chapter 2
50 minutes

Time Remaining
22 hours 25 minutes

(We're timing our inventor as he prepares a provisional patent application.) Our inventor spent 50 minutes reading and answering the questions in Chapter 2. Only 22 hours and 25 minutes left!

Our Inventor's Patent Hurdles

Our inventor proceeded quickly through the questions posed in this chapter.

Hurdle #1: Is It Commercial?

Our inventor is knowledgeable about the toy industry, has previously licensed toys, and has good reasons, based on his 25 years of experience in the toy industry, to believe that his Baby Tears doll might sell.

Hurdle #2: Did He Invent It?

Yes!

Hurdle #3: Does He Own It?

Yes! Our inventor works for himself so there is no issue as to whether it is employer owned.

Hurdle #4: Is It Useful?

Yes, the fact that the USPTO has issued many patents on toys and dolls indicates that it considers them useful as playthings and learning tools.

Hurdle #5: Does It Fit Within One of the Patent Classes?

Yes, it's a method of simulating tears. It can also be classified as a machine for simulating tears.

Hurdle #6: Is It Likely New?

Yes. Our inventor has general knowledge of the industry and has never seen this doll invention at trade shows, in catalogs, or in any patent, so he concludes it is very likely to be novel, pending the results of his prior-art search (discussed in Chapter 3).

Hurdle #7: Are Its Novel Features Likely Nonobvious?

Again, our search in Chapter 3 will provide us with more information, but the provision of a crying doll using LEDs has the following new and unexpected result: It provides a simulation of tears without using water, as prior crying dolls do. Thus, our inventor makes a preliminary conclusion that it's not obvious.

Finding Previous Inventions

"The importance of the search is a subject I know a thing or two about. Two years ago, I tried to patent an idea that, if odd, at least seemed novel: a method of spelling out words by stringing shoelaces through a grid of eyelets. The idea was compelling enough to lead me to a lawyer, who performed a search for about $900. Soon thereafter I was informed that there were no patents resembling my idea, so we went ahead and filed an application. This part of the process ultimately cost me an additional $4,600. Sad to say, the patent examiners rejected my application, unearthing six patents that were awfully similar to the one I proposed. My lawyer's gofers had simply fallen down on the job. Too bad, tough luck, goodbye $5,500."

—David Lindsay, *The Patent Files: Dispatches from the Frontiers of Invention (1999)*, The Lyons Press

Before you spend time and money filing a provisional patent application, you should confirm that your invention (or some significant part of it) is really something new. Although your PPA won't be examined, your regular patent application (RPA) (should you file one) will be examined thoroughly. If the examiner finds that somebody built, patented, or documented the same or a similar invention before you, you won't get a patent. In order to anticipate these potential problems and to avoid wasting time and money filing a PPA, it's wise to perform a prior-art search first.

💡 **TIP**

Another good reason to search for prior art: to avoid claims of patent infringement. Searching prior art not only can turn up prior art that might prevent you from getting a patent, but it can also alert you to a potential disaster. If someone holds an in-force patent for an invention that has claims that cover your invention, your manufacture, use, sale, or offer for sale of the same invention will infringe this patent. And, if you sell your invention knowing someone else has a patent, you may be liable for increased financial damages. Even if you do find an in-force patent that has claims that cover your invention, you may still wish to file a provisional patent application if you believe that your invention is a significant improvement over the patent invention. It is possible that you may be able to arrange a cross-license with the patent owner. This cross-licensing strategy has been used effectively by many inventors, including Lee De Forest who invented the triode, which infringed John Fleming's "Fleming valve" diode patent. Note: The USPTO has no concern about infringements; its main concerns are whether your invention is novel and unobvious over the prior art.

What constitutes prior art to your invention? As discussed in Chapter 2, prior art can come from just about anywhere—it includes all previous developments that are available to the public. All of the following are prior art:

- U.S. patents for inventions similar to yours
- foreign patents for inventions similar to yours
- nonpatent publications discussing inventions like yours
- any commercial sale or use of an invention like yours, and
- any public knowledge or use of a similar invention.

If you're feeling daunted by the thought of wading through all of these documents, take heart. You won't have to search all of these sources before filing a provisional application. Once you've looked for prior patents, publications, or sales of similar inventions, you've performed a thorough enough search, at least for now. And, you can do all of this preliminary searching on the Internet—with its databases of U.S. patents from 1790 to the present and its vast stores of commercial and academic information.

> When the phonograph was invented some people predicted that in the future, letters would be spoken, not written.

Keep in mind, however, that some databases permit you only to search the text of U.S. patents issued in the last 25 to 30 years. Therefore, Internet searching can sometimes be incomplete—there may be other, more relevant prior art in existence that your Internet search doesn't turn up. At some point before filing your regular patent application or selling your invention, you should initiate a more thorough prior-art search in which someone—you or a professional searcher—reviews a comprehensive Internet patent database. Whether you perform this more sophisticated search before or after filing your provisional patent application depends on the urgency you feel about getting your invention on record at the USPTO. If you need to file quickly, save the more extensive search for later.

In this chapter, we'll explain how to conduct a basic search for prior art, including:

- how to find patents on the Internet ("Internet Patent-Searching Tips" and "Searching the USPTO Website")
- how to read the patents you find—and figure out whether your invention can be distinguished from an existing patent ("How to Read a Patent")
- how to search for other prior art, such as publications or commercial uses of an invention ("Finding Prior Art That Isn't Currently Patented"), and
- how to use a patent searcher to examine records at the USPTO (or examine them yourself—"After the Preminary Search").

> ! CAUTION
> **Even the most thorough search is no guarantee.** Whether you do it yourself or hire a competent searcher, there are limitations to every search. You can never expect to uncover 100% of the prior art because you may not have access to some pending patent applications, foreign patents, or nonpatent references. Even at the USPTO in Alexandria, some prior art may be missing, misclassified, indexed incorrectly, or on loan—and therefore unavailable to the searcher you hire or you, even if you show up in person.

Internet Patent-Searching Tips

You should start your prior-art search by reviewing previously issued U.S. patents and published U.S. patent applications. All of these patent documents are available free on the Internet. Here are some tips that will help you search these records efficiently.

Find the Right Words

Before you search, analyze your invention carefully. What words would you use to describe it? Try to come up with a broad list of words commonly used to describe similar inventions. You'll need this list because successful patent searching is dependent on using the words and phrases that appear in the patents. For example, if you invented an artificial rainmaking machine, you may not find it under "artificial" or "rainmaking"; the patents covering this topic may instead refer to it as "rainfall simulation." A broad arsenal of search words will allow you to use trial and error to find the patents you need—and to work around words that have multiple meanings or are used to describe a wide range of inventions.

RESOURCE

You can speed the process of finding search terms by using a thesaurus. You can find these resources online at, for example, Merriam-Webster. com (www.m-w.com), Dictionary.com (www.dictionary.com), or YourDictionary. com (www.yourdictionary.com).

EXAMPLE: Below are terms we gathered for three invention examples:

Terms for a non-fogging shower mirror (Illustration 1): shower, mirror, looking glass, reflection, fog, fog-free, steam, water, moisture, pipes, bath, bathtub, swivel, and flexible arm.

Terms for a disposable standing trash bag (Illustration 2): trash, garbage, bag, receptacle, frame, container, disposable, collapsible, folding, and standing.

Terms for a tent that can be converted for use in different climates (Illustration 3): tent, zipper, panel, fabric, venting, weather, climate, convert, convertible, camp, shelter, and teepee.

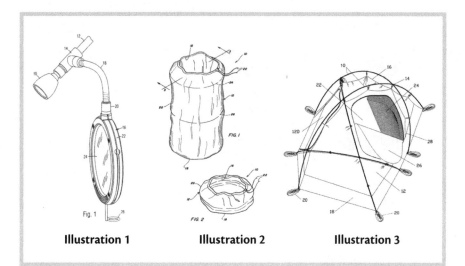

| Illustration 1 | Illustration 2 | Illustration 3 |

What's the 411? Deciphering Patent Numbers

Every U.S. patent issued since 1836 has a patent number. For example, Patent Number 6,293,280 was issued in 2001 for a "Kissing Shield and Method of Use" (Illustration 4), and Patent Number 666,666 was issued for a "Device for Picking Fruit" (Illustration 5). In patent disputes, judges and attorneys often refer to each patent by the last three digits of the registration (for example, "the '280 patent'"). Over 10,000 numbered patents were destroyed in a fire in 1836. Approximately 3,000 were recovered from other sources—the "X" patents—and are numbered sequentially with "X" prefixes, for example Patent X120.

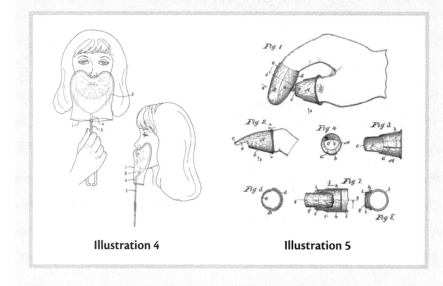

Illustration 4   Illustration 5

Search Free Before You Pay

Our favorite patent-searching site is Google Patents (www.google.com/patents), a free site that provides an accurate and fast way to perform online searches. Enter the key words (and all possible variations you can think of) and Google Patents will search approximately eight million U.S. patents and patent applications back to 1836. In addition to U.S. patents, Google also now searches patents in China, Germany, Canada, and the World Intellectual Property Organization.

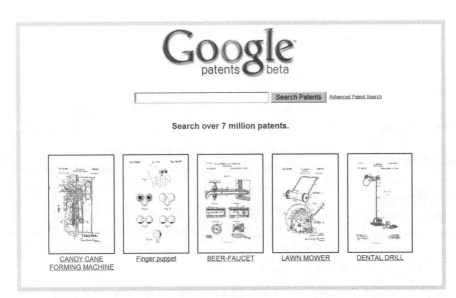

Illustration 6

To make a search from the home page (Illustration 6), simply enter your key search terms, such as "bicycle" and "fiberglass." You will quickly obtain a list of all patents that have all of your search terms. Click on any patent to get a new page with all of the parts of the patent and a link to a PDF download. The main search page also has links to a Help site and to an Advanced Patent Search.

At the Google Advanced Patent Search page, you can refine your search to look for patents with all of your key words, an exact phrase, only one of a group of words, or without a word. Also, you can search for patents by number, title, inventor, assignee, or a specific U.S. or international classification. You can restrict the search to U.S. patents or published U.S. patent applications, utility or design patents, or by a date of issue or filing date range.

> The inventor of the convenience store, Clarence Saunders, also patented the concept of price tagging items.

You can also search for free at the USPTO site (www.uspto.gov), where there is a vast database of patents. (If you do not have access to the Internet or prefer to deal with books, we recommend visiting the USPTO or a nearby Patent and Trademark Resource Center (see "Search the Internet and More at a PTRC," below).)

As explained in more detail below, if you live near the USPTO in Alexandria, Virginia, you can search on its EAST (Examiner Assisted Search Tool) but some training is required to use the terminals. The PTO gives periodic trainings; inquire at the PTO. Also the Patent and Trademark Resource Centers (PTRCs) around have WEST (Web-based Examiner Search Tool) terminals; inquire at a center for hours and training. You can find a list of PTRCs by state by searching for PTRC on the PTO's web site.

> **Tarmac road surfacing (also known as macadam) was invented when a Scottish engineer, Dr. John L. McAdam, attempted to cover spilled tar with slag from a nearby iron works.**

At the USPTO website, you can find all previously granted U.S. patents. Most of the older patents (from 1790 to 1975) have been scanned as digital illustrations. Although you can read them, you can't search the text for keywords. However, you can search the text of U.S. patents issued after 1975.

You can also extend your search of U.S. patents back to the 1920s for free at the European Patent Office (EPO) site (http://ep.espacenet.com). In addition, this site provides a searchable database for many foreign patents.

Micropatent (www.micropatent.com) is a fee-based service, which has the unique capability to offer full-text searching of U.S. patents back to 1836. However, the Micropatent historic database (pre-1976) has been obtained through optical character recognition of patent documents, so it contains many errors and incomprehensible words. Additional fee-based patent services are listed in Appendix F under "Internet Patent-Searching Resources."

An independent inventor may find the fees at services such as Micropatent astronomical. Before you break your bank paying for a fee-based service, make sure to thoroughly exhaust the free Google, USPTO, and EPO resources.

Ole Evinrude

Ole Evinrude was not the first person to create an outboard motor. But his boat motor was more reliable, simpler to build, and the first that was successfully promoted to the public.

Keep Track of Prior Art

It may seem obvious, but we'll say it anyway: You have to keep track of what you find. Set up a word processing document or a spreadsheet that includes the patent numbers and a summary of each similar invention you come across. If possible, make this document part of your inventor's notebook.

You should make copies of all relevant prior art. There are many sites where you can obtain free copies of patents. These include:

- www.google.com/patents
- www.archpatent.com
- www.pat2pdf.org
- www.freepatentsonline.com
- www.ipnewsflash.com/get_pdf.php
- free.patentfetcher.com/Patent-Fetcher-Form.php
- www.patentretriever.com, and
- www.uspto.gov.

In addition, you can order the patent from the PTO by phone (703-305-8716), fax (703- 305-8759), or letter (Mail Stop Document Services, Commissioner for Patents, P.O. Box 1450, Alexandria, VA 22213-1450) with a list of the patents you want by number and the payment for the price per patent (see the Fee Schedule at the PTO website) times the total number of patents you've ordered. The PTO will normally furnish the copies by mail, but will also fax or FedEx them for an additional fee. The PTO accepts credit cards.

Read Before You Write

If you're not familiar with the look and feel of patents, you may be surprised by their rigorous, mystifying style. But don't let the perplexing arcana put you off; the more patents you read, the more familiar you will become with their structure and language. This will help you search more efficiently because you'll know which fields of the patent—for example, the abstract or specification—are most likely to be relevant. (For more on reading patents, see "How to Read a Patent," below.)

A Picture Is Worth a Thousand Words

Sometimes, you may find it more helpful to view patent drawings than to read the text of the patent. At the USPTO website, you can see all of the drawings for a particular patent (as well as the text) by clicking "Images" while you are viewing it (see Illustration 7). (If you cannot view the image, you may need to update a plug-in for your browser.)

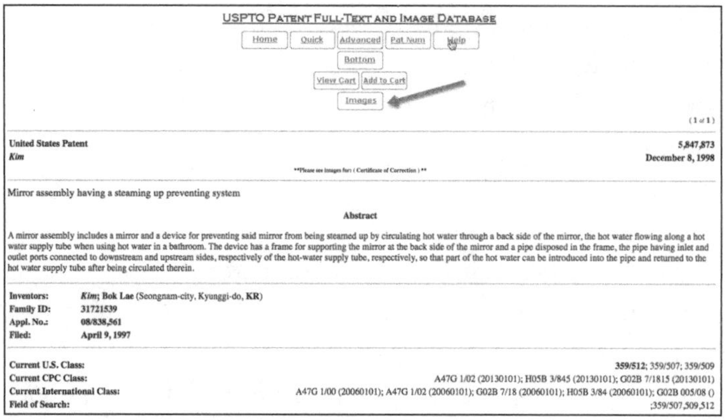

Illustration 7

Look Beyond Valid Patents

Keep in mind that you're not just searching for in-force U.S. patents. Expired patents, current patent applications, foreign patents, and nonpatented inventions are all valid forms of prior art. You can find tips for locating them in "Finding Prior Art That Isn't Currently Patented," below.

Search the Internet and More at a PTRC

The USPTO has designated about 25 Patent and Trademark Resource Centers (PTRCs)—formerly called Patent and Trademark Depository Libraries (PTDLs)—throughout the country to house copies of U.S. patent and trademark materials and to make them available to the public. The PTRCs provide access to the EAST (Examiner Assisted Search Tool) and WEST (Web-based Examiner Search Tool). These USPTO searching tools enable full-text searching of all U.S. patents. However some PTRCs charge for the use of the terminals, and the charges can add up to a considerable amount. (Note, you can use the EAST terminals at the USPTO headquarters in Virginia for free.) You can find out more about each PTRC's features by checking the USPTO website or calling the respective center (you can find a list of the PTRCs at the USPTO website).

Searching the USPTO Website

You can use two general approaches to find prior-art patents within the USPTO database:

- **Search by classification.** The USPTO categorizes all inventions using a system of classes and subclasses. Once you locate the appropriate class/subclass for your invention, you can find similar prior-art patents in the same class/subclass. (Throughout this book we will use numbers separated by a slash as shorthand for classes/subclasses. For example, 2/144 refers to Class 2, Subclass 144.) We explain how to conduct this type of search in "Search by Classification," below. (Note, as of this edition, the USPTO is switching over from the U.S. Patent Classification (USPC) to the Cooperative Patent Classification (CPC) as explained below.)

  > The idea for the microwave oven originated when an inventor noticed that his candy bar melted near a radar tube. The original ovens cost more than $3,000.

  > **EXAMPLE:** A patent examiner seeking to identify prior art for a disposable standing trash bag invention would start with Class 220 ("Receptacles"), then review subclasses such as 220/6 ("Folding receptacles"), 220/9.2 ("Collapsible or FOLDABLE receptacles"), 220/904 ("Pail or bucket of flexible or flaccid material"), and 220/908 ("Trash container"). By examining patents grouped in these subclasses, the examiner can determine whether any prior art may preclude granting a patent or force the inventor to narrow the patent claims.

- **Search by keywords and other indicia.** In addition to searching by classification, you can also search the vast collection of patents directly. This method allows you to look for matches based upon search terms and other criteria. You will find more information on this method of searching in "Searching the Patent Database by Keywords," below.

EXAMPLE: Imagine you invented a convertible tent. You could use the search engine to find all patents issued after 1976 that have "tent" and "convertible" in their specification. Further, if someone told you that, five years earlier, a rival inventor from Bolinas, California, had invented a similar tent. You can ask the search engine to find all patents that have the word "tent" in the title and were filed by an inventor from Bolinas.

What's better for you? If you are new to patent searching you will most likely find yourself gravitating to keyword searching. It is similar to Internet searching—you type in words associated with the invention—and the USPTO (or Google Patents at patents.google.com, if you choose to use it) provides a list of inventions that include those terms. The downside is if you choose the wrong keyword—for example "fire" instead of "flame"—you may overlook a worthwhile patent. Searching by classification is usually more precise because it pinpoints a specific class or subclass of inventions and you are more likely to avoid being sidetracked by numerous patents that have little relation to your invention. However, for newcomers, the USPTO index and class system may seem like a complex and challenging database system.

> **Willis Carrier's first air conditioning invention weighed 30 tons. When he died in 1950, he had over 80 air conditioning patents.**

Search by Classification

In 2015, the USPTO transitioned from its 100-year old U.S. Patent Classification system (USPC) to an international system known as the Cooperative Patent Classification (CPC). The CPC is derived from the International Patent Classification (IPC). The USPTO patent database continues to show the older USPC as well as current CPC classes. However, going forward, the USPTO will rely on CPC for classifying new utility patents. (The USPTO will continue to use USPC for classifying design and plant patents.) Both USPC and CPC systems categorize patents by class and then by a subclass.

EXAMPLE 1: Imagine you invented a kissing shield (Illustration 8) to prevent transmission of germs during kissing. The USPC system would categorize similar existing patents in Class 128 (Methods and Apparatus Used in the Inspection and Treatment of Diseases) and in Subclass 857 (Shields or guards for protecting head and face areas of the body).

EXAMPLE 2: Imagine you invented a board game that teaches players how to drive safely. The USPC system would categorize existing patents in Class 273 (Amusement Devices; Games) and Subclass 236 (Board games, pieces, or boards).

Illustration 8

Finding the Right Class and Subclass for Your Invention

Before the USPTO adopted the CPC Scheme, users could easily access and search the Manual of Patent Classification by keyword. That system provided a quick start to finding the proper patent class. Now the USPTO wants beginners to search using its Seven Step Strategy. You can learn the details of this strategy by starting at the USPTO home page (Illustration 9), clicking on the Learning and Resources tab, then from the dropdown menu, under Services and Publications, choose Support Centers. On the Support Centers page, choose Patent and Trademark Resource Centers (PTRCs). On the PTRC page, choose PTRC Basic Resources. Finally, choose The Seven Step Strategy (under Printed and Electronic Resources).

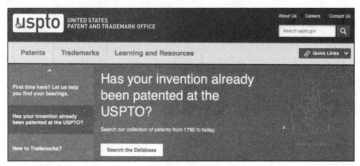

Illustration 9

Beginners may find this seven-step strategy unwieldy and for that reason, we suggest a simplified system for identifying the appropriate patent class and subclass.

Here's a simple four-step system to get started with class searching:

1. Determine a group of appropriate keywords for your inventions.
2. Use the keywords to locate patents that are similar to your invention.
3. Determine the USPC and CPC classes and subclasses for similar patents.
4. Search the USPTO database using the USPC or CPC numbers.

Skip These Steps If You Already Know of a Specific Patent

You can bypass these steps for finding the class/subclass if you already know of a patented invention that is very similar to yours. You can locate that patent using the search methods described earlier in this chapter—for example, searching by name of invention, inventor, or the company that owns the patent. Once you find the patent, you can see how the USPTO categorized it. See below, "Examine your search results and determine your class."

Determine keywords

The first step for locating the class for your invention is to come up with keywords that apply to your invention. For example, "necktie" in the case of a necktie wallet, "tent" in the case of a convertible tent, or "shower mirror" in the case of a shower mirror.

Locate similar patents

We recommend you start your initial search using Google Patents (patents. google.com). It's basically the same database as the USPTO but with a better search engine. In the search box, type in the keyword or keywords you have chosen. You can type in more than one word. For example, if we were searching for non-fogging shower mirrors, we would start with a "narrow" search by typing in "fog shower mirror." Using those search terms, we obtained the results shown in Illustration 10. If the results were too narrow (no matching inventions appeared), we would revise our search terms and try "shower mirror" or simply "mirror" until similar inventions are listed.

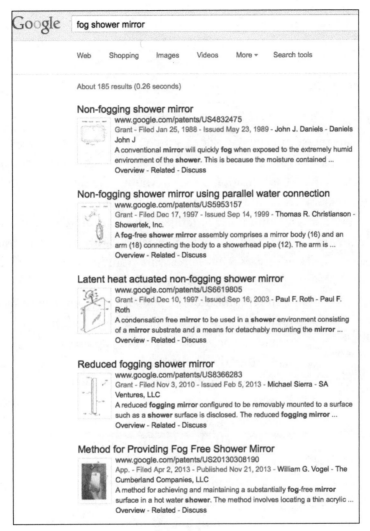

Illustration 10

Examine your search results and determine your class

Many of the inventions listed are similar to our non-fogging shower mirror so we chose one that seemed right on target—Patent No. 4,832,475 (Non-fogging shower mirror). You can view it at Google, or at the USPTO site.

Scroll down to the Classifications section. (In Illustration 11, you can see how Google and the USPTO both display classifications.)

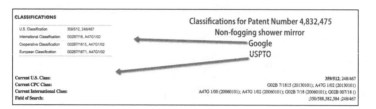

Illustration 11

One advantage of using Google to search the USPTO database is that Google has hyperlinked the class/subclass categorization. For example, if you click the U.S. Classification 359/512, you will be transported to Class 359, Optical: Systems And Elements. If you scroll down to Subclass 512, you will find it is for "humidity or temperature control," that is, devices that maintain "a desired humidity level or temperature or for increasing or decreasing the humidity level or temperature from its ambient value." If we

> Philo Farnsworth reportedly got the idea of scanning and displaying a moving image line by line (television) from harvesting hay row by row as a youth in rural Utah.

click the hyperlink for Class/Subclass 248/467 we see it is the classification for supports "for a mirror or picture holder attached to a support by adhesive means." That would not be applicable as our invention is designed to hang from the showerhead.

The same analysis can be made using the CPC numbers. Clicking the hyperlink for the Cooperative Classification will transport you to the European Patent Office (see Illustration 12). Type in the CPC number in the search box on the top of the page. That will show you the CPC class description (Optical Elements, Systems or Apparatus) and subclass ("with cooling or heating systems"). The same can be done for the remaining CPC class/subclass (A47G1/02). In this manner, you have narrowed down the searching boundaries for your prior art inventions to these specific classes. By the way, while you are at the European Patent Office you can search the worldwide patent database by typing your CPC code into the search box in the lower left corner of the web page and then clicking "Find Patents." We did that for our second CPC code (A47G1/02) and obtained the results seen in Illustration 13, several of which seemed relevant.

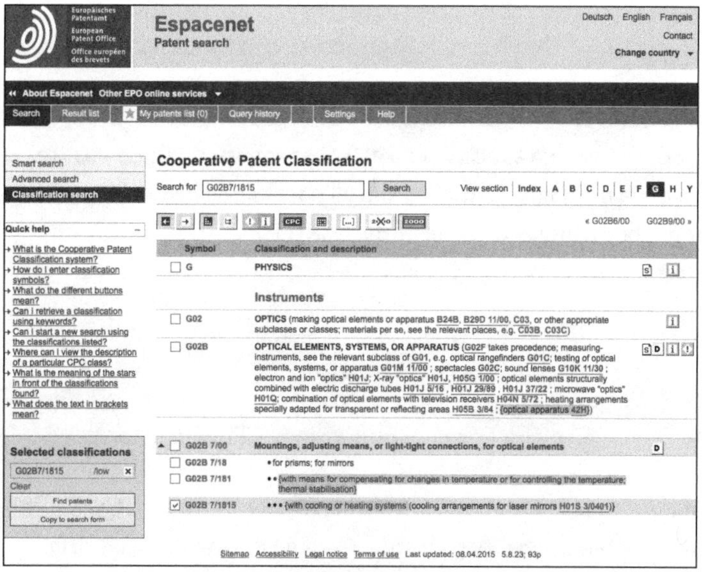

Illustration 12

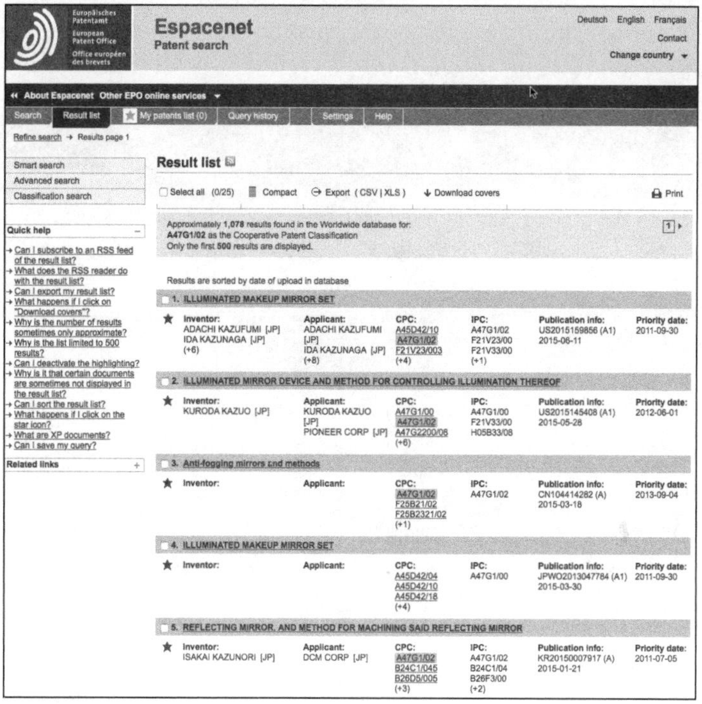

Illustration 13

No More Paper Searching by Class

Previously, the USPTO permitted the public to search through paper patents grouped by class and subclass at USPTO headquarters. These physical searches are no longer permitted and all class/subclass searching must be accomplished digitally whether at the USPTO or a PTRC.

Finding Foreign Equivalent Classifications

If you want to search through international patent databases, you'll need to use the international classification system known as the CPC (the Cooperative Patent Classification). Once you know the U.S. classification, you can easily locate the CPC equivalent at the Patent Classification home page (Illustration 14). (You can reach it directly at www.uspto.gov/web/patents/classification.) Type in the appropriate class/subclass and you will be directed to the appropriate CPC concordance.

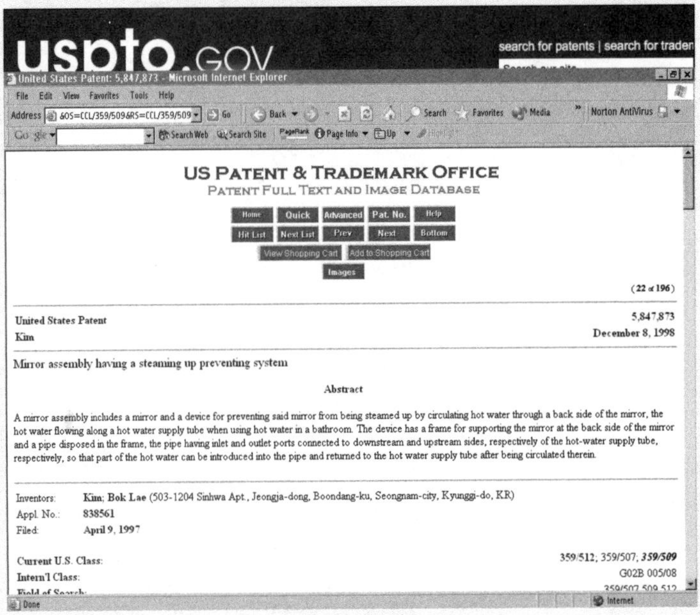

Illustration 14

Search the USPTO database using the class/subclass numbers

Once you've categorized your invention by potential class/subclass, you're ready to locate relevant prior art by plunging into the vast databases of existing and expired U.S. patents. Start at the patent-searching home page (Illustration 15). To get there, click the Patents tab on the USPTO home page, and from the drop-down menu, choose "Patent Search." Then choose "USPTO Patent Full-Text and Image Database (PatFT)." Under "Searching Full Text Patents (Since 1976)," click "Quick Search." On the Quick Search page, set the "Select years" drop-down menu to "1790 to present." Type in the class/subclass you want to search.

> Power steering was patented in 1927 but was not introduced in passenger cars until 1951.

Illustration 15

EXAMPLE: You are searching for prior-art patents for our non-fogging shower mirror. You want all patents in Class/Subclass 359/512, so you type "359/512" next to Term 1 and in Field 1, select "Current US Classification" (see Illustration 16). When you click the "Search" button, you are directed to a page with a list of patents (Illustration 17), some of which—for example, Patent 8,746,901, for a mirror assembly having a "fogless shower mirror"—are relevant.

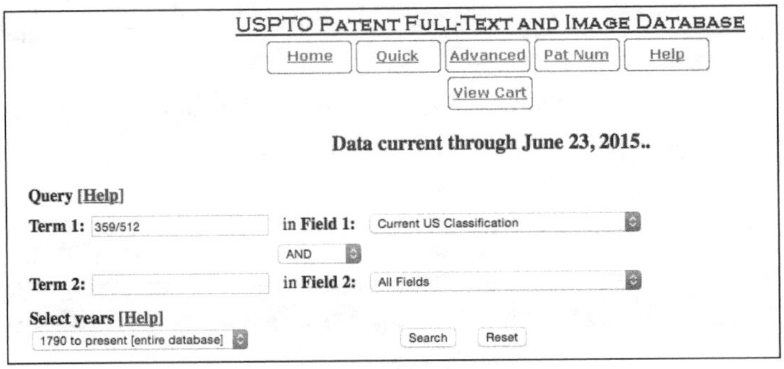

Illustration 16

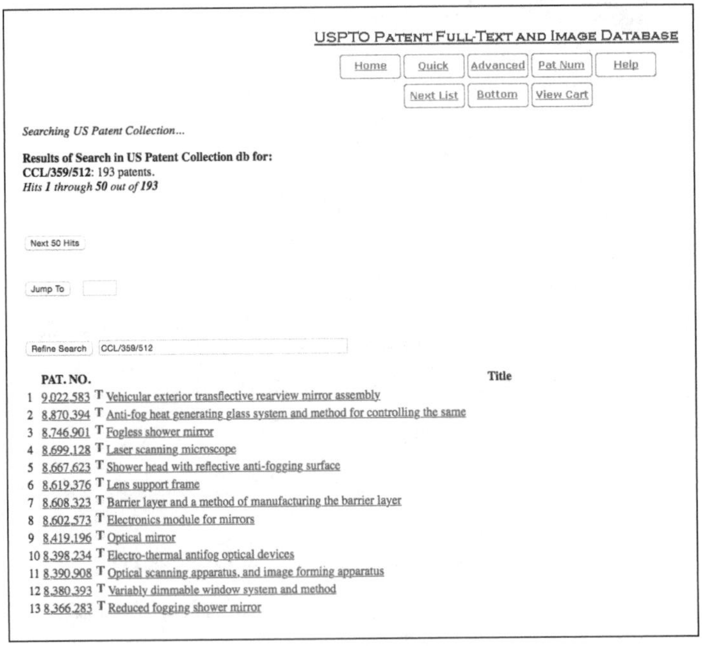

Illustration 17

Read and save relevant patents

If you have trouble reading and understanding patents, review "How to Read a Patent," below. Rest assured that it gets easier with practice: The more you read, the easier it becomes.

Which patents are relevant? You should look closely at any patent or document that has an important similarity to your invention and the way it works. In the case of a non-fogging shower mirror, for example, relevant patents would deal with inventions that prevent a mirror or glass from steaming in a humid setting. Keep in mind that you are not just seeking prior art that defeats your invention; you're also seeking prior art from which you can distinguish your invention. If you find a relevant prior-art patent and you can show that your invention is somehow different from this patent, you should cite it to the USPTO in a document known as an Information Disclosure Statement. You should submit this document either with your regular patent application or within three months of filing your regular patent application.

> **The inventor of the backless brassiere (Mary Phelps Peabody) was a descendant of Robert Fulton, inventor of the steamboat.**

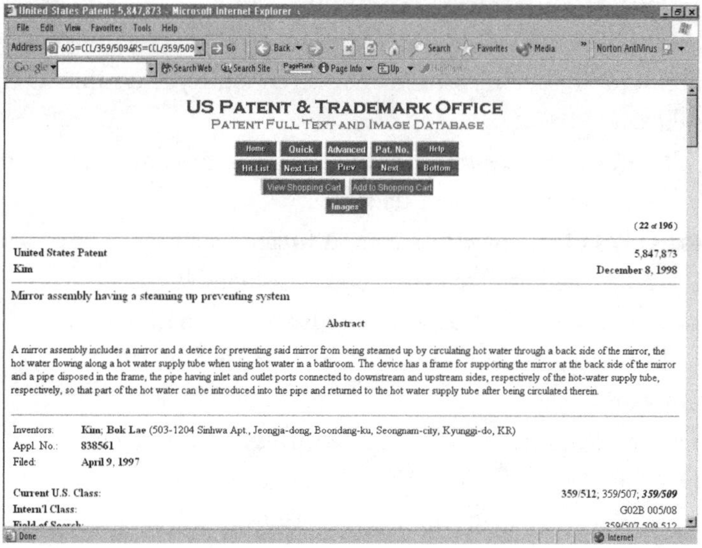

Illustration 18

Check "references cited"

The good news for patent searchers is that a particularly relevant prior-art patent will likely lead to additional prior art. Check the "References Cited" portion of the prior-art patent for leads to other inventions.

> **EXAMPLE:** One of the patents in our search for prior art for our non-fogging shower mirror, Patent 5,847,873 (a mirror assembly having a fog-preventing system), cites numerous patents that are also relevant for our mirror invention (Illustration 18).

Searching the Patent Database by Keywords

In many, if not most, circumstances, you may want to search for patents using criteria other than class/subclass. For example, it makes more sense to search by keywords if:

- You want to find patents that use a combination of certain key words, for example, "bicycle" and "carbon fiber."
- You want to find patents filed by a particular inventor.
- You want to find a patent by its number.
- You want to find all of the patents owned by a certain company.
- You want to look up a particular invention to determine its class/subclass.

The USPTO's main search page (Illustration 15) allows you to search two important patent databases:

- the USPTO Patent Full-Text and Image Database (PatFT). The PatFT consists of text-searchable patents dating back to 1976, as well as older patents dating back to 1790 (searchable only by patent number of patent class) and
- the USPTO Patent Application Full-Text and Image Database (AppFT). The AppFT consists of text-searchable published patent applications (published applications dating back to 1976).

The inventor of nonflammable film and nylon (Wallace Carothers) became depressed and took cyanide three weeks after his patent application for nylon was filed.

For keyword searching, we'll focus primarily on PatFT which offers several types of searches: "Quick Search," "Advanced Search," or "Patent Number Search."

Illustration 15

Start With "Quick Search"

Start out using Quick Search. It's comprehensive and easy to learn—and you can search two fields at one time. "Advanced Search" accesses the same information and permits you to search more than two fields at once. Unfortunately, "Advanced Search" requires considerable trial and error for first-time users.

Searching Published Patent Applications

Most regular patent applications are published 18 months after filing. If an application is not published, that means either that the application was filed within the last 18 months or that the inventor submitted, at the time of filing, a Nonpublication Request stating that the inventor will not be filing the application outside the United States.

You can search all applications published since March 15, 2001, at the USPTO website. You should search published patent applications if you're making a patentability search. To search published applications, start your search on the right side of the USPTO searching Web page titled "Patent Applications" (see Illustration 15). Search using the criteria and methods described in this chapter. Provisional patent applications are not published and therefore won't show up in your search.

Quick Search Features

When you use Quick Search, you select criteria that set the parameters for your search, including:

- **Fields.** Fields are different types of patent information—for example, "Inventor Name," "Application Date," "Abstract," "Title," or "Inventor City." We explain some of these fields in "How to Read a Patent," below, and provide additional explanations in the patent glossary in Appendix C. You can also find an explanation of each field at the USPTO website. If you don't know which field to choose, select "All Fields."
- **Terms.** Terms are the words, names, dates, or numbers that you type into the blank spaces.

  > **EXAMPLE:** You invented an inflatable whirlpool bath. To figure out what class your invention might fit into, you'd like to see inventions patented by Virgil Jacuzzi. Choose "Inventor Name" as Field 1 and type in "Jacuzzi, Virgil" as Term 1. You will recover several patents, including the world-famous invention (No. 4,211,216) that bears Mr. Jacuzzi's name.

- **Connectors.** When you search by more than one field criterion, you must choose one of three ways to connect your choices—AND,

OR, and AND NOT. You can use AND NOT to avoid getting certain patents.

> **EXAMPLE:** Imagine you invented a tennis racquet invention and you want all tennis racquet patents by inventor Howard Head. Mr. Head also had patents for metal skis. You don't want those. Choose "Inventor Name" as Field 1 and type in "Head, Howard" as Term 1. Choose "Abstract" as Field 2 (the abstract is a summary of the invention, see below) and type in "metal skis" as Term 2. Choose "AND NOT" as your connector and you will recover Head's tennis racquet patents but none of his patents for skis.

- **Select Years.** Here you select the range of years for which you wish to seek patents. Keep in mind that if you select "1790 to present," you cannot search through the text—except for the title of the patent— of pre-1976 patents. You can read those patents, but you can't search them at the USPTO. (The easiest way to locate old patents is by typing in their patent number in a Patent Number Search.)

How to Read a Patent

Patents generally include:
- the specification (this includes the description, the abstract, and the claims), and
- the drawings.

Although some practitioners refer to the description as the specification (and consider the abstract and claims as separate parts), the patent statutes define the specification as including all three parts, so we'll use the statute's terminology. In order to read and understand a patent, you will need to be able to identify these sections and tell them apart. Unfortunately, this is easier said than done—patents don't always include headings to let you know where one section stops and another starts.

We explain the description, abstract, and claims below. Patent drawings are covered separately, in Chapter 4.

The Description

The description explains how to make and use the invention—and how it can be distinguished from the prior art. The description consists of:

- **A title.** The inventor provides a short, simple summary of the invention —for example, "User-operated amusement apparatus for kicking the user's buttocks." (Yes, it's a real patent—see Illustration 19.)

- **The field of the invention.** Although no longer required, most older patents include this section. Here, the inventor explains what field the invention belongs in—for example, "the present invention pertains to a new hard-boiled-egg shelling device for quickly and easily removing the shell from a hard-boiled egg."

- **A criticism of the prior art.** The inventor describes the prior art and how the invention is distinguishable. (This helps to establish the invention's novelty and nonobviousness.)

- **"Objects and Advantages" of the invention.** The objects are found in older patents and are generally no longer used. They describe what the invention accomplishes and the advantages describe the superior qualities of the invention.

- **Description of the drawings.** Here, the inventor provides a brief explanation for each of the figures or views of the patent drawings (see Chapter 4 for more information on figures and views).

- **A detailed description of the invention and how it works.** This is the heart of the specification. Here, the inventor describes the invention's structure and explains its performance. After naming and numbering each element of the invention, the inventor describes the action of the invention's parts.

- **Any additional ramifications that are not important enough to show in the drawing.** Here, an inventor might include, for example, alternative ways that an invention can be used or put together.

Many patent attorneys conclude the patent with several boilerplate paragraphs to repeat the advantages, state less important ramifications, and state that the scope of the invention should be determined by the claims and not the specifics of the description.

Abstract

The abstract—a concise, one-paragraph summary of the structure, nature, and purpose of the invention—may prove the most helpful portion of the patent. The abstract helps you quickly get right to the heart of the invention: what it does and how it works. Below is an abstract for a masochistic patent (see Illustration 19) located by patent searcher Greg Aharonian.

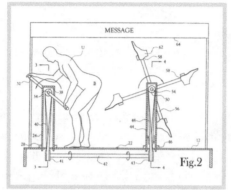

Illustration 19

Abstract

An amusement apparatus including a user-operated and -controlled apparatus for self-infliction of repetitive blows to the user's buttocks by a plurality of elongated arms bearing flexible extensions that rotate under the user's control. The apparatus includes a platform foldable at a midsection, having first post and second upstanding posts detachably mounted thereon. The first post is provided with a crank positioned at a height thereon which requires the user to bend forward toward the first post while grasping the crank with both hands, to prominently present his buttocks toward the second post. The second post is provided with a plurality of rotating arms detachably mounted thereon, with a central axis of the rotating arms positioned at a height generally level with the user's buttocks. The elongated arms are propelled by the user's movement of the crank, which is operatively connected by a drive train to the central axis of the rotating arms. As the user rotates the crank, the user's buttocks are paddled by flexible shoes located on each outboard end of the elongated arms to provide amusement to the user and viewers of the paddling. The amusement apparatus is foldable into a self-contained package for storage or shipping.

Finding the Who, What, Where, and When

You don't have to know how to read a patent to find basic data such as the title, inventor's name, address, patent filing date, patent issue date, or referenced patents. You can find these pieces of information on the front page of the patent. Search for them using either the "Quick Search" or "Advanced Search" described in "Searching the Patent Database by Keywords," above.

Claims

Patent claims establish the legal boundaries or scope of an invention. They are the standard by which patent rights are measured. When a patent owner sues for infringement, the owner contends that someone has made, used, sold, offered for sale, or imported an invention that has all of the elements of one claim or that closely fits the description of the invention contained in the claims. (In patent terms, the claims are said to "read on the infringing device.") In this manner, claims function like the boundaries in a deed for real estate—everything within them belongs to the owner.

The inventor of the lava lamp told customers, "If you buy my lamp, you won't need drugs."

You face a few challenges when you examine patent claims. First, you have to figure out how to decipher them. Claims follow strict requirements: They are sentence fragments, always start with an initial capital letter, contain one period, and don't include any quotation marks or parentheses (except in mathematical or chemical formulas). Since most claims also use obtuse terminology, we offer some tips on translating claims in Appendix C.

Another challenge may arise if you're not sure what claims you plan to make for your invention. This type of uncertainty can make it difficult to determine whether your invention infringes the claims in a patent. The structure of patent claims only adds to this confusion. There are two types of claims: independent and dependent claims. At least one independent claim is written as broadly as possible. Each independent claim is usually followed by narrower dependent claims designed to specifically recite the invention's unique features. These dependent claims incorporate the independent claims and any intervening dependent claims, but act to diversify your patent's coverage. If your independent claim is your main "recipe," the dependent claims are variations that have several functions including providing fallback weapons in case the independent claim is invalidated.

Luckily, you will rarely have to read patent claims when making your prior-art search. Usually, the claims simply repeat—in a more convoluted style—the information in the specification and drawings. Because the specification and the drawings contain more information about the invention than the claims do, it's even possible that your invention might not appear in the claims, even if it's described in the specification.

A patent examiner is primarily interested in whether your invention has been described in prior-art documents (examiners refer to these documents as "anticipating" your invention or rendering it obvious), not whether your invention infringes an in-force patent. Therefore, it is the prior art itself, not the claims, against which your invention will be judged.

Don't fall into what we call the "claims trap." If you are trying to determine if your invention is patentable, don't base your decision solely on whether your invention is covered by the claims of another patent. The claims of a patent are used only to determine whether a product or process in actual use infringes another patent. Again, the USPTO doesn't care whether your invention, if made or used, infringes any in-force patents.

RESOURCE

Need help sorting out patent claims? If you feel overwhelmed by patent claims issues, seek assistance from a patent attorney or a patent agent. We explain how to find patent attorneys and agents in Appendix E.

CAUTION

Although you aren't required to include claims in your provisional patent application, patent attorneys disagree over whether you should include them anyway. Those who oppose including them argue that any claim in a provisional patent application will probably be changed by the time the inventor files a regular patent application. These attorneys are concerned that changing the claims might be considered an amendment of the claims—which might limit the scope of the patent (*Festo Corp. v. Shoketsu Kinzoku*, 122 S.Ct. 1831 (2002)). However, other attorneys believe that you should include at least one claim in your provisional patent application to protect your rights outside the United States—some foreign patent offices may not recognize a provisional patent application as a patent application unless it includes a claim. As a general rule, we recommend that those who plan to file patent applications for their inventions outside the United States include at least one claim in the provisional patent application.

Drafting a claim or two for your PPA may also help you to understand and appreciate the essence of your invention and force you to come up with terminology that best describes your invention. If you do draft claims, be sure that every term used in your claims is also used in your specification.

Reading a Patent and Distinguishing Prior Art

As you read about previous inventions, you should begin thinking about how you can distinguish your ideas from the prior art. You can do this by taking notes on each patent to explain how your invention differs physically—for example, it has a different shape, size, or parts. You should also explain how your invention provides superior results—for example, your invention is faster, cleaner, more efficient, less expensive, or otherwise better. Although you are not required to, you can distinguish your invention from the prior art in your provisional patent application. But even if you choose not to distinguish your invention at this stage, you will need this information when preparing your regular patent application. Below is an example of how prior art was distinguished for the convertible tent invention. Note that the inventor distinguished his invention from both patented and nonpatented prior art. (You can find information on searching for nonpatented art in "Finding Prior Art That Isn't Currently Patented," below.)

The inventor of military housing (that later evolved into the Quonset hut) filed his patent application while serving on the Western Front during World War I.

EXAMPLE: Distinguishing Prior Art for Convertible Tent Invention (Illustration 20)

Patent 2,391,871 (1946) shows a canvas covering with a window that can only be opened or closed and cannot adapt to a range of climatic conditions, such as rain, heat, cold, etc.

Patent 2,666,441 (1954) shows a pocket in a tent, with a transparent sheet that is inserted in the pocket and a flap to cover the opening. This device is awkward, heavy, and difficult to adjust for differing climatic conditions.

Patent 3,800,814 (1974) shows an elongated tent with a curved roof, such as a Quonset hut, including a sidewall with a vertical zipper and two bottom horizontal zippers. This tent is difficult to adjust rapidly and easily and lacks good versatility.

Illustration 20

Patent 3,970,096 (1976) shows another elongated tent that has spaced inner and outer porous layers supported by tent poles that extend crossways over the tent. This arrangement is complex, awkward, and difficult to adjust and use.

Patent 4,077,417 (1978) shows a tent with frame members that have ends inserted in multisocket connectors. Again, it lacks versatility for different climatic conditions.

Patent 4,265,261 (1981) shows a pyramid-style tent with triangular side windows that are covered by triangular, awning-like covers. While unique, this arrangement is complex, difficult, and awkward to adjust and still lacks good versatility.

Patent 4,858,635 (1989) shows a tent with a ceiling opening that can be covered by a pivotable piece attached to a flap. The tent also has a rain fly that the pivotable piece can support. While somewhat versatile, this arrangement is not simple to use and is complex to fabricate.

Patent 5,394,897 (1995) shows interconnected tents. Modules that zip onto the tent openings connect the tents. Each tent has inner and outer panels mated by pairs of zippers. However, they connect in a complex, unreliable manner.

Patents 5,467,794 (1995) and 5,579,799 (1996) show tents with collapsible shade awnings. The awnings have hinged members. This arrangement is complex, difficult to use, and lacks good versatility.

Patent 5,765,584 (1998) shows a tent with a two-ply door (one ply is porous for air venting and one is waterproof). This complex arrangement is awkward to use, erect, and fabricate.

A Nightwatch convertible tent is made by Sierra Designs of Emeryville, California. Its inner canopy has a window with a solid panel that can be zipped open. A net panel prevents mosquitoes from entering. An outer waterproof flysheet is spaced from the inner canopy. The flysheet covers the window in rain or snow. However installing the flysheet is awkward—it must be done from outside the tent, which allows spindrift to pass through the zipper and under the bottom of the flysheet. Its netting will catch and hold the snow, so that the next time the window is open, the spindrift will fall into the tent.

Finding Prior Art That Isn't Currently Patented

To search for prior art beyond U.S. patents, your best place to start is the Internet. There, you'll find a massive storehouse of nonpatented prior art. Here are some tips that will help you sift through countless Web pages to find the information you need:

- **Check online stores.** If your idea is commercial, you may find similar inventions already for sale in an online store or outlet.

    EXAMPLE: Imagine you invented a convertible tent (Illustration 20) and you want to review prior art that is currently available for sale. By typing "convertible tent" into the search engine at the REI website (www.rei.com), you will find many patented and unpatented convertible tents (see Illustration 21).

Illustration 21

- **Embrace Google.com.** Search engines come and go, but none performs as consistently and efficiently as Google.com (www.google.com). In addition to providing links to relevant websites, Google provides thumbnail illustrations culled from the search terms (Illustration 22) as well as newsgroup commentary on the search terms (Illustration 23). For more advanced searches using multiple fields and connectors, try Google's "Advanced Search Features."

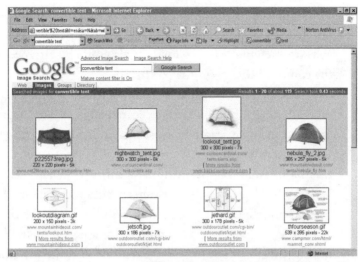

Illustration 22

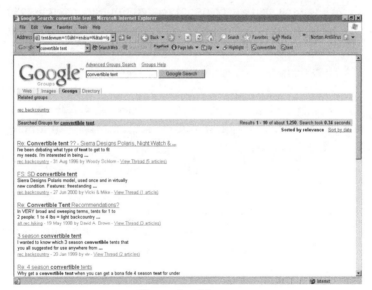

Illustration 23

- **Use Freshpatents.com.** FreshPatents (www.freshpatents.com) compiles all U.S. patent applications that are published for opposition. This publication is done before the USPTO makes its final decision to grant or deny the patent. FreshPatents is a good way to track new inventions because the company breaks down its compilations based on various categories, such as computers, software, telecom, medical, consumer, engines, and so forth. It also sorts by assignee—that is, by the company that owns the patent.

- **Use a master search engine.** In addition to individual search engines, such as Google, there are master search engines like Dogpile (www.dogpile.com) that search using several individual search engines simultaneously.

- **Use the Software Patent Institute for software inventions.** The USPTO has issued many software and Internet patents that have been invalidated (or are considered worthless) because the USPTO lacks a decent prior-art collection in this area. Don't let this happen to you—beef up your prior-art search for software inventions. With the help of the Software Patent Institute (www.spi.org), you will find a comprehensive database of related prior-art references for software, such as computer manuals, older textbooks, and older journal articles, conference proceedings, computer science theses, and other such materials.

- **Search foreign patents.** You can search a worldwide network of patents for free. At sites such as Espacenet.com (http://ep.espacenet.com), you can search the abstracts and titles of 30 million worldwide documents *in English*. In addition, you can search the full text of the resources at the World Intellectual Property Office (WIPO) and the European Patent Office in the original language (see Illustration 24). For example, we typed in "convertible tent" and obtained 44 matches (see Illustration 25). Check Espacenet.com for details. Other sources for foreign patent searching are listed in Appendix F.

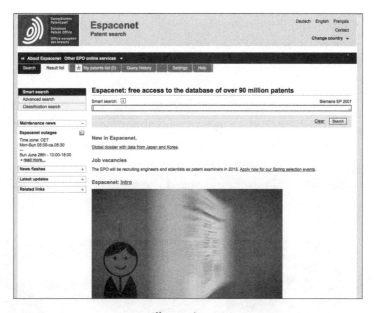

Illustration 24

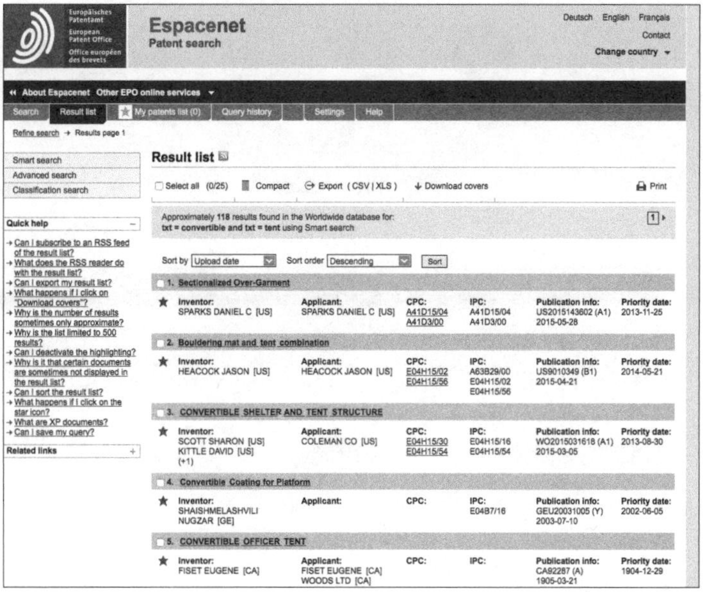

Illustration 25

- **Check the Thomas Register.** The Thomas Register (www.thomasnet. com) can enhance your prior-art searching by providing you with images and text from thousands of company catalogs as well as providing websites, CAD imagery (computer-assisted drawings), and other product information (Illustration 26). For example, when we searched for product information about tents, the Thomas Register website displayed various tent categories of products (Illustration 27), including "camping tents," "emergency tents," and "military tents." By clicking on the category and the company, you can view a mind-boggling collection of patented and nonpatented products.

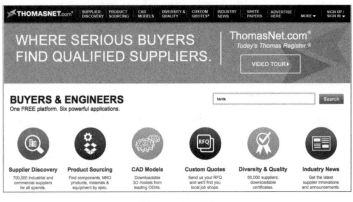

Illustration 26

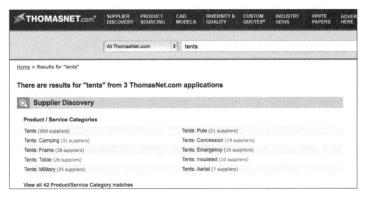

Illustration 27

> ### Beyond the Internet: Hitting the Stacks
>
> Much as we love the Internet for finding nonpatented prior art, a thorough search requires that you—or a professional searcher—visit the stacks of a local university engineering library (or similar institution) to research scientific data that may not exist online. Keep in mind that any printed publication, in any language, that was published before your date of invention is prior art to your invention. That includes technical specifications, owner's manuals, user's manuals, Web pages, textbooks, business plans, case studies, magazine articles, or any other printed publications. A visit to an engineering library, such as UC Berkeley's Kresge Engineering Library, may be essential to conduct a thorough prior-art search.

After the Preliminary Search

Once you've completed your preliminary search and reviewed your prior art, you must decide whether to proceed with your provisional patent application. Depending on what your search uncovers, you will have three options to choose from:

- If you're not worried about any of the prior art you uncovered in your preliminary search, file now and risk the filing fee ($130 for small entities and $65 for micro entities), especially if you're concerned that someone else might beat you to the USPTO. You can skip the rest of this chapter and head straight to Chapter 4 to start your patent drawings.
- If you are concerned that the prior art you have uncovered could defeat your regular patent application, you may want to put off filing until you get a professional opinion from a patent agent or lawyer (at a cost of about $200 to $500 an hour). Turn to Appendix E for information on finding a patent attorney.
- If you are not sure whether the prior art poses a threat to your invention or you want to search more thoroughly before filing your provisional patent application, hire a professional searcher or perform a more extensive search yourself. We explain these options below.

Hiring a Patent Searcher

Professional patent searchers come in two flavors: those who are licensed to practice before the USPTO (these patent attorneys and agents are known as registered representatives) and those who are not licensed, known as lay searchers. Registered representatives have passed a USPTO test demonstrating their knowledge of patent law. Lay searchers—who are usually knowledgeable in one or two fields of invention—charge less, often half of what registered representatives charge.

The inventor of the Slinky toy gave much of his profits to a Bolivian cult.

Fees for patent searchers range from $100 to $500 per search for lay searchers, and from $300 to $1,200 per search for searches by registered representatives. These fees don't include an opinion on patentability—that is, the searcher will not provide an opinion as to whether the USPTO will issue a patent. Only registered representatives are allowed to give you an opinion on patentability—lay searchers have to keep their opinions to themselves. Some patent searchers charge a flat fee; others charge by the hour. If you plan to do some of the work yourself, you'll save money by requesting hourly billing.

You can locate patent searchers in the yellow pages of local telephone directories or through Internet resources. You can also use Internet search engines (for example, Google.com or Bing.com)—look under "Patent Searchers." All registered representatives are listed at the USPTO website. (To find the list, click the drop-down menu entitled "Select a Search Collection" at the USPTO home page. Then choose "Patent Attorneys and Agents.") Keep in mind that the attorney or agent will either have to travel to the USPTO or hire an associate to make the search—this means that it may not make financial sense to hire a searcher from your home town, depending on where you live.

You'll need to give your searcher a lot of information about your invention, including:

- a description of the invention
- drawings
- information about the class/subclass, if known
- identification of the invention's novel features, and
- any required deadlines.

When you use a patent attorney or agent, requesting a search will not compromise the status of your invention as a trade secret. By law, your conversation with a registered representative is considered a confidential communication. This is not the case with an unlicensed searcher, however. If you use a lay searcher, you should ask your searcher to sign a nondisclosure agreement (a sample is provided in Appendix B).

TIP

Extra help for software and hardware patents. When searching for patents relating to software and hardware, consider Source Translation Optimization (www.bustpatents.com), a website operated by patent searcher Greg Aharonian. In addition to providing patent-searching services, Aharonian's site highlights many of the pitfalls (and bad patents) that face software inventors seeking prior art.

The Official Gazette

The USPTO puts out a weekly online publication called the *Official Gazette for Patents*, which lists pertinent bibliographic data, the abstract, and one figure or drawing for every patent issued that week. PTRCs and some other public libraries maintain older copies of the *Official Gazette for Patents* in print or on microfiche. If the drawing and claim in the *Official Gazette* look relevant, go to the actual patent online or order a copy of it.

Searching at the USPTO

You can also perform a more thorough search at the USPTO in Alexandria, Virginia, which has the EAST terminals. The advantage of searching using the EAST terminals is that you have access to a complete database that is searchable by key words or according to classification. The USPTO search facilities maintain a variety of reference materials including manuals, indexes, dictionaries, reference publications, and *Official Gazettes*. If you need help with your search, you can ask any of the search assistants in the search room or (even better) an examiner in the actual examining division.

Providing the details won't endanger the security of your invention; employees of the USPTO are not allowed to file patent applications, so you don't have to worry about them stealing your great idea. Employees of PTRCs that have the WEST system see new inventions all the time and most inventions are copied only after they are successful in the marketplace.

The USPTO's EAST terminals (the WEST terminals are available at most PTRCs) require some training and skill to use. The USPTO has about 250 EAST terminals in the public search room and gives free four-hour training sessions once per month. (Often, a user at an adjacent terminal can help a new user with the basics to get started.)

> The first fax machine was patented in 1848 by Frederick Bakewell.

The EAST-WEST systems can perform a search by class and subclass. Users of EAST can also make Boolean or keyword combination searches back to 1971 or make searches using a combination of both techniques. In terms of speed, EAST is superior to a paper search because you can flip through patents displayed on the computer monitor faster than the actual paper copies. You can also use the EAST-WEST systems to do "forward" searches—that is, if a relevant patent is found, EAST-WEST systems can find and search through all later-issued patents in which the relevant patent is cited (referred to) as a prior-art reference. Further, the systems can do "backward" searches—that is, they can search through all previously issued patents that are cited as prior art in the relevant patent. You can also use the EAST-WEST systems to search European and Japanese patents.

EAST is free to use at the USPTO, but the USPTO charges for printing out copies of patents. Hopefully, the capabilities of EAST will be soon be more widely available. In the meantime, if you want to use it, you must make a trip to Alexandria or to PTRCs with WEST and learn the system there.

Using a thesaurus, our inventor devised some searching terms for his invention, a doll that simulates tears through the use of moving lights or LED technology.

His list includes doll, toy, puppet, mannequin, tears, crying, sad, sobbing, weeping, eye, eyeball, eyelid, LED, light emitting diode, lights, and moving lights.

Following the route suggested, our inventor first searched the USPTO website. After a few false starts, our inventor located Class 446, Amusement Devices, Toys. He then found Subclass 190 for a "device comprising a simulation of an animate being or portion thereof and including either (1) an opening or passageway within or adjacent to a representation of an eye on the simulation through which a liquid is discharged to simulate weeping, or (2) a motor or mechanical motion-transmitting means to move the simulation or a part of the simulation with respect to another part." Can't get much closer than that!

After reviewing the patents in this class/subclass, he then used the second recommended method of searching—the Quick Search system. He searched using the terms "doll" and "tears," first searching in the Abstract portion of the patents and then expanding it to a mix of terms including "LED" and "doll," "light-emitting diode" and "doll," and "crying" and "doll."

He searched the "Abstracts" and "Description/Specification" fields of the patents.

Our inventor found:

- doll inventions that simulate tears with liquids
- doll inventions that simulate crying with audio, and
- doll inventions in which the eyes were composed of LEDs.

But there were no past patents in which the dolls' tears were simulated by LEDs.

Next, our inventor searched on the Internet. He located historic crying dolls, such as "Tiny Tears," but none that anticipated our inventor's creation.

Our inventor spent 150 minutes reading this chapter and performing patent searches on the Internet. Only about 20 hours left.

Time Spent on Chapter 3
**2.5 hours
(150 minutes)**

Time Remaining
19 hours 55 minutes

Drafting the Provisional Patent Application:
Part 1—Drawing Your Invention

"When I was taking a course in analytic mechanics, the professor had a big machine with a series of pipes and tubes and wires and chemical containers and springs and odd pieces of weird equipment and each student had to find the weight of the earth with this contraption. There was nothing more ridiculous to me than finding the weight of the earth because I didn't care how much the earth weighed. I had no idea that this was going to come in handy in my cartoon work later … the way people go to a great extreme to accomplish very little."

**—Rube Goldberg, "Oral History Interview With Rube Goldberg, 1970,"
interview by Emily Nathan**

Rube Goldberg may be the world's best-known invention artist. His cartoons depict contraptions that use maximum effort to produce minimal results. Regardless of their comic value, each element of a Rube Goldberg contrivance is clearly drawn and labeled with a letter or number that corresponds to accompanying explanatory text. This method gives the viewer excellent instructions on how to make and use each Rube Goldberg invention.

In this chapter, we'll help you prepare drawings that will explain your invention as clearly as any Rube Goldberg contraption. (We use the term "drawing" to refer to any illustration of your invention, whether a line drawing, a flowchart, a schematic, or a photograph.) Although there is no requirement that you include drawings with your provisional patent application, as a practical matter, it is usually necessary to do so in order to fulfill your goal of describing how to make and use your invention. Drawings communicate far more effectively than words. (If you don't believe this, imagine trying to understand how a Rube Goldberg invention works just by reading the text.)

There are no rules for provisional patent application drawings, except that they must be understandable and fit in a regular file folder. You can use black-and-white or color photographs, computer-created drawings, or handmade drawings. But whatever method you use, your drawings should conform to the basic patent drawing principles described in "Basic Patent Drafting Principles," below.

For those readers who consider themselves artistically challenged, we offer suggestions, tips, and tricks that will help you create accurate visual representations. If you have made a prototype of your invention, you can prepare drawings easily and inexpensively with the use of a camera and photo-editing and drawing software. If your invention is best illustrated by means of a schematic drawing, table, or flowchart, we provide some simple principles you can follow to prepare that type of illustration.

Obviously, your visual representation should conform to (and definitely should not contradict) your written explanation of how to make and use your invention. Because you may have to make a series of modifications to both drawings and text as you progress, it's helpful to maintain your drawings in a digital format that's easy to store and modify.

TIP
Start with drawings, then write the specification. Some inventors may prefer to start by writing the text of the application (see Chapter 5), but we believe it's easier to begin the process with the drawings. These illustrations help you focus on the elements and operation of your machine. Creating the drawings will clarify which of your invention's components are important enough to merit a mention in the text—and which are not. The drawings will also suggest ways of describing how your invention works. In short, once the completed drawings are in front of you, you'll have a much easier time writing the "specification" or text of your application.

RESOURCE
For more information on patent drawings. For a complete discussion about patent drawing, read *How to Make Patent Drawings*, by patent agent Jack Lo and attorney David Pressman (Nolo).

Basic Patent Drafting Principles

Whether you use rudimentary sketches or professionally drafted drawings, you should organize and label your drawings according to traditional patent drawing rules, discussed below.

The View

The term "brownout" is derived from H.P. Brown, who promoted the use of the electric chair.

Inventions are commonly depicted in different views or figures—for example, top views, side views, perspective views, or disassembled (exploded) views. You should present as many views as necessary to explain how to make and use your invention, including all of its embodiments. Each view provides another way of "seeing" the invention. Each view is given a discrete figure number (abbreviated as "Fig." in patent law). For example, the inventor of an egg-shelling device presents the process of removing the eggshell in Illustrations 1 and 2. Here are a few tips that will help you decide which views to include:

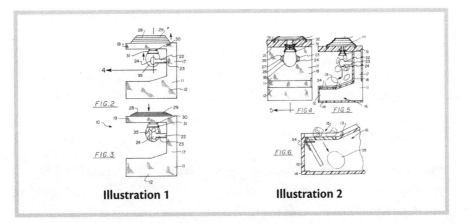

Illustration 1   Illustration 2

- In order to show the internal workings of your invention, you may use an exploded view (Illustration 3) in which the parts of the invention are separated but shown in relation to each other.
- You may also use views that are not drawings in the traditional sense, such as schematics or flowcharts (see "Drawings for Software, Business Methods, Electrical Inventions, and Chemical Compounds," later in this chapter).
- Perspective views (in which you can see several angles and sides of your invention) are preferred over straight-on side or top views.
- Hidden lines should be shown by using broken (dashed) lines instead of solid lines (Illustration 4).
- You do not need to show features that are prior art. For example, if you have invented a decoding system for a subwoofer enclosed in a traditional speaker cabinet, you do not need to include the speaker

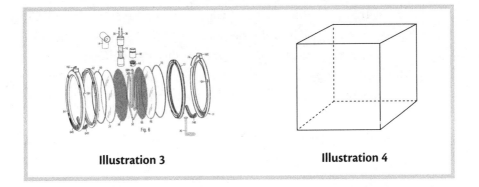

Illustration 3   Illustration 4

cabinet in your drawings unless it is essential for understanding your invention.

- If you're reducing or enlarging the dimensions of your invention, be sure that the parts are to scale—that is, reduced or enlarged in the same proportion in all parts.

Drawing Sheets

Place each figure on a sheet of paper—a "drawing sheet." Label and number each separate figure as described in "Take a Number," below. Here are some tips for creating drawing sheets:

- Use the same size paper for all of your drawing sheets. We recommend that you use the same size paper as is required for a regular patent application (RPA) since this will make it easier to modify or make your drawings for the RPA and it will provide your patent examiner with a familiar size to look at if he or she ever has to verify your PPA's disclosure. The paper sizes accepted for an RPA are US-letter size (8.5" x 11") and International A4-size (210 x 297 mm, or 8.25" x 11&11/16").

- Include a margin of approximately one inch all around each drawing sheet (don't frame the drawing area with a line).

- You can place two or more figures on a letter-size or A4 drawing sheet of 8.5" by 11" paper, as long as the page doesn't look too crowded.

- Portray each view in an upright position, large enough so that the parts can be seen clearly. If possible, always orient your drawing sheets in the portrait mode—the long sides of the sheet are vertical and the short sides are horizontal. Avoid landscape orientation since this will force anyone who looks at your drawings to have to turn their head or rotate the sheet or computer image so that the invention is shown upright. Don't connect figures on a drawing sheet (except for electrical waveforms, which may be connected with dashed lines to show relative timing).

The inventor of the Theremin, the first electronic instrument, was kidnapped from his New York apartment in 1938 and taken to a Russian labor camp where he later invented an electronic eavesdropping bug.

Take a Number

You don't have to conform to the official numbering rules used for regular patent applications, but doing so will help you save time when you prepare your regular patent application later. It will also enable anyone who views your provisional patent application to understand it and to obtain information more readily.

Sheet Numbers

Number each drawing sheet on the top using a fraction in which the numerator is the number of the drawing sheet and the denominator is the total number of drawing sheets (for example 1/4, 2/4, 3/4, and so on). Put the sheet numbers inside the top margin, in the center if possible, otherwise to the right. If you have only one drawing sheet, you do not need to number it.

Figure Numbers

Label each figure consecutively in Arabic numerals—for example Fig. 1, Fig. 2, Fig. 3—and arrange the figures in numerical order on the sheets. Use letters only as suffixes after the numbers if you want to group several related views together—for example, Fig. 1A, Fig. 1B, Fig. 2A, Fig. 2B, and so on.

Reference Numbers

Use reference numbers and letters to identify the parts or elements of your invention. The general rule is that every part you will mention or explain in your application should be numbered. The point of the reference number is to help the reader understand what you're talking about when you describe your invention. Here are some tips for labeling:
- Start with a number higher than the number of your highest Fig. number, so the reference numbers won't be confused with your figure numbers.
- Number the parts consecutively in even numbers—for example, 10, 12, 14—so that you can insert consecutive odd numbers later if necessary.

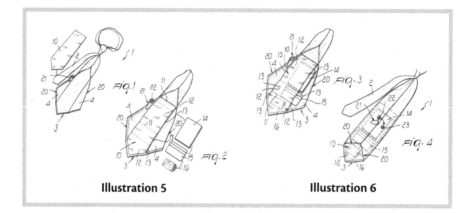

Illustration 5   Illustration 6

- Use the same number with suffix letters to associate and distinguish related parts—for example, "the machine has a left lever 10L and a right lever 10R."
- Write numbers near the part but, if possible, outside the boundaries of the drawing (for example, in Illustration 6, the artist was able to keep all of the reference numbers outside of the drawing with the exception of 21 and 22).
- Don't write a number over a line or inside a figure.
- Don't forget to number parts or items that are used in connection with your invention. For example, the inventor of a tie with concealed pockets must describe the types of items—credit cards, bills, or paper—that can be concealed in the tie (see Illustrations 5 and 6).

Getting Started

You'll need to take a fresh look at your invention to determine the best views for presenting it. You have two overlapping goals when preparing your drawings: (1) to illustrate how to make and use your invention, and (2) to visually represent every element of your invention for which you intend to claim patent rights. In a sense, these goals serve the same purpose. As writer/inventor David Lindsay puts it, "In the end, the whole shebang has to look like something that functions."

Since you want to show how your invention achieves its result, your views should demonstrate the steps in your process or the procedure for using your machine.

EXAMPLE: Imagine you invented a system for long-term remote medical monitoring of astronauts in space. Your invention includes a sensor attached to the subject's skin with an adhesive bandage, a microchip arranged on the adhesive bandage to transmit data, a central unit to receive and further transmit the data, and a portable data-recording device. In order to illustrate how this device operates, you will need to provide a drawing of the adhesive bandage with its sensor and transmitter (Illustration 7), a drawing of a person wearing the adhesive bandage and the portable data device (Illustration 9), and two flowcharts, one showing the transmission of data between sensor and receiver (Illustration 8) and another showing the transmission of data within the context of an astronaut in space (Illustration 10).

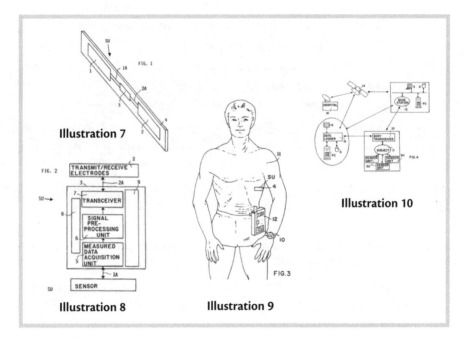

Illustration 7

Illustration 8

Illustration 9

Illustration 10

The four drawings mentioned in the example above show not only how to make and use the invention but also what is claimed in the resulting patent (Patent 6,315,719). As you can see, the drawings for this invention provide a reasonable explanation of what it looks like and how it functions—even without text.

Your first step is to imagine the potential views needed to illustrate your invention. You can accomplish this in two ways: (1) If you have a prototype, take pictures of it with a camera and organize the photos in order of the steps of operation, or (2) if you don't have a prototype, start with a series of elemental drawings (stick figures are fine). Once you have an idea which views you will need, choose a plan of attack based on your artistic skills, the nature of your invention, and your progress in modeling the invention. Here are your options:

- **If you're an inventor who can draw:** You can render drawings of your invention accurately in terms of perspective and proportion. In other words, you can probably proceed without much additional help. To get started, examine formal drawings for patented inventions similar to yours and create drawings that track their perspective and content. Don't worry about providing the same level of craftsmanship as a professional draftsperson; as long as you provide understandable representations, you'll do just fine.

- **If you have a prototype but you can't draw:** We recommend that you take photos of the invention and either use the photographs as your drawings or create drawings by tracing the photographs. We discuss these procedures in "Tips for Inventors Who Have a Prototype but Can't Draw," below.

- **If you don't have a prototype and you can't draw:** If you find yourself in this situation, you'll need to consider bringing in some technological aids or outside help. For example, you could (a) hire a prototype maker to prepare a three-dimensional model of your invention, then proceed through the steps above, (b) hire an artist to create drawings (you describe it, then the artist draws it), or (c) draw your invention using a software program or clip-art images. These options are covered in "Tips for Inventors Who Don't Have a Prototype and Can't Draw," below.

Ashok Gadgil

After an outbreak of a new strain of cholera in 1992 killed 10,000 people in India, Ashok Gadgil was inspired to create a new and inexpensive way to purify water using ultraviolet light.

- **If you need more than illustrations:** If you think you'll need schematics, flowcharts, tables, or nontraditional drawings, review "Drawings for Software, Business Methods, Electrical Inventions, and Chemical Compounds," below. You can probably create a credible flowchart or table manually or with the aid of a computer. Schematics for electrical inventions can also be drawn manually or with the aid of a plastic electronic template.

Tips for Inventors Who Have a Prototype but Can't Draw

In this section, we'll discuss some popular techniques for inventors who have a prototype but don't consider themselves artists. Keep in mind that if the design of your prototype obscures or conceals the inner workings of your invention, you'll need to provide a peek inside either by using an exploded view or by removing housings and exposing the internal workings.

> **EXAMPLE:** Stan invents an electrical pencil sharpener and encases his prototype in a stylish housing. Stan will have to remove the housing in order to provide detailed drawings of the internal invention he seeks to patent.

Take a Photograph of Your Invention

Photography is a great way to inexpensively document your invention. If you're serious about filing your provisional patent application in 24 hours, photography—using either film or digital imagery—is a fast way to obtain drawings. Below we'll discuss how to make photographic drawings with a digital or nondigital (film) camera.

Method: Film Camera

Follow these steps to create drawings using a camera and film:

1. Prepare a list of views of your invention.
2. Photograph the views, preferably with black-and-white film. (Note: Kodak T400 TMAX black-and-white film can be printed at standard photo developing outlets.)

3. Select your final prints and (a) scan the images into your computer and print the images on paper, (b) copy the images onto paper using a high-quality photocopier, (c) use the tracing methods discussed in "Trace Your Photograph by Hand," below, to create a drawing from each photograph, or (d) affix each picture to an 8.5" by 11" sheet of paper.

4. Label the figures and reference numbers on your drawing sheets.

Method: Digital Camera

Follow these steps to make drawings using a digital camera:

1. Prepare a list of views of your invention.

2. Photograph the views and download them to your computer. While color photos are acceptable in a provisional patent application, color is difficult to print and use. Therefore, we recommend that you first convert the photos to black and white by (a) selecting grayscale instead of color when downloading the image, or (b) converting the image to grayscale after you've downloaded it to your computer.

3. Select appropriate images and either (a) use the tracing methods discussed in the next section to reduce them to drawings, or (b) place each image on a separate 8.5" by 11" size sheet in a photo editing program.

4. Label the figures and reference numbers on your drawing sheets. You may label the drawings after they are printed on the sheets or before you print them, using a photo editing program.

Tips for Creating Drawings With a Camera

No matter which method you use—film or digital—these tips will help you create high-quality photographic patent drawings.

Always come as close as possible to the object—that is, make sure it takes up as much space as possible in the camera's viewfinder.

If possible, use a zoom lens when photographing small objects. If not, check to see whether your camera has a "macro" setting for extreme close-ups.

If you're photographing in sunlight, use a flash to even out the shadows.

If you own and are familiar with photo-editing software, such as Adobe *Photoshop Elements*, use that to edit and label your digital images.

Trace Your Photograph by Hand

If you want your drawings to look less like photos and more like traditional patent drawings, try tracing your photographs by hand. You'll need some supplies, all of which are available at art supply stores. These include:

- tracing paper (sometimes known as "parchment tracing paper")
- masking tape, to hold the tracing paper down on your photograph
- pencil (either wood or mechanical)
- soft or kneaded eraser, for erasing pencil marks
- ink pens (preferably drafting pens—sometimes known as "technical pens"—made for ink drawings)
- a plastic template that contains common shapes, such as circles or boxes
- a numbering template or transfer type (numbers or letters that you can press on the paper)
- white correction fluid to clean up pen markings, and
- a light source under your photograph and paper.

Tracing is best accomplished by either placing a light box under your materials (Illustration 11) or by placing your materials on glass and placing a source of light under the glass.

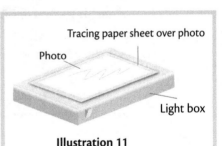

Tracing paper sheet over photo

Photo

Light box

Illustration 11

Method: Hand Tracing

To trace your drawing by hand from a photograph, follow these steps:

1. Place your photograph on a light box or, if you have no light box, on a piece of glass above a light source.
2. Tape your tracing paper to the photograph.
3. Sketch the outlines of the invention.
4. Remove the tracing paper and go over your pencil markings with an ink pen (use a ruler to create straight lines).
5. Erase any remaining pencil marks; white out any unnecessary ink lines.
6. Label the figures and reference numbers on your drawing sheets using a ruler and pen.
7. Photocopy the completed tracing sheet.

Tips for Tracing by Hand

Here are some tips to help you trace neatly and accurately:

- Don't apply too much pressure on your pencil when tracing; avoid making dark lines that are hard to erase.
- Use a plastic template whenever possible to recreate common shapes such as circles or boxes.
- When using a pen and ruler, don't let the tip of the pen touch the edge of the ruler if possible—the ink may bleed under the ruler.
- Don't apply correction fluid until the ink is dry.

Trace Your Photograph by Computer

You can also "trace" a photo on the computer using a software program such as *Photoshop* (or *Photoshop Elements*), *Freehand*, *Illustrator*, or *CorelDraw*. If you're familiar with these programs, it's usually just a matter of five steps: (1) importing the photograph, (2) creating a new layer, (3) changing the opacity on that layer so you can see the underlying photograph, (4) tracing the photograph with a drawing tool, and (5) saving (and flattening) that new layer at full opacity.

By the age of 18, Al Gross had built a shortwave radio station in his home. He later went on to invent the walkie-talkie, the proximity fuse, and the world's first pager.

Al Gross

Alternatively, you can sometimes use filters within these programs to alter your photograph (for example—the halftone filter in *Photoshop*) to create a drawing effect. (Be sure to have your color choices set to black and white). Obviously, for all of these methods, you'll need a digital copy of your photograph (obtained using a digital camera or a scanner).

Method: Tracing by Computer

To trace by computer, follow these steps:

1. Import the photograph of your figure into the computer program.
2. Create a new layer upon which you trace the underlying image.

3. Change the opacity on that layer so you can see the underlying photograph

4. Trace the photograph with a drawing tool.

5. Save (and flatten) the new layer at its full opacity.

> ⓘ **CAUTION**
> **You can't use photographs in your regular patent application.**
> Although you can submit photos (color or black and white) as drawings for a provisional patent application, they are not acceptable for a regular patent application, unless black-and-white line drawings would not adequately portray your invention.

Make a Drawing Directly From a Prototype

If you're adventurous and want to try drawing your invention from a prototype, you can use some of the drawing devices and tricks discussed in this section. Keep in mind, however, that most of these processes require some time to master. If your heart is set on meeting a 24-hour deadline, you might want to try a simpler method.

To draw directly from a prototype, you will need to project an image of your invention—this will give you a two-dimensional depiction that you can trace or draw, using the tools discussed in "Trace Your Photograph by Hand," above. There are many projection devices available to help you do this. An art projector projects an image of your prototype directly onto a drawing surface, so you can trace the image. There are several types of art projectors—some (known as opaque projectors) require that you work in a dark room. Prices on these devices range from $35 to $1,000. For an explanation of the different types of projectors and their features, see www.artograph.com/projterms.htm. (Another helpful resource for art projectors is www.artcity.com/product_info/projector_table.htm.)

Method: Drawing Directly From a Prototype

Follow these steps to draw your invention using a projected image of your prototype:

1. Place your image appropriately so that the projector captures the image.
2. Trace the image using the methods described in "Trace Your Photograph by Hand," above.
3. Complete the tracing with pen and ink.
4. Label the figures and reference numbers on your drawing sheets using a ruler and pen.

> The first color television system was invented in 1929 but did not become commercially practical until the 1960s.

Tips for Drawing From a Prototype

Here are some tips for using an art projector to draw from your prototype:

- Make sure that the projector is positioned perpendicular to the receiving plane (table or wall). If your positioning is off, one side of the projected image will appear larger than the opposite side.
- If the size of your image is determined by moving the projector closer or farther away from the image (rather than by adjusting a lens), place your projector on a rolling cart—this will allow you to move it back and forth easily, to capture the best view.
- If you always place the projector a certain distance away from the prototype, mark that distance on the floor with tape, so you can get back to the right spot quickly.

RESOURCE

Drawing outside the box. You can trace a three-dimensional image without an art projector by using a piece of glass, tracing paper, and a device to hold the glass (see Illustrations 12 and 13). For more on these methods, consult *How to Make Patent Drawings*, by patent agent Jack Lo and attorney David Pressman (Nolo).

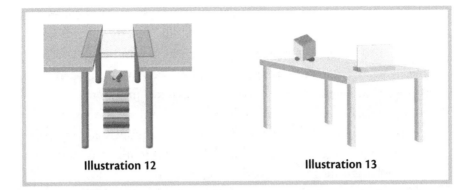

| Illustration 12 | Illustration 13 |

Tips for Inventors Who Don't Have a Prototype and Can't Draw

Can you really create patent drawings if you don't have a prototype and you don't have any drawing skills? Of course you can—but you will need some help from technology or an expert. Among your options:

- Have a prototype made (see "To Prototype or Not to Prototype," just below), then create drawings based on the prototype using the techniques discussed in "Tips for Inventors Who Have a Prototype but Can't Draw," above.
- Hire an artist to draw your invention based upon your description and rough sketches (see "Hire an Artist to Create Drawings").
- Attempt to draw your invention using some of the tips suggested in"Draw Your Invention by Collage."

To Prototype or Not to Prototype

You don't have to have a prototype to file a provisional or a regular patent application. However, preparing a prototype can help you redefine your concept for your invention. When you have to transform your idea into a physical reality, you will come up with new ideas for improvements and modifications.

The disadvantage of making a prototype is that it can be quite expensive, often costing thousands of dollars. As a general rule, you should only have a prototype made if the cost of preparing one is within your budget or if it is absolutely necessary to demonstrate that your invention works properly.

If you pay someone (usually referred to as a model maker) to prepare a working model of your invention, follow these commonsense rules:

- Use a written agreement that establishes the confidentiality of your invention—and your ownership rights to the resulting prototype. A sample agreement is provided in Appendix B.
- Give clear instructions about what you want—for example, what materials you want used and whether you expect to get a working model.
- Establish development milestones and payments clearly. For example, establish that a preliminary model should be prepared within 30 days of signing the agreement and that payment shall be made within 30 days of receipt of the final prototype.

You can locate a model maker by using an Internet search engine and typing in "model maker" or "prototype maker" as the key words.

Hire an Artist to Create Drawings

If you wish, you can use the talents of an artist—either a professional draftsperson or any competent sketch artist—to create your drawings. You describe your invention to the artist, who creates the representation. Obviously, you will need to provide as much detail as possible, since the artist is relying on your descriptions to accurately create your invention. If you hire a professional draftsperson, you should expect to pay approximately $70 to $150 per figure. You can also find a list of patent drawing services at the PatentLaw Links website (www.patentlawlinks.com/drawing.htm).

Draw Your Invention by Collage

As you can see by looking at Illustrations 7 through 10, you don't need a great deal of drawing talent to create accurate representations of some inventions. You can find the visual imagery used in these drawings—for example, a human form or a satellite image—in computer and printed clip-art sources.

You can find printed clip art in scientific clip-art books (available online and at scientific and engineering supply stores). You may also find appropriate imagery in visual dictionaries such as the *MacMillan Visual Dictionary* by Corbeil and Archambault (Dimensions).

You may find it easier to assemble drawings using software programs and digital clip art. Programs such as *CorelDRAW* or Adobe *Illustrator, Photoshop*, or *Freehand* allow you to import, modify, and manipulate scientific clip art. If you're familiar with a technical drawing program, such as *Visio*—a drawing program for engineers, architects, and scientists— then you can take advantage of the 3,800 "SmartShapes" designed to behave like bolts, pumps, and other real-world items. You can manipulate their position by using a simple drag-and-drop system. Similarly, *SmartDraw* (www.smartdraw.com) contains libraries of downloadable clip art and technical symbols (Illustration 14).

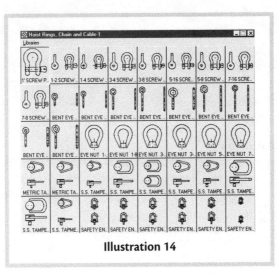

Illustration 14

For more high-powered two-dimensional or three-dimensional drawings, you can use CAD (computer-assisted drawing) programs. These programs are fairly expensive—and take many hours to learn. (The "lite" version of *AutoCAD* costs over $600; the professional versions cost thousands.)

Drawings for Software, Business Methods, Electrical Inventions, and Chemical Compounds

Nonfigurative patent drawings, such as flowcharts, electrical schematics, and tables, can be used to illustrate inventions as diverse as chemical compounds, business methods, electric circuits, and software. In this section, we explain how to create flowcharts and how to depict software inventions. We don't provide step-by-step explanations for preparing schematics and tables, but if you are a software engineer or an electrical engineer, you probably already know how to prepare these more technical drawings. You can find suitable assistance simply by examining similar inventions. We have provided examples of flowcharts and tables in Illustrations 15, 16, 17, and 18.

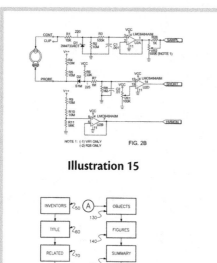

Illustration 15

TABLE II

Meat-In-Gravy Pet Food Y

INGREDIENTS	% OF MEAT EMULSION	% OF GRAVY	% OF PRODUCT
Meat and Meat By-Product	76.26	0	38.90
Fiber and Binding Agent	19.75	0	9.30
Vitamins	0.26	0	0.12
Minerals	1.23	0	0.58
Water	2.50	88.7	48.10
Maltodextrin	—	7.6	4.00
Starch	—	3.02	1.60
Lecithin	—	0.51	0.27
Caramel color	—	0.17	0.09
Total	100.00	100.00	99.96

TABLE III

Meat-In-Gravy Pet Food Z

INGREDIENTS	% OF MEAT EMULSION	% OF GRAVY	% OF PRODUCT
Meat and Meat By-Product	79.34	0	35.70
Fiber and binding Agent	20.05	0	9.50
Vitamins	0.26	0	0.12
Minerals	1.71	0	0.80
Water	2.64	88.28	47.70
Maltodextrin	—	7.83	4.12
Starch	—	3.04	1.60
Lecithin	—	0.51	0.27
Caramel color	—	0.34	0.18
Total	100.00	100.00	99.99

Illustration 16

Illustration 17

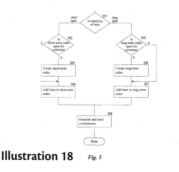

Illustration 18 Fig. 5

RESOURCE

For more on schematics. If you need help preparing electrical schematics, we suggest reviewing *A Beginner's Guide to Reading Schematics,* by Traister and Lisk (Dimensions), or *Schematic Diagrams: The Basics of Interpretation and Use,* by Richard Johnson (Dimensions).

What's the difference between a flowchart, a schematic, and a table?

- A flowchart is a diagram—usually using geometric shapes and text—that shows a step-by-step progression through a procedure.
- A schematic is a structural or procedural diagram using symbols or technical imagery.
- A table is an arrangement of data in rows and columns.

EXAMPLE: In Illustration 19, an inventor uses a schematic and a flowchart to depict a process for the production of corn dogs (those little shapes that look like rice are the corn dogs).

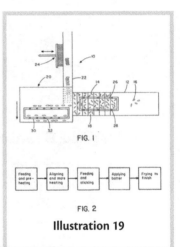

Illustration 19

Flowcharts

A flowchart can help you illustrate graphically the steps in a process or program. Each element in the process is represented by an icon or symbol such as a circle, rectangle, or diamond. The user follows the flow of the process, indicated by arrows and lines. As you can tell from Illustrations 20 and 21, a flowchart is an excellent way to illustrate many types of inventions, including software and business method inventions.

It's easy to create a flowchart using a ruler, a pen, and a plastic template with various shapes. However, for purposes of presentation, preservation, and future modification, we recommend that you create flowcharts on a computer. Almost any word processing or drawing program can create a flowchart.

For example, Microsoft *Word* (2010 version) comes equipped with "SmartArt," a graphics program that can create flowcharts. In addition, software programs such as *Illustrator, Freehand, Visio,* or most CAD programs can assist in flowchart preparation.

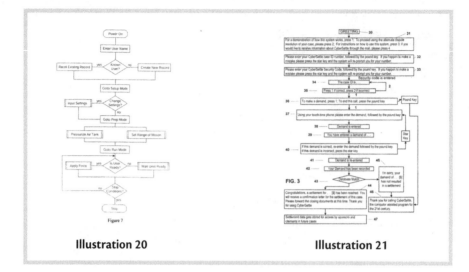

Illustration 20   Illustration 21

Method: Flowcharting a Process

Follow these steps to create a flowchart depicting your invention:

1. Start by defining the beginning and end of your process.
2. Identify any causes and effects that influence or digress from the process—for example, "if yes, Route 1, if no, Route 2."
3. Use the same shape—rectangles, circles, and so on—for similar steps in a process. For example, use rectangles for beginning and end.
4. Identify each step in the process and, if possible, indicate the timing of these steps.

> The tattoo machine was patented by Samuel F. O'Reilly in 1891 after he modified Thomas Edison's electric pen.

RESOURCE
If you'd like to learn more about preparing flowcharts, read *Flowcharts, Plain & Simple,* by Joiner Associates (Oriel, Inc.).

Tips for Creating a Flowchart

Here are some tips that will help you create a streamlined flowchart:

- Avoid using too many different shapes in your chart—if you find yourself having to resort to trapezoids and rhombuses, your viewers are not going to be able to follow your process.
- If necessary, break your process into separate functions, each with its own flowchart.
- If blocks are connected, label them as one figure; if they are disconnected, label them as separate figures.
- Ask a friend to review the chart and give you some feedback. Is it easy to follow? Is it legible?

Software Inventions: Flowcharts or Computer Code?

In order to provide the "best mode" (the inventor's preferred method) of making and using software inventions, programmers must reveal as much as possible about their inventions. The disclosure must be "full, clear, concise and exact" (35 U.S.C. § 112). This can be done with:

- a well-drafted flowchart that provides enough details to allow a reasonably skilled programmer to write the invention
- a combination of a well-drafted flowchart and a printed copy of the program code, preferably in object code format, or
- a printed copy of the source or object code.

Program code may be the clearest and most exact way to divulge a software program. However, if program code is included in a regular patent application, then the code can be copied by devious infringers once the patent application is published. (Regular patent applications are published 18 months after filing unless the inventor files a Nonpublication Request indicating that patent protection won't be sought abroad.)

The original armored gunnery vehicles were nicknamed "water tanks," later shortened to "tanks."

Despite this risk, some patent attorneys suggest including a printed copy of the source code with a provisional patent application. When you later file the regular patent application, the provisional patent application won't be published along with it—instead, it will be incorporated by reference. In other words, the USPTO will not reproduce and distribute the program code to the public if it's filed with your provisional patent application. The USPTO makes provisional patent applications available for public inspection at the USPTO in Alexandria, Virginia, only if the corresponding regular patent application is published. To avoid problems from photocopying pirates, print your code on paper that contains a grayscale watermark—for example, the programmer's copyright notice.

> **CAUTION**
>
> **This advice is untested.** Although some patent attorneys recommend filing code with your provisional patent application, we cannot advise that you do so. Neither the USPTO nor the courts have yet weighed in on whether a printed copy of the code included in a provisional patent application may be incorporated by reference into the regular patent application.

The tasks of this chapter proved time-consuming, taking almost three hours to complete. However, our inventor didn't find it difficult and enjoyed working with pen and ruler.

Our inventor began by creating the following table of the individual elements of his invention.

10	Toy doll
12	Doll head
14	Doll body
16	Cavity in doll head
18L & R	Lines of LEDs
20L & R	Doll's eyes
22	Microchip controller
24	Battery to power device
26	Motion sensor
28	Sound sensor
30	On/off switch

Then he scanned a doll photo and a profile of a doll head. He eventually converted those to hand drawings by tracing and scanning the results. He added the final numbers and lines using Microsoft's *PictureIt* program. (See Illustration 22.)

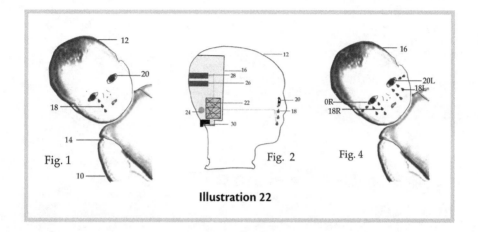

Illustration 22

Our inventor also created a flowchart indicating how the doll was turned on and off (see Illustration 23). The flowchart was created in Microsoft *Word* following our instructions in this chapter.

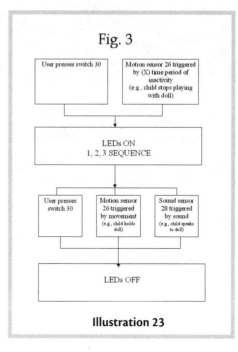

Illustration 23

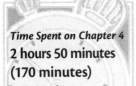

Time Spent on Chapter 4
2 hours 50 minutes
(170 minutes)

Time Remaining
17 hours 5 minutes

Our inventor spent 170 minutes reading this chapter and completing the drawings. Only about 17 hours left!

Drafting the Provisional Patent Application:
Part 2—Describing Your Invention

"A patent is a recipe. It must include all the information a skilled researcher needs to replicate what was done by the inventor and achieve the same results. Meaning the meal has to come out of the oven the same way every time, no matter who cooks it. If a patent isn't 'enabled,' meaning the instructions don't allow someone else to achieve precisely the same results as the inventor, it isn't valid."

—**Rick Murdoch and David Fisher,** *Patient Number One* **(Crown)**

In this chapter, we help you draft the text of your provisional patent application. We'll refer to this text as a "specification" even though it does not have to contain all of the elements you must include in a regular patent application specification, such as a detailed discussion of the prior art, the advantages of the invention, and a description of alternative embodiments, claims, and an abstract. If you've read the previous four chapters, then you know the rules regarding provisional patent applications, you've examined some provisional patent applications (there are 17 in Appendix A), you've researched the prior art, and you've prepared drawings of your invention. Now it's time to focus on the content and style of your provisional patent application specification so that you can accurately describe how to make and use your invention.

In order to complete your specification, you must answer the following questions (we explain how to figure out the answers and draft them in the proper format in the sections that follow):

1. What do you call your invention?
2. What are the names and addresses of the inventors?
3. What are the advantages of your invention over the prior art?
4. What drawing figures have you included?
5. What are the parts or components of your invention?
6. How do the parts or components connect or interact?
7. How does the invention achieve its result?
8. Are there alternative ways that your invention can achieve its result?

Your answers to the final four questions are especially important. Because they describe in detail the structure of your invention, how it operates, and any alternative embodiments, they are the heart of the application—and will form the basis for your patent claims if you file a regular patent application later.

As you review each question in this chapter, write down your answer and save it in a word processing document. When you're done answering questions, you can assemble the results to look like the sample provisional patent applications shown at the end of this chapter and in Appendix A.

These questions should not be too difficult to answer. You've already had to consider most of them in previous chapters. In case you run into trouble, we'll let you know which previous chapters to review for help.

> The first stapler held only one staple; 71 years later Jack Linsky perfected the stapler when he patented a device with a spring and hinge that could hold a strip of staples.

TIP
Keep your drawings handy. After reading Chapter 4, you should have prepared drawing figures providing visual representations of your invention. You'll need these figures in front of you when you draft your application.

TIP
Our convertible tent. Throughout this chapter we will show you how to complete each of the steps of a provisional patent application using our convertible tent invention as an example. The assembled version of the provisional patent application is provided in Appendix A.

What Do You Call Your Invention?

You must provide a title for your invention at the beginning of your specification and on the provisional patent application cover sheet discussed in Chapter 6. Now is not the time to get too mysterious or poetic—the purpose of an invention's title is to tell the reader what your invention does, not to generate suspense or intrigue. You should give your invention a fairly specific name that provides a snapshot of its function, type, purpose, and advantage.

EXAMPLES OF INVENTION NAMES:

- "Boredom-reducing feeding device for caged animals" (Pat. 5,894,815)
- "Multistation bird feeder with squirrel guard" (Pat. 6,269,771)
- "Voice alert system for use on bicycles" (Pat. 6,317,026)

Here are some tips for naming your invention:

- Avoid using a vague name such as "Recreational device"—it doesn't reveal much about the invention. A better title for this device (see Illustration 1) might be "Pet play device" or "Pet recreation device allowing manipulation of model mice."

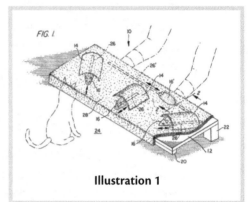

Illustration 1

- Avoid using catchy names that you might use to market your invention. For example, the inventor of a car antitheft device may sell the invention under the trademark "The Club," but that would not accurately summarize the invention. For purposes of filing a provisional patent application, a better name would be "Automobile antitheft lock."

- If you don't know what to call your invention, review prior-art patents for similar inventions. Of course, you don't want your invention to sound too similar to the prior art, but other applications will give you some idea of the terms and descriptions that might apply to your invention.

King Camp Gillette, the inventor of the safety razor, believed that the perfect invention was something that was used, thrown away, and bought again.

King Camp Gillette

EXAMPLE: Title for convertible tent: "Convertible tent for rainy, cold, and hot conditions"

- Avoid making your title too specific since a judge might interpret your invention too specifically, instead of broadly enough to cover minor changes from the description. For example, if you've invented a device for supplying food to caged monkeys that requires them to release a catch to get their food so as to reduce boredom, don't call it "Feeder requiring monkey to release catch to access food." Despite what your claims cover, a judge might be inclined to hold the patent not infringed by a dog feeder that required a dog to press a pedal to bring up the food. Instead make the title broad enough to cover the inventive concepts and all types of animals, such as "Boredom-reducing feeding device for caged animals" as above.

Eliminating "Objects" From the Provisional Patent Application

In previous editions of this book, we suggested that inventors include the "objects" of the invention—that is, a description of what the invention accomplishes. For example, the objects of a convertible tent application might include:

- to provide a tent that can be adjusted for warm, cool, cold, and precipitation conditions, and
- to provide a tent that the user can adjust for various climates while inside the tent.

We've eliminated the objects because of a series of patent court decisions in which objects language was used to limit the scope of the patent claims. For this reason, and because the objects are not mandatory, we believe that objects should no longer be included in the provisional patent application.

What Are the Names and Addresses of the Inventors?

The provisional patent application and the regular application must be filed in the name of the inventor—not a friend, an attorney, or a person who buys invention rights. When multiple inventors are involved, the provisional patent application must name at least one of the inventors. (The regular patent application must name *all* of them.) To make sure your provisional patent application conforms to your regular patent application, we recommend that you include the names of all inventors.

Avoid Using "Patent Profanity"

Avoid words in your specification that some courts have used to justify narrowing the scope of the invention (nicknamed "patent profanity"). Such words include: absolutely, advantageous, all, are, as much as, commonly, conveniently, correct, critical, desirable, difficult, essential, every, expected, few, frequently, generally, highly, invention, is, laborious, limited success with, majority, might, most, must, necessary, needed, never, none, only, partly, peculiar, preferred, rarely, required (-ment), should, significant, special, specify, surely, time-consuming, typically, uncommon, usual, and usually. Also avoid any absolute statements, such as "the disclosed system is always superior to the prior art."

What Are the Advantages of Your Invention Over the Prior Art?

The advantages of your invention are the qualities that make it superior to the prior art. You are not required to include your invention's advantages in your provisional patent application, but doing so may help to distinguish, explain, and sell your invention.

RESOURCE

In order to list your advantages, you should familiarize yourself with the prior art. If you haven't already performed a preliminary prior-art search, now's the time to do so. Review Chapter 3 if you need some help getting started.

Sometimes, your advantages will be quite obvious—for example, Bell's telephone invention transmitted sounds over wire, something that had never been accomplished before.

In other cases, you may have more subtle advantages. This means you should carefully distinguish what you've accomplished from what others have done.

You do not need to list and describe prior-art patents (as we did, for example, for the convertible tent invention in Chapter 3). However, you should summarize some of the advantages your invention has over the competition.

Advantages of convertible tent

Although others have invented converting tents, various aspects of my tent are superior because it:

- is more versatile
- is less awkward to use and handle
- is simple and easy to make and erect
- easily adjusts for a wide range of climatic conditions
- adjusts from the inside for different conditions, especially for rain
- has no outer net to catch spindrift in the winter, and
- has a flysheet that can be installed from within the tent.

Be sure to include a disclaimer to introduce your advantages section, as we have done above and avoid referring to your invention as an "invention." The simplest way to do this is by using a statement such as: "Various aspects of my [*name of invention*] may have one or more of the following advantages …."

Because of recent court decisions, (see "Eliminating 'Objects' From the Provisional Patent Application," above), we advise that you write your advantages in a manner that avoids reciting any specific details or arrangements that could be regarded as limiting; for example, don't state "One advantage is that a console is provided between the seats." Instead, state, "One advantage is that a more accessible console is provided."

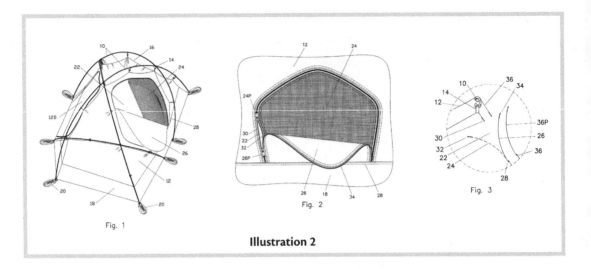

Illustration 2

Be sure that your invention, or at least one embodiment of it, will meet every stated advantage. Also use "weasel" words so that no advantage will be too broad or absolute; for example, don't state, "One advantage is to avoid the problem of ...." Rather state "One advantage is to reduce the problem of ...."

What Drawing Figures Have You Included?

For this section, all you need to do is to describe the drawing figure that you created for each view.

An example description for drawing figures (Illustration 2) for convertible tent follows.

> Drawing Figures:
>
> FIG. 1 is a perspective view from above my tent without its flysheet.
>
> FIG. 2 is a view of part of a portion of an inner canopy of the tent.
>
> FIG. 3 is a perspective view from above the tent.

The types of views that may be used are as follows: a perspective view, which shows what the invention as seen from an angle, usually above, so that several sides are shown in one figure; a plan view, which shows the invention from above, straight down; a bottom view; an elevational view, which shows the invention directly from the front, back or left or right side; and an exploded view, which shows the invention with its parts separated as if they were blown apart. A close-up view and a sectional view may also be provided if necessary or desirable. See *The Patent Drawing Book* (Nolo) for more detail about these views.

Here's another example of how to list and describe drawing figures for a mask to protect cows from flying insects (Illustration 3).

> FIG. 1 is an elevated side view of my mask in position on a cow.
>
> FIG. 2 is an elevated front view of the same.

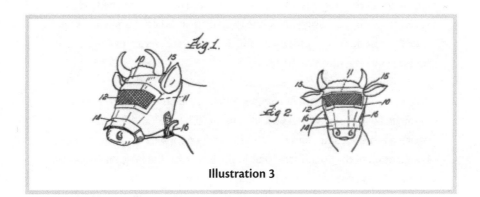

Illustration 3

What Are the Components of Your Invention and How Do They Interact?

In this section, you must prepare what's referred to as a "static description" of your invention. Basically, that's a description of the parts and how they interact, but not a description of how the invention operates as a unit.

We combined two of our nine questions here because the answers are closely related. You must describe each part of your invention and how it interacts or connects to all adjacent parts. The end result should read like the text of a model airplane kit—for example, "A left wing 10 has an elongated triangular shape and a tapering oval cross-section and is affixed via struts 12 to the center portion of a fuselage 14." As this example demonstrates, you'll need your drawing sheets. Your description should include the reference numbers you used in the drawings. (Note that you're not yet describing how the invention actually works—we'll discuss that in "How Does the Invention Achieve Its Result?" below.)

As we warned you in Chapter 4, as you proceed through your detailed description of your invention, you may find that your drawings have to be modified to make them more accurate—or more helpful to the viewer.

Get Some Help From Pete Roget

Generally, you should write your provisional patent application in your own voice—not in the language of patent attorneys. However, for the sake of precision, we suggest using an online thesaurus and dictionary when you write the description of your invention. Using these references can help you describe your invention more clearly.

For example, you may write, "Hooks 10 are attached to the bottom of box 12." A more precise statement may be "Hooks 10 are mounted on the base of container 12." By using words such as "mounted," "base," and "container," you provide a more accurate description of how the hooks are attached and the configuration of the container—that is, the base is on the bottom. In addition, the word "container" describes the function of this part better than "box."

To improve your accuracy, write your description and then use a thesaurus to enhance it. For example, on your first try, you might describe a latch as "close to a window." "Close" is not a precise term. Using a thesaurus can improve your description by providing more specific terms—such as adjacent, abutting, adjoining, against, beside, meeting, next, neighboring, proximate, or touching. You'll also need these reference books to decipher some of the language used to describe inventions in prior-art patents. Most writers use an online dictionary thesaurus, such as those found at dictionary. com. For an alternative dictionary, we like wordnik.com since it provides definitions from several sources on one page, with copious examples.

Prepare a List of Your Reference Numbers

As you prepare your static description, you may find it helpful to make a list of all the reference numbers you use and the corresponding parts (as in the example, below). This list will help you keep your names and numbers straight. You do not need to include it with your provisional patent application, but you will refer to it often as you create your list of components and describe their interaction. It's helpful to start your reference numbers with a number higher than the highest number of your figures and to use even numbers so that you can insert a reference number in order later, if necessary.

Here are reference numerals and parts for the invention "Production of corn dogs" depicted in Illustration 4.

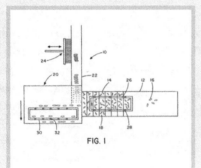

FIG. I

FIG. 2

Illustration 4

10	an apparatus for loading and aligning wieners
12	a wiener-receiving bin
14	a loading conveyer
16	accumulated wieners
18	conveyor steps
20	unit that receives and aligns wieners
22	conveyor
24	a stick-inserting device
26	heater
28	nozzles that provide a precooking mist
30	second heater
32	second set of nozzles

Here are a few tips for drafting your description:

- If you are describing the parts in a process, explain them in order. If you are describing a machine, start from the bottom and work your way up or start from the outside and work your way inside, if that makes sense.
- Start with the main parts, then describe the components of each main part, if possible. (That is, describe the forest before the trees.)
- Insert the reference number after the part name and don't use parentheses—for example, "a lever 12 is positioned above handle 10."
- Provide a reference numeral for every significant part—and don't describe a part unless you give it a reference numeral.
- Describe the relationship between interconnecting parts—for example, "lever 12 is joined to handle 10 with a hinge 6."
- Avoid using technical language if possible. If you do use a technical term, define it for the reader.
- The first time you describe a part, use an indefinite article, such as "a" or "an." For example, "A wiener-receiving bin 12 is attached." After you have introduced the part, use "the." For example, "wieners 16 then drop into the wiener-receiving bin 12." (You don't need to use "the" for parts with a number or with multiple parts. For example, "Lever 10 is connected to horizontal arms.")
- Write in the active voice as much as possible. For example, say, "A lever 10 is attached to handle 12." Don't say, "Above handle 12 is a lever 10."

Edward R. Armstrong was convinced that transatlantic passenger flights were impossible and patented several inventions for oceanic landing strips. President Teddy Roosevelt was enthusiastic but before U.S. funding was approved, aeronautical breakthroughs made transatlantic passenger flights possible.

The examples below give partial descriptions of the components for two inventions: a corn dog machine and a golf ball funnel. You can find full descriptions of these inventions by locating and reading the respective patents at the USPTO website (Pats. 6,280,786 and 6,315,677).

EXAMPLE 1: Interaction of components in an apparatus for the production of corn dogs (Illustration 4):

FIG. 1 shows an apparatus 10 for loading, aligning, and inserting sticks in wieners. A bin 12 is mounted to apparatus 10 and receives the wieners through a loading conveyer 14. Conveyor 14 extends into bin 12 and continuously holds accumulated wieners 16 so that they can be moved up a flight of conveyor steps 18 and into a receiving and aligning unit 20. Wieners 16 are transferred to unit 20 and are aligned so that wieners 16 are parallel to each other as shown. A revolving drum (not shown) is included within unit 20 to move the aligned wieners downward (see arrow) for accumulation at the lower end of the drum. The accumulated wieners are moved side-by-side to conveyor 22.

EXAMPLE 2: Golf-ball-catching funnel (used to catch golf ball directed at a driving net) (Illustration 5):

My golf-ball-catching funnel 10 is shown in a front view in FIG. 1. It contains a horizontal frame 11, a flexible funnel-shaped sheet 12 suspended within frame 11, and legs 13 that elevate frame 11 and sheet 12 off the ground. Frame 11 includes several tubes 14 (preferably plastic or metal) connected by removable corner connectors 15. Although frame 11 is shown as rectangular, it may be any other shape. Sheet 12 includes edges folded into sleeves 16 through which tubes 14 are inserted. The legs 13 are attached to respective connectors 15 by plastic or metal tubing 17. Frame 11 and connectors 15 are separable from each other for disassembly and compact storage.

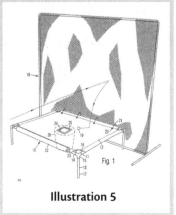

Illustration 5

Below is a partial description of the components for the convertible tent invention.

EXAMPLE: Description of convertible tent components:

> I use conventional tent poles 10 that form an arched cage. The ends of these poles are anchored to the ground. An inner canopy 12 is suspended from the poles by conventional hooks and web loops 14, shown in more detail in FIG. 3. The web loops are attached to seams or reinforcing cords 16 in canopy 12. The main portion of the floor of the tent is not shown, but it has conventional upturned sidewalls 18 that cover the bottom portion of the canopy. The canopy has a conventional door 12D on its left side. The bottom edges of the tent have conventional web loops and attachments 20 at the bottoms of the poles.

How Does the Invention Achieve Its Result?

After you've described all the parts of your invention and their intercon-nections (in the preceding Static Description section), your reader will be somewhat familiar with the parts and construction of your invention. Having prepared your reader, you now have to get down to brass tacks and describe how your invention actually operates. For example, if your goal is to create a non-fogging shower mirror or a convertible tent, you must explain how someone can operate the mirror or the tent to achieve the desired result.

EXAMPLE: Consider the Heimlich maneuver. The object of this method is to permit a user (a Good Samaritan) to expel food lodged in the throat of a choking victim without the use of instruments or equipment.

How the Heimlich method achieves its result (see Illustration 6):

A user 10 of the Heimlich method approaches a choking victim 12 who can't speak or breathe. From behind, the user wraps his arms 14 around the victim's waist 16. The user makes a fist 18 and places the thumb side of fist

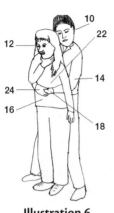

Illustration 6

18 against the victim's upper abdomen 22, below the rib cage and above the navel. The user grasps fist 18 with their other hand 24 and presses into the choking victim's upper abdomen with a quick upward thrust. The user does not squeeze the rib cage, but confines the force of the thrust to the hands. The user repeats the thrusting motion until the object is expelled.

As you can see, your description of the operation of your invention elaborates on the description of the invention's parts in much the same way that the text of a Rube Goldberg cartoon elaborates on the visual depiction. This part of the description gives your reader a step-by-step tour of your working invention.

Some inventors find it easier to merge the description of how the invention operates with the description of its parts (discussed in "What Are the Components of Your Invention and How Do They Interact?" above). (An example of a combined description is provided in the provisional patent application for the non-fogging shower mirror in Appendix A.) However, we recommend that you separate the static description from the operation section. That way, your reader becomes familiar with the parts of your invention first, which will make it much easier to understand how they operate. The combined or merged version is most suitable for simple inventions. If you go that route, make sure that the end result accurately explains how to make and use your invention.

Below is partial explanation of how the convertible tent invention achieves its result.

When early versions of transparent tape fell off, users referred to it as "Scotch," believing that the 3M company was too stingy to use enough adhesive.

> **EXAMPLE:** The user does not have to deploy the flysheet in warm weather. In cold (but not very cold) weather, and when there is no precipitation, the flysheet can be used, but with its window open. If it turns very cold, or rains or snows, the user can close the flysheet window by opening window 22 of canopy 12, pulling up flysheet panel 36P through window 22, and zipping panel 36P in place. Then users can zip solid panel 26 in place to close window 22. Even if spindrift leaks through the zipper or blows under the flysheet, it will not be able to accumulate on the net since net 24 is inside the tent. The occupants can also open a closed flysheet from inside when the precipitation stops or if it gets warmer.

What Are Alternative Ways That Your Invention Can Achieve Its Result?

So far, you have been describing your preferred method of making and using your invention, known to patent specialists as the "best mode." Even though it is what you currently consider the best mode, do not refer to it as such: just state that is a "first mode" or "one mode." Why? So a judge who may rule on your patent will not tend to look down on and discount your alternative modes if they're infringed. If you do have alternative ways that your invention can be used or assembled, refer to them as "second," "third," and so on modes, or "alternative embodiments."

It's very important to include every significant alternative embodiment for your invention—doing so will broaden the potential reach of any resulting patent. Under new decisions by the federal patent courts, a court may hold that someone who sells or makes a variation on your invention has not infringed your patent's claims, unless the variation is described in your specification.

Briefly describe alternative embodiments in a short narrative or list at the end of your provisional patent application.

> **EXAMPLE:** The inventor of the convertible tent has alternative methods of embodying his invention as described below:
> - The flysheet window can be clear.
> - Different materials, sizes, and interconnections can be used for all components.
> - In lieu of zippers, hook-and-loop fasteners, snaps, buttons, or rib or slot-slide closures can attach the panels.
> - Several windows can be used in the tent, and two complete zippers can be used on the inner panel window by providing the canopy with dual layers around the window.
> - The flysheet can be omitted and just the inner canopy can be used with its advantageous alternative net, solid panels, and its 1½ zippers.
> - The flysheet can be spaced closer or adjacent to the inner canopy by changing hooks and web loops 14.
> - In lieu of net and solid panels on the inner canopy, any two other panels can be used, such as transparent and opaque.
> - The inner canopy can have a fixed net window with an adjacent openable slot or window.

Though bar code technology was patented in 1949, it was not used for supermarket checkout until 1974.

- The flysheet can have a window that opens (e.g., a panel with a U-shaped zipper) that can be reached through the slot in the inner canopy.

You may wish to focus more closely on—and describe in greater detail—one particular alternative. For example, in the provisional patent application for the non-fogging shower mirror in Appendix A, the inventor focuses on one particular alternative—a thermal heat transfer disc.

Putting It All Together

Now you have to turn your nine answers into the text of a provisional patent application. You've already read a few applications in this book—and we provide more to consider in Appendix A. As you can see, there is no one correct style for writing your specification. Your goal is to assemble your answers to the questions in this chapter into a readable narrative form.

Just as there is no fixed style for a provisional patent application, there is also no fixed length. For example, the specification in the provisional patent application for pasteurization (provided in Chapter 1) is about one-tenth the length of the specification in the application for a non-fogging shower mirror (included in Appendix A). Pasteurization may be ten times easier to explain than the intricate mechanics of the non-fogging mirror—or the authors of these specifications may simply have different styles and levels of verbosity. Just remember, your goal is to clearly explain how to make and use your invention. As long as you do that, the number of words and tone you use to achieve that goal is up to you.

Here are a few tips to help you get started:

- Be yourself. Think of your specification as a letter that you might send to a colleague or relative, not to a patent examiner. In other words, use conversational first-person style, not legalese. For example, "I invented a rotating light socket," not "I hereby enclose my provisional patent application for the rotating light socket invention described herein."
- Use bulleted lists. You will notice that the provisional patent applications in Appendix A use bulleted lists to explain alternative embodiments and to distinguish

Wilhelm Maybach got the idea for his carburetor invention from observing a perfume pump spray.

the inventions from prior art. These lists help the reader by clarifying points and breaking up large chunks of text.

- If you have already written a technical article describing your invention, include that article with your draft. You might even be able to use that article (or a revised form of it) as your application, as long as it provides the information described in this chapter.

- Have a friend or colleague review your draft—then listen with an open mind to any criticisms of content and style. Make sure the reader agrees that you have given enough detail to allow someone with ordinary skill in the field of your invention to make and use it from your drawings and explanation.

- *always* compare your draft with other patents in your field, to make sure your language and drawings conform to the style of similarly patented inventions.

- *always* use the spell-check feature of your word processing program and verify your choice by checking a dictionary.

- Include a header or footer on every page indicating your name, the title of your invention, the page number, and the total number of pages included in your application.

- If you can't tell whether you have properly prepared your provisional patent application, consult an attorney (see Appendix E).

- Never say anything negative about your invention, no matter how candid you want to be. Always stress the positive aspects of your invention. *Wrong:* "My Fig. 2 embodiment didn't work as fast as the embodiment in Fig. 3." *Right:* "The Fig. 3 embodiment operates faster, while my Fig. 2 embodiment is more economical."

This section took considerable time—over five hours—as our inventor wrote and rewrote the specification. He answered the questions in the chapter, saved his answers in a word processing file, then assembled the results. He revised his work several times. In addition, our inventor spent considerable time analyzing related patents to be sure that his language seemed consistent with other inventors and included a unique touch—a quote from a related patent describing the field of the invention. He also spoke briefly with a prototype builder knowledgeable in electronic circuitry and showed his draft to a friend to make sure it was clear and logical.

Provisional Patent Application for a Method
of Simulating Tears in a Doll

I have invented a method of simulating tears in dolls using linear groups of blinking light emitting diodes (LEDs). These linear groups of LEDS are affixed to the doll's eyelids and extend downward on the doll's cheek. A battery-powered microchip controls the LEDs, causing the lights to blink in a pattern that simulates falling tears. The microchip can be triggered by either a sensor that detects external stimuli such as audio, movement, or by an on/off switch.

Dolls have been produced in the past that simulate crying. These dolls—for example, the Tiny Tears™ doll produced by the Ideal Company in the 1950s—have been very popular with children who enjoy role-playing. As Fusi and Jensen stated in their Tearing Eye Doll patent (Pat. 4,900,287, 1990) "Playacting performs an important role in child development, and the most effective dolls are those which simulate reality. This is why dolls which produce crying sounds are appealing, and why dolls capable of tearing also satisfy a child's need for verisimilitude."

In the past, crying dolls have relied on two concepts, ejecting water from the baby's eyes or emitting crying sounds. The Tiny Tears doll, for example, ejected water when the child placed the doll horizontally. The problems with water excretion systems are that they:
- are capable of leaking
- require refilling
- often corrode the internal working parts
- include numerous internal parts such as nozzles, reservoirs, tubing and pumps, and
- can create a play hazard.

The problems with dolls that simulate crying sounds are that they:
- may startle or frighten a young child, and
- may create alarm in adults unaware that the sound is coming from a doll.

My method of simulating tears is preferable over previous tearing dolls because it emits light instead of water or sound. In addition to avoiding the mess, hazard, and annoyance of previous methods, the small glow from the LEDs simulation provides the advantage of comforting a child using the doll in a darkened bedroom.

I've included four drawing sheets:

FIG. 1 is an elevated front view of a doll embodying the invention.

FIG. 2 is an internal view of the inside of the doll's head.

FIG. 3 is a flowchart indicating the steps in turning the simulation on and off.

FIG. 4 is another elevated front view of the doll embodying an alternate version of the invention featuring multiple LED tear simulations.

The components of my invention are:

- a toy doll 10 consisting of a doll's head 12 and body 14 contoured with human characteristics and including a cavity 16 in the doll's head for placement of elements
- LEDs 18 extending in linear groups downward from the doll's eye 20
- an LED microchip controller 22 that directs on, off, frequency, and order of blinking lights
- a battery 24 to power the microchip and LEDs
- a motion sensor 26 (or sound sensor 28) to direct the microchip controller to turn on, off, or otherwise control the blinking LEDs, and
- an ON/OFF switch 30.

The method or arrangement of wiring or connecting the above electronic components and mounting them in a doll will be well-known to those with ordinary skill in the electronic and mechanical arts. Microchip controller 22 is a standardized chip, having a ROM (Read-Only Memory) with a suitable embedded program (PROM—Programmed ROM) arranged to cause it to perform the functions indicated.

Specifically, the microchip when triggered, will light each LED for a .5 second period in a repeating 1, 2, 3 sequence.

My doll achieves its result as follows: Extending from the doll's eye 20 are three LEDs 18 affixed or embedded in the face of doll 10; these simulate the path of a falling tear drop. LEDs 18 are connected to a controlling microchip 22 and battery 24 located in a cavity 16 within the doll's head 12. The controlling microchip 22 is connected to a motion sensor 26 or sound sensor 28 affixed in head 12 and to a manual on/off switch 30. The microchip is a simple electronic distributor which illuminates the LEDs in sequence as in Table 1 as follows:

Table 1 indicates the sequence and timing of the on times of the three LEDs as the light "moves" downward from the doll's eye. The sequence repeats until halted by motion or audio sensor or by on-off switch.

TABLE 1

	LED 1 on	LED 2 on	LED 3 on
Time 1 (start)	X		
Time 2 (.5 sec. later)		X	
Time 3 (.5 sec. later)			X

The user may, if desired, simply turn the tear simulation on or off by pressing the switch 30 affixed to doll's head 12 or body 14. When the child uses switch 30, microchip controller 22 is directed to begin or stop the moving light sequence. Sensors 26 and 28 may also be used to turn on and off the moving light sequence. For example, controller 22 may be directed to turn on the LED tear simulation after a short period of inactivity—for example, the child has put the doll down. Subsequent motion—for example, the child picking up the doll—would turn off the tear simulation.

Alternatively, a sound sensor 28 may be programmed to turn off the lights—for example, the sensor is triggered by the sound of the child comforting the doll. Finally a timer, embedded on the microchip controller will turn off the timer after an extended period of inactivity.

There are many alternative ways that my crying doll using simulating lights can be implemented:

- Instead of a doll, it is also possible that the crying simulation can be implemented with a life-sized mannequin (e.g., as used in store displays), with plush toys, or with puppets.
- The doll may also include sound effects that accompany the tear simulation, for example the sound of crying.
- The battery or source of the power may vary and can include disposable, long-life, or rechargeable batteries.
- The LEDs may be all one color, e.g., white, or they may be more fanciful or whimsical as embodied in a series of colored lights.

- Instead of LEDs, the moving lights may be created with laser diodes, OLEDs, passive-matrix or active-matrix liquid crystal displays, or other nonheating low power electric lighting sources.
- The shape of each LED may be so as to create a teardrop appearance or other fanciful shape that amuses or stimulates a child.
- The linear LEDS may extend in any number of combinations on the doll's face (see Fig. 4), e.g., one strip from each eye, several strips from each eye, or strips down the front of the cheek while the doll is upright or down the sides of the cheek while the doll is in a horizontal position.
- Alternate timings may also be proposed, for example—different time separations between each LED.
- Table 2 indicates a pattern that can also be used for left and right doll eyes. This delayed timing sequence—in which one eye appears to shed a tear drop after the other can be manipulated in innumerable ways—for example, one eye might not commence until after .3, .4, .5, or .6 second from when the other eye began its LED simulation.

TABLE 2

	L1 on	L2 on	L3 on	R1 on	R2 on	R3 on
Time 1 (start)	X					
Time 2 (.5 sec. later)		X		X		
Time 3 (.5 sec. later)			X		X	
Time 4 (.5 sec. later)					X	

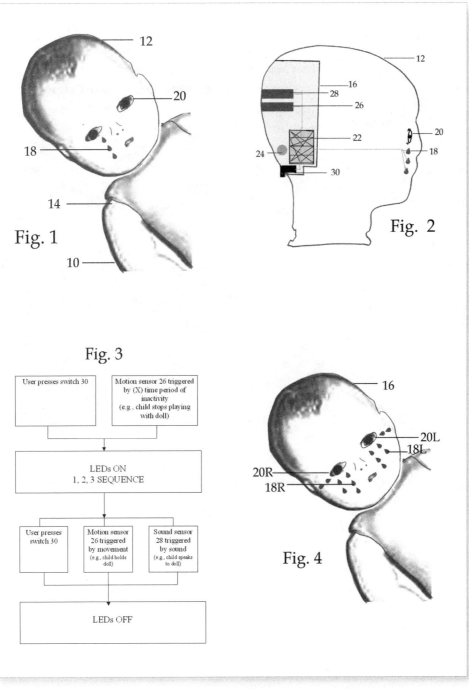

Fig. 1

Fig. 2

Fig. 3

User presses switch 30	Motion sensor 26 triggered by (X) time period of inactivity (e.g., child stops playing with doll)

LEDs ON
1, 2, 3 SEQUENCE

User presses switch 30	Motion sensor 26 triggered by movement (e.g., child holds doll)	Sound sensor 28 triggered by sound (e.g., child speaks to doll)

LEDs OFF

Fig. 4

Illustration 7

Time Spent on Chapter 5
**5 hours 10 minutes
(310 minutes)**

Time Remaining
11 hours 5 minutes

As you can imagine, our inventor spent more time drafting his specification than on any other task in this book. Our inventor spent approximately four hours reading, writing, and revising his specification. He's got more than 11 hours left to package and file, so it looks like he won't have any problem meeting our 24-hour deadline.

Filing and Beyond

"Anything worth remembering that I've ever done, I couldn't get anyone to fund it. To be a real inventor, you have to be good at not paying attention to the conventional wisdom."

—**Carver Mead, winner of the Lemelson award for his breakthroughs in semiconductor design, who said big ideas seldom have much to do with business goals.**

n this chapter, we'll explain how to file your provisional patent application with the USPTO, how to mark your invention "patent pending," and what to do if you modify your invention after you file. We'll also discuss the one-year window within which you must file your regular patent application.

How to File Your Provisional Patent Application

There are two ways to file your provisional patent application: by mail, and electronically. We'll discuss both, below.

Electronic Filing

The PTO has implemented an Electronic Filing System (EFS-Web) that enables patent applications, amendments, and other documents to be filed over the Internet. The EFS-Web represents a considerable improvement over the old system. However, it still requires some time to master, as well as time for conversion of documents to the Portable Document Format (PDF). If you're filing just one provisional patent application, it may be easier and faster for you to mail a paper copy of the application to the PTO.

The EFS-Web does have some practical advantages. Using it, you can (1) file an application anytime and from anywhere that has Internet access, (2) obtain instant confirmation of receipt of documents by the PTO, (3) send an application to the PTO without having to go to the post office to get an Express Mail receipt or having to wait for a postcard receipt, and (4) file an application without having to prepare an application transmittal, a fee transmittal, receipt postcard, or check or Credit Card Payment Form (CCPF).

Unable to open a canned drink at a picnic, Ernie Fraze invented the ring-pull can.

Before you go online, prepare the entire application as instructed, except omit the Fee Transmittal form, Receipt Postcard, and check or CCPF. You need only prepare a data sheet, the drawing, and the specification before going online.

To file electronically, follow the steps described below.

Convert Your Application to PDF Format

Convert all documents of the application (drawings, specification, including any claims and abstract) to PDF documents in your computer. It's easiest if you scan each document to a separate PDF file and give it a descriptive name, for example, Dwgs.pdf and Spec.pdf. If you use a scanner, set the scan to black and white at a resolution of 300 dpi for good clarity. To help you stay organized, put all of the PDF application computer files into a separate folder with a suitable name (for example, Derailleur PPA PDFs).

Prepare a PDF Data Sheet

The USPTO wants specific application data from every applicant and you can provide that by (1) downloading and filling out a form (and later uploading it), or (2) by simply completing the form online as part of the EFS-Web filing program.

If you want to complete it before filing, download a fillable EFS Application Data Sheet. On the USPTO home page, click "Patents," then click "Patent Forms." Choose "Patent Forms for Applications Filed On or After September 16, 2012," and download "Application Data Sheet" (the code is AIA/14). If you're having trouble downloading it, try downloading from the link below that titled "Download All Application Data Sheet Related Forms."

Save Form AIA/14 to Your Computer

Open the AIA/14 Application Data Sheet form and fill it out with the inventor name(s), a customer number if you have one, your email address if you want to receive correspondence by email, the title of the application, a docket number if you want to use one, the application type (provisional), and the total number of drawing sheets. If you have an assignee, fill in this part, but remember to send in a separate assignment. Sign the form with an "S-Signature" (e.g. "/Mildred Phillips/"), and type your name and date. The program will then automatically fill in the header blanks. Then, save the completed form using a suitable name, such as Data.pdf, in your PDF Application Holding Folder with your other PDF application forms.

Sign-On

If you want to file as an unregistered eFiler (recommended if you only plan on filing one application), then you can sign on to the EFS-Web system by going to the "About EFS-Web" page (http://www.uspto.gov/patents-application-process/applying-online/about-efs-web). You can get there by clicking "Patents" on the home page, and then on the drop down, choosing "About EFS-Web" under "Tools & Links." Once you're there, click "Launch EFS-Web Unregistered eFiler" (assuming you're unregistered).

Provide your last and first names and email address, then select "New application/proceeding." Choose "Utility," and then select provisional.

If you haven't registered as an eFiler, and you want to do that (it's worthwhile if you want to track your application or want to file many applications), then go to the EBC website center (www.uspto.gov/ebc/index.html) and under "Becoming a Registered eFiler, click "Customer Number and a Digital Certificate" and follow the "Getting Started" instructions. If you need help at any point, call the PTO's Electronic Business Center at 866-217-9197.

Application Data

On the Application Data page, you can either choose to attach your already-prepared ADS PDF or you can fill out the Web-based ADS form. If you're filling out the Web form, follow the previous instructions

("Prepare a PDF Data Sheet") and fill in the title of the invention, a docket number for the application of your choosing (optional, but a suitable docket number can be something like "Krypton derailleur"), and your name and customer number or address. Otherwise complete the fields and proceed to the "Attach Documents" page.

Take the Confusion Out of Filing Electronically

If you wish to file electronically, but find the EFS procedures off-putting, consider filing with Nolo's Online Provisional Patent Application Program. The program was created by the people who brought you this book and assists you in drafting and uploading your application and drawings. It prepares the necessary forms and forwards your filing to the USPTO. Go to Nolo (www.nolo.com) and click, "File a provisional patent app."

Attach PDF Files

On the Attach Documents page click "Choose File" and find your PDF folder which contains the PDF files of your application. Select one of your PDF application files, that is, the data file, click open, and you should see it in the "Files to Be Submitted" box adjacent to the "Choose File" button. Then, if you are uploading your Data Application file (that is, you elected not to complete the EFS-Web Application Data Sheet online) open the "Category" pull-down menu adjacent to the middle window and select "Application Part." Then open the rightmost pull-down menu

Edison's staff bet (cigars) against him as to whether his phonograph invention would work. When Edison demonstrated it, some scientists believed that he was surreptitiously using ventriloquism.

Thomas Edison

and select "Application Data Sheet." (Make sure the "No" button opposite "Does Your PDF File Contain Multiple Documents?" is checked since it's more difficult to work when everything is in one PDF document.) Then click "Add File" and a row of three windows will open. Repeat the above steps for each of your other PDF application files (that is, Dwgs.pdf and Spec.pdf), selecting the "Document Description" in the third window for each. When you've attached all of the PDF files in your PDF Application Holding Folder, click "Upload & Validate" at the bottom.

Review Documents

After a few minutes, you'll get a "Review Documents" page, which should show all of the documents you've attached. Make sure your entire application (drawings, specification, and data sheet) is there and there are no errors. If any errors are indicated, you'll have to go back and fix them. If everything is correct click "Continue."

Calculate Fees

On the "Calculate Fees" page, select your entity size, which is likely to be a micro entity or small entity.

To qualify as a **small entity,** the filer must be an independent inventor (or independent coinventors), or the company that owns invention rights must be a nonprofit or a for-profit company with 500 or fewer employees.

To qualify as a **micro entity**, the filer must be a small entity and must meet either of the following criteria:

- The applicant has not been named as the inventor on a total of more than four utility patents (regular utility patents, not provisional patent applications), design patents, or plant patents. This also does not include certain international PCT applications and applications owned by a previous employer. In addition, the applicant had to have had a gross income in the previous year of less than three times the median household income reported by the Bureau of the Census. (The median household income has been hovering around $50,000 for the past few years.) In the event that the patent application has been assigned, the assignee had to have a gross (not net) income of less than three times the U.S. median household income.

- The majority of the patent filer's employment income is from an institution of higher learning, or the applicant has assigned or is obliged to assign the patent to an institution of higher learning. An institution of higher learning is a public or nonprofit accredited institution that admits postsecondary students for programs of not less than two years.

Click the applicable box, and then click "Calculate." Your subtotal and total filing fee will be entered in the applicable boxes. Click "Continue."

Submit Application

This page will list all of your PDF files, a Fee-Info.pdf file, and the filing fee. If everything is correct, click "Submit" at the bottom to bring up a "Congratulations!" page with an assigned application number, confirmation number, and total fees due. Click "YES! I Want to Pay Now" at the bottom.

Review Fees and Select Payment Method

Unless you have a PTO Deposit Account or are set up for EFT, select "Charge Credit Card," then click "Start Online Payment Process" to bring up the payment page. Fill out the blanks and click "Confirm" at the bottom.

Become a Registered eFiler (If Time Permits)

If you plan on filing electronically and if you can wait several weeks to file, co-author David Pressman recommends you become a registered eFiler. You'll have to deal with red tape, including filling out a form to obtain a customer number, sending a notarized certificate to the PTO, obtaining access codes, and calling the PTO to confirm, but as a registered eFiler you'll be able to track your application's progress and file additional documents or corrections. To register, go to www.uspto.gov/ebc/index.html, click "Register Now," and follow the detailed instructions. If you can't wait several weeks, you can use EFS-Web to file an application as an unregistered eFiler and register later.

Acknowledgment Receipt

If everything is done correctly, you'll get an acknowledgment receipt, which is analogous to the receipt postcard used for mailed filings. the acknowledgment receipt will list the application (serial) number, the confirmation number, the application data, and parts that you've filed. Congratulations! You've bypassed the post office, filed an application electronically, and gotten an instant filing acknowledgment. Click "Print This Page" to print the page for your records. Eventually you'll get an official filing receipt by mail.

Filing by Mail

When filing by mail, you will need to include the following items in your application package:

- a completed Provisional Application for Patent Cover Sheet
- your specification (that is, the text you drafted after reading Chapter 5)
- your drawing sheets, if any (see Chapter 4)
- a Fee Transmittal form (PTO-SB/17)
- if paying by credit card, a Credit Card Payment Form (PTO-2038) or if paying by check, a check for the fee (currently $125), and
- a return receipt postcard.

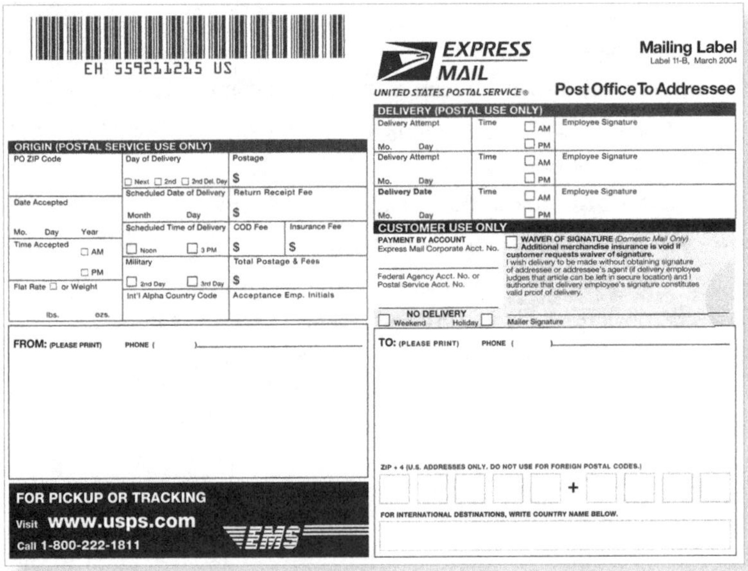

Illustration 1

Enclose everything in a U.S. Express Mail envelope (flat) with an Express Mail label and appropriate postage. Send high-quality versions of your specification (preferably printed on a laser or inkjet printer). Your specification sheets preferably should all be on the same size paper—either letter (8.5" x 11") or A4 paper is fine. Don't print on both sides of the paper. Your text should be spaced with 1.5 or double spacing and a 1-inch margin all around.

Police use computerized fingerprint systems to capture over 32,000 fugitives a year.

If you are furnishing a handwritten specification (not recommended), make sure it's in ink—or at least, that it's a good, readable photocopy of your writing. Include a header or footer on each page as described in Chapter 5.

Your drawings should be numbered as described in Chapter 4. They do not have to be the same size as your specification sheets but, for consistency, all drawing sheets should be on the same size sheets (again, letter or A4 size is preferable).

Last but not least, make sure you keep a paper copy of everything you mail.

Completing the Provisional Application for Patent Cover Sheet

You must submit a cover sheet with your provisional patent application. The USPTO has a form that we recommend you use (see Illustration 2). To obtain this form, go to the USPTO home page (www.uspto.gov) and download Form SB16 (not SB 16 EFS-Web).

The sections that follow explain how to complete the form.

Express Mail Label Number

At the top of the form, there's a space for supplying the "U.S. Express Mail Label Number." Copy the number from the Express Mail label (see Illustration 1) and write it in the box.

You don't have to use U.S. Express Mail. If you wish, or if you're not in the United States, you can mail your provisional patent application by regular mail or by an overnight express service such as Federal Express. However, using U.S. Express Mail provides two major benefits:

- Any document that you send by Express Mail that includes the Express Mail Number on the cover letter will be considered received on the day you mailed it (37 C.F.R. § 1.10). In other words, once the post office accepts your application, it's filed!
- If your application is lost in transit, you can still be accorded a filing date as of your mailing date. Send the USPTO another copy of the application, the fee, and a letter (titled "Request That Previously Express-Mailed Application Be Accorded a Filing Date"). The letter should state the details about the loss of the first application and conclude with a request that the application be granted the earlier filing date. Attach a copy of the previous Express Mail label receipt and number (37 C.F.R. § 1.10).

EXAMPLE 1: The clerk at the post office accepts David's Express Mail package on December 1, 2015. The filing date for his provisional patent application is December 1, 2015.

EXAMPLE 2: Mary sends her application by Federal Express on December 1, 2015. It's received by the USPTO on December 2, 2015. Mary's filing date is December 2, 2015.

EXAMPLE 3: Henrik sends his application to the USPTO by standard U.S. Priority or First Class Mail on December 1, 2015. It is received by the USPTO on December 6, 2015. His filing date is December 6, 2015.

EXAMPLE 4: Paul sends his application by U.S. Express Mail on December 1, 2015. As of January 15, 2016, Paul has not received his stamped receipt postcard back and his check for the filing fee has not been cashed. He inquires with the post office and learns that his application was lost in the mail. Paul sends the USPTO another copy of the complete application and fee, a copy of his dated Express Mail label and a letter ("Request That Previously Express-Mailed Application Be Accorded a Filing Date") explaining the loss. The USPTO grants Paul's request and he gets a filing date of Dec. 1, 2015.

PTO/SB/16 (03-13)
Approved for use through 01/31/2014. OMB 0651-0032
U.S. Patent and Trademark Office; U.S. DEPARTMENT OF COMMERCE
Under the Paperwork Reduction Act of 1995 no persons are required to respond to a collection of information unless it displays a valid OMB control number

PROVISIONAL APPLICATION FOR PATENT COVER SHEET – Page 1 of 2

This is a request for filing a PROVISIONAL APPLICATION FOR PATENT under 37 CFR 1.53(c).

Express Mail Label No. _____

INVENTOR(S)

Given Name (first and middle [if any])	Family Name or Surname	Residence (City and either State or Foreign Country)

Additional inventors are being named on the _____ separately numbered sheets attached hereto.

TITLE OF THE INVENTION (500 characters max):

CORRESPONDENCE ADDRESS

Direct all correspondence to:

☐ The address corresponding to Customer Number:

OR

☐ Firm or Individual Name

Address

City	State	Zip
Country	Telephone	Email

ENCLOSED APPLICATION PARTS (*check all that apply*)

☐ Application Data Sheet. See 37 CFR 1.76.   ☐ CD(s), Number of CDs _____

☐ Drawing(s)   *Number of Sheets* _____   ☐ Other (specify) _____

☐ Specification (e.g., description of the invention)   *Number of Pages* _____

Fees Due: Filing Fee of $260 ($130 for small entity) ($65 for micro entity). If the specification and drawings exceed 100 sheets of paper, an application size fee is also due, which is $400 ($200 for small entity) ($100 for micro entity) for each additional 50 sheets or fraction thereof. See 35 U.S.C. 41(a)(1)(G) and 37 CFR 1.16(s).

METHOD OF PAYMENT OF THE FILING FEE AND APPLICATION SIZE FEE FOR THIS PROVISIONAL APPLICATION FOR PATENT

☐ Applicant asserts small entity status. See 37 CFR 1.27.

☐ Applicant certifies micro entity status. See 37 CFR 1.29.
Applicant must attach form PTO/SB/15A or B or equivalent.

☐ A check or money order made payable to the *Director of the United States Patent and Trademark Office* is enclosed to cover the filing fee and application size fee (if applicable).

☐ Payment by credit card. Form PTO-2038 is attached.

☐ The Director is hereby authorized to charge the filing fee and application size fee (if applicable) or credit any overpayment to Deposit Account Number: _____.

TOTAL FEE AMOUNT ($)

USE ONLY FOR FILING A PROVISIONAL APPLICATION FOR PATENT

This collection of information is required by 37 CFR 1.51. The information is required to obtain or retain a benefit by the public which is to file (and by the USPTO to process) an application. Confidentiality is governed by 35 U.S.C. 122 and 37 CFR 1.11 and 1.14. This collection is estimated to take 10 hours to complete, including gathering, preparing, and submitting the completed application form to the USPTO. Time will vary depending upon the individual case. Any comments on the amount of time you require to complete this form and/or suggestions for reducing this burden, should be sent to the Chief Information Officer, U.S. Patent and Trademark Office, U.S. Department of Commerce, P.O. Box 1450, Alexandria, VA 22313-1450. DO NOT SEND FEES OR COMPLETED FORMS TO THIS ADDRESS. **SEND TO: Commissioner for Patents, P.O. Box 1450, Alexandria, VA 22313-1450.**
If you need assistance in completing the form, call 1-800-PTO-9199 and select option 2.

Illustration 2, Page 1 of 2

PTO/SB/16 (03-13)
Approved for use through 01/31/2014. OMB 0651-0032
U.S. Patent and Trademark Office; U.S. DEPARTMENT OF COMMERCE
Under the Paperwork Reduction Act of 1995 no persons are required to respond to a collection of information unless it displays a valid OMB control number

PROVISIONAL APPLICATION FOR PATENT COVER SHEET – Page 2 of 2

The invention was made by an agency of the United States Government or under a contract with an agency of the United States Government.

☐ No.

☐ Yes, the invention was made by an agency of the U.S. Government. The U.S. Government agency name is: _____

☐ Yes, the invention was made under a contract with an agency of the U.S. Government. The name of the U.S. Government agency and Government contract number are: _____

WARNING:

Petitioner/applicant is cautioned to avoid submitting personal information in documents filed in a patent application that may contribute to identity theft. Personal information such as social security numbers, bank account numbers, or credit card numbers (other than a check or credit card authorization form PTO-2038 submitted for payment purposes) is never required by the USPTO to support a petition or an application. If this type of personal information is included in documents submitted to the USPTO, petitioners/applicants should consider redacting such personal information from the documents before submitting them to the USPTO. Petitioner/applicant is advised that the record of a patent application is available to the public after publication of the application (unless a non-publication request in compliance with 37 CFR 1.213(a) is made in the application) or issuance of a patent. Furthermore, the record from an abandoned application may also be available to the public if the application is referenced in a published application or an issued patent (see 37 CFR 1.14). Checks and credit card authorization forms PTO-2038 submitted for payment purposes are not retained in the application file and therefore are not publicly available.

SIGNATURE   DATE

Illustration 2, Page 2 of 2

Inventor(s)

Below the box for your "Express Mail Label Number" on the cover sheet, you'll find a box titled "Inventor(s)." Fill in your name and address. If there are coinventors, you can include the names of five of them below your name. If there are more than five inventors, you will need to attach a separate sheet with the names of additional inventors. If you're unsure whether someone qualifies as a coinventor, review Hurdle #2 in Chapter 2.

Title of the Invention

In this section, provide your invention title. If you need assistance, review Chapter 5.

> When an inventor discussed jet propulsion with Adolf Hitler, the Fuhrer asked, "Why is it necessary to fly faster than the speed of sound?"

Correspondence Address

Next, you must provide an address where the USPTO can send correspondence regarding your invention. If you have a USPTO Customer Number (many law firms and corporations do), mark the "customer number" box and provide the number or use a bar code sticker. Otherwise, mark the box "Firm or Individual Name" and write the name of the individual or company that should receive mail from the USPTO. (But don't wait by the mailbox—it will probably take two to three weeks for you to get your receipt postcard back and one to two months to get your official filing receipt. If you failed to include something in your package, the USPTO's OIPE (Office of Initial Patent Examination) will send you a letter telling you what to do and what fees you are charged for the error. Supply what is needed, following the instructions in the letter.)

Enclosed Application Parts

Mark the "Specification" box and indicate how many pages you're sending. If you have drawings, mark the "Drawings" box and indicate the number of drawing sheets. Do not check the box "Application Data Sheet." (An Application Data Sheet is a voluntary submission that includes additional information about you and your invention—don't bother with it.) If you are submitting compact discs that contain supporting information—for example, program code or a biotech sequence—mark the "CD" box on the form and indicate the number of compact discs. Mark the "Other" box only if you are providing additional information for a biotech or software invention—for example, microfiche of a computer printout. Don't use this box as an invitation to submit videos, prototypes, or other information describing your invention.

Method of Payment of Fees

In this section, you must indicate your method of payment and whether you qualify for small entity or micro entity status.

To qualify as a **small entity** the filer must be an independent inventor (or independent coinventors), or the company that owns invention rights must be a nonprofit or a for-profit company with 500 or fewer employees.

To qualify as a **micro entity**, the filer must be a small entity and must meet either of the following criteria:

- The applicant has not been named as the inventor on a total of more than four utility patents (regular utility patents, not provisional patent applications), design patents, or plant patents. This also does not include certain international PCT applications and applications owned by a previous employer. In addition, the applicant had to have had a gross income in the previous year of less than three times the median household income reported by the Bureau of the Census. (The median household income has been hovering around $50,000 for the past two years.) In the event that the patent application has been assigned, the assignee had to have a gross (not net) income of less than three times the U.S. median household income.

- The majority of the patent filer's employment income is from an institution of higher learning, or the applicant has assigned or is obliged to assign the patent to an institution of higher learning. An institution of higher learning is a public or nonprofit accredited institution that admits postsecondary students for programs of not less than two years.

Small entity status entitles you to pay a filing fee of $130, rather than $260. micro entity status enables you to pay a filing fee of $65. Confirm that the fee hasn't gone up since this book went to press by clicking "Patents" on the USPTO home page and then searching for "Fee Schedule." Write or

PTO-2038 (02-2015)
Approved for use through 01/31/2018. OMB 0651-0043
United States Patent and Trademark Office; U.S. DEPARTMENT OF COMMERCE
Under the Paperwork Reduction Act of 1995, no persons are required to respond to a collection of information unless it
displays a valid OMB control number.

Credit Card Payment Form
(Do not submit this form electronically via EFS-Web)
Please Read Instructions before Completing this Form

Credit Card Information

Credit Card Type: ☐ Visa ☐ MasterCard ☐ American Express ☐ Discover

Credit Card Account #:

Credit Card Expiration Date (mm/yyyy):

Name as it Appears on Credit Card:

Payment Amount (US Dollars): $

Cardholder Signature:	Date (mm/dd/yyyy):

The USPTO does not accept an s-signature (37 CFR 1.4(e)) on credit card payment forms.
Refund Policy: The USPTO may refund a fee paid by mistake or in excess of that required. A change of purpose after the payment of a fee will not entitle a party to a refund of such fee. The USPTO will not refund amounts of $25.00 or less unless a refund is specifically requested and will not notify the payor of such amounts (37 CFR 1.26). Refund of a fee paid by credit card will be issued as a credit to the credit card account to which the fee was charged.
Maximum Daily Limit: There is a $24,999.99 daily limit per credit card account effective June 1, 2015. There is no daily limit for debit cards.

Credit Card Billing Address

Street Address 1:

Street Address 2:

City:

State/Province:	Zip/Postal Code:

Country:

Daytime Phone #:	Fax #:

Request and Payment Information

Description of Request and Payment Information:

☐ Patent Fee	☐ Patent Maintenance Fee	☐ Trademark Fee	☐ Other Fee
Application No.	Application No.	Application No.	IDON Customer No.
Patent No.	Patent No.	Registration No.	
Attorney Docket No.		Identify or Describe Mark	

If the cardholder includes a credit card number on any form or document other than the Credit Card Payment Form or submits this form electronically via EFS-Web, the United States Patent and Trademark Office will not be liable in the event that the credit card number becomes public knowledge.

Illustration 3

check the appropriate fee in the pertinent boxes on your Provisional Application for Patent Cover Sheet and on your Fee Transmittal sheet.

Check or Money Order. If you pay by check or money order, mark this box and include a check payable to "Director of the United States Patent and Trademark Office." Make sure there's enough money in your account to cover the fee—if your check bounces, you will have to pay the USPTO a stiff surcharge of $50. (You must also pay a surcharge of $25 if your payment is not included with the filing or if you forget to include the cover sheet and have to file it later.)

Deposit Account Number. Disregard this box unless you maintain a deposit account at the USPTO.

Payment by Credit Card. If you want to pay by credit card, check this box and complete an additional form (Illustration 3), Form PTO/SB/2038: Credit Card Payment Form and Instructions. If you provide credit card information without submitting Form PTO/SB/2038, the USPTO may include your credit information as part of your provisional patent application—and eventually make it available for public viewing.

To obtain Form 2038, click "Patents" on the USPTO home page, then click "Forms" and download USPTO Form 2038. Fill out Form 2038 on your computer or print it out and complete it by hand or typewriter. In the box titled "Description of Request and Payment Information" in the section "Request and Payment Information," write "provisional patent application fee." Leave the rest of this section blank. The remainder of Form 2038 is easy to complete—instructions are provided when you download the form.

If you use a credit card, be sure that your filing fee payment will not bring your charges over your credit limit; if your credit card payment is rejected, you'll have to pay the $50 fee.

Invention Made by U.S. Agency

In the bottom box on the Provisional Application for Patent Cover Sheet, you must indicate whether your invention was made by an agency of the U.S. government or under a contract with an agency of the U.S. government. If it was, check "Yes" and provide the name of the agency. If not, check the "No" box.

Signature and Telephone

Under "Respectfully Submitted," sign your name, then write or type your name and provide your telephone number.

Fee Transmittal Form

In addition to the patent application cover sheet, you should complete and enclose a Fee Transmittal form. You can download Form PTO/SB/17 from the USPTO website. To complete the form, determine if you are a small entity, or if you qualify as a micro entity and then check the appropriate box, check your method of payment, and fill in $130 or $65 under "Fee Paid" (depending on whether you are a small entity or micro entity). Provide your name, signature, telephone, and date at the bottom of the form. If paying by credit card, download Form PTO/SB/2038 and include that as well. An example of Form PTO/SB/17 is provided in Illustration 4.

Return Postcard

It's essential to include a return postcard with every document that you send to the USPTO. Once you get it back, tape it in your file; the postcard will be a permanent record that your application was received. (Your U.S. Express Mail tracking information and canceled check also provide useful evidence of receipt—tape these in your file as well.)

Write your mailing address on the front of the postcard. On the back, write: "Provisional patent application of [*your name or names*] for [*title of invention*] consisting of ____ pages of specification, ____ drawing sheets, and filing fee of $____ received today ____."

Mailing

Assemble your completed cover sheet, specification, drawing sheets, return postcard, and check (or Form 2038 if paying by credit card). Address your package to:

Commissioner for Patents
P.O. Box 1450
Alexandria, VA 22313-1450

PTO/SB/17 (03-13)
Approved for use through 01/31/2014. OMB 0651-0032
U.S. Patent and Trademark Office; U.S. DEPARTMENT OF COMMERCE
Under the Paperwork Reduction Act of 1995 no persons are required to respond to a collection of information unless it displays a valid OMB control number

FEE TRANSMITTAL

Complete if known

Application Number	
Filing Date	
First Named Inventor	
Examiner Name	
Art Unit	
Practitioner Docket No.	

☐ Applicant asserts small entity status. See 37 CFR 1.27.

☐ Applicant certifies micro entity status. See 37 CFR 1.29.
Form PTO/SB/15A or B or equivalent must either be enclosed or have been submitted previously.

TOTAL AMOUNT OF PAYMENT ($)

METHOD OF PAYMENT (check all that apply)

☐ Check ☐ Credit Card ☐ Money Order ☐ None ☐ Other (please identify): _____

☐ Deposit Account Deposit Account Number: _____ Deposit Account Name: _____

For the above-identified deposit account, the Director is hereby authorized to (check all that apply):

☐ Charge fee(s) indicated below   ☐ Charge fee(s) indicated below, **except for the filing fee**

☐ Charge any additional fee(s) or underpayment of fee(s)   ☐ Credit any overpayment of fee(s)
under 37 CFR 1.16 and 1.17

WARNING: Information on this form may become public. Credit card information should not be included on this form. Provide credit card information and authorization on PTO-2038.

FEE CALCULATION

1. BASIC FILING, SEARCH, AND EXAMINATION FEES (U = undiscounted fee; S = small entity fee; M = micro entity fee)

Application Type	FILING FEES U ($)	S ($)	M ($)	SEARCH FEES U ($)	S ($)	M ($)	EXAMINATION FEES U ($)	S ($)	M ($)	Fees Paid ($)
Utility	280	140*	70	600	300	150	720	360	180	_____
Design	180	90	45	120	60	30	460	230	115	_____
Plant	180	90	45	380	190	95	580	290	145	_____
Reissue	280	140	70	600	300	150	2,160	1,080	540	_____
Provisional	260	130	65	0	0	0	0	0	0	_____

* The $140 small entity status filing fee for a utility application is further reduced to $70 for a small entity status applicant who files the application via EFS-Web.

2. EXCESS CLAIM FEES

Fee Description	Undiscounted Fee ($)	Small Entity Fee ($)	Micro Entity Fee ($)
Each claim over 20 (including Reissues)	80	40	20
Each independent claim over 3 (including Reissues)	420	210	105
Multiple dependent claims	780	390	195

Total Claims   **Extra Claims**   **Fee ($)**   **Fee Paid ($)**
_____ -20 or HP = _____ x _____ = _____

HP = highest number of total claims paid for, if greater than 20.

Multiple Dependent Claims
Fee ($)   **Fee Paid ($)**
_____   _____

Indep. Claims   **Extra Claims**   **Fee ($)**   **Fee Paid ($)**
_____ -3 or HP = _____ x _____ = _____

HP = highest number of independent claims paid for, if greater than 3.

3. APPLICATION SIZE FEE

If the specification and drawings exceed 100 sheets of paper (excluding electronically filed sequence or computer listings under 37 CFR 1.52(e)), the application size fee due is $400 ($200 for small entity) ($100 for micro entity) for each additional 50 sheets or fraction thereof. See 35 U.S.C. 41(a)(1)(G) and 37 CFR 1.16(s).

Total Sheets   **Extra Sheets**   **Number of each additional 50 or fraction thereof**   **Fee ($)**   **Fee Paid ($)**
_____ - 100 = _____ / 50 = _____ (round **up** to a whole number)   x _____ = _____

4. OTHER FEE(S)   **Fees Paid ($)**

Non-English specification, $130 fee (no small or micro entity discount)   _____

Non-electronic filing fee under 37 CFR 1.16(t) for a utility application, $400 fee ($200 small or micro entity)   _____

Other (e.g., late filing surcharge): _____   _____

SUBMITTED BY

Signature		Registration No. (Attorney/Agent)	Telephone
Name (Print/Type)			Date

This collection of information is required by 37 CFR 1.136. The information is required to obtain or retain a benefit by the public which is to file (and by the USPTO to process) an application. Confidentiality is governed by 35 U.S.C. 122 and 37 CFR 1.14. This collection is estimated to take 30 minutes to complete, including gathering, preparing, and submitting the completed application form to the USPTO. Time will vary depending upon the individual case. Any comments on the amount of time you require to complete this form and/or suggestions for reducing this burden, should be sent to the Chief Information Officer, U.S. Patent and Trademark Office, U.S. Department of Commerce, P.O. Box 1450, Alexandria, VA 22313-1450. DO NOT SEND FEES OR COMPLETED FORMS TO THIS ADDRESS. **SEND TO: Commissioner for Patents, P.O. Box 1450, Alexandria, VA 22313-1450.**

If you need assistance in completing the form, call 1-800-PTO-9199 and select option 2.

Illustration 4

Enclose your materials and take the Express Mail flat to the post office. Don't deposit the envelope in a regular or even an Express Mail mailbox since you won't immediately receive the Express Mail receipt. Instead take the Express Mail flat directly to the desk and ask the clerk to date-stamp the sender's copy of the Express Mail receipt. This will give you a clear date on the receipt. Tape the receipt in your file so you won't lose it.

While working at the Tuskegee Institute, George Washington Carver invented the idea of crop rotation, the use of alternative crops that returned nutrients to the soil, and many products and uses for plants such as soybeans, pecans, the peanut, and sweet potato. He patented only three of his inventions: cosmetics, paints, and stains made from soybeans.

George Washington Carver

If you want to use ordinary First Class or Priority mail—for example, you can't afford Express Mail (or you're not in the United States)—affix the proper postage (consult www.usps.gov for current U.S. rates) and mail it in a regular mailbox or leave it with your RFD carrier. Alternatively, you can use a courier service, but you won't get the benefits listed above. Also, keep in mind that due to security issues, some regular (First Class) mail has been delayed when sent to U.S. government offices.

Filing a Regular Patent Application

If you want to claim the benefits of your provisional patent application's filing date (as described in Chapter 1), you must file a regular patent application within 12 months of your provisional filing date. The USPTO cannot extend the 12-month pendency period.

Congratulations! Now, Set Your Clock

Mark these two dates on your calendar:
- the date that is 12 months after you file your provisional patent application, and
- the date that is nine or ten months after you file your provisional patent application (this is when you should begin preparing your regular patent application).

Although you have 12 months to file a regular patent application, you should decide whether you're going to file well ahead of this deadline—within nine or ten months after filing your provisional patent application, if possible. Waiting any longer could turn out to be a big mistake—it may take two months or longer for you or your attorney to prepare a regular patent application.

If you miss this 12-month deadline, you can still file a regular patent application but you won't be able to claim the benefit of your provisional patent application's filing date.

Your Regular Patent Application Must Refer to Your Provisional

In order to claim the filing date of your provisional patent application, your regular patent application must specifically claim the benefit of the filing date of your provisional patent application. You can do this by inserting the following sentence in the beginning of your regular patent application under "Cross Reference To Related Applications": "This application claims the benefit of provisional patent application Ser. Nr. [#], filed [*date*]." If you forget to include this reference in your regular patent application, you have four months after the filing date of your regular patent application or 16 months after the filing date of your provisional patent application to amend the regular patent application (37 C.F.R. § 78(5)). Otherwise, you cannot claim the benefit of your provisional patent application.

Converting a Provisional Patent Application

Instead of filing a regular patent application and claiming the benefit of your provisional patent application, the USPTO permits you to convert your provisional patent application into a regular patent application. To do this, you have to file a petition with the USPTO. Users of this book should not follow this route—the provisional patent application we have helped you prepare does not include all of the information or follow the format that the USPTO requires for regular patent applications.

Your regular patent application must also name at least one inventor who was named in the provisional patent application.

Marking Your Invention "Patent Pending"

One of the benefits of filing a provisional patent application is that once you file, you can mark or refer to your application as "patent pending." If you (or a licensee) manufacture your invention, you should mark the product with the legend "U.S. Patent Pending." "Idea theft is not rampant," writes inventor Maurice Kanbar in his book, *Secrets From an Inventor's Notebook,* "but it does happen, so don't risk it … 'patent pending' status can deter thieves."

Place this legend on the product itself and, if possible, on the packaging. Obviously, if you have patented a process or method, there may not be a product to label. However, you should refer to its patent pending status in any literature or correspondence about your invention.

It is a federal crime to state that your invention has patent pending status if you have not filed a regular patent application or a provisional patent application, or if more than one year has passed since you filed a provisional patent application, unless you filed a regular patent application within that year.

Keep in mind that you cannot sue to stop infringers during the pendency period—the time between the date you file your provisional patent application and the date you get your patent. You can sue only after a patent has issued. However, once a patent issues on your invention, you can sue infringers for financial damages you suffered after your regular application was published (see Chapter 1).

What Happens If You Modify Your Invention?

You just filed your provisional patent application. On the way home from the post office, you have a brainstorm. You realize how to make your invention safer and more productive. You rush into your workshop and make the improvements. *Eureka!*

But what about the provisional patent application you just filed? Because you have modified the invention described in your provisional patent application, you will need to file a new one. You cannot amend or change the previously filed provisional patent application to include these new developments.

How can you tell whether you've made a change that requires filing a new provisional patent application? In general, if the provisional patent application you filed is no longer accurate—that is, if you must modify it to accurately describe your invention—then you have to file a new provisional patent application. In other words, if the modification alters the way you described your invention in your provisional patent application—for example, if you add or subtract parts or change the structure or operation of parts—you will not be able to rely on the date of your previous filing since it does not disclose these new developments.

International Rules to Remember

If you own a patent granted by the USPTO, you can stop others from making, using, selling, importing, or offering your invention for sale only within the United States. That same rule applies throughout the world: Patent rights only extend to a nation's territory.

Do you want to pursue foreign patent rights? And if you do want to pursue rights in foreign countries, which ones would be good candidates? In general, any decision to acquire a patent in a particular country should be based on the potential income from exploiting the invention in that nation. Ask yourself whether forgoing patent protection in a specific nation will result in a loss of substantial revenue. Making this assessment requires examining factors such as the cost of foreign patent protection and the commercial potential of your invention in a foreign country.

> **EXAMPLE:** In the United States, George pays approximately $10,000 to acquire a patent. This cost covers the patent search, preparation of application, and shepherding the application through the USPTO. In return, George acquires rights in the world's single largest national market. In contrast, if George were to seek patent protection in eight European nations (with approximately the same population as United States), his estimated cost for acquiring the patents in these countries is approximately $27,500 to $35,000.

Selling Inventions in a Foreign Country

When making a marketability-per-nation analysis, you will need to ask yourself the questions listed below. Although these questions require some degree of speculation, it is possible to acquire sufficient economic data about the trade potential, business climate, and demographics in foreign countries to make an educated guess about filing for a patent. Consider:

- **Current sales potential.** Would you be able to sell your invention in the target nation today? Without sales potential, there may be no reason to seek patent protection.

- **Future market.** Do you expect a possible future market for the invention within the next ten to 15 years? Even if the current market is weak, it may be worth pursuing a patent if a future market is expected.

- **Local partner.** Are there possibilities of finding a partner to license or create a joint venture in order to market the invention in the nation? The chances for successfully exploiting an invention usually increase when a local partner is involved.

- **Competition.** What is the status of competitors in this nation? The presence of competitors can be interpreted in different ways. It may indicate a healthy, substantial market with room for more competition. A lack of competitors, particularly in an emerging technology may prove to be a positive sign. On the other hand, a major competitor, particularly one that has dominated the market for five to ten years, could prove difficult to challenge.

- **Production costs.** Can the invention be cost-efficiently produced in this nation? Although inventions can always be imported, it may be more cost-efficient (or even necessary in some cases) to produce an invention within the nation.

- **Day-to-day operations.** Do you have the means to observe and administer the market in this country? If you must control day-to-day operations from a distance, you will have a more difficult time making a success of the market, especially if your resources are limited.

- **Ability to sue patent infringers.** How difficult is it to sue an infringer in this country? Having a patent doesn't automatically stop an infringer; you must go after the infringer in the nation where the patent was granted. This is one of the drawbacks of foreign patent protection; there is no international method to stop patent infringers. You must sue in each country where an infringement has occurred.

- **Sales and distribution.** What channels exist for getting the invention to market? Even if an invention has sales potential, you will need a way to distribute the product to buyers. The lack of strong distribution channels is a disincentive to seeking a foreign patent.
- **Marketing.** How hard will it be to gain exposure to the market? Will it be possible to reach substantial numbers of buyers through advertising, direct marketing, or other means? The more difficult it is to reach buyers, the lower your chances for success.
- **Obstacles to sales.** Are there any impediments to selling in this market? You may need to determine if there are regulatory rules (for example, safety standards for medical devices) or trade or union rules that will affect your ability to sell in a nation.
- **Licensee.** Do you have a licensee who would be willing to pay the cost of foreign filing in exchange for royalties abroad?

RELATED TOPIC
To help you research commercial potential in foreign markets, we provide relevant Internet sites in Appendix F.

Special Rules for Foreign Patents

If you are interested in pursuing foreign patent rights, remember these important rules.

You cannot obtain a foreign patent if you publish, publicly use, sell, or offer to sell your invention before filing in the United States.

If you sell, offer for sale, publicly use, or publish information about your invention before you file a provisional or regular patent application, you will not be able to obtain foreign patent rights. Outside the United States, any public release in any country will be considered prior art.

EXAMPLE: The inventors of the sailboard obtained a British patent for their invention and sought to stop infringers in the U.K. However, during their British trial, evidence was introduced indicating (1) that an article discussing sailboarding in *Popular Science Monthly* preceded the invention by several years, and (2) ten years before the patent was issued, a 12-year-old boy had built and used a similar device in England. The British patent was revoked.

If you publish, publicly use, sell, or offer to sell, your invention after filing a provisional patent application or regular patent application in the United States, you can file for a foreign patent within 12 months of the filing date in countries that belong to the Paris Convention.

The United States is a signatory nation to several international patent treaties, two of which are particularly important to inventors filing a provisional patent application: the Paris Convention and the Patent Cooperation Treaty. Most industrialized nations in the world are members of both treaties.

A U.S. inventor who files a provisional patent application or a regular patent application can file a patent application in any Paris Convention country within one year of the inventor's earliest filing date—even if a sale, public use, or publication occurred after the filing date. The inventor's application in the Convention country will be entitled to the filing date of the inventor's earliest U.S. application for purposes of prior-art examinations.

EXAMPLE: Sam files a provisional patent application in the United States on September 1, 2015. He files a regular patent application on August 10, 2016, claiming the benefit of the provisional patent application. Sam also files European, Brazilian, and Australian patent applications on August 10, 2016, and is entitled to the filing date of September 1, 2015, in these countries (all signatories to the Paris Convention).

If you don't publish, publicly use, or sell your invention, you can still acquire foreign patent rights—even if you miss the one-year Paris Convention deadline

If you miss the Paris Convention's one-year deadline you can still foreign file—but only if you haven't published, publicly used, or sold your invention. You won't be entitled to your U.S. filing date, so any relevant prior art that has been published in the meantime can be applied against the foreign application. However, if you miss the one-year Paris Convention deadline and the USPTO subsequently issues the U.S. patent, *it's too late to file a foreign application anywhere!* You can acquire patent rights *only* in the United States.

You Can Simplify Foreign Filing by Participating in a Patent Cooperation Treaty (PCT) Filing

The Patent Cooperation Treaty (PCT) enables inventors to file a relatively economical international application in their home country within one year of their home country filing date. There are two advantages to filing a PCT application:

- The inventor obtains a filing date that is good in every member country in which the inventor seeks patent protection.
- An initial international patent search will be conducted—and PCT member countries will rely heavily on this search.

The inventor in a PCT nation must eventually file separate "national" applications in each country (or group of countries) where the inventor wants coverage. However, the initial search procedure simplifies the international patent process—an initial patent search is conducted by the USPTO (or any other searching authority, such as the EPO) and PCT nations rely on this search. You can find a list of nations that are members of the PCT at the USPTO website. Click "Patents" (on the left side of the page), then click "Patent Cooperation Treaty" (it's under International Protection).

TIP

Don't procrastinate. Make foreign-filing decisions about two or three months before the end of any of the filing periods described in this section. This will give you and foreign patent agents time to prepare (or have prepared) the necessary correspondence and translations.

Our inventor downloaded and completed the cover sheet, then packaged up his provisional patent application. He spent a total of two hours reading this chapter, preparing his cover sheet, packaging, and mailing. (It took 40 minutes to deliver it to his local post office.)

In summary, our inventor filed a PPA on his Baby Tears doll in approximately 14 hours from start to finish.

Of course, our experiment is not intended as a scientifically accurate test. We were working with an experienced inventor who had considerable knowledge of his field. In addition, his invention could be expressed simply without extensive technical descriptions. Obviously, the more complex your invention, the more time-consuming it will be to prepare your drawings and specification.

In any case, as amusing as our time trial was, our concern is that you get it right. Never sacrifice accuracy for speed. Always keep in mind that without an accurate PPA that clearly teaches how to make and use the invention, your work will be worthless. Good luck!

Provisional Patent Applications

This appendix provides you with 17 inventions, some famous, some not as well known. For each, we present a provisional patent application, followed by the text from the patent upon which it was based. Comparing the documents will give you a better idea of what you should include in a provisional application and what you'll need to include in the regular patent application. We have included the drawings as furnished and filed with the patent office. As we explained in Chapter 4, these drawings can be informally prepared for purposes of the provisional patent application.

Pasteurization

As we explained in Chapter 1, Louis Pasteur discovered that by preventing exposure to air, a larger quantity and better quality of beer could be produced. Pasteur's process—later known as pasteurization—partially sterilized the beer and subsequently was used to sterilize liquids such as milk and orange juice, as well as cheese. His Improvement in Brewing Beer and Ale was patented in France in 1871 and in the United States in January 1873.

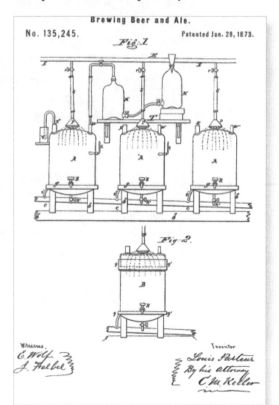

Provisional Patent Application

A Provisional Patent Application for "Pasteurization"

I discovered a better way to brew beer and ale. My process prevents the wort (the boiled extract of malt or material seasoned with malt or other qualifying ingredient seasoned with hops) from exposure to air. The result—compared to existing methods of beer production—is the production of a larger quantity of beer as well as a beer that is more aromatic and less likely to deteriorate in transit or storage.

I accomplish this by expelling the air from the boiled wort while it is confined in a closed vessel (or vessels).

The attached drawing helps to explain my invention. Three casks AAA (Fig. 1), made of iron, wood, or other suitable materials, are supported on stands below a water pipe E. The water pipe has branches, each with a valve, and at the end of each branch, a flexible hose and spray nozzle P. On another stand T is an apparatus MM that generates carbonic-acid gas. The carbonic gas is supplied to the casks and is released from the casks at the escape tubes X which extend into cups or chambers V from which the gas can be collected by a gasometer.

The wort is prepared in the usual manner and while boiling hot is placed in a cask. Carbonic-acid gas is conveyed into the cask for the purpose of expelling air. There must be a thorough penetration of carbonic-acid gas into the liquid to expel all contained air.

Then, the water pipe sprays the cask to cool it. A trough C is placed below the casks to collect the water. As the temperature is reduced to about 20 to 23 degrees Celsius (68–73 degrees Fahrenheit), the yeast or fermenting material is added to induce fermentation. After first fermentation, the beer can be sent through the valves R into casks or barrels for future use.

The beer does not have to be removed and fermentation can be completed in the cask. But in this case, a small quantity of air may be drawn into the cask to speed fermentation. The air drawn into the tube should be filtered through cotton or passed through a hot tube to kill or extract any germs that it may contain. The apparatus shown is adapted for making small quantities of beer but the capacity may be varied quite easily.

Patent

Improvement in Brewing Beer and Ale No. 135,245

Be it known that I, Louis Pasteur, of the city of Paris, France, have invented certain new and useful improvements in the Process of Making Beer for which Letters Patent were granted to me in France on the 28th day of June 1871; and I do hereby declare the following to be a full, clear and exact description thereof, reference being made to the accompanying drawing making part of this specification and the letters of reference marked thereon.

Previous to my invention in the process of making beer it has been customary to permit the exposure of the "wort"—that is the boiled extract of malt or other material seasoned with hop, or other qualifying ingredient—to the action of atmospheric air. I have discovered that by contact in the usual way with air during the process not only is the quality of the beer produced much impaired, but also that less quantity is made from a given amount of wort that can be otherwise produced.

Based on this discovery and the idea of performing the process of brewing without the presence in the wort of atmospheric air, my invention has for its object to produce a better quality and greater quantity of wort, and to afford a beer which shall also embody the quality of greater changes of climate and in transportation and use; and to these ends my invention consists in expelling the air from the boiled wort while confined in a closed vessel or vessels and then cooling it by the application of sprays of water to the exterior of such vessel or vessels as will be hereinafter more fully explained.

To enable those skilled in the art to fully understand and practice my improved process for the manufacture of beer, I will proceed to more fully describe it, referring at the same time by letters to the accompanying drawing in which I have shown an apparatus adapted to carry on my said improved process.

At Figure 1, A A A represent three casks or tanks, which may be made of galvanized iron, wood, or other suitable material, and which are supported on suitable stands *b*, as represented. Above the series of cylinders or vessel A is arranged a water supply pipe, E, from which depend branch pipes (one over each of the vessels A), provided with cocks *r*, and having attached to their lower ends flexible tubes or hose s, which in turn carry at their lower extremities spray-nozzles P. Upon a suitable stand or shelf, T, is located an apparatus M M, for the generation of carbonic acid gas, which is to be supplied therefrom to the vessels A for purposes to be presently explained and by means of tubes connected at W to the said vessels. The escape of the gas is permitted through exit or escape tubes at x which extend siphon-like into water cups or chambers v from whence the gas may be collected in a gasometer.

I have shown the connection of the gas generator with only one of the vessels; but it will be understood that the others may be similarly connected.

The spray-nozzles P are located about centrally over each of the vessels A, which should be made slightly convex or dome-shaped on top, and so that the jets of water discharged there from will fall like rain on the tops of the said vessels and trickle down their sides as illustrated by the dotted lines in Fig. 1. Around the base of each vessel A is arranged a circular trough, which catches the water and from which the water is left off by a tube, I, into a conductor or discharge trough, c, which carries it to any desired destination. R are cocks through which the contents of the vessels may be discharged into other vessels for the permanent retention of it, and R, are faucets, which are used to draw off the beer for use, when it shall have been left or allowed to remain in the vessels A, as will be presently explained.

At Fig. 2 is illustrated a modification of the vessel or cask, in which, in lieu of being closed permanently at the top, said vessel B is made with a removable top, and is provided with the usual and necessary water gauges, thermometers, man-holes, etc., common to such contrivances.

The following explanation in connection with the foregoing description of apparatus will suffice to convey a full exposition of my improved process: The wort prepared in the usual manner, and while yet boiling hot, is introduced into the vessel A, in which a current of carbonic acid gas is then conveyed for the purpose of expelling all contained air, and the water-spray is then let on to the vessels to cool them and their contents. As soon as the temperature of the charges has been reduced to about from 16 degrees to 18 degrees Reaumur, the yeast or pure ferment is added to provoke or induce fermentation. After fermentation, or the first fermentation, the contents of the vessels A may be drawn off through the cocks R into casks or barrels for future use, and in which the usual and further fermentation goes on, from which the beer becomes both clear and bright.

In lieu of drawing off the beer thus into barrels it may be allowed to remain, when the apparatus is not needed further, in the vessels A, and therein complete its fermentation, and be drawn for use through the faucets R; but in this case or where it is desired to accelerate or make more complete the first fermentation, it may be found desirable to introduce a small quantity of air into the vessel, first, however, passing the air through a hot tube, or at least filtering it through the cotton, for the purpose of either killing or extracting any germs which it may contain.

The apparatus which I have shown is adapted to the working of small quantities—say about one barrel; but it is obvious that the capacity of the apparatus may be varied at pleasure to manufacture more or less extensively.

In conducting my new mode of manufacture or process, the carbonic-acid gas generated from the fermentation of the wort may be collected properly in a gasometer, of course, and employed in lieu of or in connection with that derived from a generator, such as shown, and which is necessary for the first operation, it being important always to effect a thorough penetration of the mass by the carbonic acid gas to expel all contained air.

It will be understood that by my improved process not only are the usual cooling vessels dispensed with and all loss by evaporation prevented but that the quality of the beer and its alcoholic gradation are improved and a larger quantity produced from a given supply of material.

I have found that by my new process the beer produced possesses in an eminent degree the capacity of unchangeableness and can be transported without detriment or deterioration; and that in the use of my process by which I am enabled to brew in all season and in most any climate successfully the product is more aromatic and is perfectly limpid.

What I claim as new in the process of brewing or in the manufacture of beer is—

Subjecting the wort to a process the expulsion of the air and cooling it off, substantially as and for the purposes set forth.

In testimony whereof I have hereunto set my hand this 8th day of December 1871.

The Telephone

When offered the patent for the telephone for $100,000, William Orton, president of Western Union, was said to have replied, "What use could this company make of an electrical toy?" Orton's shortsighted decision proved to be one of the most famous blunders in American corporate history. Below we present the original telephone patent and drawings along with our version of a provisional patent application.

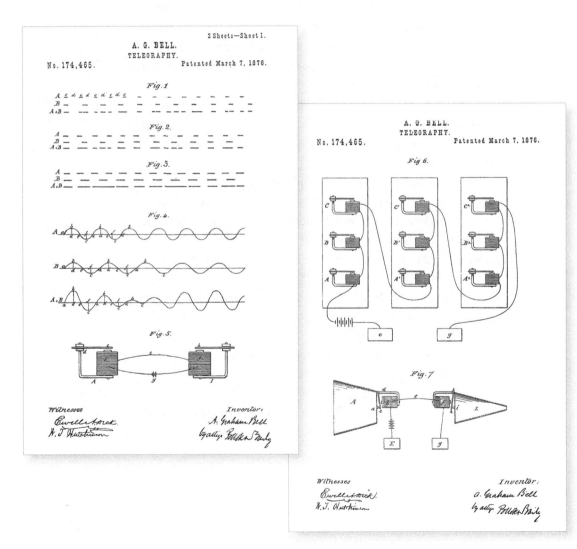

Provisional Patent Application

Improvement in Telegraphy

In my patent No. 161,739, April 6, 1875, I described transmitting two or more telegraphic signals simultaneously along a single wire by using transmitters, each of which puts out a succession of electrical pulses differing in rate from the others. Each is tuned to a pitch at which it will vibrate to produce its fundamental note by one only of the transmitting instruments. Vibratory circuit breakers convert a vibratory movement of the receiving instrument into a permanent make or break, in which is placed a Morse sounder, register, or other telegraphic apparatus. I also described a form of autograph-telegraph based upon the action of these instruments.

The patent shows an electromagnet having a steel-spring armature, which is kept in vibration by the action of a battery. This armature makes and breaks the main circuit, producing an intermittent current in the line. I have found, however, that the number of signals that can be sent simultaneously over a wire is relatively small. When a number of transmitting instruments having different rates of vibration are simultaneously making and breaking the same circuit, the effect upon the main line is practically equivalent to one continuous current.

In a pending application filed February 25, 1875, I described two ways of producing the intermittent current. One is done by actual make and break of contact, the other by alternately increasing and diminishing the intensity of the current without actually breaking the circuit, the latter being a pulsating current.

My present invention employs a vibratory or undulating current instead of an intermittent or pulsating current.

The distinction between an undulating and a pulsating current will be understood by considering that electrical pulsations are caused by sudden or instantaneous changes of intensity, and electrical undulations result from gradual changes of intensity, analogous to the changes in the density of air occasioned by simple pendulous vibrations. The electrical movement, like the aerial motion, can be represented by a sinusoidal curve or by the combination of several sinusoidal curves.

Intermittent or pulsating and undulating currents may be of two kinds, depending on whether the successive pulses all have the same polarity or are alternately positive and negative.

The advantages of the use of an undulating current in place of merely intermittent one are as follows: First, a much larger number of signals can be transmitted simultaneously on the same circuit. Second, a closed circuit and single main battery may be used. Third, communication in both directions is established without the necessity of special induction coils. Fourth, cable dispatches may be transmitted more rapidly than by means of intermittent current or by the methods at present in use. It is unnecessary to discharge the cable before a new signal can be made, so that the lagging of cable signals is prevented. Fifth, as the circuit is never broken a spark-arrester becomes unnecessary.

It has long been known that when a permanent magnet approaches the pole of an electromagnet a current is induced in the coils of the electromagnet. When the permanent magnet is made to recede, a current of opposite polarity appears in the coils. When a permanent magnet vibrates in front of the pole of an electromagnet, an undulating current is induced in the coils of the electromagnet. The undulations correspond in rapidity of succession to the vibrations of the magnet, in polarity to the direction of its motion, and in intensity to the amplitude of its vibration.

The difference between an undulating and an intermittent current may be more clearly understood by considering the condition of the current when an attempt is made to transmit two musical notes simultaneously. If the interval between the two sounds is a major third, their rates of vibration have a ratio of 4 to 5. When an intermittent current is used the circuit is made and broken four times by one transmitting-instrument in the same time that five makes and breaks are caused by the other. A and B, Figs. 1, 2, and 3, represent the intermittent currents produced, with four B pulses being made in the same time as five A pulses. C, c, c, etc., show where and for how long time the circuit is made, and d, d, d, etc. indicate the duration of the breaks of the circuit. Line A and B shows the total effect upon the current when the A and B transmitting instruments are activated simultaneously to make and break the same circuit. The resultant effect depends upon the duration of the make relative to the break. In Fig. 1 the ratio is as 1 to 4; in Fig. 2 it is 1 to 2; and in Fig. 3 the makes and breaks are of equal duration. The combined effect, A and B in Fig. 3, is very nearly equivalent to a continuous current.

When many transmitting instruments of different rates of vibration are simultaneously making and breaking the same circuit, the current in the main line becomes, for all practical purposes, continuous.

Next, consider the effect when an undulating current is employed. Electrical undulations, induced by the vibration of a body capable of inductive action can be represented graphically, without error by the same sinusoidal curve which expresses the vibration of the inducing body itself and by the effect of its vibration upon the air. As stated, the rate of oscillation of the electrical body is the same as the pitch of the sound produced. The intensity of the current varies with the amplitude of the vibration—that is, with the loudness of the sound. The polarity of the current corresponds to the direction of the vibrating body—that is, to the condensations and rarefactions of air produced by the vibration. Hence, the sinusoidal curve A or B, Fig. 4, represents graphically, the electrical undulations induced in a circuit by the vibration of a body capable of inductive action.

The horizontal line *a d e f*, etc., represents zero current. The elevation *b, b, b,* etc. indicates positive pulses. The depressions *c, c, c,* etc. show negative pulses. The vertical distance *b, d,* or *c, f* of any portion of the curve from the zero line expresses the intensity of the positive or negative impulse at the part observed. The horizontal distance *a-a* indicates the duration of the electrical oscillation. The vibrations represented by the sinusoidal curves B and A, Fig. 4, are in the ratio stated, of 4 to 5—that is, four oscillations of B are made in the same time as five oscillations of A.

The combined effect of A and B, when induced simultaneously on the same circuit, is expressed by the curve A + B, Fig. 4. This curve shows the algebraic sum of sinusoidal curves A and B. This A + B also indicates the actual motion of the air when the two musical notes considered are sounded simultaneously. Thus, when electrical undulations of different rates are simultaneously induced in the same circuit, an effect is produced exactly analogous to that occasioned in the air by the vibration of the inducing bodies. Hence, the co-existence upon a telegraphic circuit of electrical vibrations to different pitch is manifested, not by the peculiarities in the shapes of the electrical undulations, or, in other words, by the peculiarities in the shapes of the curves which represent those undulations.

There are many ways of producing undulating currents, dependent for effect upon the vibrations or motions of bodies capable of inductive action. A few of the methods that may be employed are as follows: When a wire with a continuous current vibrates in the neighborhood of another wire, an undulating current is induced in the other wire. When a cylinder, upon which are arranged bar-magnets, is made to rotate in front of the pole of an electromagnet, an undulating current is induced in the coils of the electromagnet.

I shall show and describe one form of apparatus. An electromagnet A, Fig. 5, has a coil upon only one of its legs *b*. A steel-spring armature, *c*, is firmly clamped by one extremity to an uncovered leg *d* of the magnet. Its free end is allowed to project above the pole of the uncovered leg. Armature *c* can be set in vibration in a variety of ways, one of which is by wind, and, in vibrating, it produces a musical note of a certain definite pitch.

When the electromagnet A is placed in a circuit, *g b e f g*, armature *c* becomes magnetic, and the polarity of its free end is opposed to that of the magnet underneath. When armature *c* remains at rest, no effect is produced upon the current. When it is set in vibration to produce its musical note a powerful induction action takes place, and electrical undulations traverse circuit *g b e f g*. The vibratory current passing through the coil of the electromagnet *f* causes vibration in its armature *h* when the armature *c h* of the two instruments A I are normally in unison with one another. Armature *h* is unaffected by the passage of the undulating current when the pitches of the two instruments are different.

A number of instruments may be placed upon a telegraphic circuit. When one instrument is set in vibration, all the other instruments respond. Those which have normally a different rate of vibration remain silent. Thus, if A, Fig. 6, is set in vibration, the armatures of A1 and A2 will vibrate also, but all the others will remain still. If B1 is caused to emit its musical note the instruments B B2 respond. They continue sounding so long as the mechanical vibration of B1 is continued, but become silent with the cessation of its motion. The duration of the sounds may be used to indicate the dot or dash of the Morse alphabet. Thus, a telegraphic dispatch may be indicated by alternately interrupting and renewing the sound. When two or more instruments of different pitch are simultaneously caused to vibrate, all the instruments of corresponding pitches upon the circuit are set in vibration. Each responds to that one only of the transmitting instruments with which it is in unison. Thus signals A, Fig. 6, are repeated by A1 and A2, but by no other instrument upon the circuit. The signals B2 by B and B1; and the signals of C1 by C and C2—whether A, B2, and C1 are successively or simultaneously caused to vibrate. Hence by these instruments two or more telegraphic signals or messages may be sent simultaneously over the same circuit without interfering with one another.

There are many other uses to which these instruments may be put, such as the simultaneous transmission of musical notes, differing in loudness as well as in pitch, and the telegraphic transmission of noises or sounds of any kind.

When armature c, Fig. 5, is set in motion armature h responds not only in pitch, but in loudness. Thus, when c vibrates with little amplitude, a very soft musical note proceeds from h; and when c vibrates forcibly the amplitude of the vibration of h is considerably increased, and the resulting sound becomes louder. So, if A and B, Fig. 6, are sounded simultaneously (A loudly and B softly), instruments A1 and A2 repeat loudly the signals of A, and B1 B2 repeat softly those of B.

One of the ways in which armature c, Fig. 5, may be set in motion is by wind. Another mode is shown in Fig. 7: motions can be imparted to the armature by the human voice or by means of a musical instrument.

Armature c, Fig. 7, is fastened loosely by one extremity to the uncovered leg d of electromagnet b, and its other extremity is attached to the center of a stretched membrane, a. A cone, A, is used to converge sound vibrations upon the membrane. When a sound is uttered in the cone membrane a is set in vibration, armature c is forced to partake of the motion, and thus electrical undulations are created in circuit E b e f g. These undulations are similar in sound to the air vibrations caused by the sound—that is, they are represented graphically by similar curves. The undulating current passing through electromagnet f influences its armature h to copy the motions of the armature c. A similar sound to that uttered into A is the heard to proceed from L.

Patent

Improvement in Telegraphy No. 174,465

Specification forming part of Letters Patent No. 174,465, dated March 7, 1876; application filed February 14, 1876.

To all whom it may concern:

Be it known that I, ALEXANDER GRAHAM BELL, of Salem, Massachusetts, have invented certain new and useful Improvements in Telegraphy, of which the following is a specification:

In Letters Patent granted to me April 6, 1875, No. 161,739, I have described a method of, and apparatus for, transmitting two or more telegraphic signals simultaneously along a single wire by the employment of transmitting instruments, each of which occasions a succession of electrical impulses differing in rate from the others; and of receiving instruments, each tuned to a pitch at which it will be put in vibration to produce its fundamental note by one only of the transmitting instruments; and of vibratory circuit-breakers operating to convert the vibratory movement of the receiving instrument into a permanent make or break (as the case may be) of a local circuit, in which is placed a Morse sounder, register, or other telegraphic apparatus. I have also therein described a form of autograph-telegraph based upon the action of the above-mentioned instruments.

In illustration of my method of multiple telegraphy I have shown in the patent aforesaid, as one form of transmitting instrument, an electromagnet having a steel-spring armature, which is kept in vibration by the action of a local battery. This armature in vibrating makes and breaks the main circuit, producing an intermittent current upon the line wire. I have found, however, that upon this plan the limit to the number of signals that can be sent simultaneously over the same wire is very speedily reached; for, when a number of transmitting instruments, having different rates of vibration, (2) are simultaneously making and breaking the same circuit, the effect upon the main line is practically equivalent to one continuous current.

In a pending application for Letters Patent, filed in the United States Patent Office February 25, 1875, I have described two ways of producing the intermittent current—the one by actual make and break of contact, the other by alternately increasing and diminishing the intensity of the current without actually breaking the circuit. The current produced by the latter method I shall term, for distinction sake, a pulsatory current.

My present invention consists in the employment of a vibratory or undulatory current of electricity in contradistinction to a merely intermittent or pulsatory current, and of a method of, and apparatus for, producing electrical undulations upon the line-wire.

The distinction between an undulatory and a pulsatory current will be understood by considering that electrical pulsations are caused by sudden or instantaneous changes of intensity, and that electrical undulations result from gradual changes of intensity exactly analogous to the changes in the density of air occasioned by simple pendulous vibrations. The electrical movement, like the aerial motion, can be represented by a sinusoidal curve or by the resultant of several sinusoidal curves.

Intermittent or pulsatory and undulatory currents may be of two kinds, accordingly as the successive impulses have all the same polarity or are alternately positive and negative.

The advantages I claim to derive from the use of an undulatory current in place of merely intermittent one are, first, that a very much larger number of signals can be transmitted simultaneously on the same circuit; second, that a closed circuit and single main battery may be used; third, that communication in both directions is established without the necessity of special induction-coils; fourth, that cable dispatches may be transmitted more rapidly than by means of intermittent current or by the methods at present in use; for, as it is unnecessary to discharge the cable before a new signal can be made, the lagging of cable signals is prevented; fifth, and that as the circuit is never broken a spark-arrester becomes unnecessary.

(3) It has long been known that when a permanent magnet is caused to approach the pole of an electromagnet a current of electricity is induced in the coils of the latter, and that when it is made to recede a current of opposite polarity to the first appears upon the wire. When, therefore, a permanent magnet is caused to vibrate in front of the pole of an electromagnet an undulatory current of electricity is induced in the coils of the electromagnet, the undulations of which correspond, in rapidity of succession, to the vibrations of the magnet, in polarity to the direction of its motion, and in intensity to the amplitude of its vibration.

That the difference between an undulatory and an intermittent current may be more clearly understood I shall describe the condition of the electrical current when the attempt is made to transmit two musical notes simultaneously—first upon the one plan and then upon the other. Let the interval between the two sounds be a major third; then their rates of vibration are in the ratio of 4 to 5. Now, when the intermittent current is used the circuit is made and broken four times by one transmitting-instrument in the same time that five makes and breaks are caused by the other. A and B, Figs. 1, 2, and 3, represent the intermittent currents produced, four impulses of B being made in the same time as five impulses of A. C c c, &c., show where and for how long time the circuit is made, and d d d, &c., indicate the duration of the breaks of the circuit. The line A and B shows the total effect upon the current when the transmitting-instruments for A and B are caused simultaneously to make and break the same circuit. The resultant effect depends very much upon the duration of the make relatively to the break. In Fig. 1 the ratio is as 1 to 4; in Fig. 2, as 1 to 2; and in Fig. 3 the makes and breaks are of equal duration. The combined effect A and B, Fig. 3, is very nearly equivalent to a continuous current.

When many transmitting instruments of different rates of vibration are simultaneously making and breaking the same circuit the current upon the main line becomes for all practical purposes continuous.

Next, consider the effect when an undulatory current is employed. Electrical undulations, induced by the vibration of a body capable of inductive action, can be represented graphically, without error, (4) by the same sinusoidal curve which expresses the vibration of the inducing body itself, and the effect of its vibration upon the air; for, as above stated, the rate of oscillation in the electrical body— that is, to the pitch of the sound produced. The intensity of the current varies with the amplitude of the vibration—that is, with the loudness of the sound; and the polarity of the current corresponds to the direction of the vibrating body— that is, to the condensations and rarefactions of air produced by the vibration. Hence, the sinusoidal curve A or B, Fig. 4, represents, graphically, the electrical undulations induced in a circuit by the vibration of a body capable of inductive action.

The horizontal line *a d e f*, &c., represents the zero of current. The elevation *b b b*, &c., indicates impulses of positive electricity. The depressions *c c c*, &c., show impulses of negative electricity. The vertical distance *b d* or *c f* of any portion of the curve from the zero line expresses the intensity of the positive or negative impulse at the part observed, and the horizontal distance *a a* indicates the duration of the electrical oscillation. The vibrations represented by the sinusoidal curves B and A, Fig. 4, are in the ratio aforesaid, of 4 to 5—that is, four oscillations of B are made in the same time as five oscillations of A.

The combined effect of A and B, when induced simultaneously on the same circuit, is expressed by the curve A+B, Fig. 4, which is the algebraic sum of the sinusiodal curves A and B. This curve A+B also indicates the actual motion of the air when the two musical notes considered are sounded simultaneously. Thus, when electrical undulations of different rates are simultaneously induced in the same circuit, an effect is produced exactly analogous to that occasioned in the air by the vibration of the inducing bodies. Hence, the co-existence upon a telegraphic circuit of electrical vibrations to different pitch is manifested, not by the peculiarities in the shapes of the electrical undulations, or, in other words, by the peculiarities in the shapes of the curves which represent those undulations.

There are many ways of producing undulatory currents of electricity, dependent for effect upon the vibrations or motions of bodies (5) capable of inductive action. A few of the methods that may be employed I shall here specify. When a wire, through which a continuous current of electricity is passing, is caused to vibrate in the neighborhood of another wire, an undulatory current of electricity is induced in the latter. When a cylinder, upon which are arranged bar-magnets, is made to rotate in front of the pole of an electromagnet, an undulatory current is induced in the coils of the electromagnet.

Undulations are caused in a continuous voltaic current by the vibration of motion of bodies capable of inductive action; or by the vibration of the conducing-wire itself in the neighborhood of such bodies. Electrical undulations may also be caused by alternately increasing and diminishing the resistance of the circuit, or by alternately increasing and diminishing the power of the battery. The internal resistance of a battery is diminished by bringing the voltaic elements nearer together, and increased by placing them further apart. The reciprocal vibration of the elements of a battery, therefore, occasions an undulatory action in the voltaic current. The external resistance may also be varied. For instance, let mercury or some other liquid form part of a voltaic current, the more deeply the conducting-wire is immersed in the mercury or other liquid, the less resistance does the liquid offer to the passage of the current. The vertical vibration of the elements of a battery in the liquid in which they are immersed produces an undulatory action in the current by alternately increasing and diminishing the power of the battery.

In illustration of the method of creating electrical undulations, I shall show and describe one form of apparatus for producing the effect. I prefer to employ for this purpose an electromagnet A, Fig. 5, having a coil upon only one of its legs *b*. A steel-spring armature, *c*, is firmly clamped by one extremity to the uncovered leg *d* of the magnet, and its free end is allowed to project above the pole of the uncovered leg. The armature *c* can be set in vibration in a variety of ways, one of which is by wind, and, in vibrating, it produces a musical note of a certain definite pitch.

(6) When the instrument A is placed in a voltaic circuit, *g b e f g*, the armature *c* becomes magnetic, and the polarity of its free end is opposed to that of the magnet underneath. So long as the armature *c* remains at rest, no effect is produced upon the voltaic current, but the moment it is set in vibration to produce its musical note a powerful induction action takes place, and electrical undulations tranverse the circuit *g b e f g*. The vibratory current passing through the coil of the electromagnet *f* causes vibration in its armature *h* when the armature *c h* of the two instruments A I are normally in unison with one another; but the armature *h* is unaffected by the passage of the undulatory current when the pitches of the two instruments are different.

A number of instruments may be placed upon a telegraphic circuit. When one instrument is set in vibration all the other instruments upon the circuit which are in unison with it respond, but those which have normally a different rate of vibration remain silent. Thus, if A, Fig. 6, is set in vibration, the armatures of A1 and A2 will vibrate also, but all the others will remain still. So, if B1 is caused to emit its musical note the instruments B B2 respond. They continue sounding so long as the mechanical vibration of B1 is continued, but become silent with the cessation of its motion. The duration of the sounds may be used to indicate the dot or dash of the Morse alphabet, and thus a telegraphic dispatch may be indicated by alternately interrupting and renewing the sound. When two or more instruments of different pitch are simultaneously caused to vibrate, all the instruments of corresponding pitches upon the circuit are set in vibration, each responding to that one only of the transmitting instruments with which it is in unison. Thus the signals of A, Fig. 6, are repeated by A1 and A2, but by no other instrument upon the circuit; the signals of B2 by B and B1; and the signals of C1 by C and C2—whether A, B2, and C1 are successively or simultaneously caused to vibrate. Hence by these instruments two or more telegraphic signals or messages may be sent simultaneously over the same circuit without interfering with one another.

I desire here to remark that there are many other uses to which these instruments may be put, such as the simultaneous transmission (7) of musical notes, differing in loudness as well as in pitch, and the telegraphic transmission of noises or sounds of any kind.

When the armature c, Fig. 5, is set in motion the armature h responds not only in pitch, but in loudness. Thus, when c vibrates with little amplitude, a very soft musical note proceeds from h; and when c vibrates forcibly the amplitude of the vibration of h is considerably increased, and the resulting sound becomes louder. So, if A and B, Fig. 6, are sounded simultaneously (A loudly and B softly), the instruments A1 and A2 repeat loudly the signals of A, and B1 B2 repeat softly those of B.

One of the ways in which the armature c, Fig. 5, may be set in motion has been stated above to be wind. Another mode is shown in Fig. 7, whereby motions can be imparted to the armature by the human voice or by means of a musical instrument.

The armature c, Fig. 7, is fastened loosely by one extremity to the uncovered leg d of the electromagnet b, and its other extremity is attached to the center of a stretched membrane, a. A cone, A, is used to converge sound-vibrations upon the membrane. When a sound is uttered in the cone the membrane a is set in vibration, the armature c is forced to partake of the motion, and thus electrical undulations are created upon the circuit E b e f g. These undulations are similar in sound to the air vibrations caused by the sound—that is, they are represented graphically by similar curves. The undulatory current passing through the electromagnet f influences its armature h to copy the motions of the armature c. A similar sound to that uttered into A is the heard to proceed from L.

In this specification the three words "oscillation," "vibration" and "undulation," are used synonymously, and in contradistinction to the terms "intermittent" and "pulsatory." By the term "body capable of inductive action," I mean a body which, when in motion, produces dynamical electricity. I include in the category of bodies capable of inductive action—brass, copper and other metals, as well as iron and steel.

Having described my invention, what I claim, and desire to secure by Letters Patent, is as follows:

1. A system of telegraphy in which the receiver is set in vibration by the employment of undulatory currents of electricity, substantially as set forth.

2. The combination, substantially as set forth, of a permanent magnet or other body capable of inductive action, with a closed circuit, so that the vibration of the one shall occasion electrical undulations in the other, or in itself, and this I claim, whether the permanent magnet be set in vibration in the neighborhood of the conducting-wire forming the circuit, or whether the conducting-wire be set in vibration in the neighborhood of the permanent magnet, or whether the conducting wire and the permanent magnet both simultaneously be set in vibration in each other's neighborhood.

3. The method of producing undulations in a continuous voltaic current by the vibration of motion of bodies capable of inductive action, or by the vibration or motion of the conducting-wire itself, in the neighborhood of such bodies, as set forth.

4. The method of producing undulations in a continuous voltaic circuit by gradually increasing and diminishing the resistance of the circuit, or by gradually increasing and diminishing the power of the battery, as set forth.

5. The method of, and apparatus for, transmitting vocal or other sounds telegraphically, as herein described, by causing electrical undulations, similar in form to the vibrations of the air accompanying the said vocal or other sounds, substantially as set forth.

In testimony whereof I have hereunto signed my name this 20th day of January, A.D. 1876.

ALEX. GRAHAM BELL.
Witnesses :
Thomas E. Barry.
P. D. Richards.

Car Radio

As we explained in Chapter 1, William Lear, with his friend Elmer Wavering, coinvented the first car radio in 1930 and sold the radio device under the trademark Motorola. Lear went on to invent the eight-track tape format and navigation aids for aircraft. He later founded Lear, Inc., the supplier of the Lear jet.

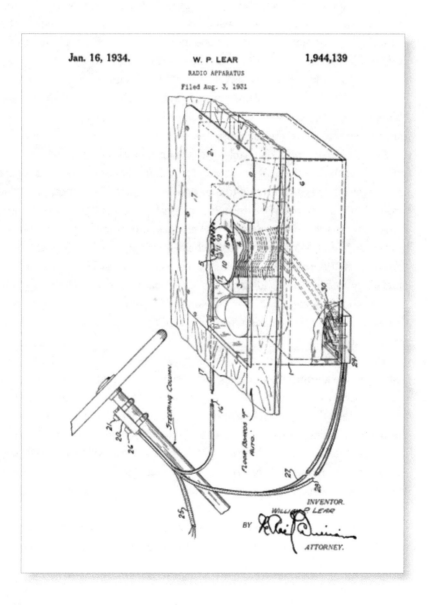

Provisional Patent Application

Radio Apparatus

I have invented a new radio receiver which is portable and can be used in automobiles and other similar vehicles. It can be operated by a remote control, which can be located within easy reach of the operator.

In automobiles, considerable vibration and jerking occurs. In the usual radio there are variable condensers or capacitors. These are usually mounted so that their axis is horizontal during normal operation. Such condensers are particularly sensitive to vibration and jerking, resulting in a change of adjustment.

I have determined that this can be eliminated by disposing the gang condenser so that its shaft is in a vertical position. This will enable practically all the jars and bumps to be taken up by the bearings of the condenser and eliminate or reduce any tendency to throw the condenser out of adjustment.

Also, the vertical position enables the remote control apparatus to be streamlined. Practically all of the remote controls used on such sets use a flexible cable, which must be connected to the condenser's shaft. The vertical mounting makes it possible to minimize the number of sharp bends and turns in this cable.

Also, when the radio is mounted in the vehicle, it must be protected from water, sand and other elements, to which anything suspended underneath an automobile is exposed. To provide such protection, I provide a container, preferably metallic, for shielding purposes. I permanently fasten the container to the automobile, preferably hanging it from the bottom of the floorboards. I mount the radio as a unit on a chassis in this container. This makes it easy to replace the vacuum tubes and service the radio.

The set is energized from any suitable source of potential, usually the storage battery of the automobile and a separate battery for the plate supply of the radio's vacuum tubes. Various connections between these sources of potential and the set must be made through the radio's protecting casing. If an ordinary cable is passed through the casing, repeated removals of the set from its container will result in sufficient clearance between the cables and the container wall to admit water, sand or other undesirable elements. In order to avoid this, I preferably provide a detachable connection, one part permanently fastened to the casing and the other part permanently fastened to the chassis. This detachable connection may consist of any suitable plug and socket arrangement, having as many terminals as may be found desirable. With such a detachable connection, the complete chassis may be removed and replaced as often as desired, without endangering the protection afforded by the casing.

The drawing shows a radio set embodying the above concepts and mounted in an automobile.

Suspended underneath the automobile's floorboards, through a suitable aperture, is a metal casing 1. It contains the radio receiving set 2. This set includes the usual elements, such as rf transformers, vacuum tubes, tube sockets, and the like. It also includes a tuning element, a gang condenser 3. The gang condenser has a rotor 4, rigidly mounted on a shaft 5. The entire radio is mounted on a chassis 6 and can be removed as a unit from casing 1 upon the removal of cover 7.

The condenser is mounted so that its rotor shaft 5 is vertical when the set is installed in the automobile.

To operate condenser 3, a pulley 10 is rigidly fastened to the upper portion of its rotor shaft 5. Pulley 10 has a pin 11, to which is anchored one end of a coil spring 12. The other end of the coil spring is anchored to a fixed portion of the set, so that there will be a tendency for the condenser to assume a position of either minimum or maximum capacity. I have shown it in the maximum position.

Pulley 10 is also provided with an anchor block on its edge. One end of a cable 16 is anchored to the anchor block. This cable is positioned in a groove 17 in the periphery of pulley 10 and extends out through the side of casing 1. Cable 16 is in a sheath 17, and the entire assembly leads to a control unit 20, here mounted on the steering column of the car. The control unit has a control knob 21 for moving cable 16 lengthwise. By actuating knob 21, the driver may adjust rotor 4 in any desired position with respect to the fixed plates of condenser 3.

To energize the set, suitable connections are made to current supplies—the automobile storage battery and a separate battery for the plates or anodes of the vacuum tubes.

A cable 25 leads to a combined volume control and switch 26 of control unit 20. From the control unit a pair of cables 27 and 28 lead to a socket 29, rigidly fastened in the bottom of casing 1. Socket 29 is tightly sealed in casing 1 so that no water or dirt can enter the casing. A cooperating plug 30 is mounted on chassis 6 so as to mate with socket member 29 when the chassis is in the normal position in the casing.

Various wires from plug 30 go to the several pieces of apparatus in the radio. When the radio chassis is removed from casing 1, plug 30 is automatically withdrawn from socket 29. Chassis 6 is rigidly mounted in casing 1 by suitable hardware (not shown).

Patent

Radio Apparatus No. 1,944,139

William P. Lear, Chicago, Ill., assignor to Grigsby-Grunow Company, Chicago, Ill., a corporation of Illinois. Application August 3, 1931. Serial No. 554,751.3 Claims (Cl. 250-14). This invention relates to radio receivers, particularly of the portable type used in automobiles and other similar vehicles. In installations of this character, it is desirable that the receiver itself be disposed in any place available therefor, and a remote control located within easy reach of the operator be provided.

In installations of this character, particularly in automobiles, considerable vibration and jerking occurs. The usual radio set, with the variable condensers mounted so that the axis is horizontal during normal operation of the set, is particularly sensitive to such jarring and frequently results in a change of condenser adjustment.

I have determined that this trouble is eliminated by disposing the gang condenser of the usual radio set in a vertical position. Practically all the jars and bumps, therefore, are taken up by the bearings of the condenser and have no tendency to throw the condenser out of adjustment.

Furthermore, the vertical position of the condenser in general makes for a more efficient disposition of the remote control apparatus with relation to the condenser itself. Practically all of the remote control apparatus used on such sets involves the use of a species of flexible cable, which must be brought to the condenser 3. By providing this particular type of mounting of the condenser, it is possible to so dispose the control unit with reference to the condenser as to have a minimum amount of sharp bends and turns in the control cable.

This invention is also concerned with the mounting of the radio in said vehicle. In mounting a set of this character, it is necessary to protect the set from water, sand and other elements encountered by anything suspended underneath an automobile where such set is usually disposed.

A container, preferably metallic, for shielding purposes, is permanently fastened to the automobile, preferably suspended from the bottom of the floorboards of an automobile. Into this container there is disposed a complete radio set mounted as a unit on a chassis. Such a mounting is desirable for the reason that tube replacements and service are facilitated.

The set is energized from any suitable source of potential, usually the storage battery of the automobile and a separate battery for the plate supply of the tube. Various connections between these sources of potential and the set must be made through said outer protecting casing. It is clear that if an ordinary cable is passed through the casing, repeated removals of the set from its container will result in sufficient clearance between the cables and the container wall to admit water, sand or other undesirable elements. In order to avoid this, I preferably provide a detachable connection, one part permanently fastened to the casing and the other part permanently fastened to the chassis. This detachable connection may consist of any suitable plug and socket arrangement, having as many terminals as may be found desirable. With such a detachable connection, a complete chassis may be removed and replaced as often as desired, without in any way endangering the scope of protection afforded by the casing.

Referring to the drawing, the figure shows a radio set embodying the inventions herein disclosed mounted in an automobile.

Suspended underneath the floorboards of an automobile, through a suitable aperture, is a casing 1, preferably of metal, in which normally rests a radio receiving set, generally designated by numeral 2. This set includes the usual elements such as transformers, vacuum tube, tube sockets and the like, and in particular includes a tuning element, here shown as a gang condenser 3. In accordance with the usual practice, the gang condenser is provided with a rotor 4, rigidly mounted upon a shaft 5. The entire radio apparatus is mounted on a chassis 6, and is adapted to be removed as a unit from casing upon the removal of cover 7.

The tuning condenser is mounted so that the rotor shaft 5 is vertically disposed during the normal disposition of the set in the automobile.

In order to actuate condenser 3, a pulley 10 is rigidly fastened to the upper portion of rotor shaft 5. Pulley 10 is provided with a pin 11, to which is anchored one end of a coil spring 12.

The other end of the coil spring may be suitably anchored to a fixed portion of the set, so that there will be a tendency for the condenser to assume a position of either minimum or maximum capacity, in this instance the latter. Pulley 10 is also provided with an anchor block disposed on the periphery thereof, into which is anchored one end of a cable 16. This cable is disposed in a groove 17 in the periphery of 105 pulley 10 and extends out through the side of casing 1. Cable 16 is preferably disposed in a sheath 17, and the entire assembly brought to a control unit 20, here shown as mounted on the steering column of an automobile. The control unit is provided with a suitable means 21 for imparting longitudinal motion to cable 16. It is clear that by actuating the means 21, here shown as a control knob, rotor 4 may be suitably adjusted in any desired position with respect to the fixed plates of condenser 3.

In order to energize the set, it is desirable to have suitable connections to current supplies, which may, in practice, be the automobile storage battery and a separate battery for energizing the plate circuits of the vacuum tubes.

Connection is made by means of a cable 25 leading to a combined volume control and switch 26 of control unit 20. From the control unit a pair of cables 27 and 28 lead to a socket member 29, rigidly fastened in the bottom of casing 1. Socket member 29 is tightly sealed in casing 1 so that no water or dirt can enter inside of the casing. Disposed on chassis 6 is a co-operating plug member 30, which is adapted to make a connection with socket member 29 when the chassis is in the normal position in casing.

Various wires from the plug 30 go to the several pieces of apparatus comprising the radio set. When the radio chassis is removed from casing 1, the plug 30 is automatically withdrawn from socket portion 29. Suitable means may be provided for rigidly maintaining chassis 6 within casing 1. The matter herein disclosed with reference to the vertical mounting of the condenser, is disclosed and claimed in a separate copending application of mine, filed of even date herewith.

I claim:

1. In combination with the floorboard of a vehicle, the bottom of said floorboard being exposed to the weather, a radio chassis comprising a metallic container, said container having a flange around the opening thereof over which a cover is adapted to fit, said container being disposed in an opening of said floorboard with the flange on the protected side of said floorboard projecting beyond the edges of said board opening, radio instrumentalities removably disposed as a unit in said container, a control cable leading from said container, said cable being permanently sealed to said container and terminating on the inside thereof in a plug, and a

cooperating plug on said radio unit adapted to connect with said plug on the container when said radio unit is in said container and disconnect therefrom when said unit is removed.

2. The structure of claim 1 in which said radio unit includes a gang condenser mounted with the axis perpendicular to the plane of the floorboard.

3. The structure of claim 1 in which said radio unit includes a gang condenser mounted with its axis perpendicular to the plane of the floorboard, the top end of said condenser being adjacent to the opening of said container, a remote control of the flexible cable type, and means for connecting said cable through the container wall with the top end of said condenser.

   WILLIAM P. LEAR.

Fly Mask

There are plenty of fly-swatting inventions for humans but what's a poor cow to do when inundated by flying pests? Our bovine friends must have appreciated Henry George O'Hare, Jr., of Amboy, Illinois, who came up with this patented solution.

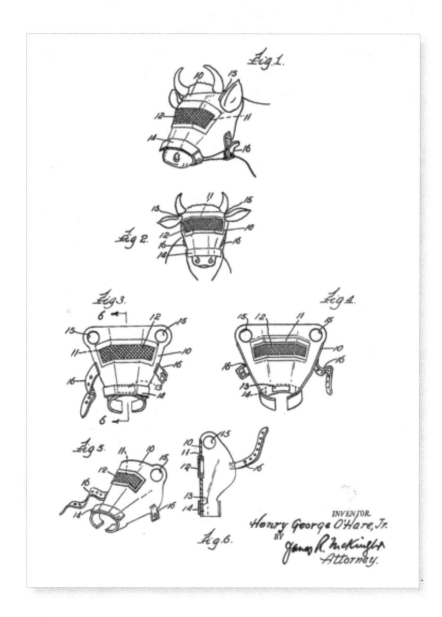

Provisional Patent Application

Fly Mask for Dairy Cows and Other Animals

I have developed a mask which can be removably attached to a dairy cow to protect it from flies and other insects.

Insects often so irritate cows as to sicken them and reduce their milk supply and cause them to lose weight and suffer ill health or die. This mask prevents these annoyances to cows and maintains their health and milk supply. The mask is much less expense than the loss of the milk or the cow.

FIG. 1 is a side view of my mask on a cow.

FIG. 2 is a front view of the same on reduced scale.

FIG. 3 is a front view on an enlarged scale.

FIG. 4 is a rear view on an enlarged scale.

FIG. 5 is a perspective view.

FIG. 6 is a sectional view on line 6-6 of FIG. 3.

Mask 10 of hard plastic material is shaped to fit over the head and face of a dairy cow or other animal. The mask has a slot 11 cut away across the front adjacent to the eyes and is covered by a fine screen 12. The screen permits the cow to see, but still protects it from insects. Another slot 13 is cut away at the lower portion of the mask and is fitted with an overlapping metal nose plate 14. On either side of the upper portion, mask 10 has openings 15 for the ears. A pair of straps 16 of heavy canvas are attached to mask 10 on opposite sides. The straps have openings and a buckle for holding the mask.

When the mask is in position, it should fit snugly and yet comfortably enough to stay in place and to prevent insects from coming in under the mask. It has sufficient room to be comfortable. It is economical, easy to put on and take off, is pleasant to wear, protects the cow from annoyance, loss of weight and infection and insures placidity in a cow and continued production of milk.

Patent

Face Fly Mask for Dairy Cows and Other Animals
No. 3,104,508

My invention relates to a mask adapted to be removably attached to a dairy cow or other animal to protect it from flies and other insects.

Flies and other insects often so irritate cows as to sicken them and reduce their milk supply and cause them to lose weight and suffer ill health or die. This mask is designed to prevent these annoyances to cows and maintain their health and milk supply. The mask is much less expense than the loss of the milk or the cow.

Among the objects of my invention is to provide a mask which will protect a dairy cow, or other animal, from being bitten by flies or other insects. Another object is to provide a mask which will particularly protect a dairy cow or other animal from attack by flies at or adjacent to the eyes, which parts are very tender and are most often attacked by flies and the like.

Another object is to provide a mask, simple and economical to construct, easy to put on and take off and acceptable and pleasant for the cow or other animal to wear.

Still another object is to protect the farmer from loss of milk due to an injured cow.

My invention also comprises such other objects, advantages and capabilities as will later more fully appear, and which are inherently possessed by my invention.

While I have shown in the accompanying drawings a preferred embodiment of my invention, yet it is to be understood that the same is susceptible of modification and change without departing from the spirit of my invention.

Referring to the drawings, FIG. 1 is a side elevational view of my mask in position on a cow.

FIG. 2 is a front elevational view of the same on reduced scale.

FIG. 3 is a front elevational view drawn on an enlarged scale.

FIG. 4 is a rear view drawn on an enlarged scale.

FIG. 5 is a perspective view.

FIG. 6 is a detailed sectional view on line 6-6 of FIG. 3.

The preferred embodiment selected to illustrate my invention comprises a mask 10 of hard plastic material shaped to fit over the head and face of a dairy cow or other animal. Said mask has a slot 11 cut away across the front adjacent the eyes and is covered by a fine screen 12 suitably attached to the mask. This screen being openwork permits the cow to see therethrough, but still protects the animal from flies or other insects. Another slot 13 cut away at the lower portion of the mask is fitted with an overlapping metal nose plate 14. On either side of the upper portion, mask 10 has openings 15 for the passage therethrough of the ears of the animal. A pair of straps 16 preferably of heavy canvas are attached to mask 10 on opposite sides, having openings and a buckle for interengagement and for removably holding the mask in place on the cow.

My mask is formed so that when it is in position on the cow, it may fit snugly and yet comfortably—snugly enough to stay in place and to prevent flies from coming in under the mask, and yet with sufficient room to be comfortable on the animal.

In use, my mask is economical, easy to put on and take off, is pleasant for the animal to wear, protects it from annoyance, loss of weight and infection and insures placidity in a cow and continued production of milk.

This is of great value and gain to the farmer who depends upon the cow for its uninterrupted production of milk.

Having thus described my invention, I claim:

A mask shaped to fit over, cover and protect the head and face of a dairy cow or other animal comprising a body member of hard plastic, said body member having a slot cut away across the front adjacent the eyes of the animal, a fine openwork screen fitted to said body member at and covering the slot, said body member having at its lower portion adjacent the nose of the animal another and smaller slot, a metal nose plate attached to said body member within the smaller slot and overlapping the smaller slot, said body member having in its upper portion a pair of spaced openings to permit passage therethrough of the ears of the animal, and strap means attached to opposite sides of said body member and adapted to interengage removably to hold the mask on the animal.

Convertible Tent

Inventor Robert H. Howe of Oregon came up with a novel idea for a convertible tent—one that can adjust for various climates while the user is inside the tent.

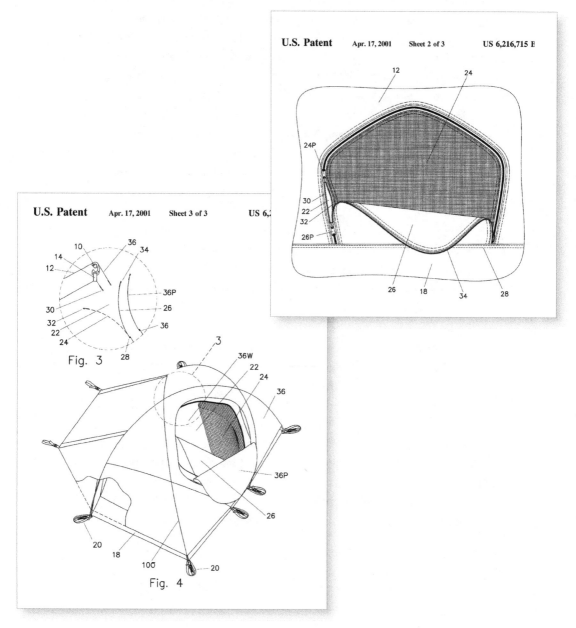

U.S. Patent   Apr. 17, 2001   Sheet 2 of 3   US 6,216,715 B

U.S. Patent   Apr. 17, 2001   Sheet 3 of 3   US 6,2

Fig. 3

Fig. 4

Provisional Patent Application

Convertible Tent for Rain, Cold and Hot Conditions

I invented a convertible tent. Someone using my tent can adjust for warm, cool, cold and precipitation conditions while inside the tent. My convertible tent includes an inner canopy and an outer canopy (referred to as a flysheet). The inner and outer canopies each have windows that align with each other. I've included zipper teeth and a chain around each window that so that the user can zip a solid or net panel over the window. The user can adjust the tent by using just the net panel in the inner canopy, just the solid panel of the inner canopy, or the solid panel of the inner canopy and the solid panel of the flysheet.

Others have invented converting tents but my invention is superior because it:

- is more versatile
- is less awkward to use and handle
- is simple, easy to make and erect
- easily adjusts for a wide range of climatic conditions
- can be adjusted for different conditions, especially for rain, from the inside
- has no outer net to catch spindrift in the winter, and
- has a flysheet that can be installed from inside the tent.

I've included four drawings:

FIG. 1 is a perspective view from above my tent without its flysheet. It shows a perspective view of the inner part of this tent. Conventional tent poles 10 form an arched cage. The ends of these poles are anchored to the ground. An inner canopy 12 is suspended from the poles by conventional hooks and web loops 14, shown in more detail in FIG. 4. The web loops are attached to seams or reinforcing cords 16 in canopy 12. The main portion of the floor of the tent is not shown, but it has conventional upturned sidewalls 18 that cover the bottom portion of the canopy. The canopy has a conventional door 12D on its left side. The bottom edges of the tent have conventional web loops and attachments 20 at the bottoms of the poles.

Canopy 12 has a convertible opening or window 22 on its right or front side (as seen in the drawing) that can be closed by either of two panels: a net panel 24 or a solid panel 26. Net panel is made of conventional mosquito netting and solid panel 26 is made of the same material as canopy 12 and is attached at its bottom to the outside of the net panel. As shown in FIG. 2, either of these panels can be alternatively zipped into window 22 so as to close the window with either a solid or a net closure.

Canopy 12 preferably is made of breathable rip-stop nylon; the tent floor is made of nylon with a waterproof coating, and the poles are made of aluminum, either solid or in sections. The tent is about 1.5 m high, and window 22 is about 75 cm high and about 1 m wide.

FIG. 2 is a view of part of a portion of an inner canopy of the tent. It shows window 22 in detail. It has a Tudor arch, but can have other shapes, such as square, rectangular, triangular, circular, oval, hemispherical, etc. Either net panel 24 or solid panel 26 can be used to close or fill the window and each has the same shape as the window. Both are attached across their bottom edges to inner canopy 12, preferably at the seam of one of the upturned sidewalls 18. Starting from the outside, stitches 28 attach the following parts together at the bottom of window 22: the top edge of part of sidewall 18, then solid panel 26, then net panel 24, and then an edge of canopy 12.

The edge of canopy 12 (other than the bottom part that is sewn by stitches 28) has a zipper chain 30, which constitutes one side of a zipper. This chain can mate with a chain 32 on net panel 24 or a chain 34 on solid panel 26. One zipper pull 24P is used to zip chain 32 of net 24 to chain 30 of canopy 12. Another pull 26P is used to zip teeth 34 of solid panel 26 to chain 30. Thus window 22 can be closed with either of panels 24 or 26 through the use of what is in effect 1½ zippers. Zipper pulls 24P and 26P are dual pulls which can be operated from inside or outside the tent. Net zipper pull 24P is started from the right side of the window and solid panel pull 26P is started from the left side.

FIG. 3 shows another, schematic view of the window panels. Ignoring optional flysheet 36 temporarily, note that canopy 12 is suspended by hook and web loop 14, which in turn hangs from pole 10. The edge of window 22 in canopy 12 has zipper chain 30 around its sides (except the bottom where stitches 28 are used). The user can fasten net panel 24 to chain 30 by means of its chain 32; this will close the window with netting. Alternatively the user can fasten solid panel 26 to chain 30 by means of its chain 34; this will close the window with a solid panel.

Users can erect the tent with canopy 12 and its dual-closable window, without the flysheet, yet it has significant advantages. When both panels 24 and

26 (net and solid) are not in the window, pull 24P of net panel 24 is to the far right (FIG. 2) and a pull 26P of solid panel 26 is to the far left (not shown).

In warm weather, the user zips net panel 24 into window 22 by holding the net panel in the window and drawing pull 24P from right to left to attach chain 32 to chain 30, thereby to install the net panel in the window. The tent then will have good ventilation and a view of the sky through the net, yet the net prevents insects from entering. When net 24 is zipped into place, solid panel 26 is left to hang down on the outside of the window. Due to the use of two-sided pulls, the user can zip net 24 into place or unzip it from the inside or outside.

In cooler weather, the user zips solid panel 26 into window 22 by unzipping the net panel (if it is in the window). Then the user holds the solid panel in the window and pulls pull 26P from left to right to attach chain 34 to chain 30. This will install the solid panel in the window. The solid shield will keep the tent warmer. When solid panel 26 is zipped into place, net panel 24 is left to hang down, inside the window. As with the net panel, the user can zip panel 26 into place or unzip it from the inside or outside.

Since the net panel is never on the outside of the canopy in cooler or cold weather, snow or spindrift will not accumulate in the net. Since both panels can be removed from inside the tent, the occupants can reach outside to adjust portions of the tent and open the window of the flysheet.

FIG. 4 is a perspective view from above of the tent and flysheet.

As shown in FIG. 4, flysheet 36 covers the tent of FIG. 1 (the pole cage and underlying canopy 12). The flysheet lies on top of hooks and web loops 14, and poles 10, and is attached to web loops 14 and poles 10 by conventional quick-release buckles (not shown) so that outlines 100 of the poles show through. Flysheet 36 has a window 36W and a flysheet panel 36P that the user can zip into the window. The zipper (not shown) extends around the window on all sides, except the bottom, and also has a dual pull (not shown) so that the user can zip the flysheet panel from the inside.

The user does not have to deploy the flysheet in warm weather. In cold (but not very cold) weather, and when there is no precipitation, the flysheet can be used, but with its window open. If it turns very cold, or rains or snows, the user can close the flysheet window by opening window 22 of canopy 12, pulling up flysheet panel 36P through window 22, and zipping panel 36P in place. Then they can zip solid panel 26 in place to close window 22. Even if spindrift leaks through the zipper or blows under the flysheet, it will not be able to accumulate on any net since net 24 is inside the tent. The occupants can also open a closed flysheet from inside when the precipitation stops or if it gets warmer.

These are not the only embodiments of my invention. Alternatively:

- The flysheet window can be clear.
- Different materials, sizes and interconnections can be used for all components.
- In lieu of zippers, hook-and-loop fasteners, snaps, buttons, rib and slot slide closures, etc. can attach the panels.
- Several windows can be used in the tent, and two complete zippers can be used on the inner panel window by providing the canopy with dual layers around the window.
- The flysheet can be omitted and just the inner canopy can be used with its advantageous alternative net and solid panels and its 1½ zippers.
- The flysheet can be spaced closer or adjacent to the inner canopy by changing hooks and web loops 14.
- In lieu of net and solid panels on the inner canopy, any other two different panels can be used, such as transparent and opaque.
- The inner canopy can have a fixed net window with an adjacent openable slot or window.
- The flysheet can have an openable window (e.g., a panel with a U-shaped zipper) that can be reached through the slot in the inner canopy.

Patent

US006216715B1

(12) **United States Patent** (10) **Patent No.:** **US 6,216,715 B1**

Howe (45) **Date of Patent:** **Apr. 17, 2001**

(54) **CONVERTIBLE TENT FOR RAIN, COLD, AND HOT CONDITIONS**

(76) Inventor: **Robert H. Howe**, 1225 NW. Foxwood Pl., Bend, OR (US) 97701-8606

(*) Notice: Subject to any disclaimer, the term of this patent is extended or adjusted under 35 U.S.C. 154(b) by 0 days.

(21) Appl. No.: **09/364,344**

(22) Filed: **Jul. 30, 1999**

(51) Int. Cl.[7] **E04H 15/30**

(52) U.S. Cl. **135/95**

(58) Field of Search 135/95, 93, 115, 135/117, 97, 124, 128

(56) **References Cited**

U.S. PATENT DOCUMENTS

2,391,871	1/1946	Benson	.... 160/368
2,666,441	1/1954	Powers	.... 135/14
3,598,133	* 8/1971	Abert .	
3,800,814	4/1974	Hibbert	.... 135/1 R
3,970,096	7/1976	Nicolai	.... 135/14 V
4,077,417	3/1978	Beavers	.... 135/3 R
4,078,572	* 3/1978	Moss .	
4,165,757	* 8/1979	Marks .	
4,265,261	5/1981	Barker	.... 135/3 R
4,269,210	* 5/1981	Marks .	

4,709,718	* 12/1987	Nichols .	
4,858,635	8/1989	Eppenbach	.... 135/104
5,394,897	3/1995	Ritchey et al.	.... 135/124
5,467,794	11/1995	Zheng	.... 135/125
5,579,799	12/1996	Zheng	.... 135/126
5,606,986	* 3/1997	Muise .	
5,765,584	6/1998	Heisler et al.	.... 135/93

* cited by examiner

Primary Examiner—Alvin Chin-Shue
Assistant Examiner—Sarah Purol
(74) *Attorney, Agent, or Firm*—David Pressman

(57) **ABSTRACT**

A convertible tent comprises an inner canopy (12) having a window (22) and a flysheet or outer canopy (36) spaced above and covering the inner canopy. The flysheet has a window (36P) in alignment with the canopy's window. The canopy's window can be closed with either a solid (26) or a net panel (24). This window has, around its edge, a row of zipper teeth (a zipper chain—30), which teeth mate with respective zipper chains (32, 34) on the solid and net panels. Thus either the solid panel or the net panel can be zipped into the inner canopy's window. A solid panel can also be zipped into the window in the flysheet. The tent can be adjusted for warm, cool, cold, and precipitation conditions from inside by using just the net panel in the inner canopy, just the solid panel of the inner canopy, or the solid panel o the inner canopy and the solid panel of the flysheet.

23 Claims, 3 Drawing Sheets

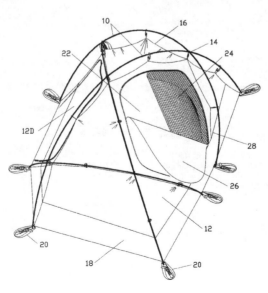

US 6,216,715 B1

1

CONVERTIBLE TENT FOR RAIN, COLD, AND HOT CONDITIONS

BACKGROUND

1. Field of Invention

This invention relates generally to tents, specifically to a tent that can be converted for use in different climactic conditions.

2. Prior Art

The art is replete with tents and other enclosure devices with conversion features for different climactic conditions, but such tents are not versatile, simple, easy to use, effective, or reliable.

Benson, in U.S. Pat. No. 2,391,871 (1946) shows a canvas covering with a window. One side of the window is attached to the canvas and the other sides are removably attached to the canvas by a zipper. This device is simple, but can only be opened or closed and thus cannot adapt to a range of climactic conditions, such as rain, heat, cold, etc.

Powers, in U.S. Pat. No. 2,666,441 (1954) shows a tent window comprising a pocket in the tent and a transparent sheet that is inserted in the pocket. A flap also can cover the opening. Although more complex and versatile, this device is awkward, heavy, and difficult to adjust for differing climactic conditions.

Hibbert, in U.S. Pat. No. 3,800,814 (1974) shows a tent that resembles an elongated building with a curved roof, such as the Quonset brand. The sidewall has a vertical zipper and two bottom horizontal zippers, as shown in FIG. **6**. While somewhat versatile, this tent is difficult to adjust rapidly and easily and lacks good versatility.

Nicolai in U.S. Pat. No. 3,970,096 (1976) shows another elongated tent; this one has spaced inner and outer porous layers. The layers are supported by tent poles that extend transversely over the tent.

This arrangement is complex and awkward and hence difficult to adjust and use.

Beavers, in U.S. Pat. No. 4,077,417 (1978) shows a tent with frame members that have ends inserted in multi-socket connectors. Again, it lacks versatility for different climactic conditions. Barker, in U.S. Pat. No. 4,265,261 (1981) shows a pyramidal tent with triangular side windows which are covered by triangular, awning-like covers. While unique, this arrangement is complex, difficult, and awkward to adjust, and still lacks good versatility.

Eppenbach, in U.S. Pat. No. 4,858,635 (1989) shows a tent having a ceiling opening that can be covered by a pivotable member attached to a flap. The tent also has a rain fly that the pivotable member can support. While somewhat versatile, this arrangement is not simple to use and is complex to fabricate.

Ritchey and Leavitt, in U.S. Pat. No. 5,394,897 (1995) shows interconnected tents. Modules that zip onto the tent openings connect the tents. The tent has inner and outer panels. They are mated by pairs of zippers as follows: inner: **72–74**; outer **78–80**. However they don't interconnect in a simple, reliable manner and do not provide a simple, versatile arrangement for a single user.

Zheng, in U.S. Pat. Nos. 5,467,794 (1995) and 5,579,799 (1996) shows a tent with collapsible shade awnings. The frame has hinged members. This arrangement suffers from the same disadvantages as Barker, supra.

Heisler and Remza, in U.S. Pat. No. 5,765,584 (1998) show a tent with a two-ply door. The first ply is porous for

2

air venting and the second ply is waterproof. The waterproof ply is attached by a zipper with two zipper slides or pulls such that the waterproof layer can be opened at the top or bottom. While somewhat versatile, this arrangement is still relatively complex and awkward to use, erect, and fabricate.

Another type of convertible tent is made by Sierra Designs of Emeryville, Calif. and sold under the trademark Nightwatch. This tent consists of an inner canopy with a window. The window has a solid panel that can be zipped open. A net panel (netting) that prevents mosquitoes from entering covers the outside of this window. This inner canopy is suspended from several arched tent poles. An outer waterproof flysheet is spaced about 7.5–13 cm away from the inner canopy, on the outside of the poles. When the solid panel is opened, the netting allows the occupants of the tent to see the sky, get ventilation, preserves the structural integrity of the tent, and keeps insects out. Thus the tent is convertible since opening the panel ventilates the tent when it is warm outside, e.g., in the summer. Closing the panel makes the tent warmer for cooler weather, e.g., in the spring and fall. The outer flysheet in installed to cover the window whenever external conditions, such as rain or snow, require more shielding. The flysheet is left partially off to enjoy the view and have ventilation when the weather is clement. However when precipitation occurs, installing the flysheet to cover the window is awkward: Since the netting covers the opening, an occupant must scramble out to arrange the flysheet to cover the window. The occupants and the inside of the tent will get wet or colder in the meantime. Even if the flysheet is installed to cover the window, spindrift (fine, wind-blown snow) will pass through the zipper of the flysheet and under the bottom of the flysheet. The netting will catch and hold the snow, so that the next time the window is open, the spindrift will fall into the tent.

OBJECTS AND ADVANTAGES

Accordingly, several objects and advantages of the invention are to provide an improved convertible tent which is more versatile, less awkward to use and handle, simple, easy to make and erect, and easily adjustable for a wide range of climactic conditions. It can be adjusted for different conditions, especially for rain, from the inside. It will not have an outer net to catch spindrift in the winter and the flysheet can be installed from inside the tent

Further objects and advantages will become apparent from a consideration of the ensuing description and the accompanying drawings.

DRAWING FIGURES

FIG. **1** is a perspective view from above of a tent according to the invention without its flysheet.

FIG. **2** is a view of part of a portion of an inner canopy of the tent showing an arrangement of zippers used on a window thereof.

FIG. **3** is a schematic, section-like partial view of the window, including a flysheet panel, showing area **3** of FIG. **4** in detail.

FIG. **4** is a perspective view from above of the tent with its flysheet.

SUMMARY

In accordance with the invention, a convertible tent comprises an inner canopy having a convertible opening or window and a flysheet or outer canopy spaced above and covering the inner canopy. The flysheet has a convertible

US 6,216,715 B1

| 3 | 4 |

opening or window in alignment with the canopy's window. The canopy's window can be closed with either a solid or a net panel. This window has, around its edge, a row of zipper teeth (a zipper chain), which teeth mate with respective zipper chains around the solid and net panels. Thus either the solid panel or the net panel can cover the inner canopy's window. A panel can be zipped into or out of the aligned window in the flysheet.

Description—FIG. 1—Inner Canopy With Dual-Closable Window

FIG. 1 shows a perspective view from above of the inner part of a tent according to the invention. A plurality of conventional tent poles 10 form an arched cage. The ends of these poles are anchored to the ground conventionally. An inner canopy, canvas, or tent body 12 is suspended from the poles by conventional hooks and web loops 14, shown in more detail in FIG. 4. The web loops are attached to seams or reinforcing cords 16 in canopy 12. The main portion of the floor of the tent is not shown, but it has conventional upturned sidewalls 18 that cover the bottom portion of the canopy. The canopy has a conventional door 12D on its left side (as seen in the drawing). The bottom edges of the tent have conventional web loops and attachments 20 at the bottoms of the poles.

In accordance with the invention, canopy 12 has a convertible opening or window 22 on its right or front side (as seen in the drawing) that can be closed by either of two panels: a net panel 24 or a solid panel 26. Net panel is made of conventional mosquito netting and solid panel 26 is made of the same material as canopy 12 and is attached at its bottom to the outside of the net panel. As shown in FIG. 2, either of these panels can be alternatively zipped into window 22 so as to close the window with either a solid or a net closure.

Canopy 12 preferably is made of breathable rip-stop nylon; the tent floor is made of nylon with a waterproof coating, and the poles are made of aluminum, either solid or in sections. In one version the tent was about 1.5 m high, and window 22 was about 75 cm high and about 1 m wide.

Description—FIGS. 2 and 3—Dual Window

FIG. 2 shows window 22 in detail. While shown as having a Tudor arch shape, it can have other shapes, such square, rectangular, triangular, circular, oval, hemispherical, etc. Either net panel 24 or solid panel 26 can be used to close or fill the window and each has the same shape as the window. Both are attached across their bottom edges to inner canopy 12, preferably at the seam of one of the upturned sidewalls 18 of the floor. Starting from the outside, the stitches 28 attach the following parts together at the bottom of window 22: the top edge of part of sidewall 18, then solid panel 26, then net panel 24, and then an edge of canopy 12.

The edge of canopy 12 (other than the bottom part that is sewn by stitches 28) has a zipper chain or row of teeth 30, which constitutes one side of a zipper. This chain can mate with a chain 32 (a mating half of the zipper) on net panel 24 or a chain 34 (another mating zipper half) on solid panel 26. One zipper pull or slide 24P is used to zip chain 32 of net 24 to chain 30 of canopy 12, while another pull 26P is used to zip teeth 34 of solid panel 26 to chain 30. Thus window 22 can be closed with either of panels 26 or 26 through the use of what is in effect 1 ½ zippers. Zipper pulls 24P and 26P are dual pulls which can be operated from inside or outside the tent. Net zipper pull 24P is started from the right side of the window and solid panel pull 26P is started from the left side.

FIG. 3 shows another, schematic view of the window panels that will aid in understanding. Ignoring optional flysheet 36 temporarily, note that canopy 12 is suspended by hook and web loop 14, which in turn hangs from pole 10. The edge of widow 22 in canopy 12 has zipper chain 30 around its sides (except the bottom where stitches 28 are used). The user can fasten net panel 24 to chain 30 by means of its chain 32, thereby closing the window with netting. Alternatively the user can fasten solid panel 26 to chain 30 by means of its chain 34, thereby closing the window with a solid panel.

Operation—FIGS. 2 and 3—Dual Window

Users can deploy the tent, as thus far described, with canopy 12 and its dual-closable window, without the flysheet, yet it has significant advantages. When both panels 24 and 26 (net and solid) are not in the window, pull 24P of net panel 24 is to the far right (FIG. 2) and a pull 26P of solid panel 26 is to the far left (not shown).

In warm weather, the user zips net panel 24 into window 22 by holding the net panel in the window and drawing pull 24P from right to left to attach chain 32 to chain 30, thereby to install the net panel in the window. The user then will obtain good ventilation and a view of the sky through the net, yet the net prevents mosquitoes and other insects from entering. When net 24 is zipped into place, solid panel 26 is left to hang down, on the outside of the window. Due to the use of two-sided pulls, the user can zip net 24 into place or unzip it from the inside or outside.

In cooler weather, the user zips solid panel 26 into window 22 by unzipping the net panel (if it is in the window) and holding the solid panel in the window and pulling pull 24P from left to right to attach chain 34 to chain 30. This will install the solid panel in the window. The user thus obtains a solid shield to keep the tent warmer. When solid panel 26 is zipped into place, net panel 24 is left to hang down, inside the window. As with the net panel, the user can zip panel 26 into place or unzip it from the inside or outside.

Since the net panel is never on the outside of the canopy in cooler or cold weather as in prior designs, snow or spindrift will not accumulate in the net. Since both panels can be removed from inside the tent, the occupants can reach outside to adjust portions of the tent and open the window of the flysheet, as will be described.

Description—FIGS. 3 and 4—Flysheet

As shown in FIGS. 3 and 4, flysheet 36 covers the tent structure of FIG. 1 (the pole cage and underlying canopy 12). Flysheet lies on top of hooks and web loops 14, and poles 10, and is attached to web loops 14 and poles 10 in conventional fashion by conventional quick-release buckles (not shown) so that outlines 10O of the poles show through (FIG. 4). Flysheet 36 has a window 36W and a flysheet panel 36P that the user can zip into the window. The zipper (not shown) extends around the window on all sides, except the bottom, and also has a dual pull (not shown) so that the flysheet panel can be zipped in place from the inside or outside.

Operation—FIGS. 3 and 4—Flysheet

The user many choose not to deploy the flysheet in warm weather. In cold (but not very cold) weather, and when there is no precipitation, the flysheet can be used, but with its window open. If it turns very cold, or rains or snows, the occupants can close the flysheet window by opening win-

US 6,216,715 B1

5

dow **22** of canopy **12**, pulling up flysheet panel **36P** through window **22**, and zipping panel **36P** in place. Then the occupants can zip solid panel **26** in place to close window **22**. Even if spindrift leaks through the zipper of the flysheet, or blows under the flysheet, it will not be able to accumulate on any net since net **24** is inside the tent. The occupants can also open a closed flysheet from inside when the precipitation stops or if it gets warmer.

Conclusions, Ramifications, and Scope

Accordingly the reader will see that, according to the invention, I have provided an improved convertible tent which is more versatile, less awkward to use and handle, simple, easy to make and erect, and easily adjustable for a wide range of climactic conditions. The user can adjust the tent for warm weather by not using the flysheet and just using the net, for cooler conditions by using the panel in the canopy and for cold or precipitation by using the flysheet and closing its panel. All variations can be implemented from the inside, without the occupants getting out of the tent and being exposed to the precipitation or cold. The tent does not have an outer net to catch snow in the winter and the user can install and remove the flysheet from inside the tent.

While the above description contains many specificities, these should not be construed as limitations on the scope of the invention, but as exemplifications of the presently preferred embodiments thereof. Many other ramifications and variations are possible within the teachings of the invention. For example, the flysheet window can be clear. Different materials, sizes, and interconnections can be used for all components. In lieu of zippers, hook-and-loop fasteners, snaps, buttons, rib and slot slide closures, etc can attach the panels. Several windows can be used in a tent, and two complete zippers can be used on the inner panel window by providing the canopy with dual layers around the window. The flysheet can be omitted and just the inner canopy can be used with its advantageous alternative net and solid panels and its 1½ zippers. The flysheet can be spaced closer or adjacent to the inner canopy by changing hooks and web loops **14**. In lieu of net and solid panels on the inner canopy, any other two different panels can be used, such as transparent and opaque, The inner canopy can have a fixed net window with an adjacent openable slot or window and the flysheet can have an openable window (e.g., a panel with a U-shaped zipper) which is reachable through the slot in the inner canopy.

Thus the scope of the invention should be determined by the appended claims and their legal equivalents, and not by the examples given.

REFERENCE NUMERALS

10 tent poles
100 outlines of poles
12 inner canopy
14 hooks and web loops
16 reinforcing cords
18 upturned sidewalls
12D door
20 web loops and attachments
22 window or convertible opening
24 net panel
24P zipper pull
26 solid panel
26P zipper pull
30 zipper chain on window
32 zipper chain on net panel

6

34 zipper chain on solid panel
36 flysheet or outer canopy
36P flysheet panel

What is claimed is:

1. A tent, comprising:

a solid canopy,

said solid canopy being supported to cover and enclose an above-ground volume,

said solid canopy having a selectively closable opening with an edge surrounding said opening,

a flysheet canopy mounted over and covering said solid canopy, said flysheet canopy having a window opening which can be reached through said selectively closable opening of said solid canopy,

said window opening of said flysheet canopy containing a flysheet panel that, from inside said solid canopy, can be can be installed in said window opening to occlude said window opening or removed from said window opening to leave said window opening patent.

2. The tent of claim **1** wherein said flysheet canopy is spaced from said solid canopy and where said flysheet panel has a plurality of sides, one of which is permanently attached to said flysheet.

3. The tent of claim **1** wherein said solid canopy has:

(a) two different panels for alternatively filling and closing said selectively closable opening, said two different panels being designated first and second panels, said first panel and said second panel each having a surrounding edge, a part of said edge of said net panel and a part of said edge of said solid panel being attached to said solid canopy surrounding said opening, said panels each having a remaining edge portion, and

(b) an attachment for alternatively attaching said remaining portion of said first panel or said remaining portion of said second panel to said edge of said solid canopy surrounding said opening, such that either said entire first panel or said entire second panel can be attached to said edge of said solid canopy surrounding said opening to fill said opening, or said opening can be left open.

4. The tent of claim **3** wherein said attachment comprises a zipper including a first panel zipper chain on said remaining edge portion of said net panel, a second panel zipper chain on said remaining edge portion of said solid panel, and a canopy opening zipper chain on said edge of said solid canopy surrounding said opening, and two zipper pulls for mating either said first panel zipper chain or said second panel zipper chain to said canopy opening zipper chain.

5. The tent of claim **3** wherein said solid canopy is supported by a plurality of tent poles which arch over said solid canopy and suspend said solid canopy from said tent poles.

6. The tent of claim **3** wherein said first panel is a net panel and said second panel is a solid panel.

7. A tent, comprising:

a solid canopy,

said solid canopy being supported to cover and enclose an above-ground volume,

said solid canopy having a convertible opening with an edge surrounding said opening,

said solid canopy having two different panels for alternatively filling and closing said opening, said two different panels being designated first and second panels, said first panel and said second panel each having a surrounding edge, a part of said edge of said net panel

US 6,216,715 B1

7

and a part of said edge of said solid panel being attached to said canopy surrounding said opening, said panels each having a remaining edge portion,

an attachment for alternatively attaching said remaining portion of said first panel or said remaining portion of said second panel to said edge of said solid canopy surrounding said opening, such that either said entire first panel or said entire second panel can be attached to said edge of said solid canopy surrounding said opening to fill said opening, or said opening can be left open, and

a flysheet canopy mounted over and covering said solid canopy, said flysheet canopy having a window opening aligned with said convertible opening of said solid canopy.

8. The tent of claim **7** wherein said attachment comprises a zipper including a first panel zipper chain on said remaining edge portion of said net panel, a second panel zipper chain on said remaining edge portion of said solid panel, and a canopy opening zipper chain on said edge of said solid canopy surrounding said opening, and two zipper pulls for mating either said first panel zipper chain or said second panel zipper chain to said canopy opening zipper chain.

9. The tent of claim **7**, further including a plurality of tent poles which arch over said solid canopy to support by and suspend said solid canopy from said tent poles, said flysheet canopy being positioned above said tent poles.

10. The tent of claim **7** wherein said window opening of said flysheet canopy contains a removable panel that can be removed and installed in said window opening of said flysheet canopy from inside said solid canopy.

11. The tent of claim **7** wherein:

said attachment comprises a zipper including a first panel zipper chain on said remaining edge portion of said net panel, a second panel zipper chain on said remaining edge portion of said solid panel, and a canopy opening zipper chain on said edge of said solid canopy surrounding said opening, and two zipper pulls for mating either said first panel zipper chain or said second panel zipper chain to said canopy opening zipper chain

said solid canopy is supported by a plurality of tent poles which arch over said canopy and suspend said solid canopy from said poles, said flysheet canopy being positioned above said tent poles, and

said window opening of said flysheet canopy contains a removable panel that can be removed and installed in said window opening of said flysheet canopy from inside said solid canopy.

12. An attachment system for attaching either a first panel or a second panel to a sheet of material, comprising:

a first panel zipper chain on an edge portion of said first panel,

a second panel zipper chain on an edge portion of said second panel,

a sheet-of-material zipper chain on an edge of said sheet of material, and

two zipper pulls for mating either said first panel zipper chain or said second panel zipper chain to said sheet-of-material zipper chain.

13. The attachment system of claim **12** wherein said sheet of material is a solid canopy for a tent, said canopy has a window, and said sheet-of-material zipper chain is mounted on an edge portion of said window, whereby either said first panel or said second panel can alternatively be zipped into said window.

14. The attachment system of claim **13**, further including a flysheet canopy mounted over and covering said solid

8

canopy, said flysheet canopy having an opening aligned with said window of said solid canopy.

15. A tent, comprising:

a solid canopy,

said solid canopy being supported to cover and enclose an above-ground volume,

said solid canopy having a convertible opening with an edge surrounding said opening,

said solid canopy having two different panels for alternatively filling and closing said opening, said two different panels being designated first and second panels, respectively, each of said first and second panels having a surrounding edge, a part of said edge of said first panel and a part of said edge of said second panel being attached to said solid canopy surrounding said opening, said panels each having a remaining edge portion,

an attachment for alternatively attaching said remaining portion of said first panel or said remaining portion of said second panel to said edge of said solid canopy surrounding said opening, such that either said entire first panel or said entire second panel can be attached to said edge of said solid canopy surrounding said opening to fill said opening with either said first or said second panel, or said opening can be left open.

16. The tent of claim **15** wherein said attachment comprises a zipper including a first panel zipper chain on said remaining edge portion of said first panel, a second panel zipper chain on said remaining edge portion of said second panel, and a canopy opening zipper chain on said edge of said solid canopy surrounding said opening, and two zipper pulls for mating either said first panel zipper chain or said second panel zipper chain to said canopy opening zipper chain.

17. The tent of claim **15** further including a plurality of tent poles supporting solid canopy, said tent poles arching over said canopy and suspending said canopy from said poles.

18. The tent of claim **17**, further including a flysheet canopy mounted over and covering said solid canopy, said flysheet canopy having an opening aligned with said convertible opening of said solid canopy.

19. The tent of claim **15** wherein said first panel is a net panel and said second panel is a solid panel.

20. The tent of claim **15** further including a plurality of tent poles supporting solid canopy, said tent poles arching over said canopy and suspending said canopy from said poles, said first panel being a net panel and said second panel being a solid panel, and wherein said attachment comprises a zipper including a first panel zipper chain on said remaining edge portion of said net panel, a second panel zipper chain on said remaining edge portion of said solid panel, and a canopy opening zipper chain on said edge of said solid canopy surrounding said opening, and two zipper pulls for mating either said first panel zipper chain or said second panel zipper chain to said canopy opening zipper chain.

21. The tent of claim **15**, further including a flysheet canopy mounted over and covering said solid canopy, said flysheet canopy having a window opening aligned with said convertible opening of said solid canopy.

22. The tent of claim **20** wherein said window opening of said flysheet contains a removable panel that can be removed and installed in said window opening of said flysheet canopy from inside said solid canopy.

23. The tent of claim **20** wherein said flysheet canopy is spaced from said solid canopy.

* * * * *

Non-Fogging Shower Mirror

Thomas Christianson wasn't the first to tackle the dilemma of shaving in the shower but his fogless mirror invention has proven to be a successful addition to the home furnishing market. Christianson licensed the patent to Showertek and you can find their Fogless Mirror in stores and on the Internet.

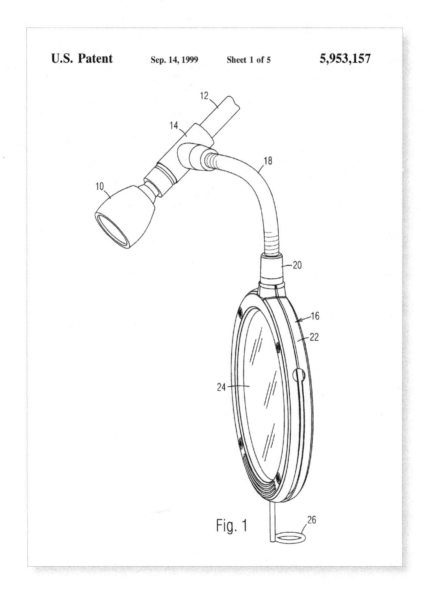

U.S. Patent   Sep. 14, 1999   Sheet 1 of 5   **5,953,157**

Fig. 1

Provisional Patent Application

Non-Fogging Shower Mirror Using Parallel Water Connection

I invented a shower mirror that uses heated shower water to keep it from fogging. When the water is turned on to the showerhead, most of the water will flow through the horizontal arm of a T-fitting via a passageway and then out of an outlet to the showerhead. Due to the higher pressure on the upstream side, some water will be forced into an upstream supply hole and down a supply tube to the mirror housing and then back through return tube to return and then to the downstream side of a barrier. The returning water from the mirror housing will rejoin the main stream of water flowing through the mirror's main passageway and both groups of water will leave to flow out of the showerhead. In this manner, the mirror surface remains fog-free without the use of a chemical coating, electric heating or waste of water. My invention is particularly useful when shaving since it enables the user to shave with a clear mirror in a steamy, watery environment, when whiskers are expanded and softened and when the shaving debris can be best washed away.

Others have invented shower mirrors that do not fog in the presence of warm water vapor but mine is superior because:

- It does not use a chemical coating that may eventually wear off on the surface of the mirror.
- It does not employ a means of heating the mirror to keep it fog free. It does not waste water that may drip from the bottom of the mirror or reduce the pressure of water coming out of the showerhead.
- It does not employ electrical lines near the water.
- It is not expensive to build and operate.
- It is not cumbersome.
- The fog-free status of the mirror is not temporary.
- It does not require soldering to be affixed to the shower head, nor does it require the mirror to be made of a solderable material, such as brass, which is expensive and unreliable.
- The whole mirror is fog free, not just a portion of it.

I've included seven drawings:

FIG. 1 is a view of my fog-free mirror assembly attached to a showerhead pipe.

FIG. 2 is a sectional view of a part of the mirror assembly where a T-fitting connects an arm of the mirror to the showerhead pipe.

FIG. 3 is a sectional view of a swivel fitting which connects the arm to the body of the mirror assembly.

FIGS. 4 and 5 are views of parts of the swivel fitting taken in the direction indicated by lines 4 and 5, respectively, of FIG. 3.

FIG. 6 is an exploded view of a body of the mirror assembly.

FIG. 7 is a perspective view of an alternative thermal transfer disc used in the body of the mirror assembly.

My fog-free mirror assembly is shown in perspective view attached to a showerhead pipe in **FIG. 1.** Warm water is supplied to a conventional showerhead 10 from a conventional showerhead pipe 12. Connected between pipe 12 and showerhead 10 is a T-fitting 14 (shown in more detail in FIG. 2). The T-fitting is connected to a mirror housing 16 by a flexible arm 18. Arm 18 is connected to housing 16 by a swivel fitting 20 (shown in more detail in FIGS. 3 to 5). The mirror housing 16 contains a mirror frame 22, a magnifying mirror 24, and other components that are shown in more detail in FIG. 2. Finally, a razor holder 26 is connected to frame 22.

The mirror assembly operates generally as follows: Some of the warm water flowing from pipe 12 to head 10 is diverted, drawn, or tapped by T-fitting 14 to a supply tube (not shown in FIG. 1) within arm 18. This diverted water flows through the supply tube to mirror housing 16. The water flows through a heat-transfer tube (not shown) in the housing. This heat-transfer tube in turn heats a heat dispersal disc that in turn heats the mirror in a relatively uniform manner to keep it fog free. Then the water returns through a return tube (not shown) in arm 18 back to the T-fitting. The return water joins the main flow of water in the T-fitting and then it flows out of head 10 in normal fashion.

The T-fitting 14 of FIG. 1 is shown in detail in **FIG. 2.** The T-fitting may be made of brass or plastic. It contains an inlet opening 28 with female threads on the right side of the top bar of the "T," and an outlet opening 30 with male threads on the left side. A passageway 32 connects inlet 28 to outlet 30 and includes a barrier wall or partition 34 having a restriction opening 34' that has a narrower cross-sectional area (19.6 sq. mm) and smaller diameter (5 mm) than passageway 32 (154 sq. mm in area and 1.4 cm in diameter). Water flowing through passageway 32 will encounter resistance (due to wall 34 and opening 34') and so will have a pressure drop across the wall. As a result the pressure will be higher on the right or upstream side of wall 34 than on the downstream or left side of wall 34.

The portion of passageway 32 on the upstream side of wall 34 is coupled via an upstream outlet or supply 32S to a mirror supply tube 36, while the downstream side is connected via a return inlet 32R to mirror return tube 38. Tubes 36 and 38 run through arm 18 (FIGS. 1 and 2) with their upper ends terminating and joined to supply 32S and return 32R, respectively, in vertical leg 40 of the "T." Vertical leg 40 has male threads and is mated with arm 18, which has female threads. The cross-sectional configurations of inlet opening 28, outlet opening 30, and vertical leg 40 are circular.

When the water is turned on to the showerhead, most of the water will flow through the horizontal arm of the T-fitting via passageway 32, including opening 34', and then out of outlet 30 to the showerhead. Due to the higher pressure on the upstream side, some water will be forced into upstream supply hole 32S and down supply tube 36 to the mirror housing and then back through return tube 38 to return 32R and then to the downstream side of barrier 34. The returning water from the mirror housing will rejoin the main stream of water flowing through passageway 32 and both components of water will leave outlet 30 to flow out of the showerhead.

FIG. 3 shows how the T-fitting 14 is connected to swivel joint 20 by arm 18. Arm 18 has a known wound spiral gooseneck-like construction (FIG. 1) so that it can be bent to and will remain stably in any desired orientation. It contains and protects supply tube 36 and return tube 38 of flexible plastic or brass. Arm 18 preferably is about 22 cm long and about 2.5 cm in diameter and tubes 36 and 38 are about 6 mm in diameter.

The swivel fitting joint 20 enables the mirror housing 16 to be rotated to any orientation with respect to arm 18 so that the user can position the mirror as desired. Joint 20 has two parts: an upper, female part 42 (shown in FIG. 4) and a mating, lower, and male part 44 (shown in FIG. 5) which rotates and fits in, or can be mated in a telescoping manner, with female part 42.

Tubes 36 and 38 within arm 18 terminate at their lower end in female part 42 which has two through holes: an inward supply hole 36S (where the water leaves female part 42) and an outward return hole 38R (where the water returns to upper part 42). The ends of tubes 36 and 38 are embedded in holes 36S and 38R, respectively. Each hole has a larger diameter top portion and a narrower diameter bottom portion with an upwardly facing shoulder or stop at the junction between these portions to limit the degree of insertion of tubes 36 and 38.

Female or upper part 42, which also may be made of brass or plastic, has a cylindrical portion 42U that projects upwards and is joined to the inside of inside arm 18. The lower end of female part 42 (FIG. 4) has a projecting skirt 46, a circular groove or moat 48 adjacent the skirt, and a central platform 50 that contains holes 38R and 36S. Note that the return hole 38R is farther out from the radius than supply hole 36S, (for a purpose to be discussed below). Platform 50 also contains a central threaded hole 50H for receiving a screw (not shown) to hold male part 44 within the female part.

The upper face of male or lower part 44 (FIG. 5) has a through hole 44H for a fastening screw (not shown). One of the upper and lower parts (42 and 44) has a pair of concentric, circular moats in floats communicating with two through holes in the other of these parts. As shown, lower part 44 has the two concentric grooves or moats 52 and 54.

Inner or supply moat 52 is the same radial distance out from the center as supply hole 36S of female part 42 so as that these parts always mate with each other. Moat 52 is also coupled to a through hole 52S in male part 44 for receiving input water from the moat and from hole 36S and supplying it to the mirror heating tube.

Outer or return moat 54 is the same distance out from the center as return hole 38R of female part 42 and is coupled to a through hole 54R for receiving water from the mirror and returning it to return hole 38R. Through holes 52S and 54R are enlarged in the lower face of male part 44 to receive and hold the ends 56S and 56R, respectively, of heat transfer tube 56 (FIG. 6). Screw hole 44H is enlarged at the lower face of male part 44 to mate with the head of the fastening screw (not shown). The swivel fitting also joins arm 18 to mirror housing 16 of the housing.

Warm water is supplied via supply tube 36 to hole 36S in upper part 42. Hole 36S always communicates with inner or supply moat 52 of the male part regardless of the relative rotated positions of the male and female parts. This is because hole 36S in female, upper part 42 is at the same radial distance from the center as is moat 52 in lower, male part 44. Thus the water will fill inner moat 52 and will then travel through hole 52S to upper or supply part 56S of the heat transfer tube 56. After traveling around the tube and heating the mirror, the warm water will flow to upper or return part 56R of tube 56 and then to hole 54R and outer moat 54.

Since outer or return moat 54 is at the same radial distance from the center as hole 38R, moat 54 is always in communication with hole 38R of the female part. Thus the returning water will pass through hole 38R and then back to return tube 38. From return tube 38 the water will, as stated, flow into hole 32R (FIG. 2) in the T-fitting and then to the downstream side of passageway 32 to the showerhead.

FIG. 6 shows an exploded view of the mirror housing and the other components. T-fitting 14 is shown in its entirety, as is arm 18 and upper and lower parts 42 and 44 of the swivel joint. The upper ends 56S and 56R of heat-transfer tube 56 are shown free, but in practice they are attached to the through holes in lower part 44 as shown in FIG. 3. Tube 56 has multiple bends so that it covers as much of the area of the mirror as possible.

On the left side of tube 56 is a thermal transfer or heat-dispersing disc 58, e.g., of woven copper mesh or cloth. Disc 58 preferably a wire density of 39 x 39 wires per square cm (100 x 100 per sq. in.), with each wire being about 114 microns (4.5 mils) in diameter.

To the left of disc 58 is magnifying mirror 24. Mirror 24 is preferably made of acrylic or glass and is shown flat, but is concave when seen from the left or front so as to provide magnification. When seen from the right or back it is convex so as to form the familiar dish shape.

To the left of mirror 24 is a gasket 60, a holding ring 62, and a front beauty ring 64. Ring 64 has a series of concentric slits 64S at its bottom part. A rubber gripping strip 64R with mating ridges is positioned between rings 62 and 64 so that when the parts are assembled (drawn together by fastening screws—not shown), the ridges of strip 64R protrude through slits 64S to provide a gripping surface on the front. Collar 16C on ring 64 may be made of plastic and ring 62 may be made of brass or plastic. The housing preferably is 15 to 17 cm in diameter.

On the right side of tube 56 is another heat dispersing disc 66, e.g., of copper mesh or cloth.

To the right of disc 66 is flat (non-magnifying) mirror 68.

To the right of mirror 68 is a gasket 70, a holding ring 72, and a rear beauty ring 74. Like ring 64, ring 74 has a series of concentric slits at its bottom part. A rubber gripping strip 74R with mating ridges is positioned between rings 72 and 74 so that when the parts are assembled, the ridges of strip 74R protrude through the concentric slits to provide a rear gripping surface.

Screws (not shown) attach the parts together, press tube 56 in good thermal contact with discs 58 and 66, press discs 58 and 66 in good contact with mirrors 24 and 68, and extend from holding ring 62 to ring 74.

FIG. 7 shows an alternative thermal transfer disc. Instead of the circular mesh sheet 58, the thermal transfer disc between tube 56 and the magnifying mirror can be a radially fluted disc, as shown in FIG. 7. This disc will also thermally couple and spread the concentrated heat from tube 56 to mirror 24. The disc has radial folds or flutes that make it flexible and thus able to contact a large area of the mirror. It is open in its center since it is not possible to extend the folds to the center.

When warm water flows through tube 56, it heats heat dispersal transfer discs 58 and 66. Each of these discs receives heat in the relatively small area of its inner side in contact with tube 56 and disperses this heat to a relatively broad area on its outer side. Since each disc's outer side is in contact with its mirror (24 or 68), it heats its mirror in a relatively uniform manner to keep it fog free. Although mirror 24 is a meniscus, disc 58 is sufficiently compressible to provide a good thermal coupling between tube 56 and mirror 24.

The mirror housing has a hole 16H so that the head of razor holder 26 can be inserted and allowed to drop down to the bottom of the housing as shown in FIG. 1. The outer diameters of rings 62 and 72 are sufficiently smaller than the inner diameters of rings 64 and 74 to provide space for the head of the razor holder to pass between the two sets of rings.

My invention operates as follows: The user installs the device by connecting the horizontal or top arms of the T-fitting in series with the showerhead (FIG. 1).

When the user turns on the water at the usual warm temperature, water flows through pipe 12, passageway 32 of T-fitting 14, and out showerhead 10. In the T-fitting, due to wall 34 and its restriction opening 34', the pressure of the water on the upstream side of wall 34 is higher than on the downstream side. Thus water will flow into opening 32S and tube 36 in arm 18, around thermal transfer tube 56 (FIG. 6), back through tube 38 and opening 32R (FIG. 2), and into the downstream side of partition 34. This returning water will recombine with the main stream flowing through passageway 32 and will flow out the showerhead. Thus no water will be wasted in heating the mirrors in housing 22.

Since arm 18 and its contained tubes 36 and 38 are flexible, the arm can be positioned as desired. Swivel connection 20 enables mirror housing 16 to be rotated to any position with respect to arm 18, as explained above.

Patent

US005953157A

United States Patent [19]

Christianson

[11] Patent Number: **5,953,157**

[45] Date of Patent: **Sep. 14, 1999**

[54] **NON-FOGGING SHOWER MIRROR USING PARALLEL WATER CONNECTION**

[75] Inventor: **Thomas R. Christianson**, Napa, Calif.

[73] Assignee: **Showertek, Inc.**, American Canyon, Calif.

[21] Appl. No.: **08/992,371**

[22] Filed: **Dec. 17, 1997**

[51] Int. Cl.⁶ **G02B 5/08**; G02B 7/182

[52] U.S. Cl. **359/509**; 359/507; 359/512

[58] Field of Search 359/507, 509, 359/512, 514, 840, 845; 4/597, 605; 219/219, 522

[56] **References Cited**

U.S. PATENT DOCUMENTS

Re. 32,906	4/1989	Jones	359/512
2,759,765	8/1956	Pawley	299/72
3,530,275	9/1970	Rust	219/219
3,594,063	7/1971	Smilie, III	359/509
4,150,869	4/1979	Hansen	359/509
4,327,961	5/1982	Kladidis	359/512
4,556,298	12/1985	Gottlieb	359/512
4,557,003	12/1985	Jones	4/605
4,655,559	4/1987	Odell	359/512
4,832,475	5/1989	Daniels	359/512

4,836,668	6/1989	Christianson	359/512

FOREIGN PATENT DOCUMENTS

1490373 11/1977 United Kingdom .

Primary Examiner—Thong Nguyen
Attorney, Agent, or Firm—David Pressman

[57] **ABSTRACT**

A fog-free shower mirror assembly comprises a mirror body (16) and an arm (18) connecting the body to a showerhead pipe (12). The arm is connected to the pipe by a T-fitting (14) that diverts warm water from the pipe to the mirror body. The T-fitting also returns the water after it passes through a heat transfer tube (56) in the mirror body. The arm is flexible and contains two inner tubes (36 and 38) for supply and return of the water. The arm is connected to the mirror body by a swivel fitting (20). The mirror body contains a thermal transfer disc (58) positioned between the heat transfer tube and the back of the mirror. Heat from the water in the heat transfer tube is thereby transferred to the mirror to keep it above the condensation point so as to maintain it fog-free. An additional mirror (68) that also is heated by heat from the heat transfer tube may be provided on an opposite side of the mirror body, also in thermal contact with the transfer tube. The two mirrors preferably are magnifying and non-magnifying, respectively.

26 Claims, 5 Drawing Sheets

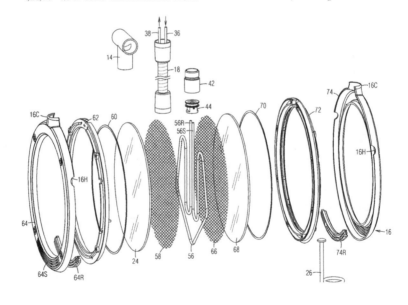

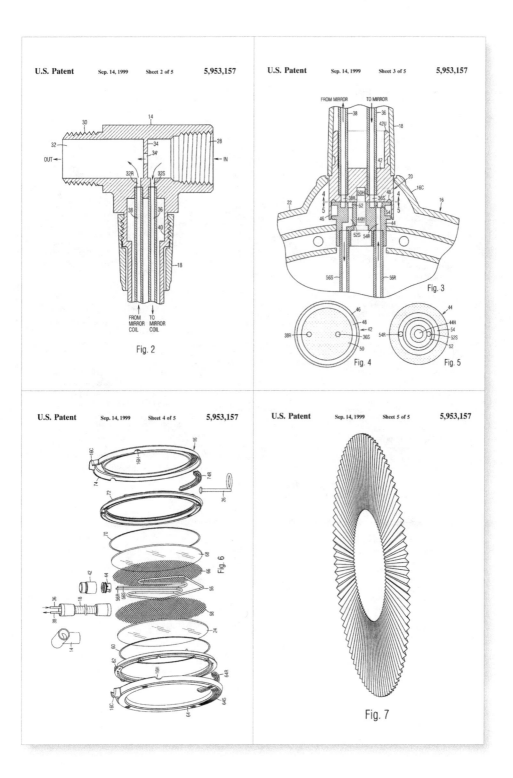

U.S. Patent   Sep. 14, 1999   Sheet 2 of 5   5,953,157

Fig. 2

U.S. Patent   Sep. 14, 1999   Sheet 3 of 5   5,953,157

FROM MIRROR   TO MIRROR

Fig. 3

Fig. 4   Fig. 5

U.S. Patent   Sep. 14, 1999   Sheet 4 of 5   5,953,157

Fig. 6

U.S. Patent   Sep. 14, 1999   Sheet 5 of 5   5,953,157

Fig. 7

5,953,157

1

NON-FOGGING SHOWER MIRROR USING PARALLEL WATER CONNECTION

BACKGROUND

1. Field of Invention

This invention relates generally to shower mirrors, specifically to a non-fogging shower mirror that employs heated shower water.

2. Background—Prior Art

Shower mirrors that do not fog in the presence of warm water vapor are known. Such mirrors use either a chemical coating on the surface of the mirror or a means of heating the mirror to keep it fog-free.

Those mirrors that use a chemical coating to prevent fogging are not entirely effective. Also the chemical coating eventually wears off, whereupon the mirror fogs as much as an untreated mirror.

Mirrors in which heat is used to keep the mirror fog free are numerous.

For example, my U.S. Pat. No. 4,836,668 (1989) shows a fog-free shower mirror that is heated by water diverted from the shower arm to the back of the mirror. While effective and successful, this mirror wastes a small quantity of water that drips out of the bottom of the mirror assembly after it heats the mirror. Also, the diverted water slightly reduces the pressure of water coming out of the showerhead.

U.S. Pat. No. 3,530,275 to Rust (1970) shows an electrically heated mirror. This arrangement is dangerous since it requires electrical lines to be near water. Also this mirror is expensive to build and operate.

U.S. Pat. No. 4,327,961 to Kladitis (1982) shows a mirror backed by a compartment that the user fills with warm water to keep the mirror fog-free. This mirror is cumbersome to use and is fog-free only temporarily since the warm water must be replenished periodically.

U.S. Pat. No. 4,556,298 to Gottlieb (1985) shows a non-fogging bathroom mirror. It employs water diverted from the shower pipe to a multiply bent tube attached to the rear of a metal mirror. The water heats the tube and the tube in turn heats the mirror. However this system is disadvantageous because the pipe must be soldered or otherwise joined in heat conducting relation to the mirror. This requires that the mirror be made of a solderable material, such as brass. This material and the soldering procedure are expensive and unreliable. Also, unless a very thick, heavy, or highly conductive mirror is used, the tube will heat the mirror generally only in the area covered by the tube, so that only this area (having a pattern corresponding to the tube) will be fog-free; the rest of the mirror will be fogged.

U.S. Pat. No. 4,557,003 to Jones (1985) shows a shower mirror in which an arm with joints and two internal water conduits is connected from the shower pipe to the mirror housing. Water flows through a supply conduit in the arm to a plenum behind the mirror to heat the mirror. Then it flows through a return conduit in the arm back to the shower pipe. This system has a disadvantage in that the entire arm, including its joints and conduits, must be sealed so as to accommodate the entire line pressure of the water line. This is difficult and expensive to accomplish while still enabling the arm to be flexible. Further, designing a sealed plenum that is strong enough to withstand line pressure yet thin enough to transfer heat is very difficult.

OBJECTS AND ADVANTAGES

Accordingly, several objects and advantages of the invention are to provide an improved shower mirror, to provide a

2

shower mirror which does not waste any water, which does not reduce the pressure of water coming out of the showerhead, which does not use electricity, which is economical, safe, and easy to use, buy, and operate, which maintains its fog-free condition as long as it is used, with no effort or action on the part of the user, which does not require soldering or pipe joining, which is made entirely fog-free, which does not use large moveable or flexible parts that carry water, which does not use a large sealed system with rotatable joints which must carry the full pressure of the water, which does not require a sealed plenum that must withstand the line pressure of the water, and which does not use chemicals or special coatings.

Other objects are to provide a shower mirror in which water does not contact a mirror directly, where it might damage the mirror, which does not use a large cavity which must carry water and be sealed under pressure, and which provides a heating system for both sides of a two-sided mirror and a fully rotatable frame for viewing either side.

Further objects and advantages will become apparent from a consideration of the ensuing description and the accompanying drawings.

DRAWING FIGURES

FIG. 1 is a perspective view of a fog-free mirror assembly attached to a showerhead pipe according to the invention;

FIG. 2 is a sectional view of a part of the mirror assembly where a T-fitting connects an arm of the mirror to the showerhead pipe;

FIG. 3 is a sectional view of a swivel fitting which connects the arm to the body of the mirror assembly;

FIGS. 4 and 5 are views of parts of the swivel fitting taken in the direction indicated by lines 4 and 5, respectively, of FIG. 3;

FIG. 6 is an exploded view of a body of the mirror assembly; and

FIG. 7 is a perspective view of an alternative thermal transfer disc used in the body of the mirror assembly.

DRAWING REFERENCE NUMERALS

10 showerhead
12 showerhead pipe
14 T-fitting
16 mirror housing
18 flexible arm
20 swivel fitting
22 mirror frame
24 magnifying mirror
26 razor holder
28 inlet opening
30 outlet opening
32 passageway
32R return inlet
32S upstream exit
34 barrier wall
34' restriction opening
36 supply tube
36S supply hole
38 return tube
38R return hole
40 vertical leg
42 female part of swivel
44 male part of swivel
44H screw hole
46 skirt

5,953,157

3

48 moat
50 central platform
50H threaded hole
52 inner moat
54 outer moat
52S supply hole
54R return hole
56 heat transfer tube
56S supply end
56R return end
58 thermal transfer disc
60 gasket
62 holding ring
64 beauty ring
64S slits
66 thermal transfer disc
68 flat mirror
70 gasket
72 holding ring
74 rear beauty ring
74R gripping strip

SUMMARY

In accordance with the invention, a fog-free shower mirror assembly comprises a mirror body and an arm connecting the body to a showerhead pipe. A T-fitting that diverts warm water from the pipe to the mirror body connects the arm to the pipe. The T-fitting also returns the water after it passes through a heat transfer tube in the mirror body, thus providing a parallel water connection. The arm is flexible and contains two inner tubes for supply and return of the water. The arm is connected to the mirror body by a swivel fitting. The mirror body contains a thermal transfer layer or plate positioned between the heat transfer tube and the back of the mirror. This layer transfers heat from the water in the heat transfer tube to the mirror to keep it above the condensation point so as to maintain it fog-free. An additional mirror that also is heated by heat from the heat transfer tube may be provided on an opposite side of the mirror body, also in thermal contact with the heat transfer tube. The two mirrors preferably are magnifying and non-magnifying, respectively.

FIG. 1—Description and Operation of Major Components

A fog-free mirror assembly according to the invention is shown in perspective view attached to a showerhead pipe in FIG. 1. Warm water is supplied to a conventional showerhead 10 from a conventional showerhead pipe 12. Connected between pipe 12 and showerhead 10 is a T-fitting 14 which is shown in more detail in FIG. 2. The T-fitting is connected to a mirror housing 16 by a flexible arm 18. Arm 18 is connected to housing 16 by a swivel fitting 20, shown in more detail in FIGS. 3 to 5. Mirror housing 16 comprises a mirror frame 22, a magnifying mirror 24, and other components that are shown in more detail in FIG. 2. Finally, a razor holder 26 is connected to frame 22.

The mirror assembly operates generally as follows: Some of the warm water flowing from pipe 12 to head 10 is diverted, drawn, or tapped by T-fitting 14 to a supply tube (not shown in FIG. 1) within arm 18. This diverted water flows through the supply tube to mirror housing 16. The water flows through a heat-transfer tube (not shown) in the housing. This heat-transfer tube in turn heats a heat dispersal disc that in turn heats the mirror in a relatively uniform manner to keep it fog-free. Then the water returns through a return tube (not shown) in arm 18 back to the T-fitting. The return water joins the main flow of water in the T-fitting and then it flows out of head 10 in normal fashion.

4

FIG. 2—Description and Operation of T-Fitting

T-fitting 14 of FIG. 1 may be made of brass or plastic and is shown in detail in the cross-sectional view of FIG. 2. It comprises an inlet opening 28 with female threads on the right side of the top bar of the "T", and an outlet opening 30 with male threads on the left side of the top bar of the "T". A passageway 32 connects inlet 28 to outlet 30 and includes a barrier wall or partition 34 having a restriction opening 34' that has a narrower cross-sectional area (19.6 sq. mm) and smaller diameter (5 mm) than passageway 32 (154 sq. mm in area and 1.4 cm in diameter). Due to wall 34 and opening 34', water flowing through passageway 32 will encounter resistance and so will have a pressure drop across the wall. As a result the pressure will be higher on the right or upstream side of wall 34 than on the downstream or left side of wall 34.

The portion of passageway 32 on the upstream side of wall 34 is coupled via an upstream outlet or supply 32S to a mirror supply tube 36, while the downstream side is connected via a return inlet 32R to mirror return tube 38. Tubes 36 and 38 run through arm 18 (FIGS. 1 and 2) with their upper ends terminating and joined to supply 32S and return 32R, respectively, in vertical leg 40 of the "T". Vertical leg 40 has male threads and is threadedly mated with arm 18, which has female threads. The cross-sectional configurations of inlet opening 28, outlet opening 30, and vertical leg 40 are circular.

In operation, the user connects the horizontal or top arms of the T-fitting in series with the showerhead (as illustrated in FIG. 1) as follows. The showerhead is unscrewed from its pipe, inlet 28 of the T-fitting is screwed onto the end of the pipe, and the showerhead is screwed onto outlet 30 of the T fitting.

When the water is turned on to the showerhead from a conventional valve (not shown), most of the water will flow through the horizontal arm of the T-fitting via passageway 32, including opening 30', and then out of outlet 30 to the showerhead. Due to the higher pressure on the upstream side, some water will be forced into upstream supply hole 32S and down supply tube 36 to the mirror housing and then back through return tube 38 to return 32R and then to the downstream side of barrier 34. The returning water from the mirror housing will rejoin the main stream of water flowing through passageway 32 and both components of water will leave outlet 30 to flow out of the showerhead.

FIGS. 3–5—Description and Operation of Arm and Swivel Joint

T-fitting 14 is connected to swivel joint 20 (FIG. 3) by arm 18. Arm 18 may be made of brass, plastic, or any other suitable material and has a known wound spiral gooseneck-like construction (FIG. 1) so that it can be bent to and will remain stably in any desired orientation. It contains and protects supply tube 36 and return tube 38, which preferably are made of flexible plastic or brass. Arm 18 preferably is about 22 cm long and about 2.5 cm in diameter and tubes 36 and 38 are about 6 mm in diameter.

Swivel joint 20 enables mirror housing 16 to be rotated to any orientation with respect to arm 18 so that the user can position the mirror as desired. Joint 20 has two parts: an upper, female part 42 (FIG. 4) and a rotatably mating, lower, and male part 44 (FIG. 5) which fits in, or is telescopingly mated with, female part 42.

Tubes 36 and 38 within arm 18 terminate at their distal or lower end in female part 42 which has two through holes: a radially inward supply hole 36S (where the water leaves female part 42) and a radially outward return hole 38R (where the water returns to upper part 42). The ends of tubes

5,953,157

5

36 and 38 are fixedly embedded in holes 36S and 38R, respectively. Each hole has a larger diameter top portion and a narrower diameter bottom portion with an upwardly facing shoulder or stop at the junction between these portions to limit the degree of insertion of tubes 36 and 38.

Female or upper part 42, which also may be made of brass or plastic, has an upwardly projecting cylindrical portion 42U that is joined to the inside of inside arm 18. The lower end of female part 42 (FIG. 4) has a projecting skirt 46, a circular groove or moat 48 adjacent the skirt, and a central platform 50 which contains holes 38R and 36S. Note that return hole 38R is radially farther out than supply hole 36S, for a purpose to be covered below. Platform 50 also contains a central threaded hole 50H for receiving a screw (not shown) to hold male part 44 within the female part.

The upper face of male or upper part 44 (FIG. 5) has a through hole 44H for a fastening screw (not shown). One of the upper and lower parts (42 and 44) has a pair of concentric, circular moats in floats communication with two through holes in the other of these parts. As shown, lower part 44 has the two concentric grooves or moats 52 and 54.

Inner or supply moat 52 is the same, lesser radial distance out from the center as supply hole 36S of female part 42 so as to always mate therewith. Moat 52 is also coupled to a through hole 52S in male part 44 for receiving input water from the moat and hence from hole 36S and supplying it to the mirror heating tube, infra.

Outer or return moat 54 is the same, greater radial distance out from the center as return hole 38R of female part 42 and is coupled to a through hole 54R for receiving water from the mirror and returning it to hole 38R. Through holes 52S and 54R are enlarged in the lower face of male part 44 to receive and hold the ends 56S and 56R, respectively, of heat transfer tube 56 (FIG. 6). Screw hole 44H is enlarged at the lower face of male part 44 to mate with the head of the fastening screw (not shown).

The swivel fitting also joins arm 18 to mirror housing 16 of the housing.

In operation, warm water is supplied via supply tube 36 to hole 36S in upper part 42. Hole 36S always communicates with inner or supply moat 52 of the male part regardless of the relative rotated positions of the male and female parts. This is because hole 36S in female, upper part 42 is at the same radial distance from the center as is moat 52 in lower, male part 44. Thus the water will fill inner moat 52 and will then travel through hole 52S to upper or supply part 56S of the heat transfer tube 56. After traveling around the tube and heating the mirror, the warm water will flow to upper or return part 56R of tube 56 and then to hole 54R and outer moat 54.

Since outer or return moat 54 is at the same radial distance from the center as hole 38R, moat 54 is always in communication with hole 38R of the female part. Thus the returning water will pass through hole 38R and then back to return tube 38. From return tube 38 the water will, as stated, flow into hole 32R (FIG. 2) in the T-fitting and then to the downstream side of passageway 32 to the showerhead.

The water will flow from supply tube 36, through heat transfer tube 56, and back through return tube 38 without interruption or impediment regardless of the orientation of the male and female parts of the swivel head due to moats 52 and 54. Thus, mirror housing 16 can be rotated infinitely with respect to arm 18 without affecting the function of the mirror.

FIG. 6—Description and Operation of Mirror Housing

FIG. 6 shows an exploded view of the mirror housing and the other components. T-fitting 14 is shown in gross view, as

6

is arm 18 and upper and lower parts 42 and 44 of the swivel joint. The upper ends 56S and 56R of heat-transfer tube 56 are shown free, but in practice they are attached to the through holes in lower part 44 as shown in FIG. 3. Tube 56 has multiple bends, i.e., a serpentine, curvilinear, or sinuous configuration, so that it covers as much of the area of the mirror as possible.

On the left side of tube 56 is a thermal transfer or heat-dispersing disc 58, e.g., of woven copper mesh or cloth. Disc 58 may preferably has a wire density of 39×39 wires per square cm. (100×100 per sq. in.), with each wire being about 114 microns (4.5 mils) in diameter.

To the left of disc 58 is magnifying mirror 24. Mirror 24 is preferably made of acrylic or glass and is shown flat, but is concave when seen from the left or front so as to provide magnification. When seen from the right or back it is convex so as to form the familiar meniscus or dish shape.

To the left of mirror 24 is a gasket 60, a holding ring 62, and a front beauty ring 64. Ring 64 has a series of concentric slits 64S at its bottom part. A rubber gripping strip 64R with mating ridges is positioned between rings 62 and 64 so that when the parts are assembled (drawn together by fastening screws—not shown), the ridges of strip 64R protrude through slits 64S to provide a gripping surface on the front. Collar 16C on ring 64 may be made of plastic and ring 62 may be made of brass or plastic. The housing preferably is 15 to 17 cm in diameter.

On the right side of tube 56 is another heat dispersing disc 66, e.g., of copper mesh or cloth.

To the right of disc 66 is flat (non-magnifying) mirror 68. To the right of mirror 68 is a gasket 70, a holding ring 72, and a rear beauty ring 74. Like ring 64, ring 74 has a series of concentric slits at its bottom part. A rubber gripping strip 74R with mating ridges is positioned between rings 72 and 74 so that when the parts are assembled, the ridges of strip 74R protrude through the concentric slits to provide a rear gripping surface.

Screws (not shown) attach the parts together, press tube 56 in good thermal contact with discs 58 and 66, press discs 58 and 66 in good contact with mirrors 24 and 68, and extend from holding ring 62 to ring 74.

In operation, when warm water flows through tube 56, it heats heat dispersal transfer discs 58 and 66. Each of these discs receives heat in the relatively small area of its inner side in contact with tube 56 and disperses this heat to a relatively broad area on its outer side. Since each disc's outer side is in contact with its respective mirror (24 or 68), it heats its mirror in a relatively uniform manner to keep it fog-free. Although mirror 24 is a meniscus, disc 58 is sufficiently compressible to provide a good thermal coupling between tube 56 and mirror 24.

The mirror housing has a hole 16H so that the head of razor holder 26 can be inserted and allowed to drop down to the bottom of the housing as shown in FIG. 1. The outer diameters of rings 62 and 72 are sufficiently smaller than the inner diameters of rings 64 and 74 to provide space for the head of the razor holder to pass between the two sets of rings.

Operation

The operation of the overall system has been generally described above in the description of FIG. 1 and the operation of the individual components has also been described above under their individual figures. The operation of the overall system will now be capitulated with reference to specific components.

After installing the mirror assembly between the shower pipe and the showerhead as explained above and as shown

5,953,157

7

in FIG. 1, the user turns on the water at the usual warm temperature. Water flows through pipe 12, passageway 32 of T-fitting 14, and out showerhead 10. In the T-fitting, due to wall 34 and its restriction opening 34', the pressure of the water on the upstream side of wall 34 is higher than on the downstream side. Thus water will flow into opening 32S and tube 36 in arm 18, around thermal transfer tube 56 (FIG. 6), back through tube 38 and opening 32R (FIG. 2), and into the downstream side of partition 34. This returning water will recombine with the main stream flowing through passageway 32 and will flow out the showerhead. Thus no water will be wasted in heating the mirrors in housing 22.

Since arm 18 and its contained tubes 36 and 38 are flexible, the arm can be positioned as desired. Swivel connection 20 enables mirror housing 16 to be rotated to any position with respect to arm 18, as explained above.

The water flowing through tube 56 (FIG. 6) will heat this tube, and, in turn, thermal transfer discs 58 and 66. These discs are good conductors and are in good thermal contact with the backs of meniscus mirror 24 and flat mirror 68, respectively, so that they will heat these mirrors relatively uniformly and thereby prevent water vapor in the shower stall from condensing anywhere on the fronts of these mirrors. For general viewing, the user can rotate the mirror housing so that the flat mirror faces the flat user, and for close-up work, the user rotates the housing so that the magnifying mirror faces the user. The present mirror is particularly useful when shaving since it enables the user to shave with a clear mirror in a steamy, watery environment, when his whiskers (or her axillary hairs) are expanded and softened and when the shaving debris can be best washed away.

FIG. 7—Alternative Thermal Transfer Disc

In lieu of circular mesh sheet 58, the thermal transfer disc between tube 56 and the magnifying mirror can be a radially fluted disc, as shown in FIG. 7. This disc will also thermally couple and spread the concentrated heat from tube 56 to mirror 24. The disc has radial folds or flutes that make it flexible and thus able to contact a large area of the mirror. It is open in its center since it is not possible to extend the folds to the center.

Conclusion, Ramifications, and Scope

Accordingly the reader will see that, according to the invention, I have provided an improved shower mirror which (a) does not waste any water, (b) reduce the pressure of water coming out of the showerhead, (c) does not use electricity, is economical, safe, and easy to use, buy, and operate, (d) maintains its fog-free condition as long as it is in use with no effort or action on the part of the user, (e) does not require soldering or pipe joining, (f) does not use large moveable or flexible parts that carry water, (g) does not use chemicals or special coatings, (h) does not use a large sealed system with rotatable joints which must carry the full pressure of the water, (i) does not use water which contacts a mirror directly, where it might damage the mirror, and (j) does not use a plenum or large cavity which must carry water.

While the above description contains many specificities, these should not be construed as limitations on the scope of the invention, but as exemplifications of the presently preferred embodiments thereof. Many other ramifications and variations are possible within the teachings of the invention. For example, the sizes and materials of all parts can readily

8

be changed. Thermal transfer plates of different shapes can be used, or such plates can be eliminated. The thermal transfer tube can be any conduit that will transfer its heat to the back of the mirror. E.g., it can be (a) made longer so as to contact a greater percentage area of the heat dispersal plate, (b) a helical coil of tubing which spirals from the outside to the center and then spirals from the center back to the outside by a continuous coil with two interspersed sections, (c) a set of parallel tubes with a supply header and a return header, or (d) a hollow flat housing with an inlet and an outlet. The mirror housing can be molded in place, around the mirrors and tube. The barrier and its hole in the T-fitting can be changed in shape. The swivel joint can be eliminated, at some loss of flexibility. In lieu of the showerhead and its pipe, the shower mirror can be connected to any other water supply duct.

Thus the scope of the invention should be determined by the appended claims and their legal equivalents, and not by the examples given.

I claim:

1. A mirror assembly for connection to a water supply duct, comprising:

a fitting for connection to a water supply duct and for drawing off a portion of any water flowing in said duct,

a hollow mounting arm, said arm containing a mirror supply tube having a distal end and also having a proximal end connected to said fitting for receiving said water drawn off from said water supply duct,

a thermal transfer conduit having supply and outlet ends, said supply end being connected to said distal end of said mirror supply tube,

a heat dispersal member in thermal contact with said thermal transfer conduit,

a mirror having a reflecting surface and a back in thermal contact with said heat dispersal member, said mirror also being connected to said distal end of said hollow mounting arm,

a mirror return tube having a proximal end and also having a distal end connected to said outlet end of said thermal transfer conduit, said mirror return tube also being positioned in said hollow mounting arm, said proximal end of said mirror return tube being connected to said fitting, said fitting also connected to return water in said return tube to said water supply duct.

2. The mirror assembly of claim 1 wherein said fitting is a T-fitting having a top passageway which can be connected in series with said water supply duct and a leg which communicates with said top passageway and said mirror supply and mirror return tubes.

3. The mirror assembly of claim 1 wherein said hollow mounting arm and said mirror supply and mirror return tubes therein are flexible.

4. The mirror assembly of claim 1 wherein said thermal transfer conduit is a tube having multiple bends.

5. The mirror assembly of claim 1, further including a mirror housing for holding said mirror and said thermal transfer conduit, said mounting arm connecting said fitting to said housing.

6. The mirror assembly of claim 5, further including a swivel fitting connecting said mounting arm to said housing, said swivel fitting enabling said housing to pivot with respect to said arm.

5,953,157

9 | 10

7. The mirror assembly of claim **6** wherein said swivel fitting comprises upper and lower rotatably connected parts, said upper part having two through holes connected to said mirror supply tube and said mirror return tube, respectively, said lower part being connected to said supply and outlet ends of said thermal transfer conduit, said lower part having a pair of circular moats in fluid communication with said two through holes of said upper part, whereby said upper and lower parts can be rotated with respect to each other, yet still allow two channels of water to flow through said parts.

8. The mirror assembly of claim **1** wherein said water supply duct is a showerhead supply pipe and a showerhead, and wherein said fitting is connected between said showerhead supply pipe and said showerhead.

9. The mirror assembly of claim **1**, further including a second mirror having a reflecting front and a back in thermal contact with said conduit, said second mirror also being connected to said distal end of said hollow mounting arm.

10. A shower mirror assembly for connection to a showerhead pipe and a showerhead, comprising:

a fitting for connection in a showerhead supply pipe for allowing water to flow through said showerhead supply pipe while also drawing some water from said showerhead supply pipe and returning said water to said showerhead supply pipe, said fitting containing first and second ducts for drawing and returning said water, respectively,

a hollow mounting arm having a proximal end connected to said fitting and also having a distal end, said hollow mounting arm containing a mirror supply tube having a distal end and also having a proximal end connected to said first duct for receiving said water drawn from said showerhead supply pipe, said hollow mounting arm also containing a mirror return tube connected to return said water drawn from said showerhead supply pipe to said second duct,

a mirror housing connected to said distal end of said hollow mounting arm,

a thermal transfer conduit in said mirror housing having supply and outlet ends, said supply end being connected to said distal end of said mirror supply tube, said outlet end being connected to said mirror return tube,

a heat dispersal member in thermal contact with said thermal transfer conduit,

a mirror in said mirror housing having a reflecting surface and a back in thermal contact with said heat dispersal member.

11. The mirror assembly of claim **10** wherein said fitting is a T-fitting having a top passageway which can be connected in series with said showerhead pipe and a leg which communicates with said top passageway and contains said first and second ducts.

12. The mirror assembly of claim **10** wherein said hollow mounting arm and said mirror supply and mirror return tubes therein are flexible.

13. The mirror assembly of claim **10** wherein said thermal transfer conduit is a tube having multiple bends.

14. The mirror assembly of claim **10**, further including a swivel fitting connecting said mounting arm to said housing, said swivel fitting enabling said housing to pivot with respect to said arm.

15. The mirror assembly of claim **14** wherein said swivel fitting comprises upper and lower rotatably connected parts,

said upper part having two through holes connected to said mirror supply tube and said mirror return tube, respectively, said lower part being connected to said supply and outlet ends of said thermal transfer conduit, said lower part having a pair of circular moats in fluid communication with said two through holes of said upper part, whereby said upper and lower parts can be rotated with respect to each other, yet still allow two channels of water to flow through said parts.

16. The mirror assembly of claim **10** wherein said fitting is connected between said showerhead supply pipe and said showerhead.

17. The mirror assembly of claim **10**, further including a second mirror in said housing and having a reflecting front and a back in thermal contact with said conduit, sad second mirror also being connected to said distal end of said hollow mounting arm.

18. In an environment which is vaporous due to warn water flowing from a pipe into said environment, a method for preventing a mirror in said environment from fogging, comprising:

tapping a portion of said warm water flowing through said pipe,

providing a thermal transfer conduit and causing said portion of water so tapped to flow through said thermal transfer conduit and back to said pipe and into said environment,

providing a heat dispersal member in thermal contact with said thermal transfer conduit, and

providing a mirror in thermal contact with said heat dispersal member,

whereby said warm water flowing through said thermal transfer conduit will heat said conduit and hence said heat dispersal member, and said heat dispersal member will heat said mirror in a relatively uniform manner to prevent it from fogging.

19. The method of claim **18** wherein said portion of water so tapped which flows through said thermal transfer conduit is done by providing a T-fitting having a top passageway which can be connected in series with said pipe and a leg which contains mirror supply and mirror return tubes therein, said tubes communicating with said thermal transfer conduit.

20. The method of claim **19** wherein said leg and said mirror supply and mirror return tubes therein are flexible.

21. The method of claim **18** wherein said thermal transfer conduit is a tube which has multiple bends.

22. The method of claim **18**, further including a mirror housing for holding said mirror and said thermal transfer conduit, and wherein said portion of water so tapped which flows through said thermal transfer conduit is done by providing a T-fitting having a top passageway which can be connected in series with said pipe and a leg which contains parts of mirror supply and mirror return tubes therein, said tubes communicating with said thermal transfer conduit, and also including a mounting arm connecting said fitting to said housing and containing parts of said mirror supply and mirror return tubes.

23. The method of claim **22**, further including a swivel fitting connecting said mounting arm to said housing, said swivel fitting enabling said housing to pivot with respect to said arm.

24. The method of claim **23** wherein said swivel fitting comprises upper and lower rotatably connected parts, said

5,953,157

11

upper part having two through holes connected to said mirror supply tube and said mirror return tube, respectively, said lower part being connected to said supply and outlet ends of said thermal transfer conduit, said lower part having a pair of moats in fluid communication with said two through holes of said upper part, whereby said upper and lower parts can be rotated with respect to each other, yet still allow two channels of water to flow through said parts.

25. The method of claim **18** wherein said pipe is a showerhead supply pipe, and wherein said portion of water so tapped which flows through said thermal transfer conduit

12

is done by providing a T-fitting having a top passageway which is connected between said showerhead supply pipe and said showerhead, said T-fitting having a leg which contains mirror supply and mirror return tubes therein, said tubes communicating with said thermal transfer conduit.

26. The method of claim **18**, further including a second mirror having a reflecting front and a back in thermal contact with said thermal transfer conduit.

* * * * *

Three-Wheeled Scooter

Just when you thought the scooter craze was over, inventor J. Beleski created an innovative improvement on this popular wheeled portable transport invention. For $200–$300, a user can buy Beleski's three-wheeled scooter (sold commercially under the trademark Trikke) and enjoy its innovative design—a rider can propel the device forward without pushing or pedaling … just by rocking from side to side. With its oversized polyurethane wheels, aircraft-grade aluminum, and exceptional stability, this scooter (known as a "cambering vehicle" in patent circles) was chosen as an Invention of the Year (2001) by *Time Magazine*.

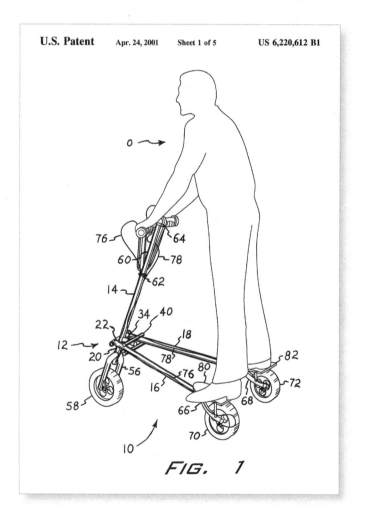

U.S. Patent   Apr. 24, 2001   Sheet 1 of 5   US 6,220,612 B1

FIG. 1

Provisional Patent Application

Cambering Vehicle and Mechanism

I, J. Gildo Beleski, Jr., have invented a cambering vehicle and mechanism.

Objects:

The invention provides a much-needed improvement in efficiency of construction for small three-wheeled operator-propelled vehicles, with its operation providing excellent exercise, as well as transportation, for the operator. It provides an improved cambering vehicle. It also provides improved folding of the vehicle for storage. It also includes improved steering or turning guidance for the vehicle. Its operating principle may be applied to skis, skates, and other sliding surface contact devices.

Relevant prior art includes:

U.S. Pat. 1303127 May, 1919 Wickman.

U.S. Pat. 1336100 Apr., 1920 Shearer.

U.S. Pat. 1664858 Apr., 1928 Headley.

U.S. Pat. 1890755 Dec., 1932 Shepherd.

U.S. Pat. 2598046 May, 1952 Frey.

U.S. Pat. 4045048 Aug., 1977 Irwin.

U.S. Pat. 4047732 Sep., 1977 Williams et al.

U.S. Pat. 4050711 Sep., 1977 Denzer.

U.S. Pat. 4050712 Sep., 1977 Denzer et al.

U.S. Pat. 4050713 Sep., 1977 Williams.

U.S. Pat. 4054300 Oct., 1977 Winchell.

U.S. Pat. 4065146 Dec., 1977 Denzer.

U.S. Pat. 4071261 Jan., 1978 Winchell.

U.S. Pat. 4076270 Feb., 1978 Winchell.

U.S. Pat. 4087104 May, 1978 Winchell et al.

U.S. Pat. 4087106 May, 1978 Winchell.

U.S. Pat. 4087108 May, 1978 Winchell.

U.S. Pat. 4088338 May, 1978 Winchell et al.

U.S. Pat. 4123079 Oct., 1978 Biskup.

U.S. Pat. 4133551 Jan., 1979 Biskup.

U.S. Pat. 4165093 Aug., 1979 Biskup.

U.S. Pat. 4540192 Sep., 1985 Shelton.
U.S. Pat. 5039121 Aug., 1991 Holter.
U.S. Pat. 5785331 Jul., 1998 Rappaport.
U.S. Pat. 5836601 Nov., 1998 Nelson.
U.S. Pat. 5871218 Feb., 1999 Lepage et al.
U.S. Pat. 6059304 May, 2000 Kakimi.
U.S. Pat. 6120044 Sep., 2000 Tsai.
2413377 – German scooter.

Advantages:

One advantage of the invention is that its novel yoke mechanism for controlling opposite curved motion of the two trailing arms, provides a more efficient and cleaner means of providing for the control of such motion as required in such vehicles.

Another advantage of the invention is that the unitary, monolithic construction of the yoke mechanism of conventional pieces welded together, results in a simple, inexpensive, and easily constructed unit, with no other parts or components required to effect the necessary action of the trailing arms.

Another advantage to the present mechanism is its attachment and ease of removal by means of a single pivot bolt, which enables the vehicle to be folded to an essentially flat configuration for storage. The yoke may be reinstalled upon its attachment point to the rear of the forward column to preclude its loss during storage, after being removed from the trailing arms.

Drawings—Figures:

FIG. 1 - is an environmental perspective view illustrating a cambering vehicle according to the invention in operation, and showing its general features.

FIG. 2 - is a detailed elevation view of the rear side of a front strut of the vehicle, showing details of a yoke mechanism interconnecting two trailing arms and the operation.

FIG. 3 - is a detailed right side elevation view of the yoke mechanism of FIG. 2, showing further details of the operation.

FIG. 4 - is a detailed exploded perspective view of the yoke mechanism of FIGS. 2 and 3, illustrating the removal of the yoke from the front structure for folding the vehicle for storage.

FIG. 5 - is a left side elevation view of the present cambering vehicle, illustrating the folded position of the vehicle in broken lines.

Drawings—Reference Numerals:
- 10 - cambering vehicle
- 12 - tricycle frame
- 14 - front column
- 16 - left trailing arm
- 18 - right trailing arm
- 20 - lower end
- 22 - trailing-arm attachment fitting
- 24 - laterally opposed trailing-arm attachment point
- 26 - laterally opposed trailing-arm attachment point
- 28 - lateral bushing
- 30 - lateral bushing
- 32 - bolt
- 34 - yoke attachment point
- 36 - internally threaded shaft
- 38 - central bushing
- 40 - trailing-arm interconnecting yoke
- 42 - single yoke attachment fastener
- 44 - upper bar
- 46 - lower bar
- 44l - left end of bar 44
- 46l - left end of bar 46
- 44r - right end of bar 44
- 46r - right end of bar 46
- 48 - lateral stop
- 50 - lateral bracing
- O - Operator

Description:
FIG. 1 provides an environmental perspective view of the present cambering vehicle 10 in operation. Vehicle 10 essentially comprises a tricycle frame 12 having a front column 14 and left and right trailing arms, respectively 16 and 18.

The trailing arms 16 and 18 are pivotally attached to the front column 14, immediately above its lower end 20. Details of the attachment of the trailing arms 16 and 18 to the front column 14 are shown more clearly in FIGS. 2 through 4 of the drawings.

A trailing-arm attachment fitting 22 is permanently secured across the front column 14 just above the lower end 20 with the attachment fitting 22 providing laterally opposed trailing-arm attachment points, respectively 24 and 26, to the front column 14. The forward ends of the two trailing arms 16 and 18 have lateral bushings, respectively 28 and 30, with a bolt 32 or other suitable fastener secured through each trailing-arm bushing 28 and 30 to secure the trailing arms 16 and 18 pivotally to the fitting 22 of the lower end 20 of the front column 14.

A yoke attachment point 34 (shown more clearly in FIG. 4 of the drawings) extends rearwardly from the front column 14 just above the lower end 20 and is positioned circumferentially about the front column 14 essentially midway between the two trailing arm attachment points 24 and 26. Yoke attachment 34 has a relatively smaller diameter, rearwardly extending, internally threaded shaft 36 to which the central bushing 38 of the trailing-arm interconnecting yoke 40 is pivotally attached by its pivot passage and removably secured by a single yoke attachment fastener 42 (e.g., threaded bolt, etc.). This attachment means is similar to that used to secure trailing arms 16 and 18 to trailing-arm attachment fitting 22 of the lower portion of front column 14.

Yoke 40 comprises an upper and a lower bar, respectively 44 and 46, with the two bars being parallel to one another and spaced apart from one another by the diameter of the central bushing 38 immovably installed (e.g., welded, etc.), which serves as a central connecting link between the two yoke bars 44 and 46. The distance between two yoke bars 44 and 46 is essentially equal to the diameters of the two trailing arms 16 and 18, with the two bars 44 and 46 capturing the two trailing arms 16 and 18 closely between them when the yoke 40 is secured to its attachment point 34 of the front column 14. The left ends 44l and 46l of the two bars 44 and 46 capture the left trailing arm 16 between them, with the right ends 44r and 46r capturing the right trailing arm 18.

The operation of the yoke 40 structure is shown clearly in the rear and right side elevation views respectively of FIGS. 2 and 3. In each of those Figures, the central or neutral position of the yoke 40, and the two trailing arms 16 and

18 captured thereby, is shown in solid lines, with the extreme arcuate upward and/or downward positions of the trailing arms 16 and 18 and corresponding positions of the yoke arms 44 and 46 being shown in broken lines.

FIG. 2 provides an example in which the vehicle 10 is leaned or cambered to the right, with the right side trailing arm 18 displaced arcuately upwardly, as shown in broken lines in FIG. 2 and by the upper trailing arm position 18 of FIG. 3. When this occurs, the right ends 44r and 46r of the yoke arms 44 and 46 must follow the upward movement of the trailing arm 18 due to their direct contact therewith. As a result, the yoke 40 pivots arcuately about its central bushing link 38 and its attachment point 34 to the rear side of the front column 14, thus causing the opposite left ends 44l and 46l of the yoke arms 44 and 46 to deflect downwardly. When this occurs, the direct contact of the two left ends 44l and 46l of the yoke arms 44 and 46 about the left trailing arm 16, cause that arm 16 to be deflected arcuately downwardly.

The amount of arcuate deflection or travel of each trailing arm 16 and 18 is identical, due to their equidistant lateral offset from the yoke attachment point 34. However, due to the pivotal actuation of the yoke 40, the two arms 16 and 18 will always travel in arcuate directions opposite to one another.

The yoke interconnection of the two trailing arms 16 and 18, provides additional advantages as well. As noted above, the yoke 40 is removably secured to the front column 14 of the vehicle 10 by means of a single fastener 42 (bolt, etc.). Removal of this single fastener 42 permits the yoke 40 to be removed from its attachment point 34, thus removing the positive interconnect between the two trailing arms 16 and 18. The ease of removal of this single yoke attachment fastener 42, and removal of the yoke 40, permits the two trailing arms 16 and 18 to be rotated simultaneously to lie generally parallel, or at least somewhat adjacent, to the front column 14. Put somewhat differently, the front column 14 may be folded downwardly to lie adjacent the two trailing arms 16 and 18, to provide a compact configuration for storage as shown in broken lines in FIG. 5 of the drawings.

It will be seen that no practicable limit is provided for the arcuate movement of the two trailing arms 16, 18 and corresponding arcuate movement of the yoke 40, by the above-described structure. Accordingly, some form of stop means is preferably provided for precluding excessive arcuate movement of the two trailing arms 16 and 18, and resulting excessive camber of the vehicle 10 during operation. FIGS. 2 and 4 illustrate the trailing-arm stop means of the present vehicle 10, comprising a lateral stop 48 which is immovably affixed to the back of the front column 14 immediately below the yoke attachment point 34. The stop 48 preferably includes lateral bracing 50, with the stop 48 and bracing 50 together comprising a generally triangular configuration, as shown.

When either the left or the right trailing arm 16 or 18 contacts the corresponding side of the stop bar 48, its arcuate movement is limited to that extent, with the interconnect of the opposite trailing arm by means of the yoke 40 serving to limit the arcuately opposite movement of that opposite arm.

The wheeled embodiment of the present vehicle 10 exemplified in the drawings has a steering shaft 52 installed concentrically through the front column 14 (shown most clearly in FIG. 4 of the drawings), with the steering shaft 52 having a lower end 54 extending from the lower end 20 of the front column 14 with an extending wheel fork 56 (shown in FIGS. 1, 2, 3, and 5) for carrying a single steerable wheel 58 therein.

The steering shaft 52 has an opposite upper end 60 which extends beyond the upper end 62 of the front column 14, with the upper end 60 of the steering shaft 52 including steering means (e.g., handlebars 64, as illustrated in FIGS. 1 and 5) extending therefrom, for the operator to steer the present vehicle 10 as desired. Turning the handlebars 64 (or other steering means which may be provided) turns the steering shaft 52 within the front column 14 and turns the front wheel fork 56 with its front wheel 58 captured therein (or other surface contact means, as noted above) to steer and turn the vehicle 10 as desired.

Each trailing arm 16 and 18 has a rearward end, respectively 66 and 68, with surface contact means extending therefrom (e.g., wheels 70 and 72, as shown in FIGS. 1 and 5, but alternatively other means such as skates, skis, etc., as noted further above). As the present vehicle 10 is capable of moderate speeds on a smooth and level surface, on the order of a fast running pace, the two rear wheels 70 and 72 each include conventional brake means, with the left and right brakes being independent of one another. The left and right brakes of the rear wheels 70 and 72 are actuated by separate and independent actuating or control means, e.g., the conventional brake-actuating lever 74 illustrated in FIG. 5 of the drawings, with it being understood that an essentially identical second lever, not shown, is provided at the right hand grip of the handlebars 64 for actuating the brake of the right rear wheel 72. The two brake-actuating means operate the brakes by means of left and right brake cables, respectively 76 and 78.

Operation:

The operator O of vehicle 10 operates the vehicle by standing atop the left and right foot rests, respectively 80 and 82, located at the rearward ends 66 and 68 of the two trailing arms 16 and 18 above their respective rear wheels 70 and 72, and gripping the steering means 64.

Operator O then pushes off with one foot and simultaneously turns the vehicle 10 to the left or right as desired to establish a given angular momentum for the vehicle 10 and operator O. Leaning into the turn moves the center of gravity of the operator O and vehicle 10 to the inside of the turn. As the angular momentum must be conserved, the shifting of the center of gravity to a smaller radius results in a linear acceleration along the arcuate path of the turn, with the acceleration corresponding to the amount of the shift of the vehicle and operator center of gravity, less any frictional losses. The cambering of the vehicle 10 to lean to the inside of the turn is provided by the arcuate travel of the two trailing arms, with their arcuate motion being limited to equal and opposite motions by means of the yoke interconnection means of the present invention.

The above-described process is continued in the opposite direction, with each shift of the operator O and vehicle 10 center of gravity to the inside of the turn (in whichever direction of turn) resulting in a linear acceleration along the arcuate path of travel of the vehicle 10. On a smooth and level surface, the resulting speed can be fairly high, with speed being controlled by the independently actuated brakes of the rear wheels, which can also assist in steering the vehicle 10, and other operator action.

Alternative Embodiments:

Alternatively, the stop means may take on other forms (e.g., a flat plate welded to the back of the column 14, etc.) as desired.

The vehicle may be constructed in the same manner as the yoke mechanism described above, i.e., welded of conventional metal tubular stock, as shown in the drawing Figures. Alternatively, other construction means (e.g., stampings, carbon fiber and/or other composites, etc.) may be used for large scale production, if so desired.

Vehicle 10 is illustrated throughout the drawings as a wheeled vehicle. Alternatively, it may be equipped with virtually any conventional type of either rolling or sliding surface contact means (e.g., inline or other wheeled skates, ice skates, skis, etc.).

The conservation of angular momentum principle of operation utilized by the present vehicle 10 is not limited to rolling means (e.g., wheels, roller skates, etc.). Alternatively, it may be applied to any low friction surface contact means, allowing it to travel over a surface with minimal frictional losses.

Patent

(12) **United States Patent**
Beleski, Jr.

(10) **Patent No.:** **US 6,220,612 B1**
(45) **Date of Patent:** **Apr. 24, 2001**

(54) **CAMBERING VEHICLE AND MECHANISM**

(76) Inventor: **J. Gildo Beleski, Jr.**, Rua Joao Parolium 131, Prado Velho Cep 80220-290 Curitiba Pr (BR)

(*) Notice: Subject to any disclaimer, the term of this patent is extended or adjusted under 35 U.S.C. 154(b) by 0 days.

(21) Appl. No.: **09/434,371**

(22) Filed: **Nov. 5, 1999**

(51) Int. Cl.[7] **B62M 1/00**

(52) U.S. Cl. **280/87.041**; 280/87.05; 280/40

(58) Field of Search .... 280/87.041, 87.042, 280/87.05, 639, 40, 652, 655, 659, DIG. 6, 124.11, 124.111; 403/61, 59, 52, 53, 151

(56) **References Cited**

U.S. PATENT DOCUMENTS

1,303,127	* 5/1919	Wickman	280/87.05
1,336,100	* 4/1920	Shearer	280/87.04
1,664,858	* 4/1928	Headley	280/87.041
1,890,755	* 12/1932	Shepherd	280/87.03
2,598,046	* 5/1952	Frey	280/38
4,045,048	8/1977	Irwin .	
4,047,732	9/1977	Williams et al. .	
4,050,711	9/1977	Denzer .	
4,050,712	9/1977	Denzer et al. .	
4,050,713	9/1977	Williams .	
4,054,300	10/1977	Winchell .	
4,065,146	12/1977	Denzer .	
4,071,261	1/1978	Winchell .	
4,076,270	2/1978	Winchell .	
4,087,104	5/1978	Winchell et al. .	
4,087,106	5/1978	Winchell .	
4,087,108	5/1978	Winchell .	
4,088,338	5/1978	Winchell et al. .	
4,123,079	10/1978	Biskup .	
4,133,551	1/1979	Biskup .	
4,165,093	8/1979	Biskup .	
4,540,192	9/1985	Shelton .	
5,039,121	8/1991	Holter .	

5,785,331	7/1998	Rappaport .	
5,836,601	* 11/1998	Nelson	280/645
5,871,218	* 2/1999	Lepage et al.	280/33.992
6,059,304	* 5/2000	Kakimi	280/124.11
6,120,044	* 9/2000	Tsai	280/87.05

FOREIGN PATENT DOCUMENTS

2413377 10/1975 (DE) .

* cited by examiner

Primary Examiner—J. J. Swann
Assistant Examiner—Michael Cuff
(74) *Attorney, Agent, or Firm*—Richard C. Litman

(57) **ABSTRACT**

A cambering vehicle includes a single steerable front wheel and a pair of rear wheels at the rearward ends of trailing arms extending from the front structure. The two trailing arms are articulated to the front structure, and may move arcuately in a plane parallel to the front wheel column of the vehicle. The two trailing arms are linked together by a novel yoke mechanism, and move in opposite directions but in equal arcuate distances relative to one another. The vehicle operates using the principle of conservation of angular momentum, with the vehicle traveling a sinusoidal path and the operator leaning to the inside of the turn. This moves the center of gravity of the vehicle and operator to the inside of the turn, thus accelerating the vehicle and operator along the path of the turn to increase the velocity of the device. The yoke mechanism of the vehicle may be quickly and easily removed, thus allowing the vehicle to be folded for storage. The yoke mechanism also allows the vehicle to be provided with a simple, fixed stop mechanism for limiting the arcuate travel of the two trailing arms. The present vehicle is also equipped with brakes for the two rear wheels, with dual operator controls independently actuating each brake. While the present invention is primarily directed to a wheeled vehicle, the operating principle is applicable to use with skis, skates, and other sliding contact devices as well, with such sliding contact devices being adaptable to the present vehicle.

19 Claims, 5 Drawing Sheets

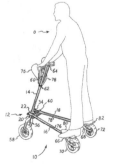

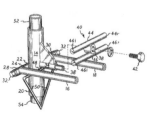

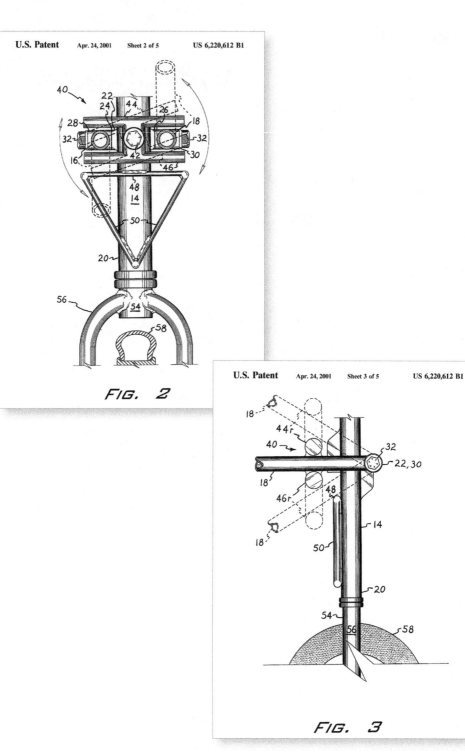

FIG. 2

FIG. 3

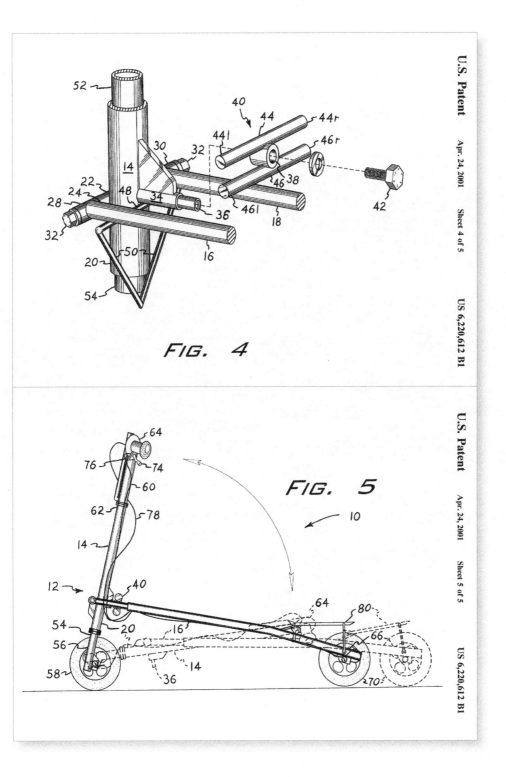

U.S. Patent　Apr. 24, 2001　Sheet 4 of 5　US 6,220,612 B1

FIG. 4

U.S. Patent　Apr. 24, 2001　Sheet 5 of 5　US 6,220,612 B1

FIG. 5

US 6,220,612 B1

1

CAMBERING VEHICLE AND MECHANISM

BACKGROUND OF THE INVENTION

1. Field of the Invention

The present invention relates generally to small, three wheeled, operator propelled vehicles, and more specifically to the class of vehicle known as "cambering vehicles," in which forward motion is provided by the alternating shifting of weight from side to side as the vehicle travels a sinusoidal path, due to the conservation of angular momentum. The present cambered vehicle includes a novel yoke linkage between the two trailing arms for the rear wheels, which links the two trailing arms together for alternating motion. The easily removable yoke also provides for ease of folding of the vehicle for storage.

2. Description of the Related Art

A type of operator propelled three wheeled vehicle known as a "cambering vehicle" has a single steerable front wheel and a pair of laterally spaced rear wheels on trailing arms which are articulated to the front column from which the front wheel extends. As the vehicle travels a sinusoidal path, the operator shifts his or her weight to the inside of each turning arc, thus shifting the center of mass to the inside of each arc. This results in a series of accelerations due to the conservation of momentum of the vehicle and operator. In this manner, forward motion is attained.

The above principle of propulsion is well known, as described in at least one of the issued patents discussed further below. Such vehicles utilize various mechanisms (cables and pulleys, gears, bellcranks, etc.) to link the two trailing arms together, with such mechanisms being cited in the related art discussed further below. However, the present cambered vehicle differs from those of the prior art in that it utilizes a novel yoke mechanism to link the motion of the two trailing arms together, with the yoke also providing for ease of folding of the present vehicle by means of the removal of a single fitting.

A discussion of the related art of which the present inventor is aware, and its differences and distinctions from the present invention, is provided below.

U.S. Pat. No. 4,045,048 issued on Aug. 30, 1977 to Clarence C. Irwin, titled "Trailing Arm Cambering Vehicle With Stabilizer Linkage Having Locking Means For Parking And Stowage," describes a cambering vehicle in which the trailing arms are linked to a bellcrank which is pivotally attached to the front column well above the attachment point of the arms to the front column. The two arms are linked to the bellcrank by pushrods. A locking plate having an arcuate slot therein with a threaded locking pin extending therethrough, permits a threaded knob to be tightened to lock the mechanism in a stationary position for upright storage of the vehicle. The folding mechanism is relatively complex in comparison to the present vehicle, in that Irwin requires both of the bellcrank connecting links to be removed.

U.S. Pat. No. 4,047,732 issued on Sep. 13, 1977 to Jerry K. Williams et al., titled "Cambering Vehicle With Hydraulic Stabilizer And Equalizer," describes a vehicle similar to that of the Irwin '048 U.S. Patent discussed immediately above, but having interconnected hydraulic cylinders linking the two trailing arms, rather than a mechanical linkage. The system functions similarly to that of the Irwin '048 U.S. Patent, with the extension of one cylinder causing the retraction of the opposite cylinder. A valve is used to shut off the flow of hydraulic fluid between the two struts to lock the position of the vehicle as desired. The valve may also be

2

adjusted to allow fluid to flow from one end to the other of the two cylinders, thereby allowing both cylinders to collapse simultaneously for folding the vehicle. The present vehicle avoids fluids and hydraulics, utilizing a yoke member for connecting the two trailing arms, and moreover does not require any form of intermediate links between the trailing arms and the yoke.

U.S. Pat. No. 4,050,711 issued on Sep. 27, 1977 to Richard E. Denzer, titled "Cambering Device For Cambering Vehicle," describes a trailing arm interconnect mechanism having two opposed arms disposed about a single pivot. The arms may be locked together to form a bellcrank to provide opposite action of the two trailing arms, or may be folded to allow the front column to be folded to the trailing arms for storage of the device. As in the other cambering vehicles discussed above, the Denzer vehicle links the trailing arms to the actuating mechanism by connecting rods, rather than using a direct yoke mechanism as in the present vehicle.

U.S. Pat. No. 4,050,712 issued on Sep. 27, 1977 to Richard E. Denzer et al., titled "Cambering Device For Cambering Vehicle," describes a mechanism very similar to that of the '711 U.S. Patent to the same first inventor, discussed immediately above. The device of the '712 Patent differs in that the central mechanism comprises a pair of meshed sector gears which may be locked together to provide the alternating action of the two trailing arms and their links to the mechanism. Unlocking the gears allows the forward structure to be folded adjacent to the two trailing arms. The device differs from the present cambering vehicle mechanism, with its single yoke configuration.

U.S. Pat. No. 4,050,713 issued on Sep. 27, 1977 to Jerry K. Williams, titled "Cambering Device For Cambering Vehicle," describes a mechanism similar to that of the '048 U.S. Patent to Irwin, discussed further above. The device of the '713 Patent comprises a pair of arcuate bellcranks which may be locked together to provide the opposite lifting and descending action of the two trailing arms, with the locking means allowing the two bellcranks to be arcuately folded together for folding the forward structure adjacent the trailing arms for storage.

U.S. Pat. No. 4,054,300 issued on Oct. 18, 1977 to Frank J. Winchell, titled "Cambering Vehicle With Trailing Arms Interconnected By Geared Stabilizer And Equalizer Mechanism," describes a mechanism comprising a pair of opposed sector bevel gears disposed upon each pivot shaft of the trailing arms, with a central spur gear linking the two sector gears to provide equal and opposite arcuate movement of the trailing arms. The mechanism includes locking means for parking the vehicle, and means for releasing the gears to allow for folding the front structure adjacent the trailing arms. No yoke mechanism is provided. The Winchell vehicle differs further in that it includes an engine driving the front wheel, which teaches away from the conservation of angular momentum principle of operation of unpowered cambering vehicles, including the present vehicle.

U.S. Pat. No. 4,065,146 issued on Dec. 27, 1977 to Richard E. Denzer, titled "Cambering Device For Cambering Vehicle," describes a mechanism similar to that described in the '713 U.S. Patent discussed further above. A pair of bellcranks works between opposite links to the two trailing arms, to cause the trailing arms to work opposite one another, as is known in the cambering vehicle art. The two bellcranks may be adjusted relative to one another to allow the vehicle to fold, in the manner generally described in the '713 U.S. Patent. As in the case of the '713 U.S. Patent and others known to the present inventor, no yoke means is disclosed.

US 6,220,612 B1

3

U.S. Pat. No. 4,071,261 issued on Jan. 31, 1978 to Frank J. Winchell, titled "Lock Bar For Cambering Vehicle," describes a mechanism quite similar to that described in the '711 U.S. Patent discussed further above, but including a lock bar which may be installed between the two trailing arms to secure them together for parking the vehicle. Again, no yoke mechanism is provided for tying together the motion of the two trailing arms, as provided by the present cambering vehicle mechanism.

U.S. Pat. No. 4,076,270 issued on Feb. 28, 1978 to Frank J. Winchell, titled "Foldable Cambering Vehicle," describes a trailing arm interconnect mechanism comprising a continuous cable run, with an idler pulley serving to reverse the direction of travel of the cable about the opposite trailing arm pulleys. The Winchell '270 U.S. Patent also discloses a bellcrank trailing arm interconnect system similar to that described in the '711 U.S. Patent discussed further above, and further discloses an engine powered embodiment similar to that of the '300 U.S. Patent to the same inventor, discussed further above. Again, no yoke mechanism is provided for linking the two trailing arms, as provided in the present cambering vehicle invention.

U.S. Pat. No. 4,087,104 issued on May 2, 1978 to Frank J. Winchell et al., titled "Method Of Manually Propelling A Cambering Vehicle," describes a pulley system for interconnecting the two trailing arms, essentially the same as that described in the '270 U.S. Patent discussed immediately above. The '104 U.S. Patent also describes the principle of conservation of angular momentum for the operation of cambered vehicles, and includes a skate equipped embodiment.

U.S. Pat. No. 4,087,106 issued on May 2, 1978 to Frank J. Winchell, titled "Cambering Vehicle," describes various embodiments incorporating the cable actuation, motor power, and skate and ski equipped embodiments generally disclosed in the '270 and '104 U.S. Patents to the same inventor, and discussed above. Although a throttle control lever is provided, no brake means is disclosed.

U.S. Pat. No. 4,087,108 issued on May 2, 1978 to Frank J. Winchell, titled "Cambering Vehicle With Trailing Arms Interconnected By Spur Gearing," describes a mechanism in which the two pivot axles of the trailing arms are non-concentric with one another, and are interconnected by mating gears. A motorized embodiment is also disclosed, similar to that of the '300, '270, and '106 U.S. Patents to the same inventor, discussed above. As in those patents and others with which the present inventor is familiar, no yoke mechanism for interconnecting the two trailing arms, is disclosed in the '108 U.S. Patent, and while a declutching lever is provided, no brake control lever is disclosed.

U.S. Pat. No. 4,088,338 issued on May 9, 1978 to Frank J. Winchell et al., titled "Cambering Vehicle With Cable Stabilizer And Equalizer," describes a vehicle utilizing a pulley system for linking the two trailing arms, similar to the mechanisms disclosed in the '270 and '104 U.S. Patents to the same first inventor, discussed further above. The same distinctions noted between those devices and the present invention are seen to apply here.

U.S. Pat. No. 4,123,079 issued on Oct. 31, 1978 to Edward J. Biskup, titled "Occupant Propelled Cambering Vehicle," describes one embodiment wherein the two trailing arms are resiliently interconnected by means of a torsion bar between the two trailing arm pivot axles, and another embodiment wherein the trailing arms are resilient. In both cases the resilient means allows the arms to move independently of one another, unlike the yoke interconnect and rigid trailing arms of the present invention.

4

U.S. Pat. No. 4,133,551 issued on Jan. 9, 1979 to Edward J. Biskup, titled "Cambering Device For Cambering Vehicle," describes a trailing arm interconnect mechanism comprising a crank arm having oppositely offset cranks which ride in slots in the opposite trailing arms. As one crank arm travels in one direction, the opposite crank arm travels in the opposite direction, thereby causing the two trailing arms to work opposite to one another. Again, no yoke mechanism is provided.

U.S. Pat. No. 4,165,093 issued on Aug. 21, 1979 to Edward J. Biskup, titled "Occupant Propelled Cambering Vehicle," describes resilient interconnect means for the two trailing arms, essentially the same as the interconnect means disclosed in the '079 U.S. Patent. The '093 Patent is a division of the '079 U.S. Patent discussed further above, and the same points raised in that discussion are seen to apply here as well.

U.S. Pat. No. 4,540,192 issued on Sep. 10, 1985 to L. H. Shelton, titled "Three-Wheeled Scooter-Type Vehicle," describes a different principle of operation for such tricycle type vehicles, in which the two rear wheels remain in the same plane, but caster inwardly and outwardly with the two trailing arms also moving laterally inwardly and outwardly relative to one another. The operation is similar to skating or cross country skiing, in which the skate or ski is angled relative to the path of travel, with lateral thrust developing a forward thrust vector to propel the skier, skater, or (in the present case) vehicle forward. This principle of operation does not apply to the present vehicle.

U.S. Pat. No. 5,039,121 issued on Aug. 13, 1991 to Donovan A. Holter, titled "Tri-Skater," describes a tricycle type vehicle in which the two trailing arms are immovably affixed to the front structure during operation. A single brake is provided on the front wheel, rather than independent brakes for the two rear wheels. The principle of operation is thus more closely related to the vehicle of the '192 U.S. Patent, discussed immediately above, than to the present vehicle invention.

U.S. Pat. No. 5,785,331 issued on Jul. 28, 1998 to Mark Rappaport, titled "Dual-Footboard Scooter," describes a tricycle type vehicle having a rigid frame, with the two rear wheels having fixed axles with no camber, caster, toe-in, or toe-out. The device is operated as a conventional scooter by pushing and coasting. A single brake is provided for the front wheel, whereas the present vehicle includes independent brakes for each rear wheel.

Finally, German Patent Publication No. 2,413,377 published on Oct. 2, 1975 illustrates a scooter and vertically undulating track, with the operator shifting his/her weight forwardly and rearwardly to shift the center of gravity of the vehicle over the crest of an undulation and thereby coast down the opposite side, the device of the German Patent Publication is constructed in the reverse of the present invention, with two forward wheels and one rearward wheel, and the frame is rigid, thus precluding any cambering action or operation by conservation of angular momentum.

None of the above inventions and patents, either singly or in combination, is seen to describe the instant invention as claimed.

SUMMARY OF THE INVENTION

The present invention comprises a cambering vehicle, wherein forward motion is achieved by lateral shift of the operator's weight to the inside of the turn as the vehicle travels a sinusoidal path. Due to the principle of conservation of angular momentum, the weight shift is partially

US 6,220,612 B1

5

translated to forward motion in the direction of travel. The above principle is well known, with numerous cambering vehicles utilizing various mechanisms to link the two trailing arms of the vehicle together to provide the desired action. However, the present vehicle utilizes a novel yoke mechanism for linking the two trailing arms together, with the present yoke mechanism providing an advance in simplicity, durability, and ease of folding for storage over the relatively complex linkages and mechanisms of the prior art.

The yoke mechanism of the present cambering vehicle provides several advantages in a single mechanism, by (1) linking the two trailing arms to articulate equally and oppositely to one another, (2) providing for folding of the vehicle for storage by the removal of a single fastener, and (3) enabling the vehicle to be provided with a simple, fixed stop means to limit the travel of the two trailing arms. The present cambering vehicle also has a separate brake for each rear wheel, with each brake being independently actuated by separate levers by the vehicle operator. While the present cambering vehicle is primarily supported by wheels, it will be seen that the principle of operation need not be limited to rollers or wheels, but may be applied to skis, skates, etc. as well.

Accordingly, it is a principal object of the invention to provide an improved cambering vehicle incorporating a yoke for interconnecting the two trailing arms to provide equal and opposite articulation thereof.

It is another object of the invention to provide an improved cambering vehicle which yoke mechanism is quickly and easily removable to provide for the folding of the vehicle for storage.

It is a further object of the invention to provide an improved cambering vehicle including stop means for limiting the arcuate travel of the two trailing arms.

An additional object of the invention is to provide an improved cambering vehicle including independent brakes for the rear wheels, with the two brakes being actuated by separate controls to provide at least some steering or turning guidance for the vehicle.

Still another object of the invention is to provide an improved cambering vehicle incorporating wheels, but which operating principle may be applied to skis, skates, and other sliding surface contact means.

It is an object of the invention to provide improved elements and arrangements thereof in an apparatus for the purposes described which is inexpensive, dependable and fully effective in accomplishing its intended purposes.

These and other objects of the present invention will become readily apparent upon further review of the following specification and drawings.

BRIEF DESCRIPTION OF THE DRAWINGS

FIG. 1 is an environmental perspective view illustrating the present cambering vehicle in operation, and showing its general features.

FIG. 2 is a detailed elevation view of the rear side of the front strut of the present cambering vehicle, showing details of the yoke mechanism interconnecting the two trailing arms and the operation thereof.

FIG. 3 is a detailed right side elevation view of the yoke mechanism of FIG. 2, showing further details of the operation thereof.

FIG. 4 is a detailed exploded perspective view of the yoke mechanism of FIGS. 2 and 3, illustrating the removal of the yoke from the front structure for folding the vehicle for storage.

6

FIG. 5 is a left side elevation view of the present cambering vehicle, illustrating the folded position of the vehicle in broken lines.

Similar reference characters denote corresponding features consistently throughout the attached drawings.

DETAILED DESCRIPTION OF THE PREFERRED EMBODIMENTS

The present invention comprises an operator powered cambering vehicle, in which the vehicle is propelled forwardly by means of the principle of conservation of angular momentum as the center of gravity of the operator and vehicle are repeatedly shifted to the inside of the turn as the vehicle travels a sinusoidal path. The present vehicle utilizes a novel means of linking the articulated portions of the structure together, in order that the trailing arms of the structure subtend equal but opposite arcs during operation.

FIG. 1 provides an environmental perspective view of the present cambering vehicle 10 in operation. The present vehicle 10 essentially comprises a tricycle frame 12 having a front column 14 and left and right trailing arms, respectively 16 and 18. The trailing arms 16 and 18 are pivotally attached to the front column 14, immediately above its lower end 20. Details of the attachment of the trailing arms 16 and 18 to the front column 14 are shown more clearly in FIGS. 2 through 4 of the drawings.

A trailing arm attachment fitting 22 is permanently secured across the front column 14 just above the lower end 20 thereof, with the attachment fitting 22 providing laterally opposed trailing arm attachment points, respectively 24 and 26, to the front column 14. The forward ends of the two trailing arms 16 and 18 have lateral bushings, respectively 28 and 30, thereacross, with a bolt 32 or other suitable fastener secured through each trailing arm bushing 28 and 30 to secure the trailing arms 16 and 18 pivotally to the fitting 22 of the lower end 20 of the front column 14.

A yoke attachment point 34 (shown more clearly in FIG. 4 of the drawings) extends rearwardly from the front column 14 just above the lower end 20 thereof, and is positioned circumferentially about the front column 14 essentially midway between the two laterally disposed trailing arm attachment points 24 and 26. The yoke attachment 34 has a relatively smaller diameter, rearwardly extending, internally threaded shaft 36 extending therefrom, to which the central bushing 38 of the trailing arm interconnecting yoke 40 is pivotally attached by its pivot passage and removably secured by a single yoke attachment fastener 42 (e.g., threaded bolt, etc.). This attachment means is similar to that used to secure the two trailing arms 16 and 18 to the trailing arm attachment fitting 22 of the lower portion of the front column 14.

The yoke 40 comprises an upper and a lower bar, respectively 44 and 46, with the two bars being parallel to one another and spaced apart from one another by the diameter of the central bushing 38 immovably installed (e.g., welded, etc.) therebetween, which serves as a central connecting link between the two yoke bars 44 and 46. The distance between the two yoke bars 44 and 46 is essentially equal to the diameters of the two trailing arms 16 and 18, with the two bars 44 and 46 capturing the two trailing arms 16 and 18 closely therebetween when the yoke 40 is secured to its attachment point 34 of the front column 14. The left ends 441 and 461 of the two bars 44 and 46 capture the left trailing arm 16 therebetween, with the right ends 44r and 46r capturing the right trailing arm 18 therebetween.

The operation of the yoke 40 structure is shown clearly in the rear and right side elevation views respectively of FIGS.

US 6,220,612 B1

7

2 and 3. In each of those Figures, the central or neutral position of the yoke **40**, and the two trailing arms **16** and **18** captured thereby, is shown in solid lines, with the extreme arcuate upward and/or downward positions of the trailing arms **16** and **18** and corresponding positions of the yoke arms **44** and **46** being shown in broken lines.

FIG. 2 provides an example in which the vehicle **10** is leaned or cambered to the right, with the right side trailing arm **18** displaced arcuately upwardly, as shown in broken lines in FIG. 2 and by the upper trailing arm position **18** of FIG. 3. When this occurs, the right ends **44r** and **46r** of the yoke arms **44** and **46** must follow the upward movement of the trailing arm **18** due to their direct contact therewith. As a result, the yoke **40** pivots arcuately about its central bushing link **38** and its attachment point **34** to the rear side of the front column **14**, thus causing the opposite left ends **44l** and **46l** of the yoke arms **44** and **46** to deflect downwardly. When this occurs, the direct contact of the two left ends **44l** and **46l** of the yoke arms **44** and **46** about the left trailing arm **16**, cause that arm **16** to be deflected arcuately downwardly.

The amount of arcuate deflection or travel of each trailing arm **16** and **18** is identical, due to their equidistant lateral offset from the yoke attachment point **34**. However, due to the pivotal actuation of the yoke **40**, the two arms **16** and **18** will always travel in arcuate directions opposite to one another.

The yoke interconnection of the two trailing arms **16** and **18**, provides additional advantages as well. As noted above, the yoke **40** is removably secured to the front column **14** of the vehicle **10** by means of a single fastener **42** (bolt, etc.). Removal of this single fastener **42** permits the yoke **40** to be removed from its attachment point **34**, thus removing the positive interconnect between the two trailing arms **16** and **18**. The ease of removal of this single yoke attachment fastener **42**, and removal of the yoke **40**, permits the two trailing arms **16** and **18** to be rotated simultaneously to lie generally parallel, or at least somewhat adjacent, to the front column **14**. Put somewhat differently, the front column **14** may be folded downwardly to lie adjacent the two trailing arms **16** and **18**, to provide a compact configuration for storage as shown in broken lines in FIG. 5 of the drawings.

It will be seen that no practicable limit is provided for the arcuate movement of the two trailing arms **16**, **18** and corresponding arcuate movement of the yoke **40**, by the above described structure. Accordingly, some form of stop means is preferably provided for precluding excessive arcuate movement of the two trailing arms **16** and **18**, and resulting excessive camber of the vehicle **10** during operation. FIGS. 2 and 4 illustrate the trailing arm stop means of the present vehicle **10**, comprising a lateral stop **48** which is immovably affixed to the back of the front column **14** immediately below the yoke attachment point **34**. The stop **48** preferably includes lateral bracing **50**, with the stop **48** and bracing **50** together comprising a generally triangular configuration, as shown.

When either the left or the right trailing arm **16** or **18** contacts the corresponding side of the stop bar **48**, its arcuate movement is limited to that extent, with the interconnect of the opposite trailing arm by means of the yoke **40** serving to limit the arcuately opposite movement of that opposite arm. It will be seen that the stop means may take on other forms (e.g., a flat plate welded to the back of the column **14**, etc.) as desired.

The cambering vehicle **10** of the present invention is illustrated throughout the drawings as a wheeled vehicle,

8

although it will be seen that the vehicle **10** may be equipped with virtually any conventional type of either rolling or sliding surface contact means (e.g., in-line or other wheeled skates, ice skates, skis, etc.), as described in U.S. Pat. No. 4,087,106 to Winchell et al., discussed in the Description of the Related Art further above. The conservation of angular momentum principle of operation utilized by the present vehicle **10** is not limited to rolling means (e.g., wheels, roller skates, etc.), but may be applied to any low friction surface contact means allowing the vehicle **10** to travel over a surface with minimal frictional losses.

The wheeled embodiment of the present vehicle **10** exemplified in the drawings has a steering shaft **52** installed concentrically through the front column **14** (shown most clearly in FIG. 4 of the drawings), with the steering shaft **52** having a lower end **54** extending from the lower end **20** of the front column **14** with a wheel fork **56** (shown in FIGS. 1, 2, 3, and 5) extending therefrom for carrying a single steerable wheel **58** therein.

The steering shaft **52** has an opposite upper end **60** which extends beyond the upper end **62** of the front column **14**, with the upper end **60** of the steering shaft **52** including steering means (e.g., handlebars **64**, as illustrated in FIGS. 1 and 5)) extending therefrom, for the operator to steer the present vehicle **10** as desired. Turning the handlebars **64** (or other steering means which may be provided) turns the steering shaft **52** within the front column **14** and turns the front wheel fork **56** with its front wheel **58** captured therein (or other surface contact means, as noted above) to steer and turn the vehicle **10** as desired.

Each trailing arm **16** and **18** has a rearward end, respectively **66** and **68**, with surface contact means extending therefrom (e.g., wheels **70** and **72**, as shown in FIGS. 1 and 5, but alternatively other means such as skates, skis, etc., as noted further above). As the present vehicle **10** is capable of moderate speeds on a smooth and level surface, on the order of a fast running pace, the two rear wheels **70** and **72** each include conventional brake means, with the left and right brakes being independent of one another. The left and right brakes of the rear wheels **70** and **72** are actuated by separate and independent actuating or control means, e.g., the conventional brake actuating lever **74** illustrated in FIG. 5 of the drawings, with it being understood that an essentially identical second lever, not shown, is provided at the right hand grip of the handlebars **64** for actuating the brake of the right rear wheel **72**. The two brake actuating means operate the brakes by means of left and right brake cables, respectively **76** and **78**.

The operator O of the present vehicle **10** operates the vehicle by standing atop the left and right foot rests, respectively **80** and **82**, located at the rearward ends **66** and **68** of the two trailing arms **16** and **18** above their respective rear wheels **70** and **72**, and gripping the steering means **64**. The operator O then pushes off with one foot and simultaneously turns the vehicle **10** to the left or right as desired to establish a given angular momentum for the vehicle **10** and operator O. Leaning into the turn moves the center of gravity of the operator O and vehicle **10** to the inside of the turn. As the angular momentum must be conserved, the shifting of the center of gravity to a smaller radius results in a linear acceleration along the arcuate path of the turn, with the acceleration corresponding to the amount of the shift of the vehicle and operator center of gravity, less any frictional losses. The cambering of the vehicle **10** to lean to the inside of the turn is provided by the arcuate travel of the two trailing arms, with their arcuate motion being limited to equal and opposite motions by means of the yoke interconnection means of the present invention.

US 6,220,612 B1

9

The above described process is continued in the opposite direction, with each shift of the operator O and vehicle **10** center of gravity to the inside of the turn (in whichever direction of turn) resulting in a linear acceleration along the arcuate path of travel of the vehicle **10**. On a smooth and level surface, the resulting speed can be fairly high, with speed being controlled by the independently actuated brakes of the rear wheels, which can also assist in steering the vehicle **10**, and other operator action.

In summary, the present cambering vehicle and its novel yoke mechanism for controlling opposite arcuate motion of the two trailing arms, provides a more efficient and cleaner means of providing for the control of such motion as required in such vehicles. The unitary, monolithic construction of the yoke mechanism of conventional weldments, results in a simple, inexpensive, and easily constructed unit, with no other parts or components being required to affect the required action of the trailing arms. Another advantage to the present mechanism is its attachment and ease of removal by means of a single pivot bolt, which enables the vehicle to be folded to an essentially flat configuration for storage. The yoke may be reinstalled upon its attachment point to the rear of the forward column to preclude its loss during storage, after being removed from the trailing arms.

The present vehicle may be constructed in the same manner as the yoke mechanism described above, i.e., welded up of conventional metal tubular stock, as shown in the drawing Figures. Other construction means (e.g., stampings, carbon fiber and/or other composites, etc.) may be used for large scale production, if so desired. The present cambering vehicle and its yoke mechanism provide a much needed improvement in efficiency of construction for such devices, with its operation providing excellent exercise, as well as transportation, for the operator.

It is to be understood that the present invention is not limited to the sole embodiment described above, but encompasses any and all embodiments within the scope of the following claims.

I claim:

1. A cambering vehicle, comprising:

a frame comprising a front column and a left and a right trailing arm;

said front column having an upper end and a lower end opposite said upper end;

each said trailing arm having a forward end and a rearward end opposite said forward end;

a left and a right trailing arm attachment point disposed opposite one another upon said front column, and immediately above said lower end thereof;

said forward end of said left and said right trailing arm being pivotally attached respectively to said left and said right trailing arm attachment point of said front column;

a yoke attachment point disposed circumferentially rearwardly substantially midway between said left and said right trailing arm attachment point of said front column;

a yoke pivotally secured to said yoke attachment point of said front column;

said yoke directly contacting and pivotally linking said left and said right trailing arm together such that said left and said right trailing arm each subtend arcs equal to one another and in directions opposite to one another when arcuately pivoted respectively about said left and said right trailing arm attachment point of said front column;

10

surface contact means extending from said rearward end of each said trailing arm;

a steering shaft having an upper end and a lower end opposite said upper end, and concentrically disposed within said front column; and

a single surface contact means extending from said lower end and steering means extending from said upper end of said steering shaft.

2. The cambering vehicle according to claim **1**, wherein said yoke comprises an upper and a lower bar connected by a central link, with each said bar being parallel to one another and capturing said left and said right trailing arm therebetween adjacent to each said forward end thereof, with said central link including a pivot passage centrally disposed therethrough for pivotally securing said yoke to said yoke attachment point of said front column.

3. The cambering vehicle according to claim **1**, including a single removable fastener for removably securing said yoke to said yoke attachment point of said front column and folding said front column adjacent said left and said right trailing arm when said yoke is removed.

4. The cambering vehicle according to claim **1**, wherein at least said surface contact means of each said trailing arm comprises a wheel, with each said wheel including a brake and each said brake being controlled independently from one another by a separate brake control disposed upon said steering means and communicating with each said brake.

5. The cambering vehicle according to claim **1**, including trailing arm stop means disposed upon said front column, for limiting arcuate movement of each said trailing arm.

6. The cambering vehicle according to claim **1**, wherein said steering means comprises handlebars.

7. The cambering vehicle according to claim **1**, wherein said surface contact means of each said trailing arm and said steering shaft is selected from the group consisting of wheels, wheeled skates, ice skates, and skis.

8. A cambering vehicle, comprising:

a frame comprising a front column and a left and a right trailing arm;

said front column having an upper end and a lower end opposite said upper end;

each said trailing arm having a forward end and a rearward end opposite said forward end;

a left and a right trailing arm attachment point disposed opposite one another upon said front column, and immediately above said lower end thereof;

said forward end of said left and said right trailing arm being pivotally attached respectively to said left and said right trailing arm attachment point of said front column;

means for interconnecting said left and said right trailing arm together such that said left and said right trailing arm each subtend arcs equal to one another and in directions opposite to one another when arcuately pivoted respectively about said left and said right trailing arm attachment point of said front column;

a single wheel extending from said rearward end of each said trailing arm;

a steering shaft having an upper end and a lower end opposite said upper end, and concentrically disposed within said front column;

a single wheel extending from said lower end and steering means extending from said upper end of said steering shaft;

brake means disposed with said wheel of each said trailing arm; and

US 6,220,612 B1

11

separate and independent brake control means for each said brake means disposed upon said steering means and communicating with said brake means for separate and independent control thereof.

9. The cambering vehicle according to claim 8, wherein said means for interconnecting said left and said right trailing arm together comprises:

a yoke attachment point disposed circumferentially rearwardly substantially midway between said left and said right trailing arm attachment point of said front column; and

a yoke pivotally secured to said yoke attachment point of said front column, and directly communicating with and pivotally linking said left and said right trailing arm together.

10. The cambering vehicle according to claim 9, wherein said yoke comprises an upper and a lower bar connected by a central link;

each said bar being parallel to one another and capturing said left and said right trailing arm therebetween adjacent to each said forward end thereof; and

said central link including a pivot passage centrally disposed therethrough for pivotally securing said yoke to said yoke attachment point of said front column.

11. The cambering vehicle according to claim 9, including a single removable fastener for removably securing said yoke to said yoke attachment point of said front column and folding said front column adjacent said left and said right trailing arm when said yoke is removed.

12. The cambering vehicle according to claim 8, including trailing arm stop means disposed upon said front column, for limiting arcuate movement of each said trailing arm.

13. The cambering vehicle according to claim 8, wherein said steering means comprises handlebars.

14. A cambering vehicle, comprising:

a frame comprising a front column and a left and a right trailing arm;

said front column having an upper end and a lower end opposite said upper end;

each said trailing arm having a forward end and a rearward end opposite said forward end;

a left and a right trailing arm attachment point disposed opposite one another upon said front column, and immediately above said lower end thereof;

said forward end of said left and said right trailing arm being pivotally attached respectively to said left and said right trailing arm attachment point of said front column;

a yoke attachment point disposed circumferentially rearwardly substantially midway between said left and said right trailing arm attachment point of said front column;

12

a yoke pivotally secured to said yoke attachment point of said front column;

said yoke directly contacting and pivotally linking said left and said right trailing arm together such that said left and said right trailing arm each subtend arcs equal to one another and in directions opposite to one another when arcuately pivoted respectively about said left and said right trailing arm attachment point of said front column;

a single removable fastener for removably securing said yoke to said yoke attachment point of said front column and folding said front column adjacent said left and said right trailing arm when said yoke is removed;

surface contact means extending from said rearward end of each said trailing arm;

a steering shaft having an upper end and a lower end opposite said upper end, and concentrically disposed within said front column; and

a single surface contact means extending from said lower end and steering means extending from said upper end of said steering shaft.

15. The cambering vehicle according to claim 14, wherein said yoke comprises an upper and a lower bar connected by a central link, with each said bar being parallel to one another and capturing said left and said right trailing arm therebetween adjacent to each said forward end thereof, with said central link including a pivot passage centrally disposed therethrough for pivotally securing said yoke to said yoke attachment point of said front column.

16. The cambering vehicle according to claim 14, wherein at least said surface contact means of each said trailing arm comprises a wheel, with each said wheel including a brake and each said brake being controlled independently from one another by a separate brake control disposed upon said steering means and communicating with each said brake.

17. The cambering vehicle according to claim 14, including trailing arm stop means disposed upon said front column, for limiting arcuate movement of each said trailing arm.

18. The cambering vehicle according to claim 14, wherein said steering means comprises handlebars.

19. The cambering vehicle according to claim 14, wherein said surface contact means of each said trailing arm and said steering shaft are selected from the group consisting of wheels, wheeled skates, ice skates, and skis.

* * * * *

Musical Condom

Many people have merged music and romance, but Paul Lyons's musical condom combines them in a truly new and nonobvious way. This may not be your typical subject for a patent—after all, how many inventors cite a *Frederick's of Hollywood* catalog as prior art?—but it's a unique contrivance.

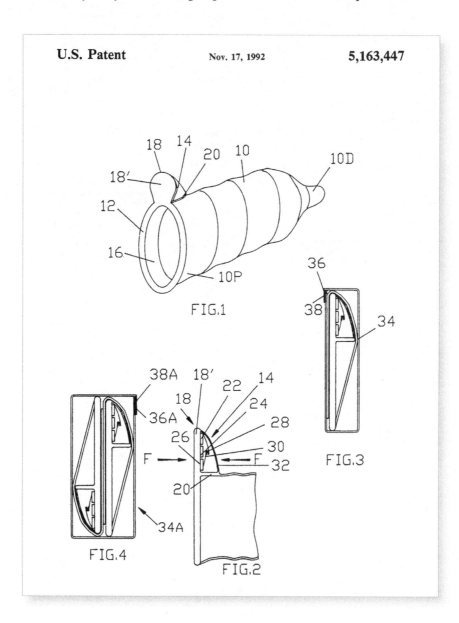

U.S. Patent   Nov. 17, 1992   **5,163,447**

FIG.1

FIG.2

FIG.3

FIG.4

Provisional Patent Application

Force-Sensitive, Sound-Playing Condom

I have invented a condom that provides entertainment and has an amusement feature.

My invention consists of a condom 10 and a miniature force-sensitive sound-playing unit 14 that's attached to the condom at its base (or proximal end) 10P. The proximal end of the condom has a semi-rigid rim 12 with a lower part with an opening 16, and an upper part that extends upward from the body of the condom and supports the sound-playing unit. The sound-playing unit contains a chip-controlled piezoelectric sound transducer which plays a melody or voiced message when—during intercourse—the contacts 28 and 30 of the sound-playing unit 14 are closed and the transducer is activated. I've provided a more detailed description, below.

Many contraceptive devices such as condoms exist but they are all designed as methods of birth control and disease prevention. Many persons who engage in coitus dislike using them because they reduce sensitivity, interrupt coitus and are bothersome to put on.

I wanted to provide a condom that:
- users will like to use
- provides amusement
- won't interfere with coitus
- has value as a fun gift
- can incorporate musical compositions of the user's choice according to the occasion, and
- has a commercial value by being amusing, entertaining, unusual and capable of producing a surprise effect.

There are other advantages to my invention and they will become apparent from my descriptions and drawings.

I've provided four drawings.
- FIG. 1 is a perspective view of my invention.
- FIG. 2 is a side view illustrating how the mechanism connects to the rim of the condom.
- FIG. 3 is a sectional view of the condom in its package.
- FIG. 4 is a sectional view of a similar package, containing two condoms.

In order to use the condom, the user opens the package 34 by unsealing flap 36 and removing wrapped condom 10. He then unwraps or unfolds the lubricated condom and slides it onto his erect penis.

During intercourse, the contact between the genital areas of the couple will create forces F sufficient to engage contacts 28 and 30, completing the circuit. Power will pass from power source 26 to chip 24, and thus cause the transducer 22 to produce sounds, for example, music, or a voiced message. This message or music may warn, compliment, stimulate, entertain or surprise the couple. The multivibrator in chip 24 ensures the continuation of music for a predetermined period of time, so that the melody will play once or repeatedly during intercourse. The upper extension 18 will not interfere with coitus.

You will see that the rim 12 and extension 18 have a figure-eight shape when seen from the closest end. The rim is made of rubber that may be reinforced internally by a stronger plastic core.

As for the music playing unit, it consists of:

- a miniature piezoelectric sound transducer 22
- a microchip 24 which controls the operation of the transducer
- a power-supplying dry-cell battery 26, and
- a switch comprising electrical contacts 28 and 30, which, when closed, complete an appropriate circuit (not shown) from battery 26 to microchip 24.

The energized microchip 24 causes the transducer 22 to emit a predetermined melody, or a voice message such as a health warning (in case transducer 22 is a speaker). The circuit of the musical unit also incorporates a multivibrator that controls an electronic bypass switch for contacts 28. This ensures that current will be supplied to chip 24 for a predetermined period of time (for example, 10 seconds), so that the music continues to play even if contacts 28 are opened. This will cause the music or voice to play even if contact is intermittent, until the next contact takes place.

The music or voice message may be played once (e.g., an overture or melody may be played for about 20 seconds), or it may be repeated continuously for several minutes to coincide with the duration of coitus. A voiced message may be a warning about safe sex, or a compliment to the couple for using a condom. Suitable melodies (if music is played) may be *"The 1812 Overture," "The Ode to*

Joy" from Beethoven's *Ninth Symphony*, the song "*Happy Birthday To You*," "*The Anniversary Waltz*," or any popular love song.

A typical sound-producing unit 14 suitable for the purposes of the invention may have overall dimensions within the range of 7 to 20 mm.

The condom is shown in packaged form in FIG. 3. Unlike conventional condoms, my invention cannot be simply rolled, because its switch is highly sensitive to pressure so the body of the condom is completely wrapped around musical unit 14 and rim 12, and sealed inside a package 34. Alternatively, the body of condom 10 may be folded against rim 12. The product is packed in a rigid boxlike container 34. Container 34 has an upper foldable flap 36, the free end of which is sealed, for example with a layer of a sealant 38, to ensure the condom remains sterile.

I've described my invention in one way but many other modifications of sound-playing condoms are possible. For example:

- The rim 12 and the extension 18 may have a shape other than a figure-eight and all components of musical unit 14 may be embedded entirely in resilient plastic, leaving only space between contacts 28 and 30. That way, all of the contacts, except the exposed contacting portions are embedded and maintained in an open state.
- The musical units themselves may have different forms, dimensions and configurations. There may be a range of musical or other sound selections that may be chosen or combined by the user.
- The rim and base may be reinforced by a wire.
- Various parts of the musical circuit may be placed around the side of the rim, i.e., piezoelectric sound transducers may be displaced laterally on one side, while the chip may be arranged on the other side.
- The package itself may take different forms and show a variety of messages.
- Instead of a disposable condom, the musical unit may be made in such a way that it can be detached and readily disconnected or connected onto other condoms by means such as adhesive tapes. In that case the package might contain, for example, ten condoms and a single musical unit.
- A speaker can be used instead of a piezoelectric transducer.
- The condom will operate in homosexual as well as heterosexual intercourse.
- In lieu of mechanical contacts 28 and 30, a strain-gauge-type activator or any other type of activator may be employed.

Patent

US005163447A

United States Patent [19]

Lyons

[11] **Patent Number:** **5,163,447**

[45] **Date of Patent:** **Nov. 17, 1992**

[54] **FORCE-SENSITIVE, SOUND-PLAYING CONDOM**

[76] Inventor: **Paul Lyons**, 295 Elm St., Southbridge, Mass. 01550-3009

[21] Appl. No.: **728,607**

[22] Filed: **Jul. 11, 1991**

[51] **Int. Cl.⁵** A61F 6/04
[52] **U.S. Cl.** **128/844**; 128/883;
446/220
[58] **Field of Search** 128/842, 844, 885, 886,
128/883, 884; 604/347–353; 446/220–226, 404

[56] **References Cited**

U.S. PATENT DOCUMENTS

494,436 3/1893 Orth 128/883
745,264 11/1903 Todd .... 128/886 X

FOREIGN PATENT DOCUMENTS

680088 10/1952 United Kingdom 128/886
2036560 7/1980 United Kingdom

OTHER PUBLICATIONS

Frederick's of Hollywood, catalog, vol. 70, Issue 356, Version 0600, ©1990, p. 68: "Wedding Surprise"

Primary Examiner—Robert A. Hafer
Assistant Examiner—David J. Kenealy
Attorney, Agent, or Firm—David Pressman

[57] **ABSTRACT**

A force-sensitive sound-playing condom comprising: a condom body (**10**) having a distal end and a proximal end, and a miniature force-sensitive sound-playing unit (**14**) attached to the condom at its proximal end. The proximal end of the condom is made in the form of a semirigid rim (**12**) having a lower part with an opening (**16**) coinciding with the cavity of the condom, and an upper part extending radially upwardly from the body of the condom and supporting the sound-playing unit (**14**). The latter contains a chip-controlled piezoelectric sound transducer which plays a melody or voiced message when during intercouse the contacts (**28** and **30**) of the sound-playing unit (**14**) are closed and the transducer is activated.

19 Claims, 1 Drawing Sheet

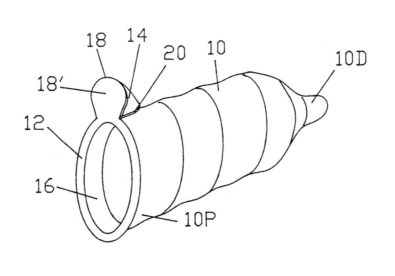

5,163,447

1

FORCE-SENSITIVE, SOUND-PLAYING CONDOM

BACKGROUND

1. Field of the Invention

The present invention relates to the field of contraceptives, particularly to condoms, and more particularly to a condom which provides entertainment and has an amusement feature.

2. Description of Prior Art

Many different kinds of contraceptive means, such as condoms, exist. They are all designed to function as methods of birth control and disease-prevention. They operate satisfactorily for these purposes, but many persons who engage in coitus dislike using them because they reduce sensitivity, interrupt coitus, and are bothersome to don.

OBJECTS AND ADVANTAGES OF THE INVENTION

It is therefore an object of the invention to provide a condom which users will like to use. Other objects are to provide a condom which provides amusement, which will not interfere with coitus, which has value as a fun gift, which can incorporate musical compositions of the user's choice according to the occasion, and which has a commercial value by being amusing, entertaining, unusual, and capable of producing a surprise effect. Further advantages and features of the invention will become apparent from a consideration of the ensuing description and drawings.

BRIEF DESCRIPTION OF DRAWINGS

FIG. 1 is a perspective view of a condom of the present invention.

FIG. 2 is a side view of a proximate portion of the condom illustrating a connection of a mechanism to the rim of the condom.

FIG. 3 is a sectional view of the condom in its package.

FIG. 4 is a sectional view of a similar package, containing two such condoms.

REFERENCE NUMERALS USED IN THE DRAWINGS AND DESCRIPTION

10—condom body
10P—proximal end of the condom
10D—distal end of the condom
12—rim
14—music-playing unit
16—opening
18—upper extension
18'—base
20—lip
22—piezoelectric sound transducer
24—chip
26—power source
28, 30—contacts
32—protective shield
34, 34a—packaging container
36, 36a—sealed flap
38—sealant

FIGS. 1 AND 2 —DETAILED DESCRIPTION OF CONDOM

A force-sensitive sound-playing condom according to the invention is shown in the attached drawings, wherein FIG. 1 is a perspective view of a force-pressure

2

sound-playing condom and FIG. 2 is a side view of the proximate portion of the condom illustrating the connection of the sound-playing mechanism to the rim of the condom. FIG. 1 shows a force-sensitive, sound-playing condom; it consists essentially of a conventional condom body 10 of latex, having a proximal end 10P and a distal end 10D, and a reinforced or rolled rim 12. Rim 12 is semi-rigid and has an opening 16 coinciding with the cavity of the condom. Extending from one portion of rim 12 is an upper extension 18. Extension 18 projects radially upwardly from the body of the condom and supports a music- or sound-playing unit 14.

Rim 12 with extension 18 has a figure-eight shape (upper loop closed) when seen from the proximal end. It is made of rubber which may be reinforced internally by a stronger plastic core (not shown). The upper part of extension 18 is solid, forming a base 18' (FIG. 2) which is molded integrally with condom 10 and rim 12, but is of thicker latex than body 10.

In order to hold base 18' upright and coplanar with rim 12, a short lip 20 is formed as the extension of the partition between the round portions of the figure-eight structure, extending a short distance distally, parallel to the side wall of the condom. Lip 20 may have a length of about 20–30 mm and may have a partly-circular, cross-sectional shape matching that of rim 12.

As shown in FIG. 2, base 18' supports elements of a standard miniature musical unit 14 which is known per se and the structure of which is beyond the scope of the invention.

As shown schematically in FIG. 2, such a unit usually consists of a miniature piezoelectric sound transducer 22, a microchip 24 which controls the operation of transducer 22, a power-supplying dry-cell battery 26, and a switch comprising electrical contacts 28 and 30, which, when closed, complete an appropriate circuit (not shown) from battery 26 to microchip 24. When energized, microchip 24 will cause transducer 22 to emit a predetermined melody, or a voice message, such as a health warning (in case transducer 22 is a speaker). The circuit of musical unit 14, or chip 24, also incorporates a monostable multivibrator which controls an electronic bypass switch for contacts 28 (not shown) which ensures that current will be supplied to chip 24 for a predetermined period of time (for example, 10 seconds), so that the music continues to play even if contacts 28 are opened. This will cause the music or voice to play even if contact is intermittent, until the next contact takes place.

The music or voice message may be played once (e.g., an overture or melody may be played for about 20 seconds), or it may be repeated continuously for several minutes to coincide with the duration of coitus. A voiced message may be a warning about safe sex, or a compliment to the couple for using a condom. Suitable melodies (if music is played) may be The 1812 Overture, "The Ode to Joy" from Beethoven's Ninth Symphony, the song, "Happy Birthday To You," "The Anniversary Waltz," or any popular love song.

It is understood that all elements are interconnected through an appropriate fine wiring or a printed circuit (not shown) mounted on base 18'.

In order to protect the unit from mechanical damage and random completion of the circuit through contacts 28, unit 14 is covered with a protective shield 32. Shield 32 can be made of semirigid rubber or plastic, stretched tightly to provide adequate rigidity against sudden en-

5,163,447

3

gagement of contacts **28** and **30**, but also having sufficient elasticity to ensure such contact when a force F (FIG. 2) is applied to the external surface of shield **32** from the distal side. Shield **32** is stretched from the distal end of lip **20** toward the upper edge of base **18'** and is seated so that unit **14** is encapsulated. Since base **18'** is installed in a cantilever manner and is made of resilient material, and since upper extension **18** is rigid, contacts **28** and **30** will also be activated if force F is applied from the proximal direction, or from both directions.

A force F sufficient to bring contacts **28** and **30** into engagement may be about 5–10 g.

The inside of condom **10** is lubricated in a conventional manner to facilitate donning.

A typical sound-producing unit **14** suitable for the purposes of the invention may have overall dimensions within the range of 7 to 20 mm.

FIGS. 3 AND 4 —PACKAGING

The condom is shown in packaged form in FIG. 3. Unlike conventional condoms, the present condom cannot be simply rolled, because its switch is highly sensitive to pressure. Thus the body of the condom is completely wrapped around musical unit **14** and rim **12**, and sealed inside a package **34**. Alternatively, the body of condom **10** may be folded against rim **12**. The product is then packed in a rigid boxlike container **34**. Container **34** has an upper foldable flap **36**, the free end of which is sealed, for example with a layer of a sealant **38**, to ensure the sterility of the product in transportation and storage. Such packaging maintains contacts **28** and **30** disengaged.

Package **34** may be molded from rigid plastic and may have the following dimensions: 44×45×20 mm, or 45×20 mm, if circular. Although only one condom is shown in FIG. 3, it is understood that, as the back surface of the rim **12** and base **18'** are coplanar, lying flat, it may be convenient to package two condoms in a back-to-back position in a single package as shown in FIG. 4.

The condom is mass produced and hence is inexpensive to manufacture. For this reason, as well as for health reasons, it should be disposed of after a single use.

The life of battery **26** may be indicated on package **34**.

OPERATION

In order to use the condom, the user opens package **34** by unsealing flap **36** and removing wrapped condom **10**. He then unwraps or unfolds the condom and slides it onto his erect penis. The lubricant inside the condom facilitates this operation.

During intercourse, the contact between the suprapubic genital areas of the couple will create forces F sufficient to engage contacts **28** and **30**, completing the circuit. Power will pass from power source **26** to chip **24**, and thus cause transducer **22** to produce sounds, e.g., music, or a voiced message. This message or music may warn, compliment, stimulate, entertain, or surprise the couple. The multivibrator in chip **24** ensures the continuation of music for a predetermined period of time, so that the melody will play once or repeatedly during intercourse.

Upper extension **18** will not interfere with coitus since it will be sandwiched between the suprapubic areas.

4

SUMMARY, RAMIFICATION, SCOPE

Thus, it has been shown that the condom of the invention provides a contraceptive combined with an amusing device, i.e., a force-sensitive sound-playing mechanism which is activated by the application of pressure during the use of the condom. The sound-playing condom is sensitive to slight pressure. The music playing unit is supported in such a manner as to not interfere with intercourse. The musical mechanism is protected by being entirely covered with a protective shield. It may have value as a fun gift incorporating other musical compositions of the user's choice according to the occasion, and may have further commercial value being amusing, entertaining, unusual, and capable of producing a surprise effect.

Although the force-sensitive sound-playing condom has been shown and described in the form of one specific embodiment, this embodiment, its parts, materials, and configurations have been given only as examples, and many other modifications of sound-playing condoms are possible. For example, rim **12** and extension **18** may have a shape other than a figure-eight; all components of musical unit **1 4** may be embedded entirely in resilient plastic, leaving only space between contacts **28** and **30** so that all of the contacts, excepting the exposed contacting portions, are embedded and thus maintained in an open state by the resiliency of the embedded mass. The musical units themselves may have different forms, dimensions, and configurations. There may be a range of musical or other sound selections which may be chosen or combined by the user. The rim and base may be reinforced by a wire. Various parts of the musical circuit may assume lateral positions around the rim, i.e., piezoelectric sound transducers may be displaced laterally on one side, while the chip may be arranged on the other side. Similarly, the package itself may take different forms and show a variety of messages. Although in the preferred embodiment shown above, it is a disposable condom, the musical unit may be made in such a way that it can be detached and readily disconnected or connected onto other condoms by means such as adhesive tapes. In that case the package might contain, for example, ten condoms and a single musical unit. A speaker can be used instead of a piezoelectric transducer. The condom will operate in homosexual as well as heterosexual intercourse. In lieu of mechanical contacts **28** and **30**, a strain-gauge-type activator or any other type of activator may be employed.

Therefore, the scope of the invention should be determined, not by the example given, but by the appended claims and their legal equivalents.

What I claim is:

1. A force-sensitive sound-playing condom, comprising:

a condom body, and

force-sensitive sound-playing means for emitting a predetermined sound, said force-sensitive sound-playing means being attached to said condom body,

said condom being donnable upon an erect penis without activating said force-sensitive sound-playing means,

said force-sensitive sound-playing means being designed to emit said predetermined sound in response to a predetermined external force created during the act of sexual intercourse.

5,163,447

5

2. The force-sensitive sound-playing condom of claim 1 wherein said condom body has a distal end and a proximal end and wherein said means is attached to said proximal end.

3. The force-sensitive sound-playing condom of claim 2 wherein said proximal end of said condom body has a semi-rigid rim having an opening coinciding with the cavity of said condom body, said means extending radially upwardly from said condom body.

4. The force-sensitive sound-playing condom of claim 3 wherein said force-sensitive sound-playing means is a miniature device having a power supply source, a piezoelectric sound transducer, a pair of force-sensitive contacts which are closed when said predetermined force is applied to at least one of said contacts, and a chip with elements which control operation of said music playing means when said contacts are closed.

5. The force-sensitive sound-playing condom of claim 4 wherein said rim is solid and said means has a semi-rigid protective cover which possesses flexibility sufficient to bring one of said contacts into engagement with the other when said predetermined force is applied to one of said contacts.

6. The force-sensitive sound-playing condom of claim 5 wherein said condom body and said protective cover are integrally molded.

7. The force-sensitive sound-playing condom of claim 5 wherein said predetermined force is 5 grams or greater.

8. The force-sensitive sound-playing condom of claim 3 wherein said means has a lip distally extending from said semi-rigid rim, said lip having a length of about 20-30 mm.

9. The force-sensitive sound-playing condom of claim 3, further including a rigid boxlike packaging container having means for sealing said condom in a state in which a part of said condom body is wrapped around said sound-playing means and said rim.

10. A force-sensitive sound-playing condom, comprising:
   a condom body having a distal end and a proximal end, said proximal end being made in the form of a semi-rigid rim having an opening coinciding with the cavity of said condom,
   force-sensitive sound-playing means for emitting a predetermined sound, said force-sensitive sound-playing means being attached to said proximal end of condom body,
   said force-sensitive sound-playing means extending radially upwardly from said proximal end of said condom body,
   said condom being donnable upon an erect penis without activating said force-sensitive sound-playing means,
   said force-sensitive sound-playing means being designed to emit said predetermined sound in response to a predetermined external force created during the act of sexual intercourse.

11. The force-sensitive sound-playing condom of claim 10 wherein said sound-playing means is a miniature device having a source of power, a piezoelectric sound transducer, a pair of force-sensitive contacts which are closed when a pressure is applied to at least one of said contacts, and a chip with elements which control operation of said sound-playing means when said contacts are closed.

12. The force-sensitive sound-playing condom of claim 11 wherein said rim is solid and said force-sensi-

6

tive sound-playing means has a semi-rigid protective cover which possesses flexibility sufficient to bring one of said contacts into engagement with the other when said predetermined force is applied to one of said contacts, said means and said rim having coplanar surfaces.

13. The force-sensitive sound-playing condom of claim 12 wherein said predetermined force is 5 grams or greater.

14. The force-sensitive sound-playing condom of claim 10 wherein said means has a lip distally extending from said rim, said lip having a length of about 20 to 30 millimeters.

15. The force-sensitive sound-playing condom of claim 10, further including a rigid boxlike packaging container having means for sealing having means for sealing said condom in a state in which a part of said condom body is wrapped around said sound-playing means and said rim.

16. A force-sensitive sound-playing condom, comprising:
   a condom body having a distal end and a proximal end, and
   force-sensitive sound-playing means attached to said proximal end of said condom body,
   said proximal end being made in the form of a semi-rigid rim having an opening coinciding with the cavity of said condom,
   said force-sensitive sound-playing means extending radially upwardly from said proximal end of said condom body,
   said force-sensitive sound-playing means comprising a miniature device having a source of energy, a piezoelectric sound transducer, a pair of force-sensitive contacts, and a chip with elements which control operation of said sound-playing means when said contacts are closed,
   said condom being donnable upon an erect penis without activating said force-sensitive sound-playing means,
   said pair of force-sensitive contacts being positioned so that at least one of said pair of contacts receives a predetermined external force created during the act of sexual intercourse, said pair of contacts closing in response to said at least one of said contacts receiving said predetermined external force, said chip being connected to said source of energy when said pair of contacts close so that said piezoelectric sound transducer will emit a predetermined sound during said act of sexual intercourse.

17. The force-sensitive sound-playing condom of claim 16 wherein said rim is solid and said means has a semi-rigid protective cover which possesses flexibility sufficient to bring one of said pair of contacts into engagement with the other when said predetermined force is applied to said cover, said semi-rigid cover and said means having surfaces which are flat and coplanar.

18. The force-sensitive sound-playing condom of claim 17 wherein said force-sensitive sound-playing means has a lip distally extending from said semi-rigid rim, said lip having a length of about 20-30 mm.

19. The force-sensitive sound-playing condom of claim 16, further including a rigid boxlike packaging container having means for sealing said condom in a state in which a part of said condom body is wrapped around said sound-playing means and said rim.

* * * * *

Fashion Business Method

Did you ever forget your size when making a clothing purchase? Do you wish you could keep your measurements on hand when making in-person or online purchases? Inventor Andrea Rose feels your pain. She invented a business method for shopping that minimizes purchasing problems.

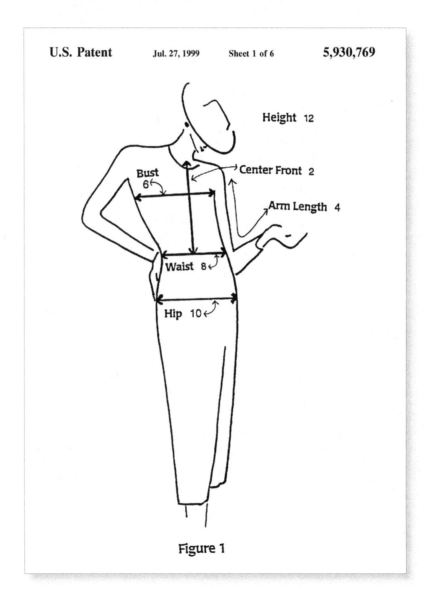

U.S. Patent   Jul. 27, 1999   Sheet 1 of 6   5,930,769

Height 12

Center Front 2

Bust 6

Arm Length 4

Waist 8

Hip 10

Figure 1

Provisional Patent Application

System and Method for Fashion Shopping

The retail clothing industry suffers from the return of merchandise due to improper fit, usually because customers do not know their size in a particular manufacturer's clothing line. Most manufacturers have their own systems for sizing; sizes are not standardized. In most stores, customers often try on three or four sizes from a manufacturer to determine the right size. This is time-consuming and frustrating. In mail or Internet orders, customers cannot try on before purchasing and must guess the size in the line. Often, the garments do not fit properly and must be returned.

Also, a large amount of inventory must be available, which is hard to sift through.

Further, salespeople often are not aware of which merchandise has been back-ordered or is in stock, so they simply tell the customer to look on the floor to see if the customer's size is available.

I have devised a method of shopping that helps a shopper select an appropriate fashion suitable for their measurements and avoid the above problems.

FIG. 1 shows a body frame illustrating body measurements that a user of my method must supply to an electronic fashion system before accessing the system.

FIG. 2 shows a main menu screen for my electronic fashion shopping system.

FIG. 3 is a submenu that depicts the fashion data for a selected fashion for the system.

FIG. 4 shows the size and fit information menu for the system.

FIG. 5 shows an analysis of fashion suggestions with design dos and don'ts based on the customer's body type.

FIG. 6 is a flowchart illustrating the system.

The system provides an interactive electronic shopping service employing a computer, interactive television, a CD-ROM database, the Internet, or other electronic medium, or alternatively a manual system. It can also be used as an in-store system that allows retailers and manufacturers to provide customers with a personalized shopping experience while freeing salespeople. The system is capable of being accessed remotely using typical telecommunication systems, e.g., office or home users may connect through analog modems, ISDN, etc. The system can be offered as a service for interactive television services, or can be accessed at home using a CD-ROM. Alternatively, the system can be accessed on the Internet by a customer to allow fully interactive and up-to-date shopping with the ability to transact business, i.e., complete selections and make purchases in a single session. The online session also allows inventory checking and sophisticated modeling and rendering.

Initially the customer inputs information including body measurements and a digital photograph of their face. A trained sales associate or personal shopper assists the customer in entering this information. For a manual system, data cards are completed. Alternatively, the customer can fill out a paper or electronic subscription form. An electronic form may be a computer file uploaded to a central system or an HTML page transmitted over the Internet. Upon registration, a membership card with personal and billing code numbers may be assigned. The personal number identifies the customer, provides security for personal information, and reduces risk. The billing code enables the customer to order merchandise without the need to reenter billing information for each transaction. The personal information includes body measurements, credit information, address, and other data. This is a permanent record which is not needed the next time the customer accesses the system. Updates or alterations may be made.

FIG. 1 shows a body frame illustrating the body measurements. The body measurements include center front 2, arm length 4, bust 6, waist 8, hip 10 and height 12. Center front 2 is measured from the hollow of the neck to the navel. Arm length 4 is measured from the end of the shoulder to the wrist. For pants, additional measurements include inseam, center length and center depth. Digital face photographs depicting the front, side and back are submitted.

The system determines a body type based on the body measurements. The body type is an individual's skeleton or bone frame plus an amount of flesh around a specific anatomical part. A manual system may employ tables, charts or formulae. Cloth or fabric is constructed to a specific shape and size that determines style. The cloth as cut is placed on a specific skeletal frame and flesh area, which determines the fashion or look. Not all shapes fit all frames, so not all styles fit all body types. Certain limitations are physical, e.g. a body may be too large for the clothing line. Some limitations are aesthetic and must be determined as a matter of "taste."

With the body type the system automatically allows the customer instant access to all suitable apparel in the system by fashion category, and further allows a modeled presentation of various clothes. The system analyzes the personal information and available garments, and recommends what shapes best compliment the customer's body type, as well as other fashion recommendations and information by any fashion consulting service. The system thus provides a personalized "chart" characterizing the customer's body type. This chart may be a physical printed document or an electronic representation. The chart also has information on the best designs to flatter her specific shape and suggestions on how to dress and shop effectively.

In essence, the system is a fashion consultant, addressing specific clothing problems, providing the customer's size in the manufacturer's line and determining if there is a fit problem so that the customer knows if alterations are needed.

Thus the system transcends simple sizing codes and analyzes the body type with respect to available garments. Fit problems are generally greater for women than for men or children, due to the larger number of styles and fabrics.

The system may also include an analysis of shrinkage or shape change of a garment over its useful life, e.g., cotton garments tend to shrink.

The fashion category for each customer is based on body measurements and for women on anatomical structure. These fashion categories are petite, short (also known as junior), average and tall. The following chart depicts the height 12 and center front 2 measurements for each fashion category:

	Height	Center Front
Petite	4'6.5" to 5'3"	12.75" to 13.5"
Short	5'3" to 5'5"	13.75" to 14.25"
Average	5'5" to 5'8"	14.75" to 15.5"
Tall	5'9" to 6'2"	16.5" to 17.25"

These categories are generally recognized American Fashion Industries categories and form a starting point for analysis. They are translated from the petite, junior petite, missy, junior, large, and half-size categories. The categories can also be used for children and men. Alternatively, for men, the categories slim, athletic, stout, and portly stout, and for children, infant, toddler, children, preteen, and teen can be used.

If center front 2 is 1" or more below the above standard, the person is short waisted and if it's 1" or more above, the person is long waisted.

Each of the fashion categories is used with a body type, e.g., a petite woman can be one of four different body types, which include the full-bust/slight hip stature, normal stature, without a waistline stature and slight bust/fuller hip stature. The petite woman has a height between 4'6.5" and 5'3". Center front 2 is between 12.75" and 13.5" and arm length 4 is between 20.5" and 22.5".

The following charts show exemplary listings of bust, waist, and hip measurements (in inches) for the extra-small- (X-small), small-, medium-, large-, extra-large- (X-large) and extra-extra-large- (XX-large) framed petite women which the system contains in its database. The extra-small is typically size 2–4, small is typically size 6–8, medium is typically size 10–12, large is typically size 12–14, extra-large is typically size 16–18, extra-extra-large is typically size 20–24, and queen is typically size 1x–4x.

Petite (Normal Stature):

	Bust	Waist	Hip	Center Front
X-Small	29 to 30	19 to 21	30 to 31	12.25 to 12.75
Small	31 to 32	21 to 23	32 to 33	12.75 to 13.25
Medium	33 to 34	23 to 25	34 to 35.5	13.25 to 13.75
Large	36 to 38	26.5 to 29	37.5 to 39	13.75 to 14.25
X-Large	39 to 41	29.25 to 32	40 to 42.25	14.25 to 14.75
XX-Large	43 to 45.25	33.25 to 36	44 to 46.25	14.75 to 15.00

Petite (Slight Bust/Fuller Hip Stature):

	Bust	Waist	Hip	Center Front
X-Small	27.5 to 29	19.5 to 21	31.5 to 33	12 to 12.5
Small	29.5 to 31	21.5 to 23	33.5 to 35	12.5 to 13
Medium	32 to 33.5	23.5 to 25	36 to 37.5	13 to 13.5
Large	35.5 to 37.5	27 to 28.5	39 to 41.5	13.5 to 14
X-Large	38 to 39.5	30 to 31.5	44 to 47	14 to 14.5
XX-Large	41 to 42.5	33 to 34.5	48 to 50.5	14.5 to 15

Petite (Full Bust/Slight Hip Stature):

	Bust	Waist	Hip	Center Front
X-Small	29 to 31	17.5 to 18.5	27 to 28.5	12.5 to 13
Small	31 to 33	19.5 to 20.5	29.5 to 31	13 to 13.50
Medium	33 to 35.5	21 to 22.5	32 to 33	13.5 to 14
Large	37 to 39.5	25 to 26.5	35.5 to 37	14 to 14.5
X-Large	41 to 43.5	28.5 to 31	38.5 to 40.5	14.5 to 15
XX-Large	45 to 48	31.5 to 34.5	42.5 to 44.5	15 to 15.5

Petite (Without Waistline Stature):

	Bust	Waist	Hip	Center Front
X-Small	29 to 30	21.5 to 23	30.5 to 32	12 to 12.5
Small	31 to 32	23.5 to 25	32.5 to 34	12.5 to 13
Medium	33 to 34	25.5 to 27.5	34.5 to 37	13 to 13.5
Large	36 to 38	29 to 32	38 to 40	13.5 to 14
X-Large	39 to 41.5	33 to 35.5	41 to 44	14 to 14.5
XX-Large	42 to 44.5	36 to 38.5	44 to 46	14.5 to 15

There are also corresponding charts for the short, average, and tall categories.

FIG. 2 shows the main menu of the system. An interface screen (touch, monitor, mouse or keyboard) requests that the customer select an area in which to shop. The customer selects clothes items to scan, which includes day suits 14, evening suits 16, day dresses 18, robes, coats 20, active sports 22, sportswear 24, casual wear and at-home wear 26, or any other category. An infrared remote control device is employed to interact and communicate with a TV version.

The system may also access other related information for analysis and presentation, including accessories and shoes, using coordinating colors.

FIG. 3 illustrates a submenu of fashions for each category; e.g., for day suits the system would show the first entry of the database for day suits in a category such as petites. The system may also provide an adaptive presentation of choices based on a determined prioritization. Each database entry or fashion has corresponding fashion data. Fashion data allows presentation of a projection of a model having the customer's body type wearing the selected fashion, on the computer screen. A manual presentation can also be done through modular graphic elements. The face of the model is the customer's or may be selected from face models. The customer can preview visually how she would look in a specific style, without having to try it on. The model may be a 2-D or 3-D projection, allowing rotations or animations. Other fashion data include the available colors of fashion 28, manufacturer 30, price 32, description 34, and sizes available 36, plus data for accessories.

The submenu allows the customer to select size and fit information menu 38, see another garment in the database for the selected clothes item 40, order 42, or start again 44, by selecting an indicator.

FIG. 4 shows a size and fit menu for the system. The system compares body measurements with the manufacturer's sizing chart or the actual garment measurements. The system uses the universal grading system and "sloper" concept; different manufacturers use different slopers, e.g., starting at size 10, for every next size, one inch is added to each side of the fabric. The computer or manual system takes into account this size differential. After size 12, it is possible that 1.5" is added to each side of the fabric and after size 16 is reached, 2" is added.

For example, a customer may be a size 6 in an Ellen Tracy dress and a size 12 in a Tahari dress. The computer tells the correct or closest size. For the size and fit submenu, the system generates a virtual mannequin 46 of the body including her face. The system also generates a pointer or arrow 48 which indicates needed alterations.

The required alterations may also be stored and employed in an automated system. The system may include feedback, where a consumer tries on selected and test garments to determine whether the fit and fashion are appropriate. The computer can then modify its future analyses.

Other fashion data, such as manufacturer, price, and description are also indicated. The customer's body measurements may also be listed. The customer also has the option to see another suit 40, ORDER 42, or START AGAIN 44, from the Size and Fit Menu.

To see another fashion in the current database for the selected clothes item, the customer selects the "See another suit." Another database entry and corresponding fashion data will be displayed.

To order, the customer selects the ORDER submenu. The customer can place an order by computer, telephone or fax. Each transaction is charged to the customer's account and can then be shipped to the customer or picked up.

The customer can select START AGAIN to select another item such as day suits, evening suits, dresses, robes, coats, active sports, sportswear, casual wear, and at-home wear. The system can suggest or advise against other fashion shapes.

FIG. 5 shows an analysis of fashion suggestions with dos and don'ts based on the customer's body type. The system will suggest fashion shapes for the customer's body type 50 and fashion shapes to avoid wearing 52. The system can output a chart of fashion dos and don'ts: e.g., for the petite fashion category, boleros, cropped jackets and short, tailored jackets with small lapels and collars are OK, but not long skirts. With prints, smaller is better since larger patterns tend to overwhelm. Vertical stripes are good, creating the illusion of height. Thin stripes are better than bold. When accessorizing, avoid oversize pieces, and use narrow belts, scarves, and smaller, delicate jewelry.

For a petite, the following would be provided:

Do wear: Pleated and dirndl skirts (add volume to waist and hips), peplums (create shape and volume), blouses with bolero vests (flatter figure).

Don't Wear: Large ruffles (overpower), large shoulder pads (distort proportion), layers (make one appear smaller).

For a petite with a small bust and large hips, the following would be provided:

Do Wear: A-line skirts and dresses (create a proportioned body), jackets 5"–7" below waist (camouflage size difference between top and bottom), separates (eliminate need for alterations that one-size, two piece outfit may require).

Don't Wear: Pleated skirts (accent fullness of hips), dirndl skirts with gathering at waist (emphasizes that area), tight skirts (call attention to difference between bust and hips).

For a petite with a large bust and small hips, the following would be provided:

Do Wear: Jackets and vests that fall 4"–7" below waist (camouflages the size difference), and dark color tops (make bust look smaller).

Don't Wear: Blousons (has elastic at bottom to hips—brings extra volume to top), white on top and black on bottom (white gives illusion of looking bigger; black gives illusion of looking smaller), horizontal shirt stripes (make top appear larger).

For a petite with a short waisted center front 2, the following would be provided:

Do wear: Jackets with 4"–7" fall below waist (elongate midsection), A-line and straight dresses (camouflage the torso), out blouses with fall 4+" below waist (disguise waist).

Don't Wear: Belts (draw attention to short waist), cropped vests and short jackets (emphasize waist and enhance short-waisted look), fitted two-piece suits with different color top and bottom (accent difference between upper and lower length).

For the petite with a long-waisted center front 2, the following would be provided.

Do wear: Jackets with fall 3"–7" below waist (even proportion), form-fitting, A-line dresses (draw attention away from long waist), one color, two-piece sets (bring a more even look to torso).

Don't Wear: Bolero or cropped jackets (emphasize length of center front), hip-huggers (make torso look longer), belts (call attention to waist and the difference in proportion).

FIG. 6 is a flowchart of the method. At step 601, the system receives a personal code to access a database linked to personal information. A personal information record is accessed (step 602). At step 603, a body type and fashion category is determined. Optionally, data relating to a body type may be supplied based on the personal information. Next, at step 604, a clothes item to shop for is received from the customer. Optionally, the system selects fashions based on body type and fashion category. At step 605, the system outputs a plurality of fashion data. Optionally, the system suggests body shapes and intended body type tips. Finally at step 606, the system receives selection information from the customer.

The system allows easy inventory control since merchandise photographs can be changed at any time by updating the database records. The system keeps track of stock sizes available, and those to be ordered. Also it may show information as to when out-of-stock items will be available. Control may be integrated with an automated storage and retrieval system, making inventory more space efficient.

The system personalizes and simplifies shopping and allows customers to consider more clothes in less time, presenting more buying opportunities, and increasing efficiency.

Claims

1. A method of fashion shopping by a customer comprising:

   - receiving personal information from the customer
   - selecting a body type and fashion category based on the personal information
   - selecting fashions from a plurality of clothes items based on the body type and fashion category
   - outputting a plurality of fashion data based on the selected fashions
   - receiving selection information from the customer, and
   - processing order information to place an order for the selected fashions.

Patent (Business Method)

US005930769A

United States Patent [19]

Rose

[11]	**Patent Number:** 5,930,769
[45]	**Date of Patent:** Jul. 27, 1999

[54] **SYSTEM AND METHOD FOR FASHION SHOPPING**

[76] Inventor: **Andrea Rose**, 245 E. 63rd St., Apt. 319, New York, N.Y. 10021

[21] Appl. No.: **08/726,674**

[22] Filed: **Oct. 7, 1996**

[51] Int. Cl.[6] G06F 17/60
[52] U.S. Cl. 705/27; 345/419; 364/400; 705/26; 707/104
[58] Field of Search 345/419; 364/400, 364/470.02, 470.03; 705/26, 27; 707/104

[56] **References Cited**

U.S. PATENT DOCUMENTS

4,149,246	4/1979	Goldman	364/470.03
4,261,012	4/1981	Maloomian	358/93
4,546,434	10/1985	Gioello	364/400
4,626,344	12/1986	Collins et al.	364/470.03
4,916,624	4/1990	Collins et al.	364/470.03
4,916,634	4/1990	Collins et al.	395/10
5,163,006	11/1992	Deziel	364/470.03
5,163,007	11/1992	Slilaty	364/470.03
5,495,568	2/1996	Beavin	364/188
5,551,021	8/1996	Harada et al.	707/104
5,680,314	10/1997	Patterson et al.	364/470.03

OTHER PUBLICATIONS

Sizing Up Clothing Sizes, Know How Magazine, Spring, 1994.

Primary Examiner—Edward R. Cosimano

[57] **ABSTRACT**

The present invention provides a method of manual fashion shopping and method for electronic fashion shopping by a customer using a programmed computer, CD-ROM, television, Internet or other electronic medium such as video. The method comprises receiving personal information from the customer; selecting a body type and fashion category based on the personal information; selecting fashions from a plurality of clothes items based on the body type and fashion category; outputting a plurality of fashion data based on the selected fashions; and receiving selection information from the customer.

45 Claims, 6 Drawing Sheets

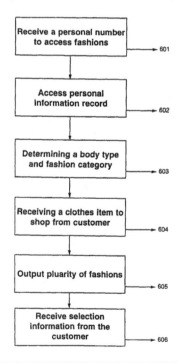

Receive a personal number to access fashions — 601

Access personal information record — 602

Determining a body type and fashion category — 603

Receiving a clothes item to shop from customer — 604

Output pluarity of fashions — 605

Receive selection information from the customer — 606

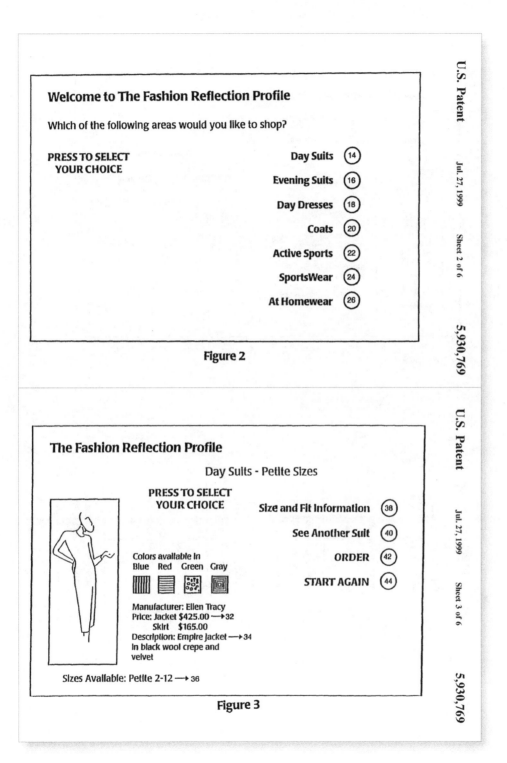

U.S. Patent

Jul. 27, 1999

Sheet 2 of 6

5,930,769

Welcome to The Fashion Reflection Profile

Which of the following areas would you like to shop?

**PRESS TO SELECT
YOUR CHOICE**

Day Suits (14)

Evening Suits (16)

Day Dresses (18)

Coats (20)

Active Sports (22)

SportsWear (24)

At Homewear (26)

Figure 2

U.S. Patent

Jul. 27, 1999

Sheet 3 of 6

5,930,769

The Fashion Reflection Profile

Day Suits - Petite Sizes

**PRESS TO SELECT
YOUR CHOICE**

Size and Fit Information (38)

See Another Suit (40)

ORDER (42)

START AGAIN (44)

Colors available in
Blue   Red   Green   Gray

Manufacturer: Ellen Tracy
Price: Jacket $425.00 →32
    Skirt $165.00
Description: Empire Jacket →34
in black wool crepe and
velvet

Sizes Available: Petite 2-12 → 36

Figure 3

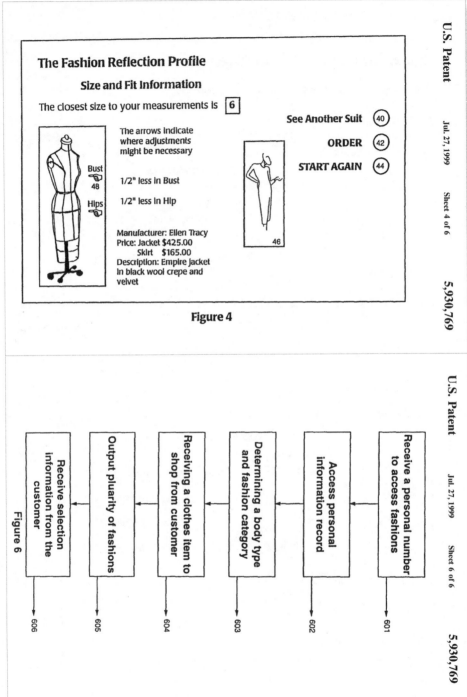

The Fashion Reflection Profile

Size and Fit Information

The closest size to your measurements is 6

The arrows indicate where adjustments might be necessary

Bust 48

1/2" less in Bust

Hips

1/2" less in Hip

Manufacturer: Ellen Tracy
Price: Jacket $425.00
Skirt $165.00
Description: Empire jacket in black wool crepe and velvet

See Another Suit (40)

ORDER (42)

START AGAIN (44)

46

Figure 4

Receive a personal number to access fashions — 601

Access personal information record — 602

Determining a body type and fashion category — 603

Receiving a clothes item to shop from customer — 604

Output pluarity of fashions — 605

Receive selection information from the customer — 606

Figure 6

U.S. Patent   Jul. 27, 1999   Sheet 5 of 6   5,930,769

Your Fashion Profile

Your unique body type is _____
variable

Suggested fashion information for your unique body type. Since you are a _____.
variable

Suggested information including such categories as fashion shapes, styles, accessories, fabrics and fabric prints, colors etc.

Please call 1-800-000-0000 the system would like more information about you to assist you. (Variable Option to Call In)

Suggested Fashion Shapes For Your unique body type are described as follows: 50

(Here a variety of fashion shapes and styles are presented)

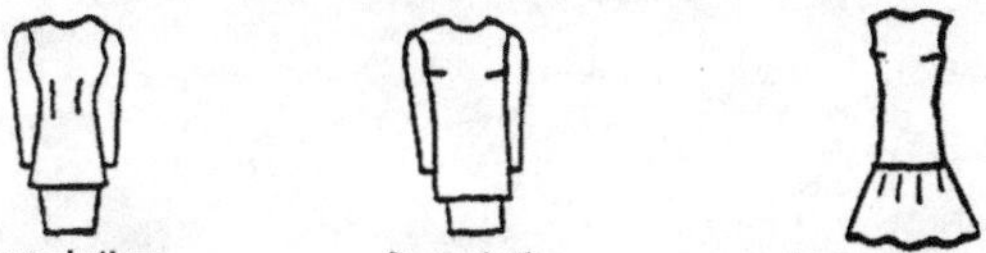

Description   Description   Description
_____   _____   _____
_____   _____   _____
_____   _____   _____

Suggested fashion shapes to avoid wearing are described as follows: 52

(Here a variety of fashion shapes and Styles are given)

Description   Description   Description
_____   _____   _____
_____   _____   _____

Your Selection Indicator

Would you like to use the Fit Profile?   Yes   No
(Example of Choices)   ☐   ☐

Please select one of the following services

           Yes   No

Fashion
Reflection

Do you want   ☐   ☐
to try this
style on?

Fit Profile

Do you want   ☐   ☐
to see fit
information?

Order

Do you want   ☐   ☐
to place an
order?

Mall Collection

Do you want   ☐   ☐
to see what
categories are
available in the
mall?

Shop

Do you want   ☐   ☐
to see
another style?

Finish

Do you want   ☐   ☐
to END the
program?

(Here a variety of
services are offered)

Figure 5

5,930,769

1

SYSTEM AND METHOD FOR FASHION SHOPPING

FIELD OF THE INVENTION

The present invention relates to a method of fashion shopping by a customer and more particularly to a method which helps select an appropriate fashion for purchase based on data relating to the customer.

BACKGROUND OF THE INVENTION

One of the biggest problems facing the retail clothing industry is the return of merchandise due to improper fit. Fit is cited as an important problem since customers often do not know their size in a particular manufacturer's clothing line. Escalating the problem, most manufacturers have developed their own systems for sizing. Regarding sales made in department stores, boutiques, or other stores, customers often try on three or four different sizes from a given manufacturer's clothing line to determine which size fits their body properly. This is both time consuming and frustrating. For the mail order catalogs and home shopping industry on television, returns are one of the biggest drawbacks of selling fashions. This is because the customers do not have the opportunity to try on garments before purchasing and must guess which size they would be in a given manufacturer's clothing line. Often, when the customers receive the garment through the mail, the garments do not fit properly and must be returned. Similar problems occur when a customer uses her computer to shop via the Internet or to shop using a CD-ROM database containing an inventory of merchandise. Thus, a need exists for a system or method to reduce the number of returns due to improper fit of the merchandise and lessen the amount of time trying on merchandise during in-store shopping.

Another drawback for in-store shopping is the large amount of inventory which must be made available. Today, customers lead very busy lives and often do not have the time to sift through all of the merchandise. Thus, a need exists for a method of allowing customers to see merchandise quickly and efficiently.

A further drawback for in-store shopping pertains to tracking inventory. Sales people often are not aware of which merchandise has been back-ordered or which merchandise is instock. Sales people tell the customer to look on the floor to see if an item in the customer's size is available. Thus, there exists a need to track inventory and order inventory if merchandise is purchased which is not in stock.

SUMMARY AND OBJECTS OF THE INVENTION

Accordingly, the present invention provides a method for electronic fashion shopping by a customer using a programmed computer, CD-ROM database, interactive television, Internet, or other electronic medium such as video or alternatively, a manual system. To attain this, the method comprises receiving personal information from the customer; selecting a body type and fashion category based on the personal information; selecting fashions from a plurality of clothes items based on the body type and fashion category; outputting a plurality of fashion data based on the selected fashions; and receiving selection information from the customer.

Accordingly, it is an object of the present invention to provide a method of electronic fashion shopping and manual shopping as a marketing and sales tool for retailers and

2

manufacturers to provide enhanced services and easy shopping for customers while increasing efficiency.

Another object of the present invention is to provide a method of electronic shopping and manual shopping which allows customers to see merchandise quickly, easily, conveniently, and facilitates opportunities for customers to buy merchandise and try on the clothes by seeing a simulated body type matching her own body type and having her own face.

Still another object of the present invention is to provide a method of electronic shopping and manual shopping which gives retailers and manufacturers the opportunity to make multiple sales, build customer loyalty and provide outstanding personal service.

Yet another object of the present invention is to furnish a method of electronic shopping and manual shopping that provides easy inventory control and reduces returns due to improper fit of the merchandise.

A further object of the present invention is to provide a method of electronic shopping and manual shopping which reduces the amount of time expended shopping.

Another object of the present invention is to provide a dynamic personalized system that helps women, men, and children save time, money, and countless hours of frustration by teaching them about their body type and the clothing styles that flatter that body type as well as showing them how to create their own unique fashion statement based on their personality and lifestyle.

These and still further objects will become apparent hereinafter.

These and other features of the present invention are described in more detail in the following detailed description when taken with the drawings. The scope of the invention, however, is limited only by the claims appended hereto.

BRIEF DESCRIPTION OF THE DRAWINGS

Various embodiments of the present invention are described and illustrated herein with reference to the drawings in which like items are indicated by the same reference, in which:

FIG. 1 shows a body frame illustrating the body measurements that must be inputted into the electronic fashion system before accessing the system;

FIG. 2 shows the main menu screen for an electronic fashion shopping system according to the present invention;

FIG. 3 is a submenu that depicts the fashion data for a selected fashion for the electronic fashion shopping system according to the present invention;

FIG. 4 shows the size and fit information menu for the electronic fashion shopping system according to the present invention;

FIG. 5 shows an analysis of fashion suggestions with design do's and don'ts based on the customer's body type according to the present invention; and

FIG. 6 is a flowchart illustrating the method of electronic fashion shopping.

DETAILED DESCRIPTION OF THE PREFERRED EMBODIMENTS

The computer software system provides an interactive electronic shopping service employing a computer, interactive television, CD-ROM database, the Internet, or other electronic medium or alternatively a manual system. It can also be used as an in-store computer system that allows

5,930,769

3

retailers and manufacturers to provide customers with a personalized shopping experience while freeing sales people. This system is capable of being accessed remotely using typical telecommunication systems. For example, office or home users may connect through analog modems, ISDN, etc. The computer system for electronic fashion shopping can be offered as a service for interactive television services such as the Home Shopping Network, or can be accessed at home using a CD-ROM containing an inventory of fashions to allow off-line shopping. Alternatively, the computer system for electronic fashion shopping can be accessed on the Internet by a customer to allow a fully interactive and up-to-date shopping experience with the ability to transact business, e.g. complete selections and make purchases in a single session. The on-line session also allows inventory checking and sophisticated modeling and rendering to be performed.

Initially the customer inputs information including body measurements and a digital photograph of the customer's face. The retail environments, trained sales associate or personal shopper assists the customer in entering the personal information into the system. For the manual system, data cards are implemented. Alternatively, the customer, without assistance, can fill out a paper or electronic subscription form. An electronic subscription form may be, for example, a computer file uploaded to a central system or an HTML form page transmitted over the Internet. Upon registration, a membership card with a personal code number and a billing code number may be assigned to the customer. The personal identification code may also be transmitted electronically. The personal code number allows the customer to access her personal information and shop using the computer system for electronic fashion shopping. The personal code number identifies the customer, provides security for personal information and allows electronic commerce with reduced risk. The billing code number enables the customer to order merchandise with ease, e.g. eliminates the need to reenter billing information for each transaction.

The personal information which is entered into the computer system includes body measurements along with credit information, address, and other pertinent facts. The personal information is a permanent record in the database of the electronic fashion shopping system and redundant input is not needed the next time the customer accesses the system. However, updates or alterations may be made as necessary or desired. Turning to the figures, FIG. 1 shows a body frame illustrating the body measurements that must be inputted into the electronic fashion system before accessing the system. The body measurements include center front **2**, arm length **4**, bust **6**, waist **8**, hip **10**, and height **12**. Center front **2** is measured from the hollow of the neck of the customer to the navel. Arm length **4** is measured from the end of the shoulder to the wrist of the arm. For pants, additional measurements may be necessary which include inseam, center length, and center depth. The customer may also submit a photograph of her face taken with a digital camera or alternatively submit a photograph that is digitized by the electronic fashion shopping service. It is preferable that multiple photographs of the face depicting the front view, side view, back view, etc. are submitted so that the system can accurately depict the face at different angles.

After the personal information is entered, the system determines a body type based on the body measurements. As determined by the system, body type is an individual's skeleton or bone frame plus an amount of flesh surrounding a specific anatomical part. A manual system may employ

4

tables, charts or formulae. Fashion is cloth or fabric constructed to a specific shape and size which determines style. The amount of cloth and shape when cut, is placed on a specific skeletal frame and flesh area, which determines the fashion or look which is the result of the process. Not all shapes fit all frames, so not all styles fit all body types. While certain limitations are physical, e.g. a body too large for the clothing-line, some limitations are aesthetic, and must be determined as a matter of "taste".

Knowing the body type enables the system to automatically allow the customer instant access to all suitable apparel in the. system by fashion category, and further allows a modeled presentation of various clothes. The system for electronic fashion shopping is based on an expert system analysis of the personal information and available garments, and also recommends what shapes best compliment the customer's body type, as well as other fashion recommendations and information by Andrea Rose fashion consulting services® and any other designers. The system thus provides a personalized "chart" characterizing the customer's body type. This chart may be a physical printed document or electronic representation. The chart also has information on the best designs to flatter her specific shape and suggestions on how to dress and shop effectively.

In essence, the computer system acts like a fashion consultant, addressing specific clothing problems, informing the customer her size in the manufacturer's clothes, and determining if there is a fit problem whereby the customer is informed of alterations needed on the garment.

The fashion industry is not standardized on the specific fit for garments, especially for individuals who vary, even slightly, from a manufacturer's ideal for a given size. Thus, a garment of a particular size from one manufacturer will not necessarily fit the same way as garments from another manufacturer, or even from the same manufacturer in a different style. Thus, it is a goal of the present invention to transcend the use of simple sizing codes and perform a complete analysis of the customer's body type with respect to available garments, to model the fit and determine acceptability. Further, in conjunction with the modeling, the system may also determine whether a garment which is a near fit may be efficiently altered to produce an acceptable fit.

The problems for garment fit are generally greater for women than for men or children, due to the larger number of styles for women and more aggressive cuts of fabric.

The system according to the present invention may also include analysis of shrinkage or shape change of a garment over its useful life, in the analysis. Thus, cotton garments which are laundered tend to shrink. Therefore, in determining the characteristics of a garment to be placed in inventory, both the as-new and environmentally cycled states may be determined and stored.

The fashion category for each customer is based on the customer's body measurements and for women the fashion categories are based on anatomical structure. These fashion categories are petite, short (also known as junior), average, and tall. The following chart depicts the height **12** and center front **2** measurements for each fashion category:

	Height	Center Front
Petite	4'6½" to 5'3"	12¾" to 13½"
Short	5'3" to 5'5"	13¾" to 14¼"

5,930,769

5

-continued

	Height	Center Front
Average	5'5" to 5'8"	14¾" to 15½"
Tall	5'9" to 6'2"	16½" to 17¼"

Since these categories are generally recognized, they form a starting point for the analysis, although the present invention is not so limited.

Note that if the center front **2** is 1" or less than the standard set forth above, the person is short waisted. If the center front **2** is 1" or more than the standard set forth above, then the person is long waisted. Additional information may be outputted by the system regarding short waisted and long waisted customers.

These fashion categories, (i.e. petite, short, average, and tall) are translated from the American Fashion Industries categories which are petite, junior petite, missy, junior, large, and halfsize. These categories can also be used for children and men. Alternatively, for men, the fashion categories are slim, athletic, stout, and portly stout. For children, the fashion categories are infant, toddler, children, pre-teen, and teen.

Each of the fashion categories are used in conjunction with a body type. For example, the petite woman can be one of four different body types, which include the full-bust/slight hip stature, normal.stature, without a waistline stature, and slight bust/fuller hip stature. The petite woman has a height between 46 ½ inches and 54 inches. The center front **2** is between 12 ¾ and 13 ½ inches and the arm length **4** is between 20 ½ and 22 ½ inches for petites. The following charts are an example listing of bust, waist, and hip measurements in inches for the extra-small (X-Small), small, medium, large, and extra-large (X-Large) and extra-extra-large (XX-Large) frame petite woman which the computer system contains in its body type database. The extra-small is typically size 2–4, small is typically size 6–8, medium is typically size 10–12, large is typically size 12–14, extra-large is typically size 16–18, extra-extra-large is typically size 20–24, and queen is typically size 1x–4x.

Petite Normal Stature:

	Bust	Waist	Hip	Center Front
X-Small	29 to 30	19 to 21	30 to 31	12¼ to 12¾
Small	31 to 32	21 to 23	32 to 33	12¾ to 13¼
Medium	33 to 34	23 to 25	34 to 35½	13¼ to 13¾
Large	36 to 38	26½ to 29	37½ to 39	13¾ to 14¼
X-Large	39 to 41	29½ to 32	40 to 42½	14¼ to 14¾
XX-Large	43 to 45¼	33½ to 36	44 to 46½	14¾ to 15

Petite Slight Bust/Fuller Hip Stature:

	Bust	Waist	Hip	Center Front
X-Small	27½ to 29	19½ to 21	31½ to 33	12 to 12½
Small	29½ to 31	21½ to 23	33½ to 35	12½ to 13
Medium	32 to 33½	23½ to 25	36 to 37½	13 to 13½
Large	35½ to 37½	27 to 28½	39 to 41½	13½ to 14

6

-continued

Petite Slight Bust/Fuller Hip Stature:

	Bust	Waist	Hip	Center Front
X-Large	38 to 39½	30 to 31½	44 to 47	14 to 14½
XX-Large	41 to 42½	33 to 34½	48 to 50½	14½ to 15

Petite Full Bust/Slight Hip stature:

	Bust	Waist	Hip	Center Front
X-Small	29 to 31	17½ to 18½	27 to 28½	12½ to 13
Small	31 to 33	19½ to 20½	29½ to 31	13 to 13½
Medium	33 to 35½	21 to 22½	32 to 33	13½ to 14
Large	37 to 39½	25 to 26½	35½ to 37	14 to 14½
X-Large	41 to 43½	28½ to 31	38½ to 40½	14½ to 15
XX-Large	45 to 48	31½ to 34½	42½ to 44½	15 to 15½

Petite without Waistline Stature:

	Bust	Waist	Hip	Center Front
X-Small	29 to 30	21½ to 23	30½ to 32	12 to 12½
Small	31 to 32	23½ to 25	32½ to 34	12½ to 13
Medium	33 to 34	25½ to 27½	34½ to 37	13 to 13½
Large	36 to 38	29 to 32	38 to 40	13½ to 14
X-Large	39 to 41½	33 to 35½	41 to 44	14 to 14½
XX-Large	42 to 44½	36 to 38½	44 to 46	14½ to 15

Note that there are corresponding charts for the short, average, and tall fashion categories.

FIG. **2** shows the main menu of a preferred embodiment of the electronic fashion shopping system. A main menu computer interface screen requests that the customer select an area in which she would like to shop. The customer selects a clothes items to scan, which include day suits **14**, evening suits **16**, day dresses **18**, robes, coats **20**, active sports **22**, sportswear **24**, casual wear and at-homewear **26** or any other fashion category. The preferred system is implemented as a typical graphical interface under Microsoft Windows software and Windows 95 software, although other operating systems and interface may be used. Selection is made using a touch screen computer monitor, mouse, or keyboard.

In an interactive television environment, an infrared remote control device is employed to interact and communicate with the system. The system, after reviewing a selection, may also access other related information for analysis and presentation. For example, accessories may be available for some clothes items, such as day suits and evening suits. In addition, shoes are also capable of being selected. When shoe shopping, basic shades that coordinate with the clothing, black, or another neutral are selected.

Each clothes item references portions of a database of fashions for each fashion category. As FIG. **3** illustrates, a submenu allows selection of a fashion for each category. For

5,930,769

7

example, if day suits was selected by the customer, then the first entry of the database of fashions for daysuits in a fashion category such as petites would be shown. The system may also provide an adaptive presentation of choices based on a determined prioritization. Each database entry or fashion has corresponding fashion data. Fashion data allows presentation of a projection of a model having the customer's body type wearing the selected fashion, portrayed on the computer screen. A manual presentation is also possible through modular graphic elements. The face of the model is the digitized photograph or photographs submitted by the customer as personal information. Where such a photograph is unavailable, the customer may select a suitable face model from a plurality of face models, for use in the presentation. This allows the customer the opportunity to preview visually how she would look in a specific style, without having to try it on. The model may be a two dimensional projection, or include three dimensional surface mapping allowing rotations or animations. Other fashion data include the available colors of the fashion **28**, the manufacturer **30**, price of the fashion **32**, the description **34**, and sizes available **36**. If accessories are included, the style number, description, and cost of the accessory are included as fashion data.

The submenu allows the customer to select the size and fit information menu **38**, see another garment in the database for the selected clothes item **40**, order **42**, or start again **44**, by selecting an indicator.

FIG. **4** shows the size and fit information menu for the electronic fashion shopping system. For each fashion, there is corresponding size and fit information menu that the customer can select to view by selecting the "Size and Fit Information" push button or icon. The system compares the customer's body measurements with the garment manufacturer's sizing chart or the actual measurements of the garment. The system uses the universal grading system and sloper concept. All sizes are derived from the sloper. Different manufacturers have a different sloper. For example, starting at size 10, for every next size, one inch is added to each side of the fabric. The computer system or manual system takes into account this size differential. After size 12, it is possible that 1 ½ inches is added to each side of the fabric and after size 16 is reached 2 inches is added to each side of the fabric.

Based on the individual's body measurements, originally gathered as personal information, the correct garment size is calculated and correctly presented. Thus, for example, a customer may be a size 6 in an Ellen Tracy dress and a size 12 in a Tahari dress. As a result, this eliminates the need to guess what size the customer is, and the necessity of trying on of several different sizes for a given manufacturer to determine which size is the right size for the selected clothes item. This is dependent upon the measurements of the customer. In an automated system, the computer tells the correct size for a manufacturer so that the customer need only bring in one size to the dressing room rather than several different sizes of the same garment, or take it home knowing her size without trying it on. The closest size is outputted to the computer screen or printer. For the size and fit submenu, the computer system will generate a virtual mannequin **46** of the customer's body including a digitized photograph of her face which shows the customer how her selected fashion will fit and look. The system may also generate a pointer or arrow **48** which indicates where alterations need to be performed and specifies how much alteration a selected fashion needs. The amount that is required to be adjusted is listed in inches, but can also be listed using the metric system.

8

Alternately, the required alterations may be stored by the computer system and employed in an automated or semi-automated tailoring system. Thus, once the alterations are determined, they need not be manually transmitted to a tailor for implementation. In addition, the system may include a so-called feedback system, wherein a consumer tries on a selected garment and a test garment to determine whether the fit and fashion are appropriate, giving feedback to the computer, which modifies its future analyses based on the feedback. For example, one or more test garments may be tried on, which allow generalization to a larger set of actual garments. In another embodiment, an electronic imaging system views the customer in selected garments or test garments, to obtain further personal information about body size and shape.

In the submenu shown in FIG. **3**, other fashion data such as manufacturer, price, and description are also indicated. Since the customer now knows her correct size in the manufacturer's garment, and the necessary alterations that are needed, if any, it is more likely that the customer would be satisfied with her purchase and less likely that a return would be necessary. The customer's body measurements may also be listed on the computer screen. The customer also has the options to See another suit **40**, ORDER **42**, or START AGAIN **44**, from the Size and Fit Information Menu.

To see another fashion in the current database of fashions for the selected clothes item, the customer selects the "See another suit" icon on the computer screen. Then, another database entry and corresponding fashion data will be displayed.

To order, the customer selects the ORDER submenu. This menu enables the customer to place an order by computer, to telephone an order, or to send an order by facsimile. Where the electronic commerce system is implemented, each transaction is charged to the customer's account and then mailed or shipped to the customer. Of course, the customer may also pick up the garment at a retail location. The billing code is entered and this generates the appropriate name, shipping address, billing address, and other pertinent information. The style number, cost, size, and color are also entered or are automatically provided for a selected fashion. For in-store situations, the sales associates can have an item ready for try-on, or wrapped and ready to go. An automated storage and retrieval system, as employed in the dry-cleaning industry, may be used to retrieve selected inventory.

To start again, the customer selects the START AGAIN icon, and the customer can then select another clothes item such as day suits, evening suits, dresses, robes, coats, active sports, sportswear, casual wear, and at-home wear.

The system optionally has a fashion reflection submenu which outputs the customer's body type to the computer screen, suggests fashion shapes for the determined body type, and suggests fashion shapes to avoid wearing. This information can be printed on an attached printer or downloaded to diskette for printing at a later time.

Turning now to FIG. **5**, this shows analysis of fashion suggestions with designer do's and don'ts based on the customer's body type. The system will output suggestion fashion shapes for the customer's unique body type **50** and suggested fashion shapes to avoid wearing **52**. After body type is determined, the system can output in a chart format fashion do's and don'ts. Using the petite fashion category as an example, the system will output that boleros, cropped jackets and short, tailored jackets with small lapels and collars would work very well. In this case, the system also

5,930,769

9

states that a petite should avoid long skirts, since the extra length will make the petite look smaller, and long garments cut the body and give the appearance of being shorter. The system will also output that when selecting prints, smaller is better since larger patterns tend to be overwhelming and will be proportionately awkward for the petite body. Vertical stripes are a good choice as they create the illusion of height. It is better to go with skinny stripes rather than bold stripes which run the risk of overpowering the petite woman. The system would also output that when accessorizing, it is important to avoid oversize pieces, and instead select narrow belts, scarves that are not too wide and smaller, more delicate jewelry.

For the normal petite, the following information would be outputted to the computer screen or be provided on a data card if the manual system is being employed:

Do wear

Pleated and dirndl skirts will aid volume to your waist and hips, which will add shape to your thin frame.

Peplums are another great look that creates shape and volume for your form.

Blouses worn with bolero vests are also flattering to your figure.

Don't Wear

Avoid large ruffles since they will overpower you with too much fabric.

Large shoulder pads will throw your body out of proportion.

Layers will make you appear smaller.

For the petite with a small bust and large hips, the following information would be outputted to the computer screen or be provided on a data card if the manual system is being employed:

Do Wear

A-line skirts and dresses create the illusion of an evenly proportioned body.

Jackets that are five to seven inches below the waist will camouflage the size difference between your top and bottom and create a better proportion.

Shop for separates. This will eliminate the need for alternations that a one-size, two piece outfit may require.

Don't Wear

Stay away from pleated skirts which will accent the fullness of your hips.

Avoid full dirndl skirts with gathering at the waist as it will emphasize that area.

Steer clear of tight skirts that will call attention to the disproportionate size difference between your bust and hips.

For the petite with a large bust and small hips, the following information would be outputted to the computer screen or be provided on a data card if the manual system is being employed:

Do Wear

Jackets that fall four to seven inches look great. This style will camouflage the size difference and create a better proportioned figure.

Vests that fall four to seven inches below the waist create a more even proportion for your figure.

Dark color tops will make your bust look smaller.

Don't Wear

Avoid blousons (a full blouse that usually has elastic at the bottom and goes to the hips) this style brings extra volume to the top that is not needed.

10

Stay away from white on the top and black on the bottom. White gives the illusion of looking bigger, while black gives the illusion of looking smaller, the combination will emphasize the difference.

Horizontal stripes in a shirt will make your top appear larger.

For the petite with a center front **2** that is short waisted, the following information would be outputted to the computer screen or be provided on a data card if the manual system is being employed:

Do wear

Jackets that fall four to seven inches below the waist elongate the midsection.

A-line and straight dresses will camouflage the torso.

Out blouses that fall at least four inches below the waist help even the look by disguising the waist.

Don't Wear

Try to avoid belts; they will draw attention to your short waist.

Cropped vests and short jackets emphasize the waist and make you look more short waisted.

Fitted two-piece suits that have a different color top and bottom should not be worn. The color contrast will accent the difference between your upper and lower length.

For the petite with a center front **2** that is long waisted, the following information would be outputted to the computer screen or be provided on a data card if the manual system is being employed:

Do wear

Jackets that fall three to seven inches below the waist look best. These styles even the proportion.

Form-fitting, A-line dresses draw attention away from the long waist.

One color, two-piece sets tend to bring a more even look to the torso.

Don't Wear

Avoid bolero or cropped jackets, since they will emphasize the length of your center front.

Hip-huggers will make a long torso look longer.

Try not to wear belts which call attention to the waist and show the difference in proportion.

This information is meant to be illustrative and not limiting. Additional or alternative information may be presented.

Turning now to FIG. **6**, this is a flowchart of a method of electronic fashion shopping for one embodiment of the present invention. At step **601**, the system receives a personal code number to access a database of fashions. The personal code number is linked to personal information relating to the customer. A personal information record is accessed **602** based on the inputted personal code number. At step **603**, a body type and fashion category is determined based on the personal information occurs. Optionally, data relating to a body type and body type may be output based on the personal information record. Next, at step **604**, a clothes item to shop from the customer is received. Optionally, the system selects fashions from the clothes items based on the body type and fashion category. At step **605**, the system outputs a plurality of fashion data based on the selected fashions. Optionally, the system suggests body shapes and intended body type tips. Finally at step **606**, the system receives selection information from the customer

The computer system for electronic fashion shopping allows easy inventory control since merchandise photo-

5,930,769

| 11 | 12 |

graphs can be changed at any time by updating the database records and the system keeps track of what is in stock, what sizes are available and what needs to be ordered. The system may also include information as to when out-of-stock items will be in the store. The inventory control may be integrated with an automated storage and retrieval system making inventory more space efficient.

The system provides better customer service since it personalizes and simplifies the shopping process. The system allows customers to consider more clothes that would fit in less time, presenting the customer with more buying opportunities, and thus increases efficiency of the system as compared to traditional shopping methods.

The computer system has application for a retailer and manufacturer selling their products on the computer, CD-ROM, the Internet, or television or through manual systems. The system also has application for a manufacturer selling his product direct, a catalog company, a fashion designer marketing their line, or an on-line network selling their own products. The computer system would aid in the success of interactive on-line home shopping by offering the home shopper what is traditionally considered as only in store services.

From the above, it should be understood that the embodiments described, in regard to the drawings, are merely exemplary and that a person skilled in the art may make variations and modifications to the shown embodiments without departing from the spirit and scope of the invention. All such variations and modifications are intended to be included within the scope of the invention as defined by the appended claims.

What is claimed is:

1. A method of fashion shopping by a customer comprising the steps of:

receiving personal information from the customer;

selecting a body type and fashion category based on the personal information;

selecting fashions from a plurality of clothes items based on the body type and fashion category;

outputting a plurality of fashion data based on the selected fashions;

receiving selection information from the customer; and

processing order information to place an order for the selected fashions.

2. A method as in claim 1 wherein the personal information includes a digitized image of the customer's face.

3. A method as in claim 1 wherein the personal information includes an electronic commerce identifier for billing purposes.

4. A method as in claim 1 wherein the fashion category provided is selected from the group consisting of petite, short, average, and tall.

5. A method as in claim 1 wherein said clothes items are a clothes category selected from the group consisting of day suits, evening suits, dresses, robes, coats, active sports, sportswear, casual wear, and at home wear.

6. A method as in claim 1 wherein said fashion data comprises providing available colors, manufacturer's prices, styles, and sizes.

7. A method as in claim 1 further comprising the step of determining on availability of selected fashions.

8. A method as in claim 1 wherein the method further comprises the step of receiving an order from the customer.

9. A method as in claim 1 further comprising the step of outputting a personal code number to identify the customer.

10. A method as in claim 1 wherein body type is a stature selected from the group consisting of full-bust/slight hip, normal, without a waistline, and slight bust/fuller hip.

11. A method as in claim 1 wherein the fashion category is selected from the group consisting of slim, athletic, stout, and portly stout.

12. A method as in claim 1 wherein the fashion category is selected from the group consisting of infant, toddler, children, pre-teen, and teen.

13. A method as in claim 1 wherein the fashions and fashion data are contained in a database.

14. A method as in claim 1 wherein the fashion data includes a garment description.

15. A method as in claim 1 wherein the fashion data includes accessory style number, accessory description, and accessory cost.

16. A method as in claim 1 further comprising the step of updating the selected fashions based on said received selection information.

17. A method as in claim 1 wherein the personal information includes the measurements of bust, hips, waist, arm length, height, and center front.

18. A method as in claim 17 wherein the measurements further comprise inseam, center length, and center depth.

19. A method as in claim 1 wherein the personal information includes a plurality of body measurements and a digitized picture of the customer's face.

20. A method as in claim 19 wherein the outputting the plurality of fashion data includes outputting a computerized simulated body type image corresponding to the customer's body measurements and the digitized picture of the customer's face.

21. A method as in claim 1 further comprising the step of determining size and fit of a selected fashion.

22. A method as in claim 21 wherein determining the size and fit comprises the steps of displaying a closest size for the selected fashion and indicating where adjustments are necessary.

23. A method as in claim 21 further comprising determining an amount the selected fashion needs to be altered.

24. A method of electronic fashion shopping by a customer using an electronic medium comprising the steps of:

receiving a personal code number to access a database of fashions;

accessing a personal information record based on the inputted personal code number;

outputting a body type and body type data based on the personal information record;

receiving a clothes item to shop from the customer;

receiving selection information from the customer; and

outputting an order for the clothes item, an invoice for the customer and an inventory record of all items ordered by the customer.

25. A method as in claim 24 wherein receiving selection information from the customer is a step selected from the group consisting of placing an order, see another fashion, start again and see size and fit information.

26. A method as in claim 24 wherein the personal information record includes a digitized image of the customer's face.

27. A method as in claim 24 wherein the personal information record includes electronic commerce information for business purposes.

28. A method as in claim 24 wherein the clothes item is a clothing category selected from the group consisting of day suits, evening suits, dresses, robes, coats, active sports, sportswear, casual wear, and at-home wear.

29. A method as in claim 24 wherein the body type data is associated with data relating to which styles to wear and which styles to avoid.

5,930,769

13

30. A method as in claim **24** wherein the body type is a stature selected from the group consisting of full-bust/slight hip, normal, without a waistline, and slight bust/fuller hip.

31. A method as in claim **24** wherein the fashion data comprises providing available colors, manufacturer's prices, styles, and sizes.

32. A method as in claim **24** wherein the method further comprises the step of receiving an order from the customer.

33. A method as in claim **24** wherein the fashion data includes a garment description.

34. A method as in claim **24** further comprising the step of updating the selected fashions based on the received selection information.

35. A method as in claim **24** wherein the personal information record contains a plurality of body measurements for the customer.

36. A method as in claim **35** wherein the body measurements include bust, hips, waist, arm length, height, and center front.

37. A method as in claim **24** further including the step of determining a fashion category based on the personal information record.

38. A method as in claim **37** wherein the fashion category is selected from the group consisting of petite, short, average, and tall.

39. A method as in claim **37** wherein the fashion category is selected from the group consisting of slim, athletic, stout, and portly stout.

40. A method as in claim **37** wherein the fashion category is selected from the group consisting of infant, toddler, children, pre-teen, and teen.

14

41. A method as in claim **24** further comprising the step of determining size and fit of a selected fashion.

42. A method as in claim **41** wherein determining the size and fit comprises the steps of displaying a closest size for the selected fashion and indicating where adjustments are necessary.

43. A method as in claim **41** further comprising determining the amount the selected fashion needs to be altered.

44. A method as in claim **41** further comprising the step of determining an availability of selected fashions.

45. A method for assisting in clothing shopping comprising:

receiving personal information from a person including a plurality of body measurements;

providing a database of clothing items, including multi-dimensional models of fit for the clothing items;

receiving a clothing type from the person;

selecting a clothing item of the clothing type from the database, the clothing item fit model of the selected clothing item, corresponding to the body type as determined by the received body measurements; and

outputting data relating to the result of modeling the person in the selected clothes item based on the personal information and the selected clothing item fit model.

* * * * *

UNITED STATES PATENT AND TRADEMARK OFFICE
CERTIFICATE OF CORRECTION

PATENT NO : 5,930,769   Page 2 of 2
DATED   : July 27, 1999
INVENTOR(S) : Andrea Rose

   It is certified that error appears in the above-identified patent and that said Letters Patent
is hereby corrected as shown below:

Column 4, line 18, "Rose" should be -- Rose® --;

           line 19, "services®" should be -- services --.

UNITED STATES PATENT AND TRADEMARK OFFICE
CERTIFICATE OF CORRECTION

PATENT NO : 5,930,769   Page 1 of 2
DATED   : July 27, 1999
INVENTOR(S) : Andrea Rose

   It is certified that error appears in the above-identified patent and that said Letters Patent
is hereby corrected as shown below:

Cover page, item 76, Inventor, "Rose" should be
--Rosengard--.

Figure 6, box 605, "pluarity" should be -- plurality --

Col. 1, line 45, "instock" should be -- in-stock. --.

Col. 4, line 12, "the." should be -- the --;

        line 27, "customer" should be -- customer of --.

Col. 5, line 28, "normal.stature," should be -- normal
stature, --.

Col. 7, line 30, "is" should be -- is a --.

Col. 10, line 56, "occurs." should be -- record. --.

Claim 7, col. 11, line 60, "on" should be   an --.

Signed and Sealed this

Fourth Day of July, 2000

Q. TODD DICKINSON

Director of Patents and Trademarks

Watch With Speed Adjustment During Travel for Reducing Jet Lag (Mitchell Electrical Patent)

For some travelers, moving the clock ahead or behind one hour whenever an international date line is crossed seems like a jolting arbitrary experience. Inventor Ross Mitchell of Massachusetts perfected a solution—a timepiece that progresses at a faster (or slower) rate to acclimatize a traveler while moving from departure to arrival.

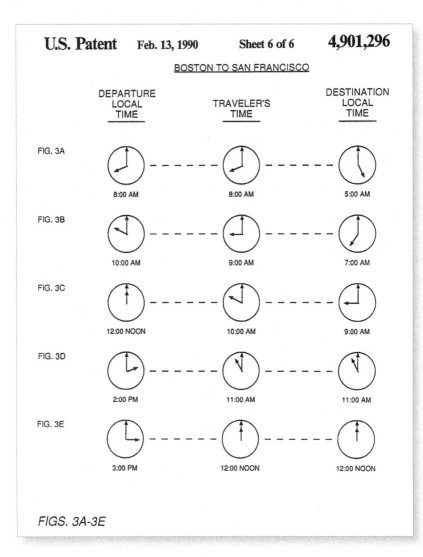

Provisional Patent Application

Watch With Speed Adjustment During Travel for Reducing Jet Lag

A major problem facing people who travel over long distances is adapting to different time zones (jet lag). They will often set their watches to the local time upon arrival at the destination. While a person arriving in New York from California may know that the local time is 5:00 PM EST, they are likely to feel that the "real" time is 2:00 PM EST. This is because the person did not experience a progression in time from the place of departure to the destination location. Thus, after having abruptly set the watch three hours ahead of the current local time of the departure location, the traveler must now attempt to believe that this new local time is the "real" time. It often takes a traveler a day or more to acclimate, both physically and psychologically, to the new local time.

While patent 4,204,398, to Lemelson (1980) shows a timepiece which changes its display automatically as it passes from one time zone to the next, it does not permit the user to gradually adapt to the new time zones. It steps back or forward in abrupt hourly increments and is complex and costly. It supposes that transmitters have been placed which have access to the current local time at any point on the earth. This, too, is a costly and cumbersome requirement. Consequently, its workings are not practical for incorporation into a relatively low cost personal timepiece.

Marvosh, in patent 4,763,311, describes a double clock, one face of which runs at either fast or slow rate for six months of each year. The purpose of this is to gradually alter the user's time standard in order to take advantage of all available daylight throughout the year. It does not address the need for a traveler to adapt to an existing time standard.

My watch includes a "traveler's time" function which is activated when a wearer leaves on an eastbound or westbound trip. The watch will advance or retard its rate so that after the trip time has elapsed, it will display the actual local time at the arrival location, and then will return to its normal operating speed.

The user enters the time difference at the departure and arrival locations and whether those hours will be gained or lost, i.e., whether one is traveling east or west. This is done by actuating a function which causes a number of hours to be displayed, prefixed with a "+" or a "−". The user then enters the length of time over which the change is to take place, i.e., the approximate trip time. Then the user activates the traveler's time function. The watch will begin to adjust to the arrival location time zone by either running faster or slower. After the trip time has elapsed, the watch will display a time which matches the local arrival time.

For example, if a person is traveling from Boston to San Francisco by airplane. The flight leaves the gate in Boston at 8:00 AM EST. The flight is due to arrive in San Francisco at 11:25 AM, PST. The user knows that the flight time should be about six hours and that the time in SF is three hours earlier than Boston time. The user enters "–3" to indicate that three hours must be lost during the trip. Then the user enters "6:00," indicating that the three hours should be lost over a six-hour period. The user then starts the function and the watch begins to run at a rate which is 6/3, or half normal speed.

Throughout the flight, the time displayed represents the time the user should consider as "real." The user need not know or be concerned with the actual local time in either location. The user should look occasionally at the watch to gain maximum benefit. The traveler's time is gradually regressing, which leaves the user at PST, six hours from the moment the function switch on the watch was actuated in Boston, i.e., 11:00 AM PST, assuming the function had been engaged at 8:00 AM EST. Thus, the user is not jolted into a new zone at the destination, but is eased into it. Upon arrival, the user feels acclimated to the San Francisco time.

For the return to Boston, the user programs the watch in the same fashion to gain an additional three hours in the approximately 4.5 hours west-to-east trip time. The watch now operates faster than normal and thus displays the correct EST after 4.5 hours elapse and the plane is nearing Boston.

A less expensive version of the watch can omit the time for the transition between the different time zones, but gains or loses time at a constant rate, e.g., one hour every hour.

The travel function includes a microprocessor circuit and function switches to receive the input data and make the rate calculations to drive the watch display at the faster or slower rate.

FIG. 1 shows the electronic system of my traveler's watch.

FIGS. 2A through 2D are flow charts which show how the traveler's time function can be implemented in the watch.

FIGS. 3A through 3E illustrate time progression during a typical use of the watch.

Microprocessor 10 (Fig. 1) is an NS COP424C and is connected to an external quartz crystal 20 to provide an HF oscillator. An LC display 30 shows hours, minutes and seconds and is driven by a decoder/driver (DD) 100 in processor 10. When the traveler's time function is active, display 30 shows only hours and minutes; the user is not distracted by seconds advancing at an abnormally fast or slow rate.

Microprocessor 10 additionally contains an oscillator circuit 110, a counter/ divider 120, a central processing unit (CPU) 130, a read-only memory (ROM) 140, registers W, X, Y and Z, designated 145, 150, 155 and 156, respectively, registers R, D, S and C, labeled 157, 158, 159 and 160, respectively, and an accumulator and flag registers (not shown). The accumulator acts as a temporary storage register where numbers can be stored in binary form and mathematical operations can be performed and the results can be directed to other registers. A latch 170, a switch decoder 180, and the internal connections are also included, as shown in FIG. 1.

Oscillator 110 provides an output square wave and divider 120 provides a 64 Hz. square wave, both with a 50% duty cycle. HF clock signal 190 clocks CPU 130 and DD 100.

CPU 130, interrupt driven, is normally waiting for instruction. Input 200, labeled "INT 1," is activated at a rate of 64 Hz. CPU 130 typically recognizes interrupts as a positive-going, logical transition between zero volts (logic "0" or "false") and 1.5 volts (logic "1" or "true").

Input 210, labeled "INT 2", is activated whenever one of switches 40 through 90 is closed. The inputs to decoder 180 are normally low or at ZERO due to resistors 41 to 91. When a switch is closed, the battery voltage is momentarily connected to the associated input on decoder 180. Decoder 180 signals CPU 130 via interrupt line #2 (205) connected to input 210, and provides logical data on multiple lines 220, to input 230 of CPU 130.

CPU 130 can send data to registers W, X, Y, Z, R, D, S and C, designated 145, 150, 155, 156, 157, 158, 159 and 160, respectively. It can also read the contents of these registers. The data in registers W, X, Y and Z is stored in latch 170. Multiple control lines 240 are used to select among the registers 145, 150, 155 and 156. Once a register is selected by address lines 240, a momentary pulse is applied to latch 170 via line 300 which connects an output of CPU 130 to the latch 170, and causes the data present at its input to be stored in the latch. The data in any of registers 145, 150, 155 or 156 represents time and can be shown as the digits on display 30. Register W 145 stores the current time. Register X 150 stores the present time, i.e., the departure time. Register Y 155 stores the destination time. Register Z stores the transition time, the trip duration. Register R 157 stores the time zone transition rate which is what CPU 130 uses. Register D 158 stores the difference between the time at the departure and destination locations, as a + or − number. Register S 159 is a counter which is incremented once for each successive tick (1/64 second). This counter increments the time at both locations. Register C 160 is a counter which will also be incremented once for each tick to increment the traveler's time. Other registers (not shown) store addresses, statuses, etc. Patent 4,316,272, to Seikosha (1982) shows these functions. Finally, CPU 130 has a ROM 140 that contains multiple instructions which govern overall operation.

FIGS. 2A and 2B show the series of instructions which are executed in response to INT 1 at input 200 (FIG. 1). FIGS. 2C and 2D show the sequence of instructions which are executed in response to INT 2, generated with each closure of any of switches 40 to 90. The interrupts are prioritized. INT 1 has the higher priority and can be activated while INT 2 is in progress. INT 2 can never be operational while INT 1 is in progress.

FIG. 2A illustrates how interrupts are handled. Upon power-up the watch loads 1:00 into registers W 145, X 150, and Y 155. Then the time in register X 150, i.e., departure time zone time, is displayed. The wait loop is entered. The processor is interrupted INT 1 at each tick. Control is then passed to the routine in FIG. 2B, after the address of the interruption is saved, in the event that an INT 2 operation had been in progress.

FIG. 2B illustrates incrementation of the departure, destination and traveler's times, as well as the termination of traveler's time after arrival. Counter S 159 is incremented once per INT 1 interruption of the CPU. When it reaches 64, one second has elapsed and it is time to increment the departure and destination time zone times, registers X 150, and Y 155, by one second. The timekeeping algorithm is a routine for incrementing minutes, hours and dates at the proper time. Counter C 160 is also incremented once per INT 1 interruption of the CPU. When it equals the value stored in register R 157, the traveler's time register W 145 is incremented one second. The value in register R 157 is determined in calculations shown in FIG. 2D below. After incrementing the traveler's time, a comparator determines if the traveler's time equals the destination time. If so, the traveler time function is cancelled, and the destination time Y 155 is latched. Operation then resumes at the normal rate.

FIG. 2C shows the sequence of instructions executed in response to INT 2, generated with each closure of one of switches 40 to 90. Switch 40 functions as a flip-flop. If travel is active, operation of this switch resets it, displaying the departure time. If the travel is not active, operation of switch 40 executes the instructions of FIG. 2D. These initialize the travel function and commence adjustment. The user may enter the trip time by operating switch 55 to cause display of the last trip time. Switches 80 and 90 may be operated to adjust this time. Logic to reset the hours after 23 and minutes after 59 is provided. The user may operate switches 45 through 90 in any order desired.

FIG. 2D shows the sequence of instructions executed in response to switch 40 when the travel is not already active. The destination and departure times are compared. If the destination time is greater, the watch determines whether this difference exceeds 12 hours. If so, it is assumed that the destination time zone is actually earlier than (west of) the departure time and a negative difference D is calculated. If the difference is less than twelve hours, a positive difference D is calculated. Similar logic is applied to combinations where the destination time zone time is less than the departure time zone time. This logic is necessary in a watch without an internal date function, since it must correctly account for a departure time zone time in one day and a destination time zone time in another. For example, a traveler departing San Francisco for Boston at 23:00 would show a destination time of 02:00. The logic in FIG. 2D correctly calculates the difference D as 3 and not −21.

Once the time difference D is known and the trip time Z has been entered, it is simple to calculate the update rate R. This is the number of ticks before incrementing the seconds counter for the travel function. This is done, the tick counter is reset, the travel time is set to the departure time and displayed, the function in progress flag is set, and the function is under way. The function will continue until the user resets it by pressing switch 40 or until the travel time equals the destination time, after the specified trip time has elapsed. The user may view the destination and/or departure time without disturbing the function, using switches 45 and/or 60. To return to the travel time, the user simply operates switch 50.

FIGS. 3A through 3E show the time which would appear on an analog embodiment during travel from Boston to San Francisco, a time difference of −3 hours. The user has set the destination time zone time into register Y 155. The user has specified a trip time of six hours into register Z 156. The function is activated at exactly 8:00 AM EST.

In FIG. 3A the traveler's time indicates the same time as the actual time in the departure location. The destination (San Francisco) time is 5:00 AM, three hours earlier.

In FIG. 3B, two hours have elapsed so that Boston time is 10:00 AM, and San Francisco time is 7:00 AM, yet the traveler's time has only increased by one hour, to 9:00 AM.

In FIG. 3C, another two hours have elapsed and one hour more has elapsed for the traveler's time display. Boston time is now 12:00 noon, and San Francisco time is 9:00 AM. The traveler's time display indicates 10:00 AM.

In FIG. 3D, six hours have elapsed in the departure and destination times zones. Boston time is now 2:00 PM, and San Francisco time is 11:00 AM. The traveler's time display has increased by one more hour and now indicates 11:00 AM, the destination time. The display is now normal.

In FIG. 3E, one hour has elapsed since arrival at the destination. Boston time is now 3:00 PM, and San Francisco is 12:00 noon. The traveler's display reads 12:00 noon. The watch has been running at a normal speed for one hour.

Patent

United States Patent [19]

Mitchell

[11] **Patent Number:** **4,901,296**

[45] **Date of Patent:** Feb. 13, 1990

[54] **WATCH WITH SPEED ADJUSTMENT DURING TRAVEL FOR REDUCING JET LAG**

[76] Inventor: Ross E. Mitchell, 4 Allston St., Newtonville, Mass. 02160

[21] Appl. No.: 325,293

[22] Filed: Mar. 17, 1989

[51] Int. Cl.[4] G04C 9/00
[52] U.S. Cl. 368/185; 368/187; 368/21
[58] Field of Search 368/185–199, 368/223, 228, 238, 21–27

[56] **References Cited**

U.S. PATENT DOCUMENTS

4,072,005	8/1978	Teshima et al.	58/42.5
4,204,398	10/1980	Lemelson	368/47
4,316,272	11/1982	Naito	368/21
4,445,785	4/1984	Chambon et al.	368/187
4,505,594	6/1985	Kawahara et al.	368/73
4,620,797	10/1986	Besson et al.	368/21
4,763,311	8/1988	Marvosh	368/228
4,821,248	9/1989	Yamasaki	368/21

OTHER PUBLICATIONS

Letter to editor Mensa Magazine, 3/86 A New Kind of Setting Time, Williams.

Primary Examiner—Bernard Roskoski
Attorney, Agent, or Firm—David Pressman

[57] **ABSTRACT**

An electronic watch includes a "traveler's time" function which can be activated when a wearer leaves on a long trip, east or west by plane, boat or the like. This function will advance or retard the operation rate of the watch so that after a user-determined trip time has elapsed, the watch will display the actual local time at the arrival location, and the watch will resume operation at its normal rate. By glancing at the watch from time to time, a traveler can become accustomed gradually to a time change caused by his travel through different time zones so that the psychological effects of "jet lag" are minimized. The watch includes a microprocessor (**10**), a quartz crystal (**20**) for providing a time standard, a display (**30**) for displaying the time, and a set of switches (**40–90**) for activating the watch's functions. The microprocessor includes a set of registers (**145 to 160**) for storing the departure, destination, and traveler's times, and for controlling operation of the watch.

15 Claims, 6 Drawing Sheets

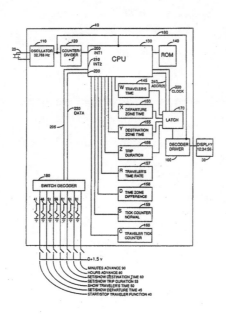

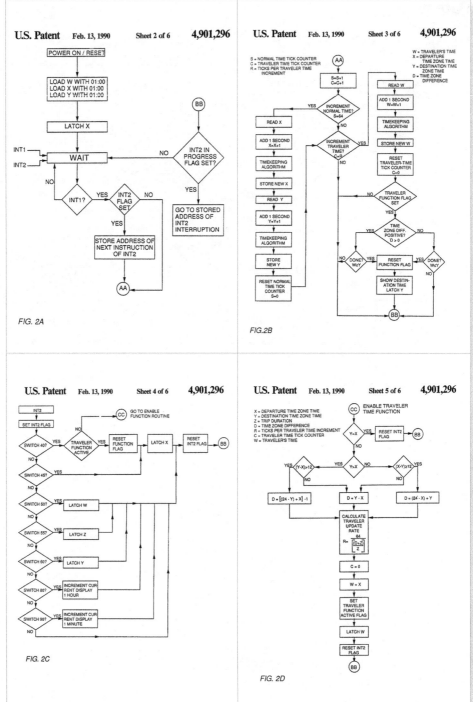

FIG. 2A

FIG.2B

FIG. 2C

FIG. 2D

4,901,296

1

WATCH WITH SPEED ADJUSTMENT DURING
TRAVEL FOR REDUCING JET LAG

BACKGROUND-FIELD OF THE INVENTION

This invention relates generally to watches, and more
particularly to watches especially suited for travelers.

BACKGROUND-DESCRIPTION OF PRIOR ART

Present-day personal timepieces, such as wrist and
pocket watches, employ a quartz crystal to generate a
precise timing signal which is stepped down in frequency to produce trains of timing signals to drive the
watch display. In the case of a watch with an analog
display, those timing signals drive a step motor which
turns the hour and minute hands of the watch. In the
case of a watch with a digital display, the timing signal
trains control a circuit which drives a LED or liquid
crystal display. An electronic watch with an analog
display is shown, for example, in U.S. Pat. No.
4,505,594, to Kawahara et al. (1985), while U.S. Pat.
No. 4,316,272, to Seikosha (1982) illustrates a watch
having a digital display.

A major problem facing people who travel over long
distances is adapting to changes in local time caused by
their passing through different time zones. This condition is commonly referred to as jet lag. Persons traveling a long distance will often set their watches to the
local time upon arrival at the destination. While a person arriving in New York from California may know
that the local time is 5:00 P.M., Eastern Standard Time,
this person is likely to feel that the "real" time is 2:00
P.M., Eastern Standard Time. This is because the person did not experience a progression in time from the
place of departure to the destination location. Thus,
after having abruptly set the watch three hours ahead of
the current local time of the departure location, the
traveler must now attempt to believe that this new local
time is the "real" time for him or her. For a long voy-
age, it often takes a traveler a day or even more to
acclimate, both physically and psychologically, to the
local time at the new location.

Some present day electronic watches include a function which enables the watch to display local time at
various cities in all of the different time zones of the
world. Examples of such watches are found in U.S. Pat.
Nos. 4,072,005 to Teshima et al. (1978); 4,316,272 to
Seikosha (1982); and 4,620,797 to Besson and Mesiter
(1986). A traveler in Boston embarking on a trip to
London at 10:00 A.M. may actuate the world time function switch of such a watch and call up London on the
watch which will thereupon display the corresponding
local time in London, i.e., 3:00 P.M. Thus the traveler
becomes aware immediately of the time difference between the two locations. However, this knowledge
really does nothing to overcome the jet lag feeling that
the traveler will experience upon reaching London.
This is because whether the traveler switches the water
to London time upon departing from Boston, while in
the air over the Atlantic, or upon reaching England, the
watch, because it switches the two local times
substantially instantaneously, does not help the traveler
to become accustomed psychologically to the new local
time.

There does exist a timepiece which changes its time
display automatically as it passes from one time zone to
the next. This time piece is described in U.S. Pat. No.
4,204,398, to Lemelson (1980), and includes a radio

2

receiver which responds to signals generated from a
remote transmitter located, for example, in the aircraft
in which the user is traveling. As the aircraft passes
from one time zone to the next, this timepiece can automatically change its display to show the current time in
the new time zone. However, this watch does not permit the user to gradually adapt to the new time zones.
The watch is stepped back or forward in abrupt hourly
increments. Further, this watch is quite complex and
costly. It supposes that transmitters have been placed
which have access to the current local time at any point
on the earth. This, too, represents a costly and cumbersome requirement. Consequently, its workings are not
practical for incorporation into a relatively low cost
personal timepiece, such as a wrist or pocket watch.
Marvosh, in U.S. Pat. No. 4,763,311, describes a double
clock, one face of which runs at either fast or slow rate
for six months of each year. The purpose of this is to
gradually alter the user's time standard in order to take
advantage of all available daylight throughout the year.
It does not address the need for travelers to adapt to an
existing time standard.

OBJECTS AND ADVANTAGES

Accordingly, one object and advantage of this invention is to provide a timepiece which can be carried on
the person and which reduces jet lag caused by travel
between different times zones.

Other objects are to provide a watch which will assist
the wearer to acclimate to local time changes caused by
easterly or westerly travel over relatively great distances between two locations, to provide such a watch
which enables a wearer to acclimate to the change in
local time over the course of the trip, and to provide a
watch of this type which will not cost appreciably more
than a conventional electronic watch having a plural
function display capability.

Further objects will become apparent from the ensuing description, claims and accompanying drawings.

SUMMARY

Briefly, in accordance with the present invention, an
electronic watch includes a "traveler's time" function
which can be activated when a wearer leaves on an east
or westbound trip. This function will advance or retard
the operation rate of the watch so that after a user-
determined trip time has elapsed, the timepiece will
display the actual local time at the arrival location, and
from that point, will return automatically to its normal
operating speed.

In one watch implementation, the user enters the time
difference at the departure and arrival locations and
whether those hours will be gained or lost, i.e., whether
one is traveling east or west. This is done by actuating
a function which causes a number of hours to be displayed, prefixed with a "+" or a "−". Following this,
the user enters the length of time over which the change
to the new time zone is to take place, i.e., the approximate trip time. Then the user presses a function button
to activate the traveler's time function. At that moment,
the watch will begin to adjust to the arrival location
time zone by either running faster or slower than normal. After the preset trip time has elapsed, the watch
will display a time which matches the local time in the
time zone of the arrival location. At this point, the traveler time function is automatically canceled and the
watch resumes operation at its normal rate.

4,901,296

3

4

For example, assume that a person is traveling from Boston to San Francisco by airplane. The flight leaves the gate in Boston at 8:00 A.M., Eastern Standard Time. The flight is due to arrive in San Francisco at 11:25 A.M., Pacific Standard Time. Upon boarding the flight, the user knows that the flight time should be about six hours and that the time in San Francisco is three hours earlier than Boston time, using a function button, the user enters "−3" to indicate that three hours must be lost during the course of the trip. Then, using another function button, the user enters "6:00", indicating that the three hours should be lost over a six-hour time period. The user than starts the function and the watch begins to run at a rate which is 6/3, or half normal speed.

Throughout the flight, the time displayed by the watch represents the time the user should consider as "real." It is advantageous that the user not know or be concerned with the actual local time in either the departure location or the arrival location during this transition period. Most airplanes are isolated environments and are, therefore, particularly well suited to providing the user with an opportunity to experience the "traveler's time" displayed by the watch as being "real." In this connection, it is incumbent upon the user to look occasionally at the time shown on the watch in order to gain maximum benefit from this watch feature. In this example, the traveler's time is gradually regressing, which leaves the user at Pacific Standard Time, six hours from the moment the function switch on the watch was actuated in Boston, i.e., 11:00 A.M. PST, assuming the function had been engaged at 8:00 A.M. EST. Thus, the user is not jolted into a new time zone at the destination, but rather, is eased into this new local time. As a result, upon arrival, the user feels more acclimated to the San Francisco local time since the user has experienced a gradual progression into the destination time zone.

For the return to Boston, the user programs the watch in the same fashion to gain an additional three hours in the approximately four and a half hours west-to-east trip time. The watch now operates faster than normal and thus displays the correct Eastern Standard Time after four and a half hours elapes and the plane is nearing its Boston destination.

The function can be engaged substantially prior to the commencement of travel and/or be set to terminate after the trip has been completed, so that users crossing time zones extremely rapidly, such as those traveling at very high latitudes or by means of supersonic transport, can provide themselves a sufficient period of time over which to adapt to the new time zone.

A less expensive version of the watch might operate so as not to permit the user to enter the amount of time allowed for the transition between the different time zones, but would gain or lose time at a constant rate, e.g., one hour every hour. Further, this rate could be provided as a default transition rate even on watches which allowed the user to set the rate. In this way, if the user were willing to accept the default, it would not be necessary to enter the transition period (travel time). Also, the watch can be implemented in conjunction with a conventional date function so that the date will be incremented or decremented if the destination time would cause the date to be other than the one at the departure location.

The function can as well be incorporated into a conventional electronic watch having a world time display function. In this embodiment, the user would not have to know the local time difference between the departure and arrival locations of his trip; the watch would display these times, often simultaneously. To use the watch, the traveler would then simply enter the expected trip time into the watch, select the destination, and engage the function. The watch would thereupon operate at a faster or slower rate to gain or lose the necessary time over the course of the trip such that the watch would display the correct local time at the arrival location upon completion of the entered trip time.

Still further, the traveler's time function can be incorporated into a conventional electronic watch having a multiple time zone display function. In this embodiment, the user would set the arrival location's time into the second time zone display. To use the watch, the traveler would then simply enter the travel time (or accept the default) and engage the function. The watch would then automatically determine the difference between the time zones and the likely direction of travel, i.e., east or west. This is the embodiment which will be covered in the detailed explanation which follows.

The preferred implementation of the travel function includes a microprocessor circuit and associated function switchs to receive the input data and make the rate calculations described above to develop the timing signals to drive the watch display at the computed faster or slower rate. The electronic circuitry for doing this is well known in the art so that the incorporation of this invention into an otherwise conventional electronic watch should not unduly complicate the watch or materially add to its overall cost.

BRIEF DESCRIPTION OF THE DRAWINGS

FIG. 1 is a block diagram showing the electronic system of a digital watch according to the invention.

FIGS. 2A through 2D are flow charts which denote one means by which the traveler's time function can be implemented in the watch of FIG. 1.

FIGS. 3A through 3F are diagrams illustrating time progression during a typical use of the function.

FIG. 1 - BLOCK DIAGRAM OF WATCH

FIG. 1 shows one preferred embodiment of the invention. Many timepieces manufactured today utilize microprocessors. These typically contain an internal memory, a number of internal registers, counters, latches, decoders, etc. One such microprocessor, shown at 10, is the model COP424C, manufactured by National Semiconductor Corporation, 2900 Semiconductor Drive, Santa Clara, Calif. 95051, U.S.A. The application of these microprocessors to timekeeping is well known to those familiar with both horology and microprocessor technology.

The term "tick" will be used to denote 1/64 second. This is the rate at which the watch will be interrupted and at which the routine for adjusting the time will be executed.

Microprocessor 10 is supplied with an external quartz crystal 20 to provide a high frequency oscillator circuit. Other external components include batteries (not shown) which provide the energy to run the circuitry of the timepiece; a display 30 which, in this embodiment, would preferably be a liquid crystal horological display capable of showing hours, minutes and seconds; and a set of switches 40 through 90. The functions associated with each of switches 40 through 90 will be described in detail below. Display 30 is activated by a decoder/-driver 100 in microprocessor 10. When the traveler's

4,901,296

5

time function is active, display 30 is programmed to show only hours and minutes, so that the user is not distracted by seconds advancing at an abnormally fast or slow rate.

Microprocessor 10 additionally contains an oscillator circuit 110, a counter/divider 120, a central processing unit (CPU) 130, a read-only memory (ROM) 140, registers W, X, Y, and Z, designated 145, 150, 155, and 156, respectively, registers R, D, S and C, labeled 157, 158, 159 and 160, respectively, and an accumulator and flag registers (not shown). The accumulator acts as a temporary storage register in where numbers can be stored in binary form and mathematical operations can be performed on these numbers and from where the results can be directed to other registers. A latch 170, a switch decoder 180, and the internal connections are also included, as shown in FIG. 1.

Oscillator 110 provides an output square wave with 50% duty cycle, in well-known fashion. Divider 120 provides at its output a 64 Hz. square wave, again with a 50% duty cycle, in well-known fashion. High frequency clocking signal 190 is connected to CPU 130 and decoder/driver 100 to cause them to operate at a high speed. CPU 130 must be able to perform operations at a high rate of speed in order to complete numerous tasks each second. Decoder/driver 100 must also activate all parts of display 30 in a time short compared with a second. The operation of these two components is well known to those familiar with logic circuits.

CPU 130 is "interrupt" driven. It is normally waiting for instruction. It can optionally be "powered down" between interrupts to conserve battery energy. Input 200, labeled "INT 1" for "interrupt number 1," is activated at a rate of 64 Hz. CPU 130 typically recognizes interrupts as a positive-going, logical transistions between zero volts (logic "0" or "false") and +1.5 volts (logic "1" or "true").

Input 210, labeled "INT 2" for "interrupt number 2," is activated whenever one of switches 40 through 90 is closed. The inputs to decoder 180 are normally held "low" or at logic "0" by resistors 41 through 91. When a switch is closed, the battery voltage, typically 1.5 volts, is momentarily connected to the associated input on decoder 180. In response, decoder 180 signals CPU 130 via interrupt line #2 (205) connected to input 210, and provides logical data on multiple lines 220, to input 230 of CPU 130, in well-known fashion.

CPU 130 can send data to registers W, X, Y, Z, R, D, S, and C, designated 145, 150, 155, 156, 157, 158, 159, and 160, respectively. It can also read the contents of these registers. The data in registers W, X, Y, and Z can be stored in latch 170. Multiple control lines 240 are used to select among the registers 145, 150, 155, and 156 in well-known fashion. Once a register is selected by address lines 240, a momentary pulse is applied to latch 170 via line 300 which connects an output of CPU 130 to the "latch" input of latch 170, and causes the data present at the input of latch 170 to be stored in the latch indefinitely, in well-known fashion. In this way, the data present in any of registers 145, 150, 155, or 156, which are representative of time, can be shown as the digits of time on display 30. In the present embodiment, register W 145 is used to show the current traveler's time. Register X 150 is used to store the "present" time of day, i.e., the departure time zone time. Register Y 155 is used to store the current time at the destination. Register Z is used to store the transition time, i.e., the duration of the trip.

6

Register R (157) is used to store the time zone transition rate which will be calculated by CPU 130 using data from Registers X, Y, Z, and D. Register D (158) is used to store the difference between the time at the departure location, and the time at the destination location, as a signed (+ or −) number. Register S (159) is a counter which will be incremented once for each successive tick of the timepiece, i.e., once per 1/64 second. This counter is used to increment the time at the departure and destination locations. Register C (160) is a counter which will also be incremented once for each tick of the timepiece. This counter is used to increment the traveler's time. There are other registers (not shown) capable of storing addresses, statuses, etc. The setting and operation of watches of type are quite well known. See U.S. Pat. No. 4,316,272, to Seikosha (1982), for example, whose disclosure is incorporated by reference herein.

Finally, CPU 130 is provided with ROM 140 which. ROM 140 contains multiple instructions which govern the operation of the timepiece. This concept is also well known to those skilled in the art of microprocessor technology.

FIGS. 2 - FLOW CHARTS

The principle of the present invention is best understood by consideration of the flow charts in FIGS. 2A through 2D and FIGS. 3A through 3E. FIGS. 2A and 2B show the series of instructions which are executed in response to INT 1 at input 200 (FIG. 1). FIGS. 2C and 2D show the sequence of instructions which are executed in response to INT 2, generated with each closure of a switch 40 through 90. The interrupts are prioritized. INT 1 has the higher priority and can be activated while INT 2 is in progress. INT 2 can never be operational while INT 1 is in progress.

FIG. 2A is a flowchart which illustrates how interrupts are handled. Upon initial power-up the watch loads 1:00 into registers W (145), X (150), and Y (155). Then the time in register X (150), i.e., departure time zone time, is displayed. The wait loop is entered. The processor will be interrupted (INT 1) each 1/64 second. Control will then be passed to the routine described in FIG. 2B, after the address of the interruption is saved, in the event that an INT 2 operation had been in progress.

FIG. 2B illustrates the means by which the departure, destination and traveler's current time is incremented, as well as the means by which the traveler's time function is terminated after arrival in the destination time zone. Counter S (159) is incremented once per INT 1 interruption of the CPU. When it reaches 64, one second has elapsed and it is time to increment the departure, register X (150), and the destination, register Y (155), time zone time by one second. The "timekeeping algorithm" referred to is a routine for incrementing minutes, hours, and dates at the proper time. All electronic timepieces must perform this function and their operation is well known in the art. Counter C (160) is also incremented once per INT 1 interruption of the CPU. When it equals the value stored in register R (157), it is time to increment the traveler's time register W (145) by one second. The value in register R (157) is determined in calculations shown in FIG. 2D below. After incrementing the traveler's time, a comparator determines if the function has completed, i.e., if the traveler's time substantially equals the destination time zone time. If so, the traveler time function is cancelled,

4,901,296

7

and the destination time zone time (Y **155**) is latched. Operation then resumes at the normal rate.

FIG. 2C shows the sequence of instructions which are executed in response to INT 2, generated with each closure of one of switches **40** through **90**. Operation of the various function switches cause the functions shown to be executed. It should be noted that switch **40** functions as a flip-flop. If the traveler time function is active, operation of this switch reset it, leaving, in this embodiment, the user displaying the departure time zone time. If the traveler time function is not active, operation of switch **40** causes the instructions explained in FIG. 2D to be executed. These instructions initialize the traveler time function and commence operation of the adjustment. The user may enter the trip time by operating switch **55** to cause display of the last trip time. Switches **80** and **90** may be operated to adjust this time. Logic to reset the hours after **23** and minutes after **59** is provided but is not shown in view of its conventionality. The user may operate switches **45** through **90** in any order desired.

FIG. 2D shows the sequence of instructions which are executed in response to closure of switch **40** when the traveler time function is not already active. The destination time zone time is compared to the departure time zone time. If the destination time zone time is greater than the departure time zone time, the watch determines whether this difference exceeds 12 hours. If so, it is assumed that the destination time zone is actually earlier than (west of) the departure time zone and a negative difference (D) is calculated. If the difference is less than twelve hours, it is assumed that the destination time zone is later than (east of) the departure time zone and a positive difference (D) is calculated. Similar logic is applied to combinations where the destination time zone time is less than the departure time zone time. This logic is necessary in a watch without an internal date function, since it must correctly account for a departure time zone time in one day and a destination time zone time in another. For example, a traveler departing San Francisco for Boston at 23:00 would show a destination time zone time of 02:00. The logic shown in FIG. 2D would correctly calculate the difference (D) as +3 and not −21. Of course, watches capable of incorporating the date into the difference calculation do not require that this assumption be made.

Once the time difference (D) is known and the trip time (Z) has been entered, it is simple to calculate the update rate (R). This is the number of "ticks" (1/64 second) before incrementing the seconds counter for the traveler function. This done, the tick counter is reset, the traveler time is set to the departure time and displayed, the function in progress flag is set, and the function is under way. The function will continue until the user resets it by pressing switch **40** or until the traveler's time arrives at the destination time zone time, after the specified trip time has elapsed. Note that the user may elect to view destination and/or departure time zone time at any point during the trip without disturbing the function. This is accomplished by operating switches **45** and/or **60**. To return to the traveler's time display, the user simply operates switch **50**.

FIGS. 3 - DISPLAYED AND ZONE TIMES

FIG. 3A through 3E show the time which would appear on an analog embodiment of the watch during a typical operation of the function. In this example, the user is traveling from Boston to San Francisco, a time

8

difference of −3 hours. The user has set the destination time zone time into register Y (**155**). The user has specified a trip time of six hours into register Z (**156**). The function is activated at exactly 8:00 AM EST.

In FIG. 3A it can be seen that the traveler's time indicates the same time as the actual time in the departure location. Note that the destination (San Francisco) time is 5:00 AM, three hours earlier.

In FIG. 3B, two hours have elapsed so that Boston time is 10:00 AM, and San Francisco time is 7:00 AM, yet the traveler's time has only increased by one hour, to 9:00 AM. The traveler is being slowly eased into the San Francisco time zone. By allowing the transition to take place progressively throughout the flight, the watch is assisting the traveler to adapt to the new time zone.

In FIG. 3C, another two hours have elapsed and one hour more has elapsed for the traveler's time display, i.e., the traveler's time display is continuing to approach San Francisco time zone time. Boston time is now 12:00 noon, and San Francisco time is 9:00 AM. The traveler's time display indicates 10:00 AM. The traveler continues to consult the watch in a normal fashion, notices the change in time and continues to become psychologically acclimated to the time indicated in the display.

In FIG. 3D, it can be seen that six hours have elapsed in the departure and destination times zones. Boston time is now 2:00 PM, and San Francisco time is 11:00 AM. The traveler's time display has increased by one more hour and now indicates 11:00 AM, the exact time in the destination location. The watch display now proceeds at a normal rate. The traveler has been gradually brought into the destination time zone and will not experience any jolt when the local time is announced to the passengers. The traveler is already acclimated to the San Francisco local time.

In FIG. 3E, one hour has elapsed since arrival at the destination time zone's time. Boston time is now 3:00 PM, and San Francisco is 12:00 noon. The traveler's display reads 12:00 noon. The watch has been running at a normal rate for one hour. The traveler is operating on San Francisco time, fully psychologically acclimated to the local time zone. It can be seen that the traveler's watch will continue to indicate destination time zone time until such time as the function is activated again.

CONCLUSIONS, RAMIFICATIONS, AND SCOPE

As described above, the traveler time function can be incorporated into a standard electronic watch having a data function so that the date will be incremented or decremented if the local time change caused by passage through time zones also results in a date change.

The traveler's time function can also be incorporated into otherwise conventional digital watches, including those having a world time display, e.g., such as the watch sold under the trademark CASIO DATA BANK by Casio, Inc., Fairfield, N.J. This watch displays local time and also the corresponding local times in all of the different time zones of the world.

In addition to a digital watch, my traveler's time function can be incorporated into an analog watch, such as the one described in U.S. Pat. No. 4,505,594, to Kawahara et al. (1985). Further, the function can be incorporated into clocks having either an analog or digital display.

Thus it is seen that may invention provides a timepiece which can be carried on the person, which re-

4,901,296

9

duces jet lag caused by travel between different time zones. My timepiece assists the wearer to acclimate to local time changes caused by easterly or westerly travel, by permitting the wearer to acclimate over the course of the trip. Further, my timepiece is economical to construct and need not cost appreciably more than a conventional electronic watch having a plural function display capability.

Also, it should be understood that the implementation shown in merely one example, and should not be considered as limiting in any way the scope of the invention. For example, the invention can be used to adjust a timepiece from different time standards other than time zones, e.g., from standard time to daylight savings time and vice versa within a given time zone. In this application, the timepiece can contain a function button to activate the loss or gain of one hour over a specified period, e.g., five hours, to give the user time to acclimate to the time change. The number of switches can be reduced by assigning several functions to each switch, with the mode of the switches determined by the setting of a mode switch. The display can be capable of showing three or more time zones. Audible time indications may be included in the watch, setting means may vary, etc. Therefore, the scope of the invention should be determined by the appended claims and their legal equivalents and not by the examples given.

I claim:

1. In a timepiece for continuously advancing an indication of time at a standard rate, an improvement for assisting a traveler to accommodate to a change of an applicable time standard caused by travel, for a given travel time, from a time zone at a place of departure to a different time zone at a place of destination, comprising:

input means for entering travel data representing at least two of the following data: a time zone of departure, a time zone of destination and the travel time;

storage means for storing travel data representing the local time at said departure time zone, the time at said destination time zone, and said travel time;

calculation means, responsive to said travel data in said storage means, for automatically calculating and supplying, during said travel time, output data representing a non-standard rate of advance of time for said timepiece based upon said travel data such that said non-standard rate of advance will correspond to the rate at which time would progress if the time standard experienced by said traveler gradually changed during said travel time from the time standard in said departure time zone to the time standard in said destination time zone;

display means, responsive to said output data off said calculation means, for indicating time at said non-standard rate for said travel time,

such that the time indicated by said timepiece varies gradually during travel between the correct local time at said departure time zone and the correct local time at said destination time zone, and such that said traveler, by observing said timepiece during said travel time, will tend to experience less of the psychological symptoms of jet lag than if said traveler experienced an abrupt change of applicable time standards.

2. The timepiece of claim 1 wherein said calculation means is also arranged to revert, automatically, to incre-

10

ment said displayed time at said normal rate when said given travel time has elapsed.

3. The timepiece of claim 1 wherein said storage means is arranged to receive the time standard in said departure and destination time zones and thereupon automatically select said give travel time based upon the difference in said time standards and a prearranged estimated travel time.

4. The timepiece of claim 1 wherein said storage means is arranged to receive the time standard in said departure and destination time zones and said give travel time.

5. The timepiece of claim 1, further including means for causing said calculation means to cause said display means also to show times under both said time standard in said departure and said destination time zones.

6. The time piece of claim 1, further including selection means for causing said display means to display either time under said time standard in said departure time zone, time under said time standard in said destination time zone, or time as determined by said non-standard rate.

7. The timepiece of claim 1 further including clock means arranged to produce a standard time signal representing the progression of time at said standard rate and wherein said storage means is arranged to receive said standard time signal and input data representing (1) a time correction for the time difference between said two time zones, (2) the direction of said time correction, and (3) said given travel time.

8. A timepiece for a traveler experiencing at least one abrupt change of time standards caused by travel, within a given travel time, from one time zone to a different time zone, comprising:

clock means for producing a normal time signal representing the progression of time at a normal rate;

storage means arranged to receive said normal time signal and input data representing (1) a time correction for the time difference between said two zones, (2) the direction of said time correction, and (3) said given travel time;

calculation means arranged to produce a modified time signal having a frequency which is greater or lesser than that of said normal time signal by an amount determined by said time correction and said given travel time;

loading means for loading said input data into said storage means;

display means responsive to said normal and said modified time signals for displaying time; and

selection means for selectively applying said normal time signal and said modified time signal to said display means so that said modified time signal is applied to said display means during said travel time, whereby the time displayed by said display means will change gradually to effect said time correction in a gradual manner over said travel time,

such that said traveler, by observing said timepiece during said travel time, will tend to experience less of the psychological symptoms of jet lag than if said traveler experienced an abrupt change of applicable time standards.

9. The timepiece of claim 8 wherein said display means is arranged to provide an analog display.

10. The timepiece of claim 8 wherein said display means is arranged to provide a digital display.

4,901,296

11

11. A timepiece for a traveler experiencing an abrupt change of time standards caused by travel, in a given travel time, from one time zone to a different time zone, comprising:

display means responsive to a time signal for display- 5 ing time represented by said time signal;

processing means connected to provide a plurality of time signals to said display means,

one of said time signals being a normal time signal representing time advancing at a normal rate as 10 would be experienced by a person remaining in one of said time zones,

another of said time signals being a modified signal representing time advancing at a modified rate as would be required to adjust, in said given travel 15 time, the time standard from that in said one time zone to that in said different time zone;

data entering means arranged to enter travel data representing said change in time standards and said given travel time into said processing means; and 20 selection means arranged to cause said display means to display the time represented by said modified time signal during said travel time, and said normal time signal thereafter, whereby the time displayed

25

30

35

40

45

50

55

60

65

12

by said display means will change gradually to effect said time correction in a gradual manner over said travel time,

such that said traveler, by observing said timepiece during said travel time, will tend to experience less of the psychological symptoms of jet lag than if said traveler experienced an abrupt change of applicable time standards.

12. The timepiece of claim 11 wherein said display means is arranged to display a plurality of times as represented by said normal and said modified time signals.

13. The timepiece of claim 11 wherein said processing means is arranged to supply three time signals to said display means, two of said signals being normal time signals representing time advancing at a normal rate as would be experienced by persons remaining in said two time zones, the third of said time signals being said modified signal, said display means being arranged to display the times represented by said three time signals.

14. The timepiece of claim 11 wherein said display means is arranged to provide an analog display.

15. The timepiece of claim 11 wherein said display means is arranged to provide a digital display.

* * * * *

UNITED STATES PATENT AND TRADEMARK OFFICE

CERTIFICATE OF CORRECTION

PATENT NO. : 4,901,296   Page 1 of 3

DATED   : February 13, 1990

INVENTOR(S) : Ross E. Mitchell

It is certified that error appears in the above-identified patent and that said Letters Patent is hereby corrected as shown below:

Col. 1, line 48, change "Mesiter" to --Meister--.

Col. 1, line 58, change "water" to --watch--.

Col. 2, line 18, after "this" insert --clock--.

Col. 3, line 13, change "than" to --then--.

Col. 3, line 43, change "elapes" to --elapses--.

Col. 4, line 24, change "switchs" to --switches--.

Col. 5, line 31, change "instruction" to --instructions--.

Col. 6, line20-21, after "which" delete ".ROM 140"

Col. 8, line 67, change "may" to --my--.

Col. 9, line 55, change "off" to --of--.

UNITED STATES PATENT AND TRADEMARK OFFICE

CERTIFICATE OF CORRECTION

PATENT NO. : 4,901,296   Page 2 of 3

DATED   : February 13, 1990

INVENTOR(S) : Ross E. Mitchell

It is certified that error appears in the above-identified patent and that said Letters Patent is hereby corrected as shown below:

Col. 10, line 6, change "give" to --given--.

Col. 10, line 11, change "give" to --given--.

Figure 2D, change "D = [(24 - Y) + X] -1" to --D = -1 [(24-Y) + X]--

Signed and Sealed this

First Day of December, 1992

Attest:

DOUGLAS B. COMER

Attesting Officer   *Acting Commissioner of Patents and Trademarks*

PATENT NO. 4,901,296   Page 3 of 3

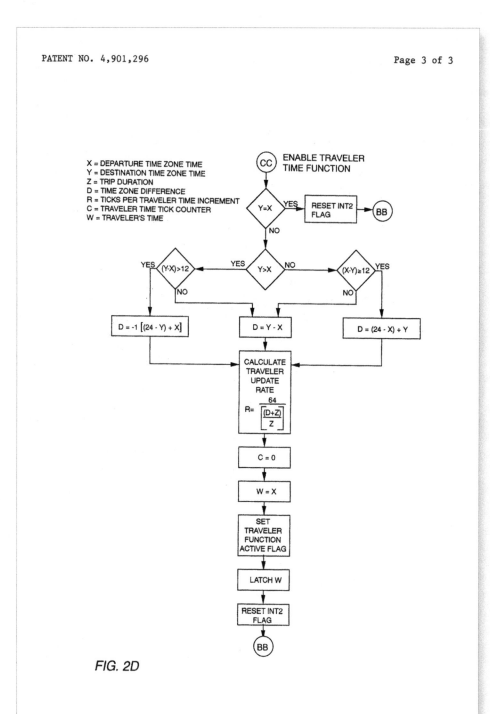

FIG. 2D

Pre-Monopoly Board Game

This is the Landlord's Game created by Lizzie Magie and well-known among socialists of the 1920s. Many contend that the concept was later pilfered to create Monopoly and repatented in 1936. When issuing the Monopoly patent, "the PTO goofed," says coauthor David Pressman.

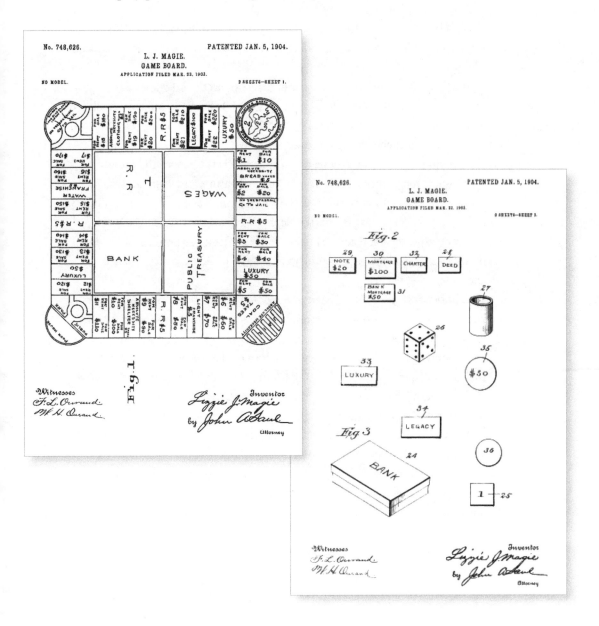

Provisional Patent Application

Board Game

I have invented a game in which the player having the greatest amount of wealth at the end of the game, after a certain predetermined number of circuits of a board has been made, is the winner.

Fig. 1 is a plan view of the board, showing the different spaces. Fig. 2 shows the various movable pieces. Fig 3. is a view of a box used in the game and designated a bank.

The board is divided into a number of spaces or sections. Four spaces in the center indicate Bank, Wages, Public Treasury, and Railroad. Four boxes are placed in these spaces, one of which is designated 24.

The movable pieces in the game are as follows:

Four pairs of dice, four shaking boxes, four checkers to check the throws made, boxes representing Bank, Wages, Public Treasury, and Railroad. Also various, colored chips or tickets represent lots, money, deeds, notes, individual mortgages, bank mortgages, charters, legacies and luxuries. Ref. # 25 indicates lot tickets; 26 indicates dice; 27 shaking boxes; 28 deeds; 29 notes; 30 individual mortgages; 31 bank mortgages; 32 charters; 33 luxuries; 35 money; 36 checkers; and 34 legacies.

Each player is given $500. Twenty-two lot tickets are placed face downward and each player draws one until twelve have been taken. The rest are put back in the wages box. Each player looks at their tickets and may purchase the lot corresponding to their ticket if they can afford to. If a player does not purchase, they do not have to pay rent, but simply put the ticket back. When these twelve lots have been bought or the privilege refused and the owner's deeds are placed upon those purchased, the game begins.

The series of spaces on the board are colored to distinguish them. The lot spaces "1" to "22," preferably green, are for sale at the highest figure marked or for rent at the lowest figure marked. If a player chooses to buy or rent a lot, they must pay the price into the Public Treasury and put their deed on the lot if buying.

Absolute Necessity spaces are blue and indicate absolute necessities—such as bread, coal, shelter and clothing. When a player lands upon these they must pay five dollars into the Public Treasury as a tax.

No Trespassing spaces represent property held out so that when a player lands on these they must go to jail until they throw a double or until they pay into the Public Treasury $50. When a player comes out, they must count from the space immediately in front of the jail.

R. R.: When a player lands on these spaces they must pay $5. If a player throws a double, they get a pass with the privilege of jumping once from one RR to another, provided they would in ordinary moving pass a R.R.

Luxury spaces are preferably purple. If a player lands on a Luxury space they pay $50 to the Treasury and receive a luxury ticket, which counts $60 at the end of the game. The player may purchase the luxury. If they do they lose a move.

Franchise spaces, preferably yellow, are public necessities. The first player who stops upon one puts a charter on it without charge. All through the game they have the privilege of taxing all the other players $5 whenever they land on it.

Public Park: A player may stop here for free.

Legacy: If a player stops here, they get $100 and a legacy ticket.

Mother Earth: Each time a player goes around the board they receive $100 wages.

Poorhouse: If at any time a player has no money or property they go to the poorhouse until they make such throws as will enable them to finish the round.

Rent: When a player stops upon a lot owned by any other player, they must pay the rent. If two players stop on the same lot, the second must pay half of the rent. If a third player's throw lands them on the lot, they must move to the previous space.

In case of lot 1 the player gets the whole rent.

Borrowing: A player may borrow from the Bank in multiples of $100 and mortgage one or more lots with a total value at least ten dollars more than is borrowed. A bank mortgage is placed on the property, and the player pays $5 interest every time they receive their wages.

One player may borrow from another, giving a mortgage on any property owned and making the best bargain as to interest, terms of payment, etc. The player loaning the money places his mortgage on the borrower's deed. If a loan is paid before passing the beginning, the borrower saves the interest.

Five times around: When a player has been around five times, they may move in either direction, provided they are clear of debt until each other player has been around five times. A player who passes the beginning five times receives no more wages. The game is finished when the last player has passed the beginning point the fifth time.

Counting up: The deeds are removed from the lots and each player is credited with the value of their lots. His cash and luxuries are added. The player with the largest total is the winner.

Some have found it interesting to play the game without using the lot tickets: players simply purchase lots as they come to them in ordinary moving. Each player is provided with $100. The number of times around the board may also be changed.

Emergencies: Should any emergency arise, the players must settle the matter between themselves. If any player refuses to obey the rules they must go to jail until they throw a double or pay a fine—see No Trespassing.

Patent

Game-Board. 748,626 Application filed March 23,1903. Serial No. 149,177. (No model.)

To all whom it may concern

Be it known that I, LIZZIE J. MAGIE, a citizen of the United States, residing at Brentwood, in the county of Prince George and State of Maryland, have invented certain new and useful Improvements in Game Boards, of which the following is a specification.

My invention, which I have designated "The Landlord's Game," relates to Games-Boards, and more particularly to games of chance.

The object of the game is to obtain as much wealth or money as possible, the player having the greatest amount of wealth at the end of the game after a certain predetermined number of circuits of the board have been made being the winner.

In the drawings forming a part of this specification, and in which like symbols of reference represent corresponding parts in the several views, Figure 1 is a plan view of the board, showing the different spaces marked thereon. Figure 2 shows the various movable pieces used in the game; and Fig. 3 is a view 2b of one of the boxes, the same being designated as the "Bank."

The implements of the game consist of a board which is divided into a number of spaces or sections and four (4) spaces in the center indicating, respectively, "Bank," "Wages," "Public Treasury," and "Railroad." Within these four spaces are preferably placed four (4) boxes, one of which is shown in the drawings and represented by the numeral 24.

The movable pieces used in the game, only one piece of each set for convenience of illustration being shown in the drawings, are as follows:

Four pairs of dice, four shaking boxes, four checkers to check the throws made, boxes representing, respectively, "Bank," "Wages," "Public Treasury" and "Railroad," and also various, colored chips or tickets representing lots, money, deeds, notes, individual mortgages, bank mortgages, charters, legacies and luxuries. These chips are not to be limited to any certain number or colors.

25 indicates lot tickets; 26, the dice; 27, shaking boxes; 28, deeds; 29, notes; 30, individual mortgages; 31, bank mortgages; 32, charters; 33, luxuries; 35, money; 36, checkers; and 34 legacies.

The game is played as follows: Each player is provided with five hundred dollars. The lot tickets, twenty-two (22) in number, are placed face downward upon the board, and each player draws one until twelve have been taken. The rest are put back in the wages box. Each player looks at the tickets he has drawn and may purchase the lot corresponding to his ticket if he can afford to or so chooses. If he does not purchase, he does not have to pay rent, but simply puts the ticket back into the wages box again. When these twelve lots have been bought or the privilege refused and the owner's deeds placed upon those purchased, the game begins.

The series of spaces upon the board are colored to distinguish them; but of course other means of making them distinctive may be employed. The lot spaces "1" to "22," which are preferably green, are for sale at the highest figure marked upon them or for rent at the lowest figure marked upon them. If a player chooses to buy a lot, he must pay into the "Public Treasury" the price of it and place his deed upon it. If he chooses to rent it, he must pay the rent to the "Public Treasury."

Absolute necessities: These spaces, which are preferably blue, indicate absolute necessities—such as bread, coal, shelter, and clothing—and when a player stops upon any of these he must pay five dollars into the "Public Treasury." (This represents indirect taxation.)

No Trespassing: Spaces marked "No trespassing" represent property held out of use, and when a player stops on one of these spaces he must go to jail and remain there until he throws a double or until he pays into the "Public Treasury" a fine of fifty dollars.

When he comes out, he must count from the space immediately in front of the jail.

Railroad: "R. R." represents transportation, and when a player stops upon one of these spaces he must pay five dollars to the R. R. If a player throws a double, he "Gets a pass" and has the privilege of jumping once from one railroad to another, provided he would in his ordinary moving pass a "R.R." If he stops upon it, however, he must pay five dollars.

Luxuries: These spaces, preferably purple, represent the luxuries of life, and if a player stops on a "Luxury" he pays fifty dollars to the "Public Treasury," receiving in return a luxury ticket, which counts him sixty dollars at the end of the game.

The player may purchase the luxury or not, as he chooses or can afford; but if he does not purchase it he loses his move.

Franchises: These spaces, preferably yellow, indicate the light franchise and water franchise and are public necessities. The first player who stops upon one of these franchises puts his charter upon it, and all through the game he has the privilege of taxing all the other players five dollars whenever they chance to stop upon it. It costs him nothing and counts him nothing at the end of the game.

Public Park: A player may stop in the "Public Park" without paying anything.

Legacy: If a player stops upon the "Legacy," he gets one hundred dollars cash and a legacy ticket.

Mother Earth: Each time a player goes around the board he is supposed to have performed so much labor upon Mother Earth, for which after passing the beginning point he receives his wages, one hundred dollars, and is checked upon the tally sheet as having been around once.

Poorhouse: If at any time a player has no money with which to meet expenses and has no property upon which he can borrow, he must go to the Poorhouse and remain there until he makes such throws as will enable him to finish the round.

Rent: When a player stops upon a lot owned by any of the players, he must pay the rent to the owner. If he stops upon one of his own lots, of course he pays nothing. If two players stop upon the same lot, the second must pay to the first one-half of the rent, (in case of an odd number, giving to the first the benefit of the fraction.) If a third player's throw brings him on the same lot, he cannot occupy it, but must remain upon the space next to it, counting his throw one less.

In case of Lot 1 the player gets the whole rent.

Borrowing: A player may borrow from the "Bank" in amounts of one hundred dollars, and for every one hundred dollars borrowed the "Bank" takes a mortgage on one or more of the borrower's lots, the total value of which must be at least ten dollars more than is borrowed. For every one hundred dollars borrowed from the "Bank" a bank mortgage is placed upon the property on which the loan is made, and the player puts his note in the "Bank," paying upon each note five dollars (interest) every time he receives his wages.

One player may borrow from another, giving a mortgage on any property he may own and making the best bargain he can as to interest, terms of payment, etc. The player loaning the money places his individual mortgage on the top of the borrower's deed to show that he has a mortgage on that property. Should a loan be repaid before passing the beginning-point, the borrower saves the interest.

Five times around: When a player has been around the board five times, he may move in either direction, provided he is clear of debt, until each of the other players has been around five times; but having passed the beginning point the required number of times, he receives no more wages. The game is finished when the last player has passed the beginning point the fifth time.

Counting up: As the deeds are removed from the lots each player is credited with the value of the lots owned by him. His cash on hand is counted, and the amount set down under the total value of the lots. Then the luxuries are counted (remember that each one counts sixty), and the amount set down under cash. Add together these three amounts—lots, cash and luxuries—and the player who has the largest sum-total is the winner. Playing without the lot tickets: Some have found it more interesting to play the game without using the lot tickets at all, players simply purchasing lots as they come to them in the ordinary moving. In this case the player is provided with one hundred dollars to begin with. The number of times around the board may also be regulated by the will of the players.

Emergencies: Should any emergency arise which is not covered by the rules of the game, the players must settle the matter between themselves; but if any player absolutely refuses to obey the rules as above set forth he must go to jail and remain there until he throws a double or pays his fine, as explained in paragraph "No Trespassing."

Having now fully described my invention, what I claim as new, and desire to secure by Letters Patent, is:

1. A game board, having corner spaces, one constituting the starting point, and a series of intervening spaces indicating different denominations, some of the spaces of the different series corresponding, and distinguished by coloring or other marking, so that the corresponding divisions on the four spaces may be readily recognized.

2. A game board, provided with corner spaces, intervening spaces of different denominations, some of the spaces of the different series corresponding, and distinguished by coloring or other marking, so that the corresponding spaces in the different divisions may be recognized, and a series of movable pieces having reference to the different divisions upon the board.

3. A game board, having a series of divisions of different denominations upon its outer border, one constituting the starting point, four divisions within said series for the reception of boxes, a series of movable pieces having reference to the spaces upon the board, and a chance device to control the movement of the pieces.

4. A game board, provided with corner spaces, intervening spaces of different denominations, and distinguished by distinctive marking, so that the corresponding divisions on the different spaces may be recognized, movable pieces having reference to the spaces, a chance device to control the movement of the pieces, checkers, and tickets representing money, deeds, notes, mortgages, bank mortgages, charters, legacies and luxuries, adapted to be used in connection with the same.

In testimony whereof I affix my signature in presence of two witnesses.

LIZZIE J. MAGIE.

Advertising System for Airport

So much luggage to push and so little space to advertise: That was the dilemma faced by two German inventors who believed that the advertising space at airports could be increased exponentially if every advertising board could contain multiple advertising messages, each triggered by a transponder on the cart carrying your luggage (see Patent 6,275,201, below). In other words, as you approached an airport advertisement it could change repeatedly as you passed or be customized for you—for example, if you landed on a flight from Germany, the message might appear in German.

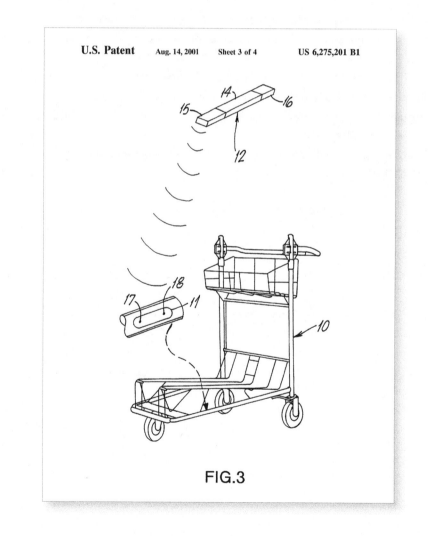

U.S. Patent   Aug. 14, 2001   Sheet 3 of 4   US 6,275,201 B1

FIG.3

Provisional Patent Application

Advertisement System for an Airport Facility

We, Wolfgang Kratzenberg and Siegfried Stein, have invented an advertisement system for an airport facility.

Objects:

The invention will provide an advertisement system for an airport facility which would permit multiple use of the available-for-advertising surface, thereby permitting the surface to be offered to different customers and advertisers. It would also provide an advertisement system for an airport facility which would permit offering of the available-for-advertisement surface to customers and advertisers at different pricing scales dependent on a selected advertisement message.

Relevant prior art includes:

U.S. Pat. 6,088,008 - Apparatus and method for remotely controlled variable message display

U.S. Pat. 4,791,417 - Display device

U.S. Pat. 4,754,582 - Telephone booth with advertising displays

U.S. Pat. 4,750,151 - Apparatus for selectively retrieving stored information to a plurality of output units in response to touching display panel areas associated with the information to be retrieved

U.S. Pat. 3,868,675 - Display system with combined dynamic and static display

Advantages:

One advantage is that it permits presentation of multiple advertising messages in an airport facility thereby overcoming any limitations as to the number of permitted display panels. Another advantage is that advertising messages can be triggered based upon the nature of the arriving or departing passenger (for example, German language advertisements can be presented to passengers arriving from Germany). Another advantage is that by placing the transponder triggering mechanism on luggage carts, the timing of the changing advertising panels can be controlled based upon the number and frequency of the carts in any facility area.

Drawings—Figures:

FIG. 1 - a schematic view of a ground plan of an airport facility

FIG. 2 - a schematic view of an information board having an advertisement area and an associated therewith transmitter-receiver unit

FIG. 3 - a schematic view of a control arrangement for a pushcart

FIG. 4 - a diagram of the vertical reach of a stationary transmitter-receiver installation

FIG. 5 - a diagram of the horizontal reach of a stationary transmitter-receiver installation

Drawings—Reference Numerals:

1 - central area

2 - departure building

3 - check-in desks

4 - shops and restaurants

5 - passageways

6 - aisles

7 - gates

8 - display panels

10 - luggage pushcarts

11 - transponder

12 - transmitter/receiver units

13 - ceiling

14 - single transmitter

15 - receiving antenna

16 - receiving antennas

19 - conductor sets

Description:

FIG. 1 shows a simplified schematic view of a ground plan of an airport facility which includes, e.g., a central area 1 in a departure building 2 in which a plurality of check-in desks 3 are provided. A plurality of shops and restaurants 4 are also located in the central area 1.

A plurality of gates 7 are provided on the periphery of the central area 1. The gates 7 are connected with the central area 1 and with each other by passageways 5 and aisles 6. Starting from the check-in desks 3 or the central region 1 of the ground plan of the airport facility and in all of the passageways 5 and aisles 6, the advertisement areas are provided. The advertisement areas include display panels 8 which, in addition to a standard advertisement, store at least one and, preferably a plurality of different advertisement messages. The advertisement messages are changed in such a manner that in an arbitrary order, one of the stored advertisement messages is displayed.

The display or exchange of the stored advertisement messages is effected in the advertisement system by a wireless remote control system. The remote control system includes transponders 11 that are provided in the luggage pushcarts 10 and that serve as special means, emitting coding signals in response to an inquiry. The transponders 11 can simply send a single signal for turning on a corresponding advertisement message. In addition to transponders 11 provided on the pushcarts 10, the remote control system includes suitable devices, in particular, transmitter/receiver units 12 that are capable of inquiring and receiving coded dated from a transponder 11. The transmitter/receiver units 12 are associated with respective information boards containing advertisement panels or with pure advertisement boards containing only advertised messages.

The transmitter/receiver units 12, that are associated with the information and/or advertisement boards, are connected with the respective information and/or advertisement boards by respective conductor sets 19, as shown in FIG. 2, and are capable of inquiring and receiving coded data from a transponder 11.

The transmitter/receiver units 12, which are associated with the information and/or advertisement boards by respective conductor sets 19, are shown in FIG. 2, and are arranged on the walls or ceiling of the building, as shown in FIG. 2.

As shown in FIGS. 4 and 5, the transmitter/receiver units 12 have limited vertical and horizontal reach regions that have a somewhat lobar-like shape.

As shown in FIG. 3, a stationary transmitter/receiver unit 12 has a single transmitter 14 and two receiving antennas 15, 16 aligned with the transmitter 14 and arranged on opposite sides of the transmitter 14. The transmitter/receiver units 12 are mounted on the ceiling 13 in the region of the passageways 5 and aisles 6 so that each receiving antenna 15 or 16 is associated with a direction of movement of the pushcarts 10. Correspondingly, the transponder 11 is provided with two directed poles 17 and 18. The transponder 11 is arranged on a respective pushcart 10 parallel to a longitudinal axis of the pushcart 10 so that it is aligned in parallel with the transmitter/receiver unit 12.

Operation:

Many advertisement display panels 8 can be triggered to display different advertisements based on information transmitted by transponders 11 located on luggage pushcarts 10. Each of the display panels has a standard advertisement message and at least one different stored advertisement message. Each panel also has a means for arbitrarily changing the messages so that only one of the advertisement messages is displayed at a time.

The controlled turn-on time, which is dependent on an arbitrary number and distribution of airport passengers throughout the central area 1 of the airport facility, is associated with turn-on/off advertisement areas available in different areas of the airport facility for advertising.

The arbitrary number can be defined by a number of usable luggage pushcarts 10 so that an advertisement space is rented for a price corresponding to an arbitrary number of pushcarts passing through the area. The pushcarts are equipped with a device for activating a predetermined advertisement message on that turn-on/off advertisement area when a pushcart passes.

This, on one hand, insures a multiple arbitrary use of advertisement areas of panels and, on the other hand, permits matching the price for an advertisement to rent payments of a certain number of pushcarts, i.e., to determine the probability of how long a certain advertisement area will be used for a certain advertisement. Thus, the probability of display of an advertisement message increases with an increased number of rented luggage pushcarts 10.

An advertisement message is displayed for a limited time, and the switching of the advertisement on and off is effected by using a wireless remote control system, with the advertisement message being activated by a mobile single transmitter 14. This can be effected, in a simplest case, by providing on a pushcart a signal generator, e.g., a magnet which activates a switch-on device (transmitter/receiver unit 12) associated with a respective advertisement area or panel upon the pushcart 10 passing by. This simplest form of activation permits the activation of a very limited number of exchangeable advertisement messages.

Many interrogatable transponders 11 with means for emitting coded signals are arranged on the luggage pushcarts, with respective transponders 11 being associated with a respective advertisement message.

Many devices for receiving coded signals emitted from the transponders 10, are associated with the advertisement areas or panels. These devices are formed as transmitter/receiver units 12. This makes it possible to store in separate advertisement areas or panels, an arbitrary number of advertisement messages.

Optimally, use of the advertisement areas or panels is increased when a limited display time is assigned to each separate advertisement message. An automatic time limitation of separate advertisement messages is achieved by providing a counter downstream of a respective sender/transmitter unit that stores the entry of activation signals in case the activation signals are inputted more quickly than they can be implemented.

In order to prevent luggage pushcarts 10 inadvertently left within a reach region of an interrogating station from triggering a lasting display of a particular advertisement message, according to a further advantageous embodiment of the present invention, each transmitter 14, in addition to the counter, is associated with a timer which, upon identification of a static activation signal, limits a message repetition to a predetermined interval, e.g., to 30 minutes.

Preferably, each advertisement area or display panel 8 is programmed with a standing advertisement message that is automatically turned on in case no activation signal for triggering any advertisement message is received.

The transmitter/receiver devices are stationary, mounted on a ceiling of the turnoffs and crossings of the passageway and the aisles of the airport facility. Each of the transmitter/receiver units includes a transmitter and two receiver antennas mounted on opposite sides of the transmitter in alignment therewith. Each transmitter/receiver unit is so mounted on the ceiling in respective turnoffs and crossings that each receiver antenna is associated with a movement direction of a pushcart.

Alternative Embodiments:

Alternatively, instead of wireless remote control system for controlling the advertisement panels, a system including a light transmitter and a light receiver may be implemented. Instead of placing the transponder on luggage pushcarts, the switching signal emitting means can be provided on other items associated with displacement of passengers within an airport facility, e.g., on air tickets.

Patent

US006275201B1

(12) **United States Patent**
Kratzenberg et al.

(10) **Patent No.:** **US 6,275,201 B1**
(45) **Date of Patent:** **Aug. 14, 2001**

(54) **ADVERTISEMENT SYSTEM FOR AN AIRPORT FACILITY**

(75) Inventors: **Wolfgang Kratzenberg**, Schauenburg; **Siegfried Stein**, Vellmar, both of (DE)

(73) Assignee: **Expresso Deutschland Transportgeräte GmbH**, Kassel (DE)

(*) Notice: Subject to any disclaimer, the term of this patent is extended or adjusted under 35 U.S.C. 154(b) by 0 days.

(21) Appl. No.: **09/211,890**

(22) Filed: **Dec. 15, 1998**

(30) **Foreign Application Priority Data**

Dec. 18, 1997 (DE) .... 297 22 340 U

(51) **Int. Cl.**[7] **G09G 5/00**
(52) **U.S. Cl.** **345/2**; 40/606
(58) **Field of Search** 40/463, 446, 453, 40/447, 606; 345/1, 89, 2, 56

(56) **References Cited**

U.S. PATENT DOCUMENTS

3,868,675 * 2/1975 Firmin 345/56

4,750,151	* 6/1988	Baus	364/900
4,754,582	* 7/1988	Cameron	52/27
4,791,417	* 12/1988	Bobak	345/89
6,088,008	* 7/2000	Reeder	40/447

* cited by examiner

Primary Examiner—Amare Mengistu
(74) *Attorney, Agent, or Firm*—Sidley Austin Brown & Wood, LLP

(57) **ABSTRACT**

An advertisement system for an airport facility having a plurality of gates connected by passageways and aisles and provided in departure and arrival buildings with restaurants and shops, with information carriers emitting written and picture messages and provided on information boards, and with a plurality of luggage pushcarts for transporting luggage of airport passengers inside the facility, the advertisements system including a plurality of advertisement panels each having a standard advertisement message and at least one different advertisement message stored in the advertisement panels, and elements which arbitrary change the messages so that one of the advertisement messages is displayed at a time.

8 Claims, 4 Drawing Sheets

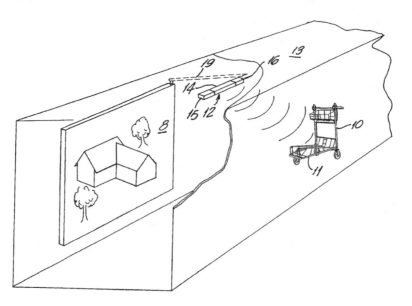

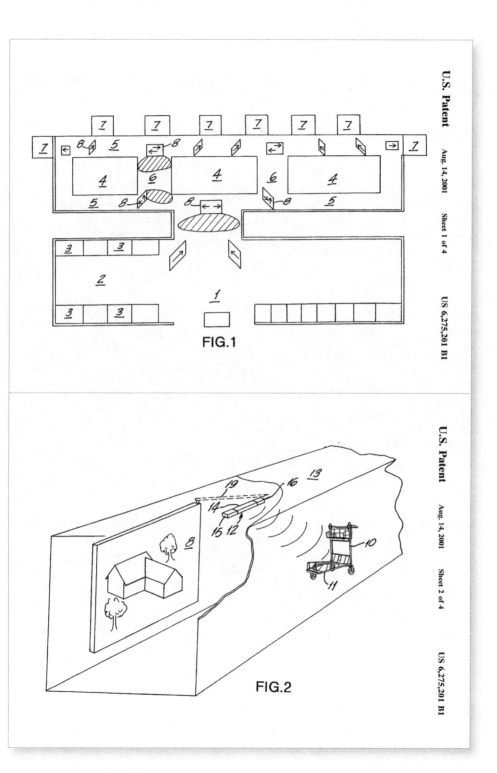

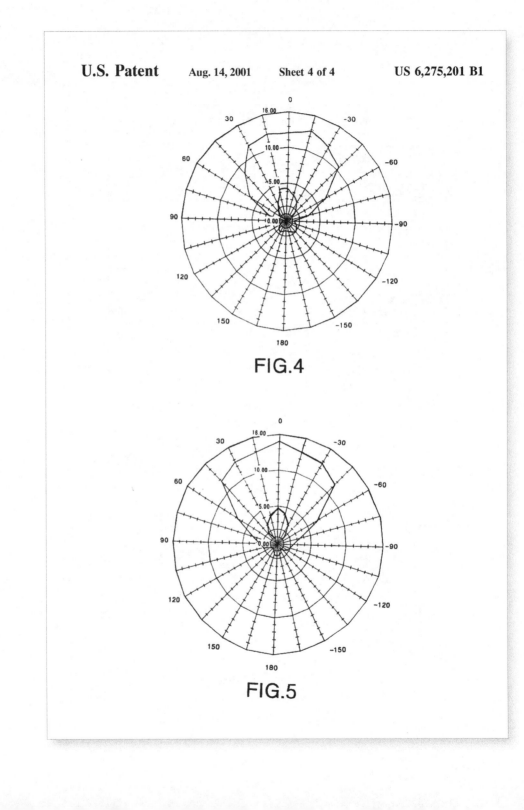

U.S. Patent Aug. 14, 2001 Sheet 4 of 4 US 6,275,201 B1

FIG.4

FIG.5

US 6,275,201 B1

1

ADVERTISEMENT SYSTEM FOR AN AIRPORT FACILITY

BACKGROUND OF THE INVENTION

1. Field of the Invention

The present invention relates to an advertisement system for an airport facility having a plurality of gates connected by passageways and aisles and provided in departure and arrival buildings with restaurants and shops, with information carriers emitting written and picture messages and provided on information boards and with a plurality of luggage pushcarts for transporting luggage of airport passengers inside the facility.

2. Description of the Prior Art

With an ever increasing use of airplanes as means of transportation and the accompanying increase in air traffic, the size of airport facilities is also necessarily increases. Therefore, the use of the airport facilities for advertisement purposes evokes greater and greater interest. Therefore, the airport businesses try hard to offer different, interesting advertisement board or panels. However, despite the spaciousness of an airport facility, the surface available for advertising is limited. As a result of the finite nature of the surface in an airport facility available for advertising, there exists a need in a most effective use of the available-for-advertising surface. The present conventional use of the available-for-advertising surface for single messages prevents an increased or multiple use of the limited surface available-for-advertisement.

Accordingly, an object of the present invention is an advertisement system for an airport facility which would permit a multiple use of the available-for-advertising surface, thereby permitting offering of the available-for-advertising surface to different customers and advertisers.

Another object of the present invention is an advertisement system for an airport facility which would permit offering of the available-for-advertisement surface to customers and advertisers at different pricing scales dependent on a selected advertisement message.

SUMMARY OF THE INVENTION

These and other objects of the present invention, which will become apparent hereinafter, are achieved by providing an advertisement system including a plurality of advertisement panels each having a standard advertisement message and at least one different advertisement message stored in the advertisement panels, and means for arbitrary changing the messages so that one of the advertisement messages is displayed at a time. According to the present invention, a controlled turn-on time, which is dependent on an arbitrary number and distribution of airport passengers throughout the airport facility, is associated with turn-on/off advertisement areas available in different areas of the airport facility for advertising. The arbitrary number can be defined by a number of usable luggage pushcarts so that an advertisement space is rented for a price corresponding to an arbitrary number of pushcarts passing through the area. The pushcarts are equipped with a device for activating a predetermined advertisement message on that turn-on/off advertisement area which a pushcart passes. This, on one hand, insures a multiple arbitrary use of advertisement areas of panels and, on the other hand, permits to match the price for an advertisement to payments for rent of a certain number of pushcarts, i.e., to determine the probability of how long a certain advertisement area will be used for a certain adver-

2

tisement. Thus, the probability of display of an advertisement message increases with the increase of a number of rented pushcarts.

For an advantageous multiple use of the available advertisement areas, in accordance with advantageous development of the present invention, it is further contemplated that an advertisement message is displayed for a limited time, and the switching of the advertisement on and off is effected by using a wireless remote control system, with the advertisement message being activated by a mobile transmitter. This can be effected, in a simplest case, by providing an a pushcart a signal generator, e.g., a magnet which activates a switch-on device associated with a respective advertisement area or panel upon the pushcart passing by. However, this simplest form of activation means permits to activate a very limited number of exchangeable advertisement messages.

Therefore, according to a further embodiment of the present invention, a plurality of interrogatable transponders with means for emitting coded signals are arranged on the luggage pushcarts, with respective transponders being associated with a respective advertisement message. It is further contemplated that a plurality of suitable devices for interrogating of the transponders, i.e., for receiving coded signal emitted therefrom, are associated with the advertisement areas or panels. These devices are formed as transmitter/receiver units. This makes possible to store in separate advertisement areas or panels, an arbitrary number of advertisement messages.

An optimal use of the advertisement areas or panels is increased when a limited display time is assigned to each separate advertisement message. According to the invention, an automatic time limitation of separate advertisement messages is achieved by providing a counter downstream of a respective sender/transmitter unit and which stores the entry of activation signal in case the activation signals are inputted in a quicker sequence then they can be implemented.

In order to prevent that pushcarts, which inadvertently were left within a reach region of an interrogating station, trigger a lasting display of a particular advertisement message, according to a further advantageous embodiment of the present invention, each sender/transmitter device, in addition to the counter, is associated with a timer which, upon an identification of a static activation signal limits a message repetition to a predetermined interval, e.g., to 30 minutes.

Preferably, each advertisement area or panel is programmed with a standing advertisement message which is automatically turned on in case no activation signal for triggering any advertisement message is received.

According to a further development of the present invention, the transmitter/receiver devices are stationary mounted in all of turn-offs and crossings of the passageway and the aisles of the airport facility on a ceiling. Each of the transmitter/receiver units include a transmitter and two receiver antennas mounted on opposite sides of the transmitter in alignment therewith. Each transmitter/receiver unit is so mounted on the ceiling in respective turn-offs and crossings that each receiver antenna is associated with a movement direction of a pushcart.

The present invention contemplates the use, instead of wireless remote control system for controlling the advertisement panels, of a system including a light transmitter and a light receiver.

In accordance with a still further development of the advertisement system with a multiple use of the available advertisement areas by switching time-limited advertise-

US 6,275,201 B1

3

ment messages, it is contemplated that the switching signal emitting means, e.g., transponder, can be provided on other items associated with displacement of passengers within an airport facility, e.g., on air tickets.

BRIEF DESCRIPTION OF THE DRAWINGS

The features and objects of the present invention will become more apparent, and the invention itself will be best understood from the following detailed description for the preferred embodiments when read with reference to the accompanying drawings, wherein:

FIG. **1** shows a schematic view of a ground plan of an airport facility;

FIG. **2** shows a schematic diagrammatic view of an information board having an advertisement area and an associated therewith transmitter-receiver unit;

FIG. **3** shows a schematic view of a control arrangement for a pushcart;

FIG. **4** shows a diagram of a vertical reach of a stationary transmitter-receiver installation; and

FIG. **5** shows a diagram of a horizontal reach of a stationary transmitter-receiver installation.

DETAILED DESCRIPTION OF THE PREFERRED EMBODIMENTS

FIG. **1** shows a simplified schematic view of a ground plan of an airport facility which includes, e.g., a central area **1** in a departure building **2** in which a plurality of check-in desks **3** are provided. A plurality of shops and restaurants **4** are also located in the central area **1**. A plurality of gates **7** are provided on the periphery of the central area **1**. The gates **7** are connected with the central area **1** and with each other by passageways **5** and aisles **6**. Starting from the check-in desks **3** or the central region **1** over the ground plan of the airport facility and in all of the passageways **5** and aisles **6**, the advertisement areas are provided. The advertisement areas include display panels **8** which in addition to a standard advertisement, store at least one and, preferably a plurality of different advertisement messages. The advertisement messages are arbitrary changed in such a manner that in an arbitrary order, one of the stored advertisement messages is displayed.

The display or exchange of the stored advertisement messages is effected in the embodiment of the advertisement system shown in the drawings by a wireless remote control system. The remote control system includes transponders **11** which are provided in the luggage pushcarts **10** and which serve as special means emitting coding signals in response to an inquiry. The transponders **11** can simply send a single signal for turning on a corresponding advertisement message. In addition to transponders **11** provided on the pushcarts **10**, the remote control system includes suitable devices, in particular, transmitter/receiver units **12** which are capable of inquiring and receiving coded dated from a transponder **11**. The transmitter/receiver units **12** are associated with respective information boards containing advertisement panels or with pure advertisement boards containing only advertised messages. The transmitter/receiver units **12**, which are associated with the information and/or advertisement boards, are connected with the respective information and/or advertisement boards by respective conductor sets **19**, are shown in FIG. **2**, and are capable of inquiring and receiving coded data from a transponder **11**. The transmitter/receiver units **12**, which are associated with the information and/or advertisement boards by respective con-

4

ductor sets **19**, as shown in FIG. **2**, and are arranged on the walls or ceiling of the building, as shown in FIG. **2**. As shown in FIGS. **4** and **5**, the transmitter/receiver units **12** have limited vertical and horizontal reach regions which have a somewhat lobar-like shape.

As particularly shown in FIG. **3**, a stationary transmitter/receiver unit **12** has a single transmitter **14** and two receiving antennas **15**, **16** aligned with the transmitter **14** and arranged on opposite sides of the transmitter **14**. The transmitter/receiver units **12** are so mounted on the ceiling **13** in the region of the passageways **5** and aisles **6** that each receiving antenna **15** or **16** is associated with a direction of movement of the pushcarts **10**. Correspondingly, the transponder **11** is provided with two directed poles **17** and **18**. The transponder **11** is arranged on a respective pushcart **10** parallel to a longitudinal axis of the pushcart **10** so that it is aligned in parallel with the transmitter/receiver unit **12**.

Though the present invention was shown and described with references to the preferred embodiments, various modifications thereof will be apparent to those skilled in the art and, therefore, it is not intended that the invention be limited to the disclosed embodiments or details thereof, and departure can be made therefrom within the spirit and scope of the appended claims.

What is claimed is:

1. An advertisement system for an airport facility having a plurality of gates connected by passageways and aisles and provided in departure and arrival buildings with restaurants and shops, with information carriers emitting written and picture messages and provided on information boards, and with a plurality of luggage pushcarts for transporting luggage of airport passengers inside the facility, the advertisement system comprising:

a plurality of advertisement panels each having a standard advertisement message and at least one different advertisement message stored in the advertisement panels; and

means for arbitrary changing the message so that one of the advertisement messages is displayed at a time,

wherein a controlled turn-on time, which is dependent on an arbitrary number and distribution of airport passengers, is associated with turn-on/off advertisement areas for advertisement panels available in the airport facility,

wherein a limited turn-on time is associated with each advertisement message, and

wherein the message changing means comprises a plurality of sets of interrogatable transponders with the transponders of each set emitting particularly coded signals, which correspond to a particular message, and arranged on a group of luggage pushcarts of the plurality of luggage pushcarts available in the airport facility, whereby the particular message is displayed dependent on a frequency the luggage pushcarts of the group of luggage pushcarts passing a particular location.

2. An advertisement system as set forth in claim **1**, wherein the message changing means comprises a plurality of sender/transmitter units associated with respective ones of the plurality of advertisement panels and capable of interrogating the transponders.

3. An advertisement system as set forth in claim **2**, wherein the message changing means comprises a plurality of counters associated with the plurality of the sender/transmitter units, respectively, for storing an entry of activated signals when the activated signals are inputted in a quicker sequence than they can be implemented.

US 6,275,201 B1

5

4. An advertisement system as set forth in claim **3**, wherein each sender/transmitter unit is associated, in addition to the counter, with a timer which, upon an identification of a static activation signal for a certain advertisement message, limits a message repetition to a predetermined interval.

5. An advertisement system as set forth in claim **2**, wherein the transmitter/receiver devices are stationary mounted in all turn-of and crossings of the passageway and the aisles of the airport facility on a ceiling, and wherein each of the transmitter/receiver comprises a transmitter and two receiver antennas mounted on opposite sides of the transmitter in alignment therewith, each transmitter/receiver unit is so mounted on the ceiling in respective turn-offs and crossings that each receiver antenna is associated with a movement direction of a luggage pushcart.

6

6. An advertisement system as set forth in claim **1**, wherein each advertisement panel is so programmed that a predetermined advertisement message is automatically activated in case of an absence of an activation signal for any of the advertisement messages.

7. An advertisement system as set forth in claim **1**, wherein the message changing means comprises a wireless remote control system.

8. An advertisement system as set forth in claim **7**, wherein the remote control system comprises a plurality of transmitter/receiver units having their own power source and arranged on luggage pushcarts available in the airport facility for transporting luggage of passages, the plurality of the transmitter/receiver units cooperating with a central transmitter/receiver installation.

* * * * *

Mashed Potato Machine

Homemakers already have machines that peel apples, process carrots, and make rice. So why isn't there a device that produces America's beloved side dish, mashed potatoes? Carmina O'Connor (née Figueroa) patented a machine that does just that (and it produces a dish of mashed potatoes in about 20 minutes). O'Connor's invention was a finalist in Hammacher Schlemmer's Search for Invention 2001 competition and was chosen by *Time Magazine* as one of its Inventions of the Year (2001).

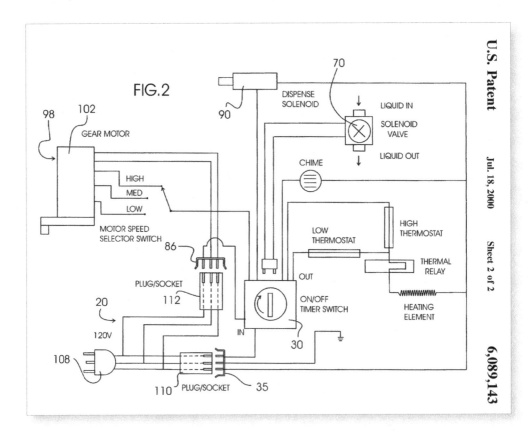

Provisional Patent Application

Mashed Potato Machine

I, Carmina Figueroa, have invented a mashed potato machine.

Objects and Advantages:
The invention provides a machine that, when set up with the required potatoes, milk, butter and other seasonings for mashed potatoes, proceeds to boil the potatoes, add the flavoring ingredients and whip the potatoes to a degree set by the user. The invention enables people to prepare real mashed potatoes with selected flavorings without spending the time or energy necessary to prepare the mashed potatoes manually.

Relevant prior art includes:
U.S. Pat. 3638557, Ljung.
U.S. Pat. 3814360, Samuelian, Sr. et al
U.S. Pat. 3891171, Samuelian et al.
U.S. Pat. 3924838, Waniishi et al.
U.S. Pat. 4026532, Madan.
U.S. Pat. 4131034, Rolf.
U.S. Pat. 4151792, Nearhood.
U.S. Pat. 4422343, Falkenbach et al.
U.S. Pat. 4591273, Meyer et al.
U.S. Pat. 4645352, Valbona et al.
U.S. Pat. 4693610, Weiss.
U.S. Pat. 4714205, Steinko.
U.S. Pat. 4936688, Cornell.
U.S. Pat. 5332310, Wells.
U.S. Pat. 5498074, Moller et al.
U.S. Pat. 5524530, Nijzingh et al.
U.S. Pat. 5533805, Mandel.
U.S. Pat. 5711602, Rohring et al.
U.S. Pat. 5816136, Stallings.

Drawings—Figures:
FIG. 1 - is an exploded perspective view of an exemplary embodiment of the mashed potato machine of the present invention.

FIG. 2 - is a schematic diagram of the electrical elements of the mashed potato machine of FIG. 1.

Drawings—Reference Numerals:

10 - mashed potato machine

12 - bottom cooker assembly

14 - drained water receiving container

16 - cooking container

18 - combination lid/mixer assembly

20 - dual plug power cord

22 - cooker housing

24 - heater element

26 - interior sidewall

28 - container receiving cavity

30 - timer unit

32 - drain solenoid valve connecting socket

34 - bottom power connecting socket

35 - power connecting socket

36 - pair of lifting handles

38 - pair of lid latching protrusions

40 - suction cup feet

44 - drained water receiving cavity

46 - drain valve connecting fitting

48 - sidewall

60 - cooking cavity

62 - solenoid controlled valve assembly

64 - first conduit

66 - second conduit

68 - attachment fitting

74 - control line plug

82 - pair of latch assemblies

80 - lid portion

86 - lid power cord connecting socket

88 - ingredient dispensing chambers

94 - steam vent

96 - viewing window

98 - mixer assembly

100 - detachable beater members

106 - mixer gear motor

108 - wall outlet plug

110 - bottom connecting plug

112 - lid connecting plug

Description:

FIGS. 1 and 2 reference a mashed potato machine 10 that includes a bottom cooker assembly 12, a drained water receiving container 14, a cooking container 16, a combination lid/mixer assembly 18, and a dual plug power cord 20.

Bottom cooker assembly 12 including a cooker housing 22 having a heater element 24 (shown in dashed lines) provided on the interior sidewall 26 of a container receiving cavity 28 formed therein, a power connecting socket 35, a timer unit 30 in connection with heater element 24 having a drain solenoid valve connecting socket 32 and a bottom power connecting socket 34, a pair of lifting handles 36, a pair of lid latching protrusions 38, and a number of suction cup feet 40.

Drained water receiving container 14 is of metal construction and is sized to fit entirely within a bottom portion of container receiving cavity 28 of cooker housing 22 below heating element 24 and has a drained water receiving cavity 44 formed therein in connection with a drain valve connecting fitting 46 formed through a sidewall 48 thereof. Cooking container 16 is sized to fit entirely within a top portion of the container receiving cavity 28 such that the cooking container sidewalls 50 contact heating element 24 of cooker housing 12 when cooking container 16 is seated on top of drained water receiving container 14. Cooking container 16 has a cooking cavity 60 formed therein in connection with a solenoid controlled valve assembly 62, including a first conduit 64 in connection with cooking cavity 60 and a second conduit 66 terminating in an attachment fitting 68 that can mate with connecting fitting 46 of drained water receiving container 14. A solenoid controlled valve assembly 70 is provided between first and second conduits 64, 66 and has a control line plug 74 insertable into connection with drain solenoid valve connecting socket 32 of timer unit 30.

Combination lid/mixer assembly 18 includes a lid portion 80 sized to cover a top opening of container receiving cavity 28, a pair of latch assemblies 82 positioned to engage the pair of lid latching protrusions 38 to secure lid portion 80 in sealing, nonrotating relationship with bottom cooker assembly 22, a lid power cord connecting socket 86, a pair of ingredient dispensing chambers 88 positioned atop lid portion 80 each in connection with a dispensing orifice sealed by a dispensing solenoid valve 90 (FIG. 2) controlled by timer unit 30 to dispense the contents of the ingredient dispensing chambers 88 as needed, a steam vent 94 through the lid portion 80, a viewing window 96 for viewing the cooking container 16, and a mixer assembly 98 controlled by timer unit 30 and including a pair of detachable beater members 100.

In use, beater members 100 extend into the cooking cavity 60 when lid portion 80 is secured to bottom cooker assembly 22 and are moveable throughout the cooking cavity 60 when a mixer gear motor 106 (FIG. 2) is in operation. Dual plug power cord 20 includes a wall outlet plug 108, a bottom connecting plug 110 and a lid connecting plug 112. Timer unit 30 controls the operating sequence of heater element 24, solenoid controlled valve assembly 70, dispensing solenoid valve 90, and mixer assembly 98 to produce mashed potatoes once the mashed potato machine is initially set up.

Operation:

A user of the mashed potato machine 10 plugs the wall outlet plug 110 into a wall socket, places cleaned potatoes in the bottom cooker assembly 12 and adds water to the cooking cavity 60. After turning on the machine 10, the timer unit 30 activates a heater element 24 provided on the interior sidewall 26. The heater element 24 causes the water to boil, cooking the potatoes, after which the water is ejected via a drain solenoid valve into a drained water receiving container 14 being sized to fit entirely within a bottom portion of the container receiving cavity 44 of the cooker housing 22.

A dispensing solenoid valve assembly 62 controlled by the timer unit 30 dispenses the contents of the ingredient dispensing chambers 88 (for example, milk and/or butter) positioned atop the lid portion 80.

The user, viewing the mix of potatoes and ingredients through a viewing window 96 watches the mixer assembly 98 controlled by the timer unit 30 and including a pair of detachable beater members 100 extending into the cooking cavity 60 when the lid portion is secured to the bottom cooker operate to mash and mix the ingredients powered by a mixer gear motor 106.

Patent

US006089143A

United States Patent [19]

Figueroa

[11] **Patent Number:** **6,089,143**

[45] **Date of Patent:** **Jul. 18, 2000**

[54] **MASHED POTATO MACHINE**

[76] Inventor: **Carmina B. Figueroa**, 30W026 Laurel Ct., Warrenville, Ill. 60555

[21] Appl. No.: **09/442,996**

[22] Filed: **Nov. 18, 1999**

[51] Int. Cl.[7] **A47J 27/00**; A47J 43/044; B01F 7/20; B01F 7/24; B01F 7/32

[52] U.S. Cl. **99/327**; 99/332; 99/348; 366/145; 366/146; 366/199; 366/206; 366/297

[58] Field of Search 99/326–333, 337–340, 99/348, 468; 366/144–149, 292, 297–301, 197–200, 206; 241/101.1

[56] **References Cited**

U.S. PATENT DOCUMENTS

3,638,557	2/1972	Ljung	99/348
3,814,360	6/1974	Samuelian, Sr. et al.	366/200 X
3,891,171	6/1975	Samuelian et al.	248/131
3,924,838	12/1975	Waniishi et al.	259/108
4,026,532	5/1977	Madan	366/207
4,131,034	12/1978	Rolf	366/288
4,151,792	5/1979	Nearhood	99/348
4,422,343	12/1983	Falkenbach et al.	241/101.1
4,591,273	5/1986	Meyer et al.	366/331
4,645,352	2/1987	Valbona et al.	366/343
4,693,610	9/1987	Weiss	99/348
4,714,205	12/1987	Steinko	241/95
4,936,688	6/1990	Cornell	99/348
5,332,310	7/1994	Wells	366/344
5,498,074	3/1996	Moller et al.	366/224
5,524,530	6/1996	Nijzingh et al.	99/348
5,533,805	7/1996	Mandel	366/197 X
5,711,602	1/1998	Rohring et al.	366/251
5,816,136	10/1998	Stallings	99/335

Primary Examiner—Timothy Simone
Attorney, Agent, or Firm—Joseph N. Breaux

[57] **ABSTRACT**

A machine that is set up with the required potatoes, milk, butter and other seasonings for mashed potatoes and that when turned on proceeds to boil the potatoes, add the flavoring ingredients and whip the potatoes to a degree set by the user.

1 Claim, 2 Drawing Sheets

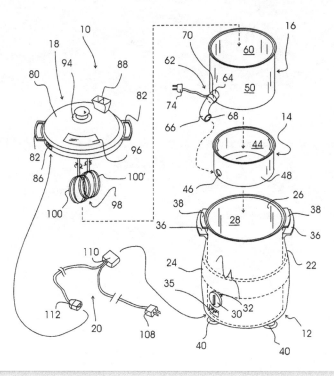

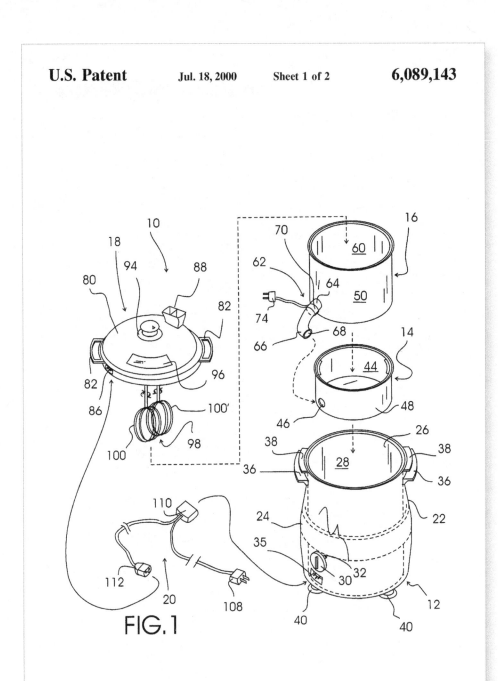

FIG.1

6,089,143

1

MASHED POTATO MACHINE

TECHNICAL FIELD

The present invention relates to cooking accessories and more particularly to a mashed potato machine that includes a bottom cooker assembly, a drained water receiving container, a cooking container, a combination lid/mixer assembly, and a dual plug power cord; the bottom cooker assembly including a cooker housing having a heater element provided on the interior sidewall of a container receiving cavity formed therein, a timer unit in connection with the heater element, a drain solenoid valve connecting socket and a bottom power connecting socket, a pair of lifting handles, a pair of lid latching protrusions, and a number of suction cup feet; the drained water receiving container being sized to fit entirely within a bottom portion of the container receiving cavity of the cooker housing and having a drained water receiving cavity in connection with a drain valve connecting fitting formed through a sidewall thereof; the cooking container being sized to fit entirely within a top portion of the container receiving cavity of the cooker housing when seated on top of the drained water receiving container and having a cooking cavity formed therein in connection with a solenoid controlled valve assembly including a first conduit in connection with the cooking cavity and a second conduit terminating in an attachment fitting mateable with the connecting fitting of the drained water receiving container; the solenoid controlled valve assembly including a control line plug insertable into connection with the drain solenoid valve connecting socket of the timer unit; the combination lid/mixer assembly including a lid portion sized to sealing cover a top opening of the container receiving cavity, a pair of latch assemblies positioned to engage the pair of lid latching protrusions to secure the lid portion in sealing relationship with the bottom cooker assembly, a lid power cord connecting socket, a pair of ingredient dispensing chambers positioned atop the lid portion each in connection with a dispensing orifice sealed by a dispensing solenoid valve controlled by the timer unit to dispense the contents of the ingredient dispensing chamber as needed, a steam vent through the lid portion, a viewing window for viewing the cooking container, and a mixer assembly controlled by the timer unit and including a pair of detachable beater members; the beater members extending into the cooking cavity when the lid portion is secured to the bottom cooker assembly and being moveable throughout the cooking cavity when in operation by a gear mechanism; the dual plug power cord including a wall outlet plug, a bottom connecting plug and a lid connecting plug; the timer unit controlling the operating sequence of the heater element, the solenoid controlled valve assembly, the dispensing solenoid valve, and the mixer assembly.

BACKGROUND ART

Real mashed potatoes are enjoyed by many people who do not like to spend the time or energy necessary to prepare the mashed potatoes from scratch. It would be a benefit to these individuals to have a machine that could be set up with the required potatoes, milk, butter and other seasonings and that would then proceed to boil the potatoes, add the flavoring ingredients and whip the potatoes to a degree set by the user.

GENERAL SUMMARY DISCUSSION OF INVENTION

It is thus an object of the invention to provide a mashed potato machine that includes a bottom cooker assembly, a

2

drained water receiving container, a cooking container, a combination lid/mixer assembly, and a dual plug power cord; the bottom cooker assembly including a cooker housing having a heater element provided on the interior sidewall of a container receiving cavity formed therein, a timer unit in connection with the heater element, a drain solenoid valve connecting socket and a bottom power connecting socket, a pair of lifting handles, a pair of lid latching protrusions, and a number of suction cup feet; the drained water receiving container being sized to fit entirely within a bottom portion of the container receiving cavity of the cooker housing and having a drained water receiving cavity in connection with a drain valve connecting fitting formed through a sidewall thereof; the cooking container being sized to fit entirely within a top portion of the container receiving cavity of the cooker housing when seated on top of the drained water receiving container and having a cooking cavity formed therein in connection with a solenoid controlled valve assembly including a first conduit in connection with the cooking cavity and a second conduit terminating in an attachment fitting mateable with the connecting fitting of the drained water receiving container; the solenoid controlled valve assembly including a control line plug insertable into connection with the drain solenoid valve connecting socket of the timer unit; the combination lid/mixer assembly including a lid portion sized to sealing cover a top opening of the container receiving cavity, a pair of latch assemblies positioned to engage the pair of lid latching protrusions to secure the lid portion in sealing relationship with the bottom cooker assembly, a lid power cord connecting socket, a pair of ingredient dispensing chambers positioned atop the lid portion each in connection with a dispensing orifice sealed by a dispensing solenoid valve controlled by the timer unit to dispense the contents of the ingredient dispensing chamber as needed, a steam vent through the lid portion, a viewing window for viewing the cooking container, and a mixer assembly controlled by the timer unit and including a pair of detachable beater members; the beater members extending into the cooking cavity when the lid portion is secured to the bottom cooker assembly and being moveable throughout the cooking cavity when in operation by a gear mechanism; the dual plug power cord including a wall outlet plug, a bottom connecting plug and a lid connecting plug; the timer unit controlling the operating sequence of the heater element, the solenoid controlled valve assembly, the dispensing solenoid valve, and the mixer assembly.

Accordingly, a mashed potato machine is provided. The mashed potato machine includes a bottom cooker assembly, a drained water receiving container, a cooking container, a combination lid/mixer assembly, and a dual plug power cord; the bottom cooker assembly including a cooker housing having a heater element provided on the interior sidewall of a container receiving cavity formed therein, a timer unit in connection with the heater element, a drain solenoid valve connecting socket and a bottom power connecting socket, a pair of lifting handles, a pair of lid latching protrusions, and a number of suction cup feet; the drained water receiving container being sized to fit entirely within a bottom portion of the container receiving cavity of the cooker housing and having a drained water receiving cavity in connection with a drain valve connecting fitting formed through a sidewall thereof; the cooking container being sized to fit entirely within a top portion of the container receiving cavity of the cooker housing when seated on top of the drained water receiving container and having a cooking cavity formed therein in connection with a solenoid controlled valve assembly including a first conduit in connection with the

6,089,143

3

cooking cavity and a second conduit terminating in an attachment fitting mateable with the connecting fitting of the drained water receiving container; the solenoid controlled valve assembly including a control line plug insertable into connection with the drain solenoid valve connecting socket of the timer unit; the combination lid/mixer assembly including a lid portion sized to sealing cover a top opening of the container receiving cavity, a pair of latch assemblies positioned to engage the pair of lid latching protrusions to secure the lid portion in sealing relationship with the bottom cooker assembly, a lid power cord connecting socket, a pair of ingredient dispensing chambers positioned atop the lid portion each in connection with a dispensing orifice sealed by a dispensing solenoid valve controlled by the timer unit to dispense the contents of the ingredient dispensing chamber as needed, a steam vent through the lid portion, a viewing window for viewing the cooking container, and a mixer assembly controlled by the timer unit and including a pair of detachable beater members; the beater members extending into the cooking cavity when the lid portion is secured to the bottom cooker assembly and being moveable throughout the cooking cavity when in operation by a gear mechanism; the dual plug power cord including a wall outlet plug, a bottom connecting plug and a lid connecting plug; the timer unit controlling the operating sequence of the heater element, the solenoid controlled valve assembly, the dispensing solenoid valve, and the mixer assembly.

BRIEF DESCRIPTION OF DRAWINGS

For a further understanding of the nature and objects of the present invention, reference should be made to the following detailed description, taken in conjunction with the accompanying drawings, in which like elements are given the same or analogous reference numbers and wherein:

FIG. 1 is an exploded perspective view of an exemplary embodiment of the mashed potato machine of the present invention.

FIG. 2 is a schematic diagram of the electrical elements of the mashed potato machine of FIG. 1.

EXEMPLARY MODE FOR CARRYING OUT THE INVENTION

With general reference to FIGS. 1 and 2, mashed potato machine 10 includes a bottom cooker assembly, generally designated 12; a drained water receiving container, generally designated 14; a cooking container, generally designated 16; a combination lid/mixer assembly, generally designated 18; and a dual plug power cord, generally designated 20.

Bottom cooker assembly 12 including a cooker housing 22 having a heater element 24 (shown in dashed lines) provided on the interior sidewall 26 of a container receiving cavity 28 formed therein, a power connecting socket 35, a timer unit 30 in connection with heater element 24 having a drain solenoid valve connecting socket 32 and a bottom power connecting socket 34, a pair of lifting handles 36, a pair of lid latching protrusions 38, and a number of suction cup feet 40.

Drained water receiving container 14 is of metal construction and is sized to fit entirely within a bottom portion of container receiving cavity 28 of cooker housing 22 below heating element 24 and has a drained water receiving cavity 44 formed therein in connection with a drain valve connecting fitting 46 formed through a sidewall 48 thereof. Cooking container 16 is sized to fit entirely within a top portion of the container receiving cavity 28 such that the cooking container sidewalls 50 contact heating element 24 of cooker housing

4

12 when cooking container 16 is seated on top of drained water receiving container 14. Cooking container 16 has a cooking cavity 60 formed therein in connection with a solenoid controlled valve assembly, generally designated 62, including a first conduit 64 in connection with cooking cavity 60 and a second conduit 66 terminating in an attachment fitting 68 mateable with connecting fitting 46 of drained water receiving container 14. A solenoid controlled valve assembly 70 is provided between first and second conduits 64,66 and has a control line plug 74 insertable into connection with drain solenoid valve connecting socket 32 of timer unit 30.

Combination lid/mixer assembly 18 includes a lid portion 80 sized to sealing cover a top opening of container receiving cavity 28, a pair of latch assemblies 82 positioned to engage the pair of lid latching protrusions 38 to secure lid portion 80 in sealing, non-rotating relationship with bottom cooker assembly 22, a lid power cord connecting socket 86, a pair of ingredient dispensing chambers 88 positioned atop lid portion 80 each in connection with a dispensing orifice sealed by a dispensing solenoid valve 90 FIG. 2) controlled by timer unit 30 to dispense the contents of the ingredient dispensing chambers 88 as needed, a steam vent 94 through the lid portion 80, a viewing window 96 for viewing the cooking container 16, and a mixer assembly 98 controlled by timer unit 30 and including a pair of detachable beater members 100.

In use, beater members 100 extend into the cooking cavity 60 when lid portion 80 is secured to bottom cooker assembly 22 and are moveable throughout the cooking cavity 60 when a mixer gear motor 106 (FIG. 2) is in operation. Dual plug power cord 20 including a wall outlet plug 108, a bottom connecting plug 110 and a lid connecting plug 112. Timer unit 30 controls the operating sequence of heater element 24, solenoid controlled valve assembly 70, dispensing solenoid valve 90, and mixer assembly 98 to produce mashed potatoes once the mashed potato machine is initially set up.

It can be seen from the preceding description that a mashed potato machine has been provided that includes a bottom cooker assembly, a drained water receiving container, a cooking container, a combination lid/mixer assembly, and a dual plug power cord; the bottom cooker assembly including a cooker housing having a heater element provided on the interior sidewall of a container receiving cavity formed therein, a timer unit in connection with the heater element, a drain solenoid valve connecting socket and a bottom power connecting socket, a pair of lifting handles, a pair of lid latching protrusions, and a number of suction cup feet; the drained water receiving container being sized to fit entirely within a bottom portion of the container receiving cavity of the cooker housing and having a drained water receiving cavity in connection with a drain valve connecting fitting formed through a sidewall thereof; the cooking container being sized to fit entirely within a top portion of the container receiving cavity of the cooker housing when seated on top of the drained water receiving container and having a cooking cavity formed therein in connection with a solenoid controlled valve assembly including a first conduit in connection with the cooking cavity and a second conduit terminating in an attachment fitting mateable with the connecting fitting of the drained water receiving container; the solenoid controlled valve assembly including a control line plug insertable into connection with the drain solenoid valve connecting socket of the timer unit; the combination lid/mixer assembly including a lid portion sized to sealing cover a top opening of the container receiving cavity, a pair of latch assemblies posi-

6,089,143

| 5 | 6 |

tioned to engage the pair of lid latching protrusions to secure the lid portion in sealing relationship with the bottom cooker assembly, a lid power cord connecting socket, a pair of ingredient dispensing chambers positioned atop the lid portion each in connection with a dispensing orifice sealed by a dispensing solenoid valve controlled by the timer unit to dispense the contents of the ingredient dispensing chamber as needed, a steam vent through the lid portion, a viewing window for viewing the cooking container, and a mixer assembly controlled by the timer unit and including a pair of detachable beater members; the beater members extending into the cooking cavity when the lid portion is secured to the bottom cooker assembly and being moveable throughout the cooking cavity when in operation by a gear mechanism; the dual plug power cord including a wall outlet plug, a bottom connecting plug and a lid connecting plug; the timer unit controlling the operating sequence of the heater element, the solenoid controlled valve assembly, the dispensing solenoid valve, and the mixer assembly.

It is noted that the embodiment of the mashed potato machine described herein in detail for exemplary purposes is of course subject to many different variations in structure, design, application and methodology. Because many varying and different embodiments may be made within the scope of the inventive concept(s) herein taught, and because many modifications may be made in the embodiment herein detailed in accordance with the descriptive requirements of the law, it is to be understood that the details herein are to be interpreted as illustrative and not in a limiting sense.

What is claimed is:

1. A mashed potato machine comprising:

a bottom cooker assembly;

a drained water receiving container;

a cooking container;

a combination lid/mixer assembly; and

a dual plug power cord;

said bottom cooker assembly including a cooker housing having a heater element provided on said interior sidewall of a container receiving cavity formed therein, a timer unit in connection with said heater element, a drain solenoid valve connecting socket, a bottom power connecting socket, a pair of lifting handles, and a pair of lid latching protrusions;

said drained water receiving container being sized to fit entirely within a bottom portion of said container receiving cavity of said cooker housing and having a drained water receiving cavity in connection with a drain valve connecting fitting formed through a sidewall thereof;

said cooking container being sized to fit entirely within a top portion of said container receiving cavity of said cooker housing when seated on top of said drained water receiving container and having a cooking cavity formed therein in connection with a solenoid controlled valve assembly including a first conduit in connection with said cooking cavity and a second conduit terminating in an attachment fitting mateable with said connecting fitting of said drained water receiving container;

said solenoid controlled valve assembly including a control line plug insertable into connection with said drain solenoid valve connecting socket of said timer unit;

said combination lid/mixer assembly including a lid portion sized to sealing cover a top opening of said container receiving cavity, a pair of latch assemblies positioned to engage said pair of lid latching protrusions to secure said lid portion in sealing relationship with said bottom cooker assembly, a lid power cord connecting socket, a pair of ingredient dispensing chambers positioned atop said lid portion each in connection with a dispensing orifice sealed by a dispensing solenoid valve controlled by said timer unit to dispense said contents of said ingredient dispensing chamber as needed, a steam vent through said lid portion, a viewing window for viewing said cooking container, and a mixer assembly controlled by said timer unit and including a pair of detachable beater members;

said beater members extending into said cooking cavity when said lid portion is secured to said bottom cooker assembly and being moveable throughout said cooking cavity when in operation by a gear mechanism;

said dual plug power cord including a wall outlet plug, a bottom connecting plug and a lid connecting plug;

said timer unit controlling said operating sequence of said heater element, said solenoid controlled valve assembly, said dispensing solenoid valve, and said mixer assembly.

* * * * *

Method of Viewing Panoramic Images

Selling real estate online became a lot easier once real estate agents could offer virtual tours of prospective homes. These virtual tours allow a viewer, by moving a mouse, to view different rooms in the home from different angles. These amazing tours had a few disadvantages, though. For example, it was difficult to understand how all the views or rooms in a virtual tour related to each other—that is the layout of the house— or which direction you were facing (north, south, east, or west). Jerry Jongerius's software invention solves that problem by providing—along with the detailed or "virtual" view—an additional window (a "map image") that displays the viewing position, direction, and field of view that the detailed view window displays. When the user changes the field of view in the detailed view window, the highlighted sector in the map image changes in synchronism. The resulting interactive windows allow a person to easily and quickly view and understand the field of view, position, and direction of the image being displayed in the detail view window. Below we provide a sample provisional patent application for the invention followed by a copy of the actual patent.

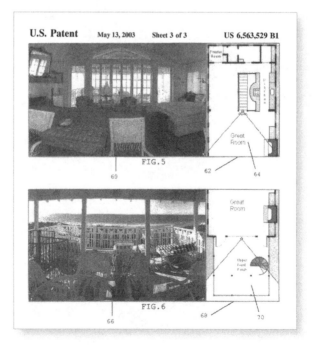

Provisional Patent Application

Interactive System for Displaying Detailed View and Direction in Panoramic Images

I, Jerry Jongerius, have invented an interactive system for displaying detailed view and direction in panoramic images.

Objects:

The invention provides an improved virtual image viewing and panning system. In this system, part of a panoramic image is represented in a detailed image, the location of which is shown in an improved map image. It is much easier for the user to understand direction without any prior knowledge of the physical location of the panoramic image. The detailed image and the map image are never out of sync because any change in the detailed image is immediately reflected in the map image, and any change in the map image is immediately reflected in the detailed image.

Relevant prior art includes:

U.S. Patents

U.S. Pat. 5,040,055 - Panoramic interactive system

U.S. Pat. 5,444,478 - Image processing method and device for constructing an image from adjacent images

U.S. Pat. 5,495,576 - Panoramic image-based virtual reality/telepresence audio-visual system and method

U.S. Pat. 5,563,650 - Method and device for producing panoramic images, and a method and device for consulting panoramic images

U.S. Pat. 5,588,914 - Method and system for guiding a user in a virtual reality presentation

U.S. Pat. 5,754,189 - Virtual environment display apparatus and method

U.S. Pat. 5,764,217 - Schematic guided control of the view point of a graphics processing and display system

U.S. Pat. 5,917,495 - Information presentation apparatus and method

U.S. Pat. 6,121,966 - Navigable viewing system

U.S. Pat. 6,246,413 - Method and system for creating panoramas

U.S. Pat. 6,392,658 - Panorama picture synthesis apparatus and method, recording medium storing panorama synthesis program 9

U.S. Pat. 6,434,265 - Aligning rectilinear images in 3D through projective registration and calibration

Other publications:

bamboo.com, Inc. website, www.bamboo.com/take_a_tour/index.html; first seen on Internet Mar. 1, 1999

Harvard Office of News and Public Affairs web site, www.hno.harvard.edu/tour/qtrv_tour/index.htm; first seen on Internet Aug. 26, 1999

Advanced Relational Technology Inc. web site, http://www.chiefarchitect.com, Jul. 1999

Advantages:

One advantage of the invention is that it provides an improved virtual image viewing and panning system.

Another advantage of the invention is that it provides a system in which part of a panoramic image is represented in a detailed image, the location of which is shown in an improved map image.

Another advantage of the invention is that it provides a detail viewer in which a user will understand the field of view shown in a particular view and in which direction it is taken.

Another advantage of the invention is that it is much easier for the user to understand direction without any prior knowledge of the physical location of the panoramic image.

Another advantage of the invention is that the detailed image and the map image are never out of sync because any change in the detailed image is immediately reflected in the map image, and any change in the map image is immediately reflected in the detailed image.

Drawings—Figures:

FIG. 1 - (prior art) shows a computer linear display or photo of a full (360 degree) panoramic image of a shopping area, ready to be viewed with a detail viewer.

FIG. 2 - (prior art) shows a similar photo of a detailed or enlarged view of a portion of the panoramic image of FIG. 1.

FIG. 3 - depicts a window showing a map which includes the area covered by the panoramic image of FIG. 1, and one method of indicating the area and direction of the detailed field of view of FIG. 2.

FIG. 4 - shows a computer display window showing a presently preferred layout of a detailed view adjacent to a map of the panoramic image of FIG. 1, with the detailed view taken from a different direction than FIG. 2, and the map indicating this different direction.

FIG. 5 - depicts a window showing a detailed view of part of a room in the inside of a house in accordance with the invention, together with an adjacent map showing the location of the room in a floor plan of the house.

FIG. 6 - depicts a window showing a detailed view of a covered porch of the house of FIG. 5, together with an adjacent map showing the location of the porch in the house floor plan.

Drawings—Reference Numerals:

10 - compass rose

30 - dot representing camera

32 - field of view angle

34 - highlighted view area or arc

36 - new highlighted view area or arc

38 - new map

40 - new detailed field of view

60 - detailed view of Great Room

62 - map of floor plan including room 60

64 - highlighted sector in map 62

66 - detailed view of porch

68 - map of area including porch

70 - highlighted sector in map 68

Description:

Prior to describing the viewer of the invention, I will first describe a typical panoramic image, a detail view window and the problem with using these images, which is solved by the present viewer.

FIG. 1 (prior art) shows a sample full (360 degree) panoramic image of an area, in this case a portion of a shopping area, Ruskin Place, in Seaside, Fla. It was taken with multiple successively rotated exposures using a digital camera to take a series of pictures and splicing the pictures together to form the 360 degree image, but it can also be taken with fewer exposures using a camera with a panoramic or 180 degree (or narrower) lens.

Alternatively it can be taken with a plurality of separate cameras operating simultaneously, each with a relatively narrow field of view, with their separate images electronically spliced together to form the 360 degree composite image.

The image of FIG. 1 is displayed in a linear window in a computer screen by a conventional image display program from a computer file formed by scanning the panoramic photo (not shown) or inputting an electronic file representing the image directly into the computer. The image of FIG. 1 is typically used in any of many ways, for example, to orient a newcomer to an area, or to plan modifications to an area.

The image of FIG. 1, being a fully clear 360 degree image, shows much more than can be seen by a human since a human's view angle is limited to about 140 degrees, and of this, only the angle from about 30 degrees to 50 degrees is clear or in focus.

FIG. 2 (prior art) shows a detailed or close-up view of a center portion (about 80 degrees) of the panoramic image of FIG. 1. It can also be displayed on the same computer screen in a separate window by the same imaging program. Note that the detailed view of FIG. 2 is identical to a center portion of the panoramic image of FIG. 1, albeit enlarged.

The detailed view of FIG. 2 is very useful since it shows the details of a portion of the panoramic image of FIG. 1. The portion shown in FIG. 2 is in the center of the panoramic image of FIG. 1, but if the user is interested in any other portion of the panoramic image, the detail view can be moved to view any other portion easily. For example, if users want to see a detail of an area to the right of the center area shown in FIG. 2, they simply position the cursor of their mouse in FIG. 2. Then they depress and hold down the mouse button (usually the left button on a multiple-button mouse), and move or drag the cursor to the right. This will cause the portion of the panoramic image of FIG. 1 shown in FIG. 2 to change and move, just as if the users were actually standing and turning to the right.

While the above views are useful, they do not show the user which portion of the panoramic image they are viewing and how the area viewed is changing. Thus to determine what portion of the panoramic image is being viewed, the user must locate the buildings or features shown in FIG. 2 in FIG. 1. This may not be too difficult with the simple and unique arrangement of buildings and features in FIGS. 1 and 2, but can be very difficult with other areas, such as those which show flora or the inside of a building.

As stated, one system shows a map of the area with the detailed area indicated, but when the detailed area is changed, the indication on the map does not change unless special additional steps are taken. This is highly disadvantageous since it requires users to take intermediate steps and interrupt their viewing and scanning. This causes the users to lose their orientation and severely limits their understanding of the area.

Description—FIG. 3—Map Image and FIG. 4—Combined Views of Shopping Area

FIG. 3 shows a partial map of a town, which, in accordance with the invention, depicts a bird's-eye view of the area covered by the panoramic image of FIG. 1. It shows the buildings seen in FIG. 1, plus some additional surrounding area not seen in the panoramic image of FIG. 1. The map image of FIG. 3 may also be displayed on the same computer screen in a separate window. It is displayed using an imaging program in the same manner as the images of FIGS. 1 and 2. The map of FIG. 3 includes a compass rose or crosshairs 10 to show geographical directions.

The position of the camera from which the panoramic image has been taken is represented by a dot 30, preferably in a contrasting color, such as yellow as shown. The camera indicated has a field of view or viewing angle of about 80 degrees, generally in a south-south-east (SSE) direction so as to view an area 34 of FIG. 3 covered by angle 32. Viewed area 34 is highlighted (i.e., it is lighter than the rest of the map, which is made darker) to show the area of FIG. 1 that FIG. 2 details.

FIG. 4 is similar to FIGS. 2 and 3, except that it combines the two windows into one window with two sections, a left section 40—the detailed field of view and a right section 38—the map. The single window of FIG. 4 is the presently preferred embodiment since, by combining both windows into one, it is simpler in appearance. As will be explained, detailed field of view 40 shows a new area of the panoramic view of FIG. 1 slightly to the left of the view of FIG. 2, while map 38 shows a new highlighted view area 36, rotated slightly counterclockwise (CCW) from view area 34 of FIG. 2.

Operation:

As indicated above, users can change the field of view of FIG. 2—that is, they simply position the cursor (not shown) of their mouse (not shown) anywhere in FIG. 2. Then they depress and hold down the mouse button (usually the left button on a multiple-button mouse), and move or drag the cursor to the right or to the left. This will cause the portion of the panoramic image of FIG. 1 shown in FIG. 2 to change and move, just as if they actually stood at location 30 and turned to the right or left.

When a user changes the field of view of FIG. 2 in this manner, the highlighted sector or arc displayed in the map (FIG. 3) simultaneously rotates and always shows the actual sector displayed in FIG. 2.

For example, assume that the user positions the cursor anywhere in FIG. 2 to the left of the right border and drags the cursor slightly to the left. FIG. 2 will change as follows: the image will move to the right as the cursor is moved to the left so as to display an area to the left of the center area of FIG. 1, as shown by new detailed view window 40 in FIG. 4.

The detailed view will change in the same manner as if a person standing at location 30 in FIG. 3 and looking in the SSE direction to see field of view 34 of FIG. 3 turned their head slightly to the left. The person would then view in the generally ESE direction as shown by field of view 36 in map 38 at the right-hand side of FIG. 4.

Simultaneously highlighted sector or arc 34 of FIG. 3 will rotate CCW to highlight new field 36 in FIG. 4 and the actual area being viewed. The highlighted area will still cover an angle or arc 32, which will be approximately 80 degrees, but may change slightly because of imperfections in the images. Thus when the viewed arc is moved, one of the lines bounding the highlighted arc may move faster or slower than the other line to reflect this.

As stated, movement of the field of view can be effected by dragging the cursor in the detailed view of FIG. 2, or in the detailed view window 40 of FIG. 4. Movement of the field of view can also be effected by clicking and dragging the cursor in the map of FIG. 3 or map window 38 of FIG. 4. That is, the user would position the cursor anywhere in the map of FIG. 3, or anywhere in map window 38 of FIG. 4. The user left clicks and holds down the mouse button and drags the cursor approximately clockwise (CW) or CCW. The highlighted arc will rotate in the selected direction. E.g., if the highlighted sector is looking in the SSE direction as shown in FIG. 3 and the cursor is dragged up or CCW, the highlighted arc will move slightly CCW, as shown by arc 36 in image 38 of FIG. 4. Thus the field of view can be changed by clicking and dragging in either the map or the detailed field of view window.

In FIG. 4, detail view window 40 is positioned adjacent and joined to map 38. As stated, this is the presently preferred arrangement, but the arrangement of FIGS. 2 and 3, where the windows are separated, will also operate in an identical manner.

Thus whenever the user changes the field of view in FIG. 2 (or window 40 of FIG. 4) in either direction, the highlighted sector or view shown in FIG. 3 (or window 38 of FIG. 4) will automatically and simultaneously change to show the new field of view. This will enable a user to always see exactly what part of the panoramic image he or she is viewing. The user will obtain a much better understanding of the field of view and direction, and hence of the area being viewed.

The above example can be experienced interactively online at the following site: http://www.duckware.com/patent.html.

Relocation of Camera—FIGS. 1 to 4

In addition to showing a panoramic map of the geographical area and a detailed view of any selected portion of the area in another window, the program can be used to move the map as if the camera were moved to another location. The map will change accordingly to show a new map of the area, as seen from the new camera location.

Alternative Embodiments:

Many other variations on the invention are possible. For example, the panoramic image can be from a live video source and not just a static image.

The map image can be generated from a geographic information system and not just a static image.

As shown, the "highlighted" area of the map is actually made by darkening the rest of the map, but the detailed view area can be highlighted by making it lighter, in a different color, with darker lines, with border lines only, by shading, etc.

The view can be changed by other than a mouse, e.g., by use of elevators in the side margins of the window of said detailed field of view, by keyboard commands, by voiced commands, by head or foot movements, etc.

Instead of the geographic urban image shown, the images can be of a rural or natural area or the inside or outside of a building.

In the case of an inside-building image, it can be of a furnished or empty home, an apartment, etc.

The viewer can be used on any type of image displayer, including CRT monitors, flat screen, mosaic, projection displays, mobile or vehicle displays (the map would be of an actual large geographic territory), interactive television displays, laptop, desktop or mainframe computers, dedicated computers, dumb terminals or clients with the software in a server, etc.

Patent

US006563529B1

(12) **United States Patent**
Jongerius

(10) **Patent No.:** US 6,563,529 B1
(45) **Date of Patent:** May 13, 2003

(54) **INTERACTIVE SYSTEM FOR DISPLAYING DETAILED VIEW AND DIRECTION IN PANORAMIC IMAGES**

(76) Inventor: **Jerry Jongerius**, P.O. Box 4879, Seaside, FL (US) 32459-4879

(*) Notice: Subject to any disclaimer, the term of this patent is extended or adjusted under 35 U.S.C. 154(b) by 0 days.

(21) Appl. No.: **09/416,505**

(22) Filed: **Oct. 8, 1999**

(51) Int. Cl.[7] H04N 7/00; H04N 7/18; H04N 5/45; G09G 5/00

(52) U.S. Cl. 348/36; 348/144; 348/565; 345/629

(58) Field of Search 348/36, 37, 38, 348/39, 580, 147, 144, 563, 564, 565; 345/629, 419, 619, 848, 420; 382/154, 284, 294; H04N 7/18

(56) **References Cited**

U.S. PATENT DOCUMENTS

5,040,055 A		8/1991	Smith	358/87
5,444,478 A	*	8/1995	Lelong et al.	348/39
5,495,576 A	*	2/1996	Ritchey	345/420
5,563,650 A	*	10/1996	Poelstra	348/36
5,588,914 A		12/1996	Adamczyk	463/32
5,754,189 A		5/1998	Doi et al.	354/473
5,764,217 A		6/1998	Borrel et al.	345/156
5,917,495 A		6/1999	Doi et al.	345/419
6,121,966 A		9/2000	Teodosio et al.	345/838
6,246,413 B1	*	6/2001	Teo	345/419
6,392,658 B1	*	5/2002	Oura	345/629
6,434,265 B1	*	8/2002	Xiong et al.	382/104

OTHER PUBLICATIONS

bamboo.com, Inc. web site, www.bamboo.com/take_a_tour/index.html, first seen on Internet Mar. 1, 1999.
Harvard Office of News and Public Affairs web site www.h-no.harvard.edu/tour/qtrv_tour/index.htm, First seen on Internet Aug. 26, 1999.
Advanced Relational Technology Inc. web site, http://www.chiefarchitect.com, Jul. 1999.

* cited by examiner

Primary Examiner—Gims S. Philippe
(74) *Attorney, Agent, or Firm*—David Pressman

(57) **ABSTRACT**

A method and system for indicating the camera position, direction, and field of view in a map or panoramic image comprises a map image window which displays a map or panoramic image of the site to be studied (house, apartment, city, etc.). A detailed view window displays a portion of the map image, taken from a point in the site. A highlighted sector in the map image represents the viewing position, direction, and field of view that the detailed view window displays. When the user changes the field of view in the detailed view window, the highlighted sector in the map image changes in synchronism. The resulting interactive windows allow a person to easily and quickly view and understand the field of view, position, and direction of the image being displayed in the detail view window.

28 Claims, 3 Drawing Sheets

(3 of 3 Drawing Sheet(s) Filed in Color)

Microfiche Appendix Included
(1 Microfiche, 18 Pages)

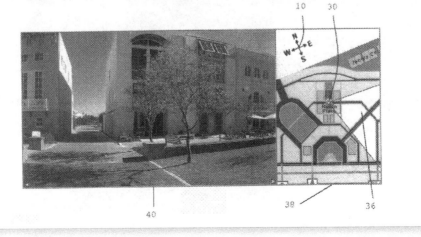

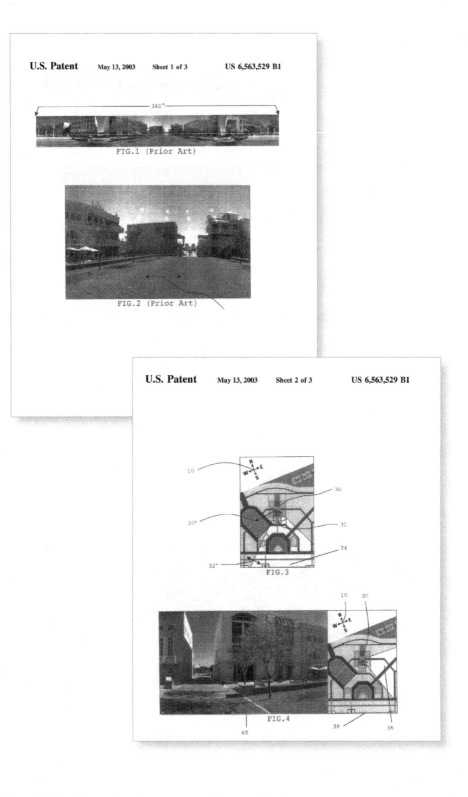

U.S. Patent   May 13, 2003   Sheet 1 of 3   US 6,563,529 B1

FIG.1 (Prior Art)

FIG.2 (Prior Art)

U.S. Patent   May 13, 2003   Sheet 2 of 3   US 6,563,529 B1

FIG.3

FIG.4

US 6,563,529 B1

1

INTERACTIVE SYSTEM FOR DISPLAYING
DETAILED VIEW AND DIRECTION IN
PANORAMIC IMAGES

MICROFICHE APPENDIX

Included with this application is a single-fiche microfiche appendix of 18 frames, which contains the programs pmvr.java (11 frames) and FloorPlan.java (7 frames); these implement the present invention.

COLOR DRAWINGS

The file of this patent contains at least one drawing (photograph) executed in color. The Patent and Trademark Office will, upon request and payment of the necessary fee, provide copies of this patent with color drawings.

RESERVATION OF COPYRIGHT

BACKGROUND

1. Field of Invention

This invention relates to viewing panoramic images, specifically to an improved method for displaying a detailed field of view and a direction when viewing panoramic images.

2. Description of Prior Art

Using panoramic images to present virtual (computer-simulated) tours of real physical environments is becoming commonplace. Many virtual tours use 360° panoramic images and employ a detail viewer. The viewer displays a portion of the panoramic image and provides a method for panning throughout the image. Panning is usually accomplished by using a mouse or keyboard input device.

A common viewer used to create these tours is sold by Apple Computer Corp. of Cupertino, Calif. under the trademark QUICKTIME VR. It provides a way to view panoramic images from a web site by using a web browser. Other companies provide services and software to create virtual tours for the real estate industry. E.g., such software is found under the trademark BAMBOO at the Internet site www.bamboo.com, and IPIX at www.ipix.com.

While these systems provide tours that contain many detailed views of rooms, it is difficult to understand how all the views or rooms relate to each other and which direction the user is facing. E.g., if a prospective real estate purchaser takes a virtual tour of a house and goes to the living room, then the dining room, then the kitchen, etc., the software enables the prospect to visit these rooms in any order and to see them in detail. However it does not indicate how the rooms interrelate physically, in which direction the prospect is proceeding as they move through the house, and where the rooms are in relation to each other and in the overall scheme, i.e., the layout of the house.

Thus, although these virtual tours have a good appearance, they do not help the individual to understand fully the field of view, direction, and relation of the detailed views to the overall layout because the tours display only

2

detailed views of panoramic images. Some web sites display panoramic images along with maps of the panoramic image, but the maps are static and are only used to select which image to view. I.e., the static map image does not help the individual to fully understand the field of view, direction, and relation to the overall layout.

An architectural design software package, sold under the trademark CHIEF ARCHITECT at www.chiefarch.com, allows a user to in effect to place a virtual camera on a spot on a floor plan and have a window appear on the screen to indicate the camera's field of view in a map window. (Two short, fixed-length diverging lines on the floor plan indicate a sector seen by the camera and thus indicate the camera's field of view.) But if the user changes the field of view in this window by resizing it, moving controls bars, or using an "elevator" (a block in the vertical side column), the "camera's" orientation on the floor plan remains unchanged and will thereby become inaccurate. This program also has a reverse disadvantage: If the user moves the camera on the floor plan, the map window does not immediately change to reflect the new camera position or orientation until after the user clicks in the map window. Thus the display can be very misleading because the two windows (the detailed view and the map window) will often be out of synchronization (sync).

OBJECTS AND ADVANTAGES

Accordingly, several objects and advantages of my invention are:

(a) to provide an improved virtual image viewing and panning system,

(b) to provide such a system in which part of a panoramic image is represented in a detailed image, the location of which is shown in an improved map image,

(c) to provide a detail viewer in which a user will understand the field of view that is shown in this view and in which direction it is taken,

(d) to provide such a viewer in which it is much easier for the user to understand direction without any prior knowledge of the physical location of the panoramic image, and

(e) to provide such a viewer in which the detailed image and the map image are never be out of sync because any change in the detailed image is immediately reflected in the map image, and any change in the map image is immediately reflected in the detailed image.

Other objects and advantages are:

(f) to provide a viewer for viewing detail in a panoramic image in association with a map that shows the location of the detailed image in the panoramic image,

(g) to provide such a viewer in which, when the detailed image changes, the map shows a highlight indicating this new detailed image, and

(h) to provide such a viewer in which detailed image or field of view is highlighted or otherwise indicated to provide a frame of reference for those who have never physically been to the location.

Further objects and advantages will become apparent from a consideration of the drawings and ensuing description.

DRAWINGS

FIG. 1 (prior art) shows a computer linear display or photo of a full (360°) panoramic image of a shopping area, ready to be viewed with a detail viewer in accordance with the invention.

US 6,563,529 B1

3

FIG. 2 (prior art) shows a similar photo of a detailed or enlarged view of a portion of the panoramic image of FIG. 1.

FIG. 3 depicts a window showing a map which includes the area covered by the panoramic image of FIG. 1, and one method of indicating the area and direction of the detailed field of view of FIG. 2, in accordance with the invention.

FIG. 4 shows a computer display window showing a presently preferred layout of a detailed view adjacent a map of the panoramic image of FIG. 1, with the detailed view taken from a different direction than FIG. 2 and the map indicating this different direction, in accordance with the invention.

FIG. 5 depicts a window showing a detailed view of part of a room in the inside of a house in accordance with the invention, together with an adjacent map showing the location of the room in a floor plan of the house.

FIG. 6 depicts a window showing a detailed view of a covered porch of the house of FIG. 5, together with an adjacent map showing the location of the porch in the house floor plan.

REFERENCE NUMERALS

10 compass rose
30 dot representing camera
32 field of view angle
34 highlighted view area or arc
36 new highlighted view area or arc
38 new map
40 new detailed field of view
60 detailed view of Great Room
62 map of floor plan incl. room **60**
64 highlighted sector in map **62**
66 detailed view of porch
68 map of area incl. Porch
70 highlighted sector in map **68**

SUMMARY

In accordance with the invention, I provide an improved method for showing a detailed field of view of a panoramic image and a map of the area covered by the panoramic image that indicates the direction and area over which the detailed field of view is taken. The detailed field of view is presented in one window and displays a portion of the panoramic image. The map is presented in another window and has a sector that is highlighted or contrasted from the rest of the map to indicate the point of origin and direction of the detailed image. When the user changes the field of view in the detailed field of view window, the highlighted sector changes accordingly. The resulting interactive windows allow a person easily and quickly to view and understand the field of view and direction of the image being displayed in the detailed field of view window. The panoramic image may be of an outside or inside area.

Description—FIGS. **1** & **2**—Prior-art Panoramic & Detailed Views of Shopping Area

Prior to describing the viewer of the invention, I will first describe a typical panoramic image and a detail view window and the problem with using these images, which is solved by the present viewer.

FIG. 1 (prior art) shows a sample full (360°) panoramic image of an area, in this case a portion of a shopping area, Ruskin Place, in Seaside, Fla. It was taken with multiple successively rotated exposures using a digital camera to take

4

a series of pictures and splicing the pictures together to form the 360° image, but it can also be taken with fewer exposures using a camera with a panoramic or 180° (or narrower) lens. Alternatively it can be taken with a plurality of separate cameras operating simultaneously, each with a relatively narrow field of view, with their separate images electronically spliced together to form the 360° composite image.

The image of FIG. 1 is displayed in a linear window in a computer screen by a conventional image display program from a computer file formed by scanning the panoramic photo (not shown) or inputting an electronic file representing the image directly into the computer. The image of FIG. 1 is typically used in any of many ways, e.g., to orient a newcomer to an area, or to plan modifications to an area. The image of FIG. 1, being a fully clear 360° image, shows much more than can be seen by a human since a human's view angle is limited to about 140°, and of this, only about 30° to 50° is clear or in focus.

FIG. 2 (prior art) shows a detailed or close-up view of a center portion (about 80°) of the panoramic image of FIG. 1. It can also be displayed on the same computer screen in a separate window by the same imaging program. Note that the detailed view of FIG. 2 is identical to a center portion of the panoramic image of FIG. 1, albeit enlarged.

The detailed view of FIG. 2 is very useful since it shows the details of a portion of the panoramic image of FIG. 1. The portion shown in FIG. 2 is in the center of the panoramic image of FIG. 1, but if the user is interested in any other portion of the panoramic image, the detail view can be moved to view any other portion easily. E.g., if the user wants to see a detail of an area to the right of the center area shown in FIG. 2, they simply position the cursor of their mouse in FIG. 2. Then they depress and hold down the mouse button (usually the left button on a multiple-button mouse), and move or drag the cursor to the right. This will cause the portion of the panoramic image of FIG. 1 shown in FIG. 2 to change and move, just as if the user were actually standing and turning to the right.

While the above views are useful, they do not show the user which portion of the panoramic image they are viewing and how the area viewed is changing. Thus to determine what portion of the panoramic image is being viewed, the user must locate the buildings or features shown in FIG. 2 in FIG. 1. This may not be too difficult with the simple and unique arrangement of buildings and features in FIGS. 1 and 2, but can be very difficult with other areas, such as those which show flora, the inside of a building, etc.

As stated, one system shows a map of the area with the detailed area indicated, but when the detailed area is changed, the indication on the map does not change unless special additional steps are taken. This is highly disadvantageous since it requires the user to take intermediate steps and interrupt their viewing and scanning. This causes the user to lose their orientation and severely limits their understanding of the area.

Description—FIG. **3**—Map Image & FIG. **4**— Combined Views of Shopping Area

FIG. 3 shows a partial map of a town, which, in accordance with the invention, depicts a bird's-eye view 3f the area covered by the panoramic image of FIG. 1. I.e., it shows the buildings seen in FIG. 1, plus some additional surrounding area not seen in the panoramic image of FIG. 1. The map image of FIG. 3 may also be displayed on the same computer screen in a separate window. It is displayed using an imaging program in the same manner as with the images of FIGS. 1

US 6,563,529 B1

5

and **2**. The map of FIG. **3** includes a compass rose or crosshairs **10** to show geographical directions.

The position of the camera from which the panoramic image has been taken is represented by a dot **30**, preferably in a contrasting color, such as yellow as shown. The camera indicated has a field of view or viewing angle of about 80°, generally in a South-South-East (SSE) direction so as to view an area **34** of FIG. **3** covered by angle **32**. Viewed area **34** is highlighted (i.e., it is lighter than the rest of the map, which is made darker) to show visually the area of FIG. **1** that FIG. **2** details.

FIG. **4** is similar to FIGS. **2** and **3**, except that it combines the two windows into one window with two sections, a left section **40**—the detailed field of view, and a right section **38**—the map. The single widow of FIG. **4** is the presently preferred embodiment since, by combining both windows into one, is simpler in appearance. As will be explained, detailed field of view **40** shows a new area of the panoramic view of FIG. **1** slightly to the left of the view of FIG. **2**, while map **38** shows a new highlighted view area **36**, rotated slightly counter-clockwise (CCW) from view area **34** of FIG. **2**.

Basic Operation—FIGS. 1 to 4

As indicated above, the user can change the field of view of FIG. **2**. I.e., the user simply positions the cursor (not shown) of their mouse (not shown) anywhere in FIG. **2**. Then they depress and hold down the mouse button (usually the left button on a multiple-button mouse), and move or drag the cursor to the right or to the left. This will cause the portion of the panoramic image of FIG. **1** shown in FIG. **2** to change and move, just as if the user actually stood at location **30** and turned to the right or left.

When the user changes the field of view of FIG. **2** in this manner, the highlighted sector or arc displayed in the map (FIG. **3**) simultaneously rotates and always shows the actual sector displayed in FIG. **2**.

E.g., assume that the user positions the cursor anywhere in FIG. **2** to the left of the right border and drags the cursor slightly to the left. FIG. **2** will change as follows: the image will move to the right as the cursor is moved to the left so as to display an area to the left of the center area of FIG. **1**, as shown by new detailed view window **40** in FIG. **4**.

The detailed view will change in the same manner as if a person standing at location **30** in FIG. **3** and looking in the SSE direction to see field of view **34** of FIG. **3** turned their head slightly to the left. The person would then view in the generally ESE direction as shown by field of view **36** in map **38** at the right-hand side of FIG. **4**.

Simultaneously highlighted sector or arc **34** of FIG. **3** will rotate CCW to highlight new field **36** in FIG. **4** and the actual area being viewed. The highlighted area will still cover an angle or arc **32**, which will be approximately 80°, but may change slightly because of imperfections in the images. Thus when the viewed arc is moved, one of the lines bounding the highlighted arc may move faster or slower than the other line to reflect this.

As stated, movement of the field of view can be effected by dragging the cursor in the detailed view of FIG. **2**, or in the detailed view window **40** of FIG. **4**. Movement of the field of view can also be effected by clicking and dragging the cursor in the map of FIG. **3** or map window **38** of FIG. **4**. I.e., the user would position the cursor anywhere in the map of FIG. **3**, or anywhere in map window **38** of FIG. **4**. The user left clicks and holds down the mouse button and drags the cursor approximately clockwise (CW) or CCW.

6

The highlighted arc will rotate in the selected direction. E.g., if the highlighted sector is looking in the SSE direction as shown in FIG. **3** and the cursor is cragged up or CCW, the highlighted arc will move slightly CCW, as shown by arc **36** in image **38** of FIG. **4**. Thus the field of view can be changed by clicking and dragging in either the map or the detailed field of view window.

In FIG. **4**, detail view window **40** is positioned adjacent and joined to map **38**. As stated, this is the presently preferred arrangement, but the arrangement of FIGS. **2** and **3**, where the windows are separated, will also operate in an identical manner.

Thus whenever the user changes the field of view in FIG. **2** (or window **40** of FIG. **4**) in either direction, the highlighted sector or view shown in FIG. **3** (or window **38** of FIG. **4**) will automatically and simultaneously change to show the new field of view. This will enable to user to always see exactly what part of the panoramic image they are viewing. The user will obtain a much better understanding of the field of view and direction, and hence of the area being viewed.

The above example can be experienced interactively online at the following site:

http://www.duckware.com/patent.html.

Relocation of Camera—FIGS. 1 to 4

In addition to showing a panoramic map of the geographical area and a detailed view of any selected portion of the area in another window, the program can be used to move the map as if the camera were moved to another location. The map will change accordingly to show a new map of the area, as seen from the new camera location, with the camera location being located in the approximate center of the new map.

In the example shown in the above site, the camera's position can be moved to inside a building and the detailed view (FIG. **2** or **40** in FIG. **4**) will show the room and the map (FIG. **3** or **38** in FIG. **4**) will show a map of the room. The detailed view will change to reflect the new camera location and can be moved throughout the new map as before. The above programs (in microfiche in the file of this patent) will effect this operation. This is illustrated in FIG. **3** by new camera location **30'**, which has been moved from original camera location **30** by the arrow connecting original location **30** with new location **30'**.

Automatic Panning—FIGS. 1 to 4

The manual movement of the detailed view discussed above under Basic Operation can be done automatically within the program. This automatic panning is configured by the designer of the HTML page containing the detailed pmvr viewer by inserting the following line into the param section of the pmvr applet (section of the HTML document):

```
<param name="auto" value="1">
```

For example, an automatic panning capability can be added to the test.html document described below by inserting this single line just after the "pixdeg" line.

When automatic panning occurs, field-of-view sector **32** will rotate around slowly in either direction, as indicated by arrows **32'** in FIG. **3**. During this movement, the detailed view (FIG. **2** or **40** in FIG. **4**) will automatically pan in a corresponding movement. This movement can be seen at the above duckware site. The manual panning operation can still be used and will override the automatic panning operation.

Method of Installing and Using System—FIGS. 1 to 4

To install and use the system, a programmer need merely install the above two source programs (pmvr.java and

US 6,563,529 B1

7

FloorPlan.java) into a working directory on any computer having the following installed programs: (1) a Java compiler (to translate the Java source code into Java class files), and (2) a Java-enabled web browser.

Then the Java source files are compiled into Java-class files. This is done by using a program, Java Development Kit (JDK), sold by Sun Microsystems, and issuing the following commands:

    javac pmvr.java

    javac FloorPlan.java

After these commands are run, the current working directory will contain the compiled programs. Namely, pmvr.java will be compiled and produce a file named pmvr.class, and FloorPlan.java will be compiled and produce a file named FloorPlan.class.

Then a 360° panoramic image, such as the one of FIG. **1**, is installed on the computer's hard disk in the working directory under the name panoramic.jpg, in JPEG format.

Next a map image, such as the one in FIG. **3**, is installed on the computer's hard disk in the working directory under the name map.gif, in GIF format. This map image is produced using a drawing program, such as that sold under the trademark MICROSOFT PAINT by Microsoft Corp. of Bellevue, Wash., from a map of the actual site shown in the panoramic image. E.g., an actual map is scanned with a scanner and opened with the drawing program. The resulting image is changed using the drawing program to eliminate any extraneous information and to provide the desired colors. Alternatively the map can be drawn by hand. The image is saved in GIF format under the name map.gif. (The actual names of the images are not important, but they must match the names used within the test.html document to be created next.)

The next step is to create an HTML document that uses both pmvr.class and FloorPlan.class to view the panoramic image and the map within a Java-enabled web browser. For example, the user creates an HTML document named test.html as follows:

```
<html>
<body>
<applet code=pmvr.class height=250 width=400>
<param name="image" value="panoramic.jpg">
<param name="view" value="360">
<param name="pixdeg" value="0=90,2000=90">
</applet>
<applet name=FloorPlan code=FloorPlan.class height=
    250 width=200>
<param name="image" value="map.gif">
<param name="x" value="50">
<param name="y" value="100">
</applet>
</body>
</html>
```

Within the first pmvr applet (third line above) the 'height' (250) is usually set to be the height in pixels of the sample panoramic image. The 'width' (400) is usually set to around 20% the width of the panoramic image (2000, for example). Thus the applet presents a partial view of the panoramic.

The 'image' param value (next line above) is set to the file name of the saved panoramic image, which will be 'panoramic.jpg'.

The 'view' param value is set to '360' to indicate that the panoramic represents 360° of view.

The 'pixdeg' value is set to '0=90,2000=90' to indicate that the leftmost pixel (0) of the panoramic image is pointing

8

due north (90) and that the rightmost pixel (2000) of the panoramic image is also pointing due north (90).

Within the second FloorPlan applet, the 'height' (250) is set to be the same as the pmvr applet, since they will usually be seen side by side next to each other.

The 'width' (200) is set to be the pixel width of the map image.

The 'image' param value must be set to the file name of the saved map image, which will be 'map.gif'.

The 'x' (50) and 'y' (100) param values specify the x and y pixel locations within the map image that represents the standing or viewing position (camera location) of the panoramic image.

The final step is to view the test HTML document, test.html, within a Java enabled web browser.

The web browser will show a view similar to FIG. **4**, provided the panoramic image of FIG. **1** and the map of FIG. **3** are used. The interactive operation between the map image and the detailed view will operate as described above.

Alternatively the 'appletviewer' program within Sun's Java Development Kit can be used to view the test.html document. For example, running the command 'applet-viewer test.html' results in two windows similar to FIGS. **2** and **3** being displayed.

In the attached programs, lines **122–130** and **290–316** of pmvr.java and lines **147–157** and **267–272** of FloorPlan.java generally constitute synchronization means. This means changes the portion of the panoramic image highlighted in the map in response to changes in the portion of the panoramic image shown in the detailed view, and vice-versa.

Lines **484–491** of pmvr.java generally constitute means for automatically changing the field of view at a predetermined interval.

Lines **417–433** of pmvr.java generally constitute means for enabling an operator to end such automatic changing.

FIGS. **5** & **6**—Windows of Building Floor Plan and Rooms

The program can also be used to move through the rooms in a building. In this case the detailed view will show individual rooms and the map will show where the viewed room is in the overall floor plan.

FIG. **5** shows a computer screen window containing on its left side a detailed view **60** of a portion of a 'Great Room' of a private Gulf-front residence in Seaside, Fla. The detailed view shows a sector or arc, approximately 80° wide, of a 360° panoramic image (not shown). An adjacent map **62** on the right side of the window shows a floor plan with a highlighted sector **64** representing the area of view in detailed view **60**.

When a mouse is moved within detailed view **60**, the shape of the mouse cursor normally will be an arrow, but will change to a hand when the cursor is in a location where clicking will result in moving to a new room or location. For example, when the mouse cursor is moved to over a door to the left or right of the windows in the center of detailed view **60**, it will change to a hand. Clicking on either door will cause the window of FIG. **5** to change to the window of FIG. **6**.

FIG. **6** depicts a widow showing a detailed view **66** and adjacent floor plan map **68** of a covered porch that is adjacent to the Great Room of FIG. **5**. Note that map **68** of FIG. **6** differs from map **62** of FIG. **5** in that map **68** is moved just outside the room to show the adjacent porch. In map **68**, a sector **70** is highlighted to indicate the area of the porch in detailed view **66**.

US 6,563,529 B1

9

10

In addition to clicking on areas within a detailed view to move from one area to another area, it is also possible to click within areas on the map to move from area to area. For example, moving the mouse cursor over the 'Great Room' text in map **68** of FIG. **6** will result in the mouse cursor changing to a hand cursor. Clicking on the 'Great Room' text will result in the window of FIG. **5** being re-displayed.

The method of storing the map and detailed views of FIGS. **5** and **6** in the computer is similar to that of providing the images of FIGS. **1** to **4**, discussed above when creating test.html, with the following exceptions:

(a) For FIG. **5**, both 'image' params are set to view the new panoramic and map images; the 'height' is set to '304', 'pixdeg' is set to '0=102,750=0,1063=320, 1200=301,2400=102'; 'x' is set to '102'; and 'y' is set to '181 '.

(b) For FIG. **6**, both 'image' params are set to view the new panoramic and map images; the 'height' is set to '300'; 'pixdeg' is set to '0=5,1137=175'; 'x' is set to '100'; and 'y' is set to '347'.

The above examples can be experienced interactively online at the above duckware site.

CONCLUSION, RAMIFICATIONS, AND SCOPE

Thus the reader will see that I have provided an improved detail viewer for a panoramic image that can be used to view any part of the image by simply moving it across the image. While the image is viewed, a map of the area covered by the panoramic image is displayed with the detailed field of view highlighted. When the detailed field of view is changed, the highlighted area in the map simultaneously changes to show the area being viewed. This enables the user to be more easily acclimated to and understand an area being viewed and also to understand more fully the direction in which the detailed view is taken. The user can do this without any prior knowledge of the physical location of the panoramic image. The map and the detailed field of view are never out of sync because a change in the map is immediately reflected in the detailed view and a change in the detailed view is immediately reflected within the map. The map substantially includes the panoramic image area and has a highlight that always indicates the field of view and changes to the latter. This gives the user an excellent frame of reference that is highly useful if they have never physically been to the location before. The system can be used to view any type of area, inside or outside, or even celestial.

While the above description contains many specificities, these should not be construed as limitations on the scope of the invention, but rather as an exemplification of one preferred embodiment thereof. Many other variations are possible. For example, the panoramic image can be from a live video source and not just a static image. The map image can be generated from a geographic information system and not just a static image. As shown, the "highlighted" area of the map is actually made by darkening the rest of the map, but the detailed view area can be highlighted by making it lighter, in a different color, with darker lines, with border lines only, by shading, etc. The view can be changed by other than a mouse, e.g., by use of elevators in the side margins of the window of said detailed field of view, by keyboard commands, by voiced commands, by head or foot movements, etc. Instead of the geographic urban image shown, the images can be of a rural or natural area, in the inside or outside of a building. In the case of an inside-building image, it can be of a furnished or empty home, an apartment, etc. The viewer can be used on any type of image

displayer, including CRT monitors, flat screen displays, mosaic displays, projection displays, mobile or vehicle displays (the map would be of an actual large geographic territory), interactive television displays, laptop, desktop, or mainframe computers, dedicated computers, dumb terminals or clients with the software in a server, etc.

Accordingly, the scope of the invention should be determined not by the embodiments illustrated, but by the appended claims and their legal equivalents.

I claim:

1. A method for displaying a detailed view of an area within a territory, taken from a predetermined location within said territory, and indicating the area and direction in which said detailed view is taken from within said territory, comprising:

    providing a display that can display a map of a territory and a detailed view of an area within said territory, said detailed view being taken from a predetermined location within said territory,

    displaying said map of said territory on said display,

    displaying said detailed view, as taken from said predetermined location within said territory, as an image on said display,

    providing an input means for a human operator to change the angular direction and area of said detailed view as seen from said location within said territory,

    using said input means to change said angular direction and said area of said detailed view, thereby to move virtually through said territory,

    indicating on said map said angular direction and said area of said detailed view, thereby providing, on said map, an indication of said angular direction and said area of said detailed view as seen from said location within said territory,

    causing any change in said angular direction and said area of said detailed view to be simultaneously indicated by a corresponding change in said indication on said map, such that both said detailed view and said indication on said map change substantially simultaneously,

    thereby to create a highly interactive display, which allows a human operator to better understand, by looking at said map, the area and direction of said detailed view.

2. The method of claim **1** wherein said indicating on said map is done by causing said detailed view on said map to have a different brightness than the rest of said map.

3. The method of claim **2** wherein said rest of said map is darkened relative to said detailed view so that said detailed view is effectively highlighted.

4. The method of claim **1** wherein said change of angular direction or area of said detailed view is effected by manipulating the image of said detailed view.

5. The method of claim **1** wherein said change of angular direction or area of said detailed view is effected by manipulating said detailed view image on said map.

6. The method of claim **1** wherein said map of said territory is a geographical image.

7. The method of claim **1** wherein said map of said territory is an image of the inside of a building.

8. The method of claim **2** wherein said map and said detailed field are selectively arranged to change direction automatically and continuously.

9. The method of claim **1** wherein said input means for a human operator to change the angular direction and area of said detailed view is also arranged to change said location from where said detailed view is taken, said input means is

US 6,563,529 B1

11

used to change said augural direction and origin of said detailed view, and said map and said detailed view image are arranged to indicate any changes in angular direction and origin of said detailed view.

10. A system for indicating the origin, area, and angular direction of a detailed view of an area within a territory, as seen from a point within said territory, and for also indicating changes in said origin, area, and angular direction, comprising:

detail display means for displaying a detailed view of an area within a territory, as seen from a point within said territory, and for enabling a user to change the origin, area, and angular direction of said area shown in said detailed view,

map display means for displaying a map of said territory and indicating the origin, area, and angular direction of said area within said territory, as shown in said detailed view, and

synchronization means for changing, in said map, the origin, area, and angular direction of said territory shown in said detailed view, said changing occurring in response to and in correspondence with changes in the origin, area, and angular direction of said territory shown in said detailed view, or for changing said detailed view in response to and in correspondence with changes in the origin, area, and angular direction of said detailed view of said area of said territory shown in said map.

11. The system of claim **10** wherein said map display means is arranged to indicate the area of said territory shown in said detailed view in a different brightness than the rest of said map.

12. The system of claim **11** wherein said map display means is arranged to darken the rest of said image relative to said area so that said area is effectively highlighted.

13. The system of claim **10** wherein said synchronization means is responsive to manipulations of said detailed view.

14. The system of claim **10** wherein said synchronization means is responsive to manipulations of said area in said detailed view.

15. The system of claim **10** wherein said map is an image of a territory selected from the group consisting of geographic and inside-building images.

16. The system of claim **10** wherein said synchronization means is arranged to change direction and field of view of said map and said detailed view automatically and continuously.

17. A system for indicating the origin, area, and angular direction of a detailed view of an area within a territory, and for also indicating changes in said origin, area, and angular direction, as seen from a point within said territory, comprising:

a display for displaying a detailed view of an area of a territory, as seen from a point within said territory, and for enabling a user to change the origin, area, and angular direction of said area within said territory, as shown in said detailed view,

map display means for displaying a map of said territory and indicating the origin, area, and angular direction said area of said territory shown by said detailed view, and

a synchronizer for changing, in said map, the origin, area, and angular direction of said area of said area within

12

said territory shown in said detailed view in response to and in correspondence with changes in said origin, area, and angular direction of said territory shown in said detailed view.

18. The system of claim **17** wherein said map display means is arranged to indicate the portion of said territory shown in said detailed view in a different brightness than the rest of said map.

19. The system of claim **18** wherein said map display means is arranged to darken the rest of said image relative to said field of view so that said the field of view is effectively highlighted.

20. The system of claim **17** further including:

a timer for automatically changing said field of view at a predetermined interval, and

a timer stop for enabling an operator to end said automatic changing of said field of view.

21. The system of claim **17** wherein said territory represents a room in a building and said map image is a floor plan of said building.

22. The system of claim **17** wherein said territory represents a part of a geographical area and said map represents said geographical area.

23. A system for indicating the origin and area of a detailed view of an area within in a territory, as seen from a point within said territory, comprising:

a display for displaying a detailed view of an area within a territory as seen from a point within said territory, and for enabling a user to change the location of said point, said area, and the angular direction of said area as seen from said point, as shown in said detailed view,

a map display for displaying a map of said territory and indicating said point, said area, and said angular direction of said area as seen from said point, as shown in said detailed view, and

a synchronizer for changing, in said map, said point, said area, and said angular direction of said area within said territory indicated by said detailed view in response to and in correspondence with changes in said point origin, said area, or said angular direction as shown in said detailed view.

24. The system of claim **23** wherein said map display is arranged to indicate said area of said territory shown in said detailed view in a different brightness than the rest of said map.

25. The system of claim **24** wherein said map display is arranged to darken the rest of said image relative to said area of said territory so that said area is effectively highlighted.

26. The system of claim **23** further including:

a module for automatically changing said area at a predetermined interval, and

a module for enabling an operator to end said automatic changing of said area.

27. The system of claim **23** wherein said territory represents a plan of a floor of a building and said detailed view shows a room on said floor of said building.

28. The system of claim **23** wherein said territory represents a geographical area and said detailed view shows a sector of said geographical area.

* * * * *

Puppet Construction Kit

Humans have always been fascinated by puppets—figures whose movements are controlled by strings, rods, or hand movements. Puppets are believed to have evolved from tribal ritual masks that had hinged jaws or jointed skulls and were used in religious ceremonies. John Edward Kennedy has created a method (and accompanying kit) that enables an inexperienced puppeteer—starting with a block of sculptable material—to create a movable-jaw puppet. Below is a sample provisional patent application followed by the actual patent.

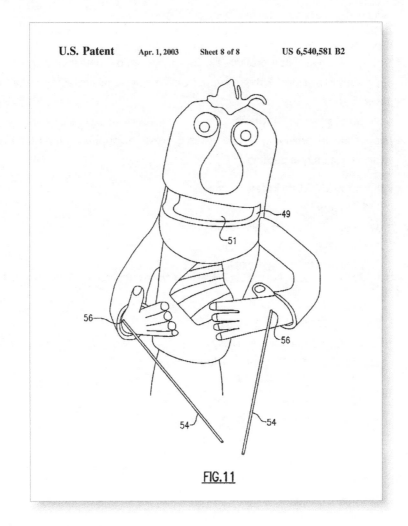

U.S. Patent   Apr. 1, 2003   Sheet 8 of 8   US 6,540,581 B2

FIG.11

Provisional Patent Application

Puppet Construction Kit and Method of Making a Personalized Hand-Operated Puppet

I, John Edward Kennedy, have invented a puppet construction kit and method of making a personalized hand-operated puppet.

Objects:

The invention provides a convenient means to make a personalized hand-operated puppet by an unskilled person. It provides a kit of components that one may use with typical household tools to make a personalized puppet that reflects the characteristics of the intended puppeteer.

Advantages:

One advantage is that it provides the inexperienced puppeteer with the opportunity to create a unique puppet with the personal characteristics and design features of the puppeteer.

Another advantage is that by providing a kit of components to make a puppet, and by providing a step-by-step process, the puppeteer has the freedom to develop a unique puppet.

Relevant prior art includes:

U.S. Patents

U.S. Pat. 2729023 Jan., 1956 Lerner et al.

U.S. Pat. 3698127 Oct., 1972 Harp.

U.S. Pat. 3942283 Mar., 1976 Rushion.

U.S. Pat. 4010570 Mar., 1977 Kohler.

U.S. Pat. 4054006 Oct., 1977 Estlund.

U.S. Pat. 4173842 Nov., 1979 Bahner.

U.S. Pat. 4207704 Jun., 1980 Akiyama.

U.S. Pat. 4226046 Oct., 1980 Delhome.

U.S. Pat. 4276715 Jul., 1981 Rogers.

U.S. Pat. 4326356 Apr., 1982 Mason.

U.S. Pat. 4504240 Mar., 1985 Thomas.

U.S. Pat. 4838827 Jun., 1989 Schlaifer.

U.S. Pat. 4938515 Jul., 1990 Fazio.

U.S. Pat. 4944710 Jul., 1990 Sommers.

U.S. Pat. 4964832 Oct., 1990 Bickoff.

U.S. Pat. 4987615 Jan., 1991 Massey.

U.S. Pat. 5080626 Jan., 1992 Maddi.

U.S. Pat. 5171151 Dec., 1992 Barthold.

U.S. Pat. 5322465 Jun., 1994 McGill.

U.S. Pat. 5348510 Sep., 1994 DuPont.

U.S. Pat. 5662477 Sep., 1997 Miles.

U.S. Pat. D393026 Mar., 1998 Ingram.

U.S. Pat. 5964634 Oct., 1999 Chang.

U.S. Pat. 6000983 Dec., 1999 Pressman et al.

U.S. Pat. 6010387 Jan., 2000 Nemec et al.

U.S. Pat. 6108817 Aug., 2000 Kostelac.

U.S. Pat. 6234858 May, 2001 Nix.

Foreign Patent Documents

588877 Jun., 1977 CH.

3343988 Jun., 1984 DE.

29912632 Oct., 1999 DE.

WO 93/15490 Aug., 1993 WO.

Other References

Harriet Gamble, Puppet Revolutionary: An interview with John E. Kennedy, Jun.–Summer 2000, Arts & Activities, pp. 38–40 44.

Nick Barone Puppets, www.puppetbuilder.com, (c) 2000.

Cedric Flower and Alan Fortney, Puppets: Methods and Materials, 1983, Davis Publications, pp. 8, 9, 29, 46, 47, and 99.

Drawings—Figures:

FIG. 1 - is a perspective view of a block of sculptable material, such as a flexible foam, and a template pattern for tracing along a major face of the block.

FIG. 2 - is a perspective view of the cut block of FIG. 1 showing major and minor block segments, where each segment shows a flat base wall and a common upper Z-shaped wall.

FIG. 3 - is a perspective view showing the beginning formation of a puppet head, where the minor block segment has been folded essentially 189 degrees to a position where portions of the flat base wall are contiguous to one another.

FIG. 4 - is a perspective view of the folded block segments, where the two segments have been provided with slots for receiving the operator's fingers and thumb.

FIGS. 4A and 4B - are perspective views of a second embodiment for a starting block for making the puppet, where FIG. 4B shows the preliminary folded block provided with finger and thumb slots.

FIGS. 4C and 4D - are perspective views of a third embodiment for a two-piece starting block for making the puppet of this invention, where the finger and thumb slots have been precut.

FIG. 5 - is a perspective view showing some initial tracing of facial features on the exposed faces of the block segments, where personal touches for the puppet begin to develop.

FIG. 6 - is a perspective view showing a first step in cutting into the block segments around the facial tracings of FIG. 5.

FIG. 7 - is a perspective view showing additional cutting of the block segments and the development of a shaped head for the puppet.

FIG. 8 - is a perspective view of the cut and trimmed puppet head, where a step of the cutting and trimming is to provide eye sockets for eyeballs and painting of the puppet.

FIG. 9 - is a perspective view of the partially flexed head, or major and minor block segments, and the application of a mouth liner in the form of a fabric.

FIG. 10 - is a rear perspective view of the flexed head showing the attachment of a sleeve member to the finger and thumb slots.

FIG. 11 - is a perspective view of a finished hand-operated puppet, where the puppet includes a pair of rigid wires extending from the wrists of the puppet to allow manipulation of the hands of the puppet.

Drawings—Reference Numerals:
    10 - block of sculptable material
    12 - front faces
    14 - rear faces
    16 - pair of parallel long sides
    18 - pair of parallel short sides
    20 - template pattern
    22 - lower continuous edge

24 - pair of parallel side edges

26 - Z-shaped upper edge

28, 30 - pair of head sections

32 - thin section

34 - lateral slot

36 - mouth opening

38 - lateral slot

40 - rear

42 - opening

43 - central slot

45 - thin flexible section

47 - elongated block section

49 - second member

50 - fabric sleeve

51 - piece of fabric

52 - simulated arms

54 - rigid wires

56 - wrists

Description and Operation:

The starting materials for a first embodiment for making the personalized puppet are illustrated in FIG. 1. The kit of components includes a block 10 of sculptable material, such as a flexible foam, which is generally rectangular in shape, with front and rear faces 12, 14, respectively, a pair of parallel long sides 16, and a pair of parallel short sides 18. While dimensions may vary, a preferred size is about 6 by 12 inches. The depth of thickness, as will be apparent, is at least equal to the breadth of the operator or puppeteer's hand, that is, about 4 to 5 inches. To cut the head portion out of the block 10, a template pattern 20 for tracing the head portion is provided. The template pattern 20 consists of a planar sheet having a lower continuous edge 22 of a size approximately equal to the long side, a pair of parallel side edges 24, and a Z-shaped upper edge 26. This design results in a pair of head sections 28, 30 joined by a thin section 32, where the thin section is further defined by the lateral slot 34 undercut into the larger head section 28. With the tracing marked on the block 10, the head sections 28, 30 may be cut out to reveal one or two integral head sections 28, 30 (see FIG. 2).

With a preferred template pattern 20, two mirror image head portions may be cut from a single block 10.

FIG. 3 illustrates the first step in forming the cut block into a puppet head. Specifically, the smaller head section 30 is folded at the thin section 32 and slot 34 about 180 degrees to form a mouth opening 36. With the respective head sections so folded, the rear of the larger head section 28, as an extension of the slot 34, is provided with a lateral slot 38, where the breadth and depth of the slot is of a size capable of receiving the four fingers of the operator (see FIG. 4). Additionally, the rear 40 of the smaller head section 30 includes an opening 42 for receipt of the operator's thumb in an operative mode. Thus, by movement of the operator's fingers and thumb, the operator can simulate a moving mouth. Further, by holding the head sections as shown in FIG. 4, it is now possible to finish the facial designs features.

FIG. 4A illustrates a second embodiment for the starting block 10 of sculptable material, such as foam, for the puppet-making step of this invention, where the block has been provided with central slot 43 terminating in a thin flexible section 45 (see also FIG. 4B). Additionally, the block, as best seen in FIG. 4B, has been provided with a finger slot 38' and thumb opening 42', the purpose of which has been noted above. Alternatively, a third embodiment for the starting material is illustrated in FIGS. 4C and 4D. In this embodiment, the starting block 10" may comprise a two-piece member consisting of an elongated block section 47, pre-cut with a finger slot 38" and thumb opening 42" for the reasons discussed above. The second member 49 is a smaller member to be glued or otherwise secured to the elongated block section 47 as shown in FIG. 4C. In all cases, the sculptable block 10, 10', 10" may be readily bent or formed to allow the operator to place his hand into the finger slot and thumb opening for designing and sculpting the puppet according to the teachings of this invention.

FIGS. 5 to 11, show three embodiments for designing and personalizing a puppet according to this invention. FIG. 5, for example, illustrates the three surfaces for the embodiment of FIGS. 1 to 4 on which facial tracings and shaping are performed. Though the further description will be limited to the design and shaping of the first embodiment, it will be understood that essentially the same steps are followed for the second and third embodiments. Returning now to the first embodiment, the larger head section 28 has an upper face section 44 and a lower face section 46, while the smaller head section 30 has a single face section 48, where the latter represents the lip of the puppet. Having identified the three surfaces, one is now ready to draw or trace the facial features, such as the nose, lip, and eyes, including eye sockets. This is where the unique or personalized characteristics of the puppet are developed. Once drawn, the respective head sections may be carved and shaped, such as by scissors (see FIGS. 6 and 7). FIG. 7 shows some final trimming touches to the puppet's head.

Providing eye sockets is part of the carving and trimming operation. Into the sockets a pair of eyeballs, forming a part of the kit of components, are inserted, glued and painted (note FIG. 8).

FIGS. 9 to 11 illustrate the final steps in making the personalized puppet. To simulate the mouth of the puppet, a piece of fabric 49, preferably a dark color and of a size about equal to the block's long side and depth, is glued and placed in the mouth opening 36 (see FIG. 9), followed by trimming the edges. As an added touch, a smaller piece of fabric 51, such as pink or comparable skin color, may be glued inside the mouth to represent the tongue of the puppet (see FIG. 11). To operate the puppet, an elongated fabric sleeve 50, with a pair of simulated arms 52 is provided. The sleeve 50 may be glued into the lateral finger slot 38 and thumb opening 42 (see FIG. 10). To further personalize the puppet, hair may be added to the head of the puppet, and dress features may be included on the sleeve 50. As best seen in FIG. 11, a pair of rigid wires 54 may be secured to the respective wrists 56 of the puppet, by means known in the art, to allow manipulation of the arms by the operator's other hand. Thus, the final product is a hand-operated puppet, where a first hand is inserted into the sleeve 50 to manipulate the head, and the other hand may be used to move the arms to help animate the puppet. Though not illustrated as a separate item, the kit of components may include a pair of sculptable or flexible hands (see FIG. 11).

Alternative Embodiments:

As noted, the invention can be implemented in at least three different embodiments. In addition, as an alternative to the generally rectangular block of the first embodiment, the starting sculptable material may comprise a precut foam block having a slot dividing the block into two sections, joined by a thin flexible web. A third embodiment may comprise an elongated block of foam and a second smaller block to be secured to the elongated block.

Patent

US006540581B2

(12) **United States Patent**

Kennedy

(10) **Patent No.:** **US 6,540,581 B2**

(45) **Date of Patent:** Apr. 1, 2003

(54) **PUPPET CONSTRUCTION KIT AND METHOD OF MAKING A PERSONALIZED HAND OPERATED PUPPET**

(76) Inventor: **John Edward Kennedy**, 3121 Castle Oak Ave., Orlando, FL (US) 32808

(*) Notice: Subject to any disclaimer, the term of this patent is extended or adjusted under 35 U.S.C. 154(b) by 0 days.

(21) Appl. No.: **09/881,487**

(22) Filed: **Jun. 14, 2001**

(65) **Prior Publication Data**

US 2002/0193044 A1 Dec. 19, 2002

(51) Int. Cl.[7] **A63H 3/14**
(52) U.S. Cl. **446/327**; 446/85
(58) Field of Search 446/327, 100, 446/97, 85

(56) **References Cited**

U.S. PATENT DOCUMENTS

2,729,023 A		1/1956	Lerner et al.
3,698,127 A		10/1972	Harp
3,942,283 A		3/1976	Rushion
4,010,570 A		3/1977	Kohler
4,054,006 A		10/1977	Estlund
4,173,842 A	*	11/1979	Bahner 446/391
4,207,704 A	*	6/1980	Akiyama 446/369
4,226,046 A	*	10/1980	Delhome 446/327
4,276,715 A	*	7/1981	Rogers 446/329
4,326,356 A	*	4/1982	Mason 446/73
4,504,240 A		3/1985	Thomas
4,838,827 A		6/1989	Schlaifer
4,938,515 A	*	7/1990	Fazio 2/21
4,944,710 A		7/1990	Sommers
4,964,832 A		10/1990	Bickoff
4,987,615 A	*	1/1991	Massey 2/206
5,080,626 A		1/1992	Maddi
5,171,151 A		12/1992	Barthold
5,322,465 A		6/1994	McGill 446/100
5,348,510 A		9/1994	DuPont 446/100

5,662,477 A		9/1997	Miles 434/185
D393,026 S	*	3/1998	Ingram D21/598
5,964,634 A		10/1999	Chang 446/85
6,000,983 A	*	12/1999	Pressman et al. 446/118
6,010,387 A	*	1/2000	Nemec et al. 428/100
6,108,817 A	*	8/2000	Kostelac 446/338
6,234,858 B1	*	5/2001	Nix 446/101

FOREIGN PATENT DOCUMENTS

CH	588877 A	*	6/1977	.... A63H/03/36
DE	3343988 A1	*	6/1984	.... A63H/03/14
DE	29912632 U1	*	10/1999	.... A63H/03/00
WO	WO 93/15490		8/1993	

OTHER PUBLICATIONS

Harriet Gamble, Puppet Revolutionary: An interview with John E. Kennedy, Jun.–Summer 2000, Arts & Activities, pp. 38–40 44.*
Nick Barone Puppets, www.puppetbuilder.com, (c) 2000.*
Cedric Flower and Alan Fortney, Puppets: Methods and Materials, 1983, Davis Publications, pp. 8, 9, 29, 46, 47, and 99.*

* cited by examiner

Primary Examiner—Derris H. Banks
Assistant Examiner—Urszula M Cegielnik
(74) *Attorney, Agent, or Firm*—Jason A. Bernstein; Bernstein & Associates, PC

(57) **ABSTRACT**

A kit for making a personalized hands operated puppet, the kit comprising a sculptable block of material, such as a flexible foam, that may be readily cut and trimmed to form a head portion that can be manipulated by the hand of the puppeteer. The kit may further include a piece of fabric to be glued to the mouth opening to help stimulate the mouth of the puppet, a pair of eye balls to be inserted in eye sockets, an elongated sleeve, with simulated arms, for receiving the puppeteer's hand to operate the mouth motions of the puppet, and a pair of rigid wire members that may be used by the puppeteer's other hand to manipulate the arms of the puppet. A process for making the puppet is also disclosed.

18 Claims, 8 Drawing Sheets

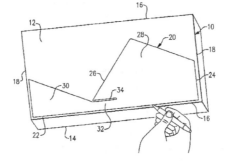

U.S. Patent   Apr. 1, 2003   Sheet 1 of 8   US 6,540,581 B2

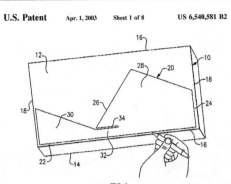

FIG.1

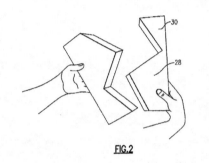

FIG.2

U.S. Patent   Apr. 1, 2003   Sheet 2 of 8   US 6,540,581 B2

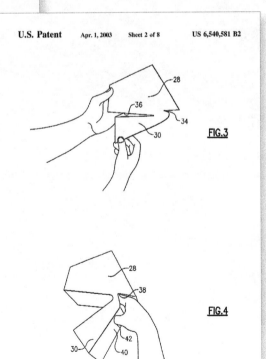

FIG.3

FIG.4

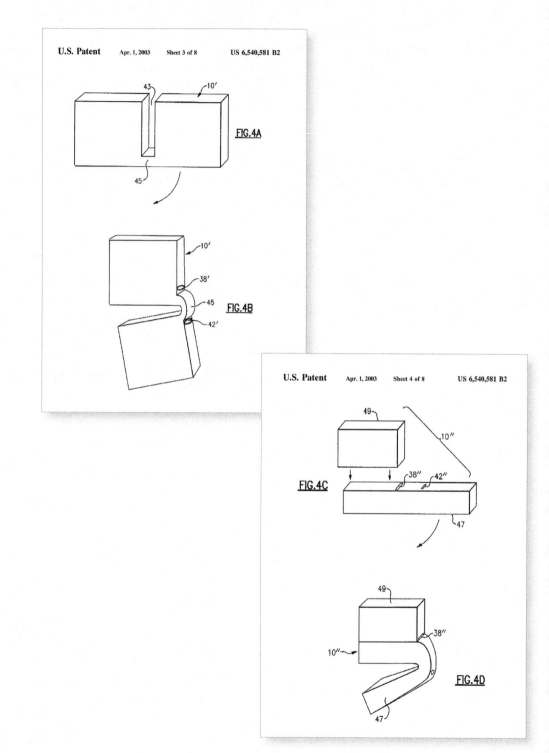

FIG.4A

FIG.4B

FIG.4C

FIG.4D

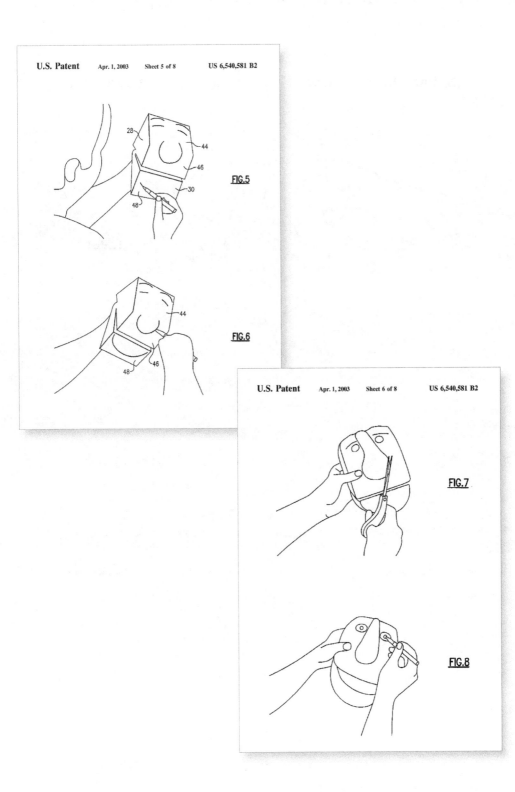

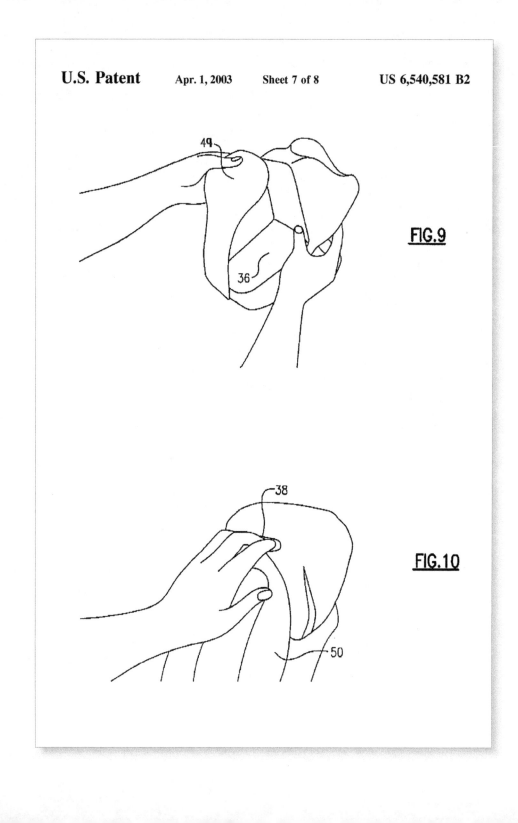

FIG.9

FIG.10

US 6,540,581 B2

1

PUPPET CONSTRUCTION KIT AND METHOD OF MAKING A PERSONALIZED HAND OPERATED PUPPET

FIELD OF THE INVENTION

The present invention is directed to the field of hands operated puppets, formed from a sculptable material, such as a flexible foam block, and to a method of making a personalized puppet.

BACKGROUND OF THE INVENTION

The present invention relates to a puppet construction kit, and to a method of fabricating the components thereof into a personalized puppet character that may reflect individual design features. At an early age many people experienced their first hand puppet fabricated from a white sock with a face marked thereon, but there was little input by the person operating the puppet. A search of the prior art revealed only a single patent that offered some creativity in making a hand puppet with limited personal touches. Such patent is U.S. Pat. No. 5,322,465, to McGill, which teaches a hand puppet kit to maximize creative play by the operator. The patent covers a hand puppet kit including a sock-like body member formed of a flexible material to have a hand receiving opening at one end thereof. The kit also includes a separate sheet of flexible material together with at least one pattern for creating a piece in a predetermined shape from the separate sheet of flexible material. With these features, the hand puppet kit further includes at least one portion of a hook and loop fastener to be secured to the piece.

The reaming developed prior art, as reflected in the following U.S. Patents, relate to a number of commercial hand puppets, without any or at best limited creativity by the operator or puppeteer, namely;

a) U.S. Pat. No. 5,080,626, to Maddi, is directed to a puppet of the type having a flexible elongated neck manipulated through movement from within by the puppeteer's forearm, and the puppet having depending legs adapted to serve as a rest or support for the forearm as well as the puppet's appearance.

b) U.S. Pat. No. 4,944,710, to Sommers, teaches the mouth construction for a puppet that is capable of being hand operated. The invention includes a pair of identical semi-rigid pieces having a lip region periphery having separate layers of fabric sewn to the pieces adjacent the lip periphery and one of the fabric layers is slit and pulled over the periphery to enclose the edge. The pieces are sewn together to define a hinge, and the assembly is mounted upon plates within a puppet mouth opening.

c) U.S. Pat. No. 4,504,240, to Thomas, relates to a hand puppet in which a plurality of different facial components can be removably attached to a head portion to produce different characters, such as monsters, funny looking characters, science fiction characters, etc. The hand puppet has a relatively rigid head portions, and the facial components can be attached anywhere on the head portion, and in any orientation relative to the head portion. A sleeve depends from the head portion, and has an opening at its distal end, and into which an operator's hand can be inserted to support the puppet. The sleeve is preferably formed of fabric which depicts an outer garment for the puppet and the sleeve has a pocket for storing the detachable facial components. Further, the sleeve is designed so that when the pocket

2

is closed, it is basically hidden from view. Thus, the detachable facial components that are not being used to form the puppet's face are stored in a way which does not detract from the appearance of the puppet, and yet makes them readily accessible for changing the puppet's face.

d) U.S. Pat. No. 4,054,006, to Estlund, is directed to a puppet having a head from which a collar-like element extends downwardly below the mouth area for the receipt of the operator's arm. The mouth of the head is manipulated by one hand of the operator to simulate talking, biting, turning and the like. The head has hard, bulging eyes and a soft nose which are secured above the mouth area. The head and collar element are made of fabric material which may be of any type, the one herein illustrated is a woven cloth having long strands of fibers simulating hair over the outside thereof. Below the mouth area a pair of flexible extending arms are attached to opposite sides of the collar at the base of the head. Each arm is made of a cloth material which is doubled over and stitched along the bottom edge leaving an opening in which a rod is slidably secured. The rods have rubber tips on the inner and outer ends which require a substantial force for removal. The rods and arms are operated by one hand while the mouth and head of the puppet are actuated by the other hand of the operator.

e) U.S. Pat. No. 4,010,570, to Kohler, teaches a puppet comprising a head and a costume, the head comprising a container filled with a resilient foam material squeezed therein, the material having a slitted portion extending into the container from its opening, the slitted portion providing a finger-receiving receptacle for manipulation of the head by a finger, and the costume being in the form of a mitten for receiving a hand, the head and costume being in assembled relation when a hand is inserted into the mitten and a finger of the hand is inserted into the slitted portion of the head.

f) U.S. Pat. No. 3,942,283, to Rushton, relates to a hand puppet, resembling a stuffed animal has a pocket extending therein into which the head of a manipulator is inserted. The pocket is configured to extend into the legs and head of the animal so that the legs and head may be moved by the fingers of the manipulator. Behind the pocket, there is a cavity which is filled with polyurethane foam or the like so that the back portion of the animal retains its shape as the animal is manipulated.

g) U.S. Pat. No. 3,698,127, to Harp, is directed to a puppet with a substantially spherical head having a movable mouth which is operated by a pulling string. The string is attached to the lower jaw if the lower jaw is to be moved or it is attached to the upper part of the head if the upper part of the mouth is to move with respect to the lower part. The head is supported upright on a rod extending downward therefrom so that the lower end of the rod may be gripped to hold the puppet upright or said lower end maybe set into a support. The head may be rotated with respect to the cup-shaped member by rotating the rod and suitable arms may be attached to the cup-shaped member so that this member appears as the upper part of the puppet body.

The prior art is significantly devoid of providing the inexperienced puppeteer with the opportunity to create a unique puppet with the personal characteristics and design features of the puppeteer. The present invention, with a kit of components to make a puppet, and by a step by step

US 6,540,581 B2

3

process, gives the puppeteer the freedom to develop such unique puppet. The manner by which the present invention achieves the goals hereof will become apparent in the description which follows, particularly when considered in conjunction with the accompanying drawings.

SUMMARY OF THE INVENTION

The present invention relates to a kit of components for making a personalized hands operated puppet, and to a step by step process for making same. The method, in a first embodiment, comprises the steps of selecting a generally rectangular block of sculptable material, such as a flexible foam, and tracing a head portion of the block by a template pattern. Thereafter, the block is cut and trimmed to produce a head portion having a pair of sections that are foldable upon one another to simulate a head to be activated by the movement of the operator's hand. To simulate features of the puppet, a fabric mouth lining is provided, including a simulated tongue. Included with the kit may be a pair of eye balls to be inserted into complementary carved eye sockets, an elongated sleeve member to be glued to the head portion, where the sleeve member includes a pair of simulated arm extensions, and a pair of rigid wire members for attaching to the arms for manipulating the arms. As an alternative to the generally rectangular block of the first embodiment, the starting sculptable material may comprise a pre-cut foam block having a slot dividing the block into two sections, joined by a thin flexible web. A further alternative, or third embodiment, may comprise an elongated block of foam and a second smaller block to be secured to the elongated block.

Accordingly, an object of the present invention is to provide a convenient means to make a personalized hands operated puppet by an unskilled person.

A further object hereof is the provision of a kit of components that one may use with typical household tools to make a personalized puppet that reflects the characteristics of the intended puppeteer.

These and other objects of the invention will become more apparent in the description which follows, particularly when read in conjunction with the accompanying drawings.

BRIEF DESCRIPTION OF DRAWINGS

The several Figures illustrate sequentially the various steps in making a personalized, hands operated puppet, where the respective Figures show the following:

FIG. 1 is a perspective view of a block of sculptable material, such as a flexible foam, and a template pattern for tracing along a major face of the block, where the tracing begins the method for a first embodiment of the present invention.

FIG. 2 is a perspective view of the cut block of FIG. 1 showing major and minor block segments, where each said segment shows a flat base wall and a common upper Z-shaped wall.

FIG. 3 is a perspective view showing the beginning formation of a puppet head, where the minor block segment has been folded essentially 189° to a position where portions of said flat base wall are contiguous to one another.

FIG. 4 is a perspective view of the folded block segments, where the two segments have been provided with slots for receiving the operator's fingers and thumb.

FIGS. 4A and 4B are perspective views of a second embodiment for a starting block for making the puppet according to this invention, where FIG. 4B shows the preliminary folded block provided with finger and thumb slots.

4

FIGS. 4C and 4D are perspective views of a third embodiment for a two-piece starting block for making the puppet of this invention, where the finger and thumb slots have been pre-cut.

FIG. 5 is a perspective view showing some initial tracing of facial features on the exposed faces of the block segments, where personal touches for the puppet begin to develop.

FIG. 6 is a perspective view showing a first step in cutting into the block segments about the facial tracings of FIG. 5.

FIG. 7 is a perspective view showing additional cutting of the block segments and the development of a shaped head for the puppet.

FIG. 8 is a perspective view of the cut and trimmed puppet head, where a step of the cutting and trimming is to provide eye sockets for receiving eye balls and the painting thereof.

FIG. 9 is a perspective view of the partially flexed head, or major and minor block segments, and the application of a mouth liner in the form of a fabric.

FIG. 10 is a rear perspective view of the flexed head showing the attachment of a sleeve member to the finger and thumb slots.

FIG. 11 is a perspective view of a finished hands operated puppet made by the method of the present invention, where the puppet further includes a pair of rigid wires extending from the wrists of the puppet to allow manipulation of the hands of the puppet.

DETAILED DESCRIPTION OF PREFERRED EMBODIMENT

The present invention is directed to a puppet construction kit of components for making a personalized puppet, and to the various steps in producing said puppet for hand operation by the puppeteer. The invention will now be described with regard to the several Figures, such as by the sequence of steps to produce same, where like reference numerals represent like components or features throughout the various views.

The starting materials for a first embodiment for making the personalized puppet of the present invention are illustrated in FIG. 1. The kit of components includes a block **10** of sculptable material, such as a flexible foam, which is generally rectangular in shape, with front and rear faces **12**, **14**, respectively, a pair of parallel long sides **16**, and a pair of parallel short sides **18**. While dimensions may vary, a preferred size is about 6 by 12 inches. The depth of thickness thereof, as will be apparent hereafter, is at least equal to the breadth of the operator or puppeteer's hand, i.e., about 4 to 5 inches. To cut the head portion out of the block **10**, a template pattern **20** for tracing the head portion is provided. The template pattern **20** consists of a planar sheet having a lower continuous edge **22** of a size approximately equal to said long side, a pair of parallel side edges **24**, and a Z-shaped upper edge **26**. This design results in a pair of head sections **28**, **30** joined by a thin section **32**, where said thin section is further defined by the lateral slot **34** undercut into the larger head section **28**. With the tracing marked on the block **10**, the head sections **28**, **30** may be cut out to reveal one or two head integral head sections **28**, **30**, see FIG. 2. With a preferred template pattern **20**, two mirror image head portions may be cut from a single said block **10**.

FIG. 3 illustrates the first step in forming the cut block into a puppet head. Specifically, the smaller head section **30** is folded at the thin section **32** and slot **34** about 180° to form a mouth-opening **36**. With the respective head sections so

US 6,540,581 B2

5

folded, the rear of the larger head section **28**, as an extension of the slot **34**, is provided with a lateral slot **38**, where the breadth and depth of the slot is of a size to slidably receive the four fingers of the operator, see FIG. **4**. Additionally, the rear **40** of the smaller head section **30** includes an opening **42** for receipt of the operator's thumb in an operative mode. Thus, by movement of the operator's fingers and thumb, the operator can simulate a moving mouth. Further, by holding the head sections as shown in FIG. **4**, it is now possible to finish the facial designs features.

FIG. **4A** illustrates a second embodiment for the starting block **10'** of sculptable material, such as foam, for the puppet making step of this invention, where the block has been provided with central slot **43** terminating in a thin flexible section **45**, see also FIG. **4B**. Additionally, the block, as best seen in FIG. **4B**, has been provided with a finger slot **38'** and thumb opening **42'**, the purpose of which has been noted above. Alternatively, a third embodiment for the starting material is illustrated in FIGS. **4C** and **4D**. In this embodiment, the starting block **10''** may comprise a two-piece member consisting of an elongated block section **47**, pre-cut with a finger slot **38''** and thumb opening **42''** for the reasons discussed above. The second member **49** is a smaller member to be glued or otherwise secured to the elongated block section **47** as shown in FIG. **4C**. In all cases, the sculptable block **10, 10', 10''** may be readily bent or formed to allow the operator to place his hand into the finger slot and thumb opening for designing and sculpting the puppet according to the teachings of this invention.

FIGS. **5** to **11**, for the three embodiments for designing and personalizing a puppet according to this invention. FIG. **5**, for example, illustrates the three surfaces for the embodiment of FIGS. **1** to **4** on which facial tracings and shaping are performed. Though the further description will be limited to the design and shaping of the first embodiment, it will be understood that essentially the same steps are followed for the second and third embodiments. Returning now to the first embodiment, the larger head section **28** has an upper face section **44** and a lower face section **46**, while the smaller head section **30** has a single face section **48**, where the latter represents the lip of the puppet. Having identified the three surfaces, one is now ready to draw or trace the facial features, such as the nose, lip, and eyes, including eye sockets. This is where the unique or personalized characteristics of the puppet are developed. Once drawn, the respective head sections may be carved and shaped, such as by a scissors, see FIGS. **6** and **7**. FIG. **7** shows some final trimming touches to the puppet's head.

Providing eye sockets is part of the carving and trimming operation. Into the sockets a pair of eye balls, forming a part of the kit of components, are inserted, glued and painted, note FIG. **8**.

FIGS. **9** to **11** illustrate the final steps in making the personalized puppet of the present invention. To simulate the mouth of the puppet, a piece of fabric **49**, preferably a dark color and of a size about equal to the block's long side and depth, is glued and placed in the mouth opening **36**, see FIG. **9**, followed by trimming the edges. As an added touch, a smaller piece of fabric **51**, such as pink or comparable skin color, may be glued inside the mouth to represent the tongue of the puppet, see FIG. **11**. To operate the puppet, an elongated fabric sleeve **50**, with a pair of simulated arms **52** is provided. The sleeve **50** may be glued into the lateral finger slot **38** and thumb opening **42**, see FIG. **10**. To further personalize the puppet, hair may be added to the head of the puppet, and dress features may be included on the sleeve **50**. Thereafter, as best seen in FIG. **11**, a pair of rigid wires **54**

6

may be secured to the respective wrists **56** of the puppet, by means known in the art, to allow manipulation of the arms by the operator's other hand. Thus, the final product is a hands operated puppet, where a first hand is inserted into the sleeve **50** to manipulate the head, and the other hand may be used to move the arms to help animate the puppet. Though not illustrated as a separate item, the kit of components for this invention may include a pair of sculptable or flexible hands, see FIG. **11**.

It is recognized that changes, variations and modifications may be made to the puppet components and process of utilizing same in making a personalized puppet, particularly by those skilled in the art, without departing from the spirit and scope of the invention. Accordingly, no limitation is intended to be imposed thereon except as set forth in the accompanying claims. All patents, applications and publications referred to herein are in incorporated by reference in their entirety.

What is claimed is:

1. A method of fabricating a personalized, hands operated puppet, said method comprising the steps of:

a) selecting a generally rectangular block of a sculptable material, where said block has front and rear faces, each defined by a pair of parallel long sides, a pair of parallel short sides, and a thickness greater than the breadth of the operator's hand;

b) tracing a Z-shaped pattern from a said short side to the opposite said short side, where a first trace is angled upwardly from a first said side toward a midpoint in proximity to a first said long side, a second trace downwardly from said midpoint to an internal location in proximity to said second long side, and a third trace upwardly from said internal location to a midpoint along said second side wall;

c) cutting through said block along said traces to provide essentially two equal pieces of sculptable material;

d) undercutting said block from said internal location parallel to said long walls and in a direction toward said first side wall;

e) folding the block portion defined by the third trace upon said second long side, to define the lower jaw and head portions for the puppet;

f) cutting a slot in said head portion as an extension of said undercutting, where said slot is of a size to receive the operator's fingers;

g) cutting an opening in said lower jaw portion to receive the operator's thumb, whereby movement of the fingers and thumb will simulate the opening and closing of said lower jaw;

h) tracing facial features along exposed faces of said head portion;

i) personalizing the character of the head and jaw portions by removing excess sculptable material about said facial features to reveal a shaped head; and,

j) applying a sheet of fabric to said block portion that defines the mouth to simulate the inside of the mouth of said puppet.

2. The method of claim **1**, after removing excess sculptable material about said facial features, including the further step of providing a pair of sockets for receiving eyes.

3. The method of claim **2**, including a final step of selecting a fabric sleeve to receive the operator's arm, said sleeve adjacent one end being provided with a pair of elongated extensions to simulate the arms of the puppet, and gluing the end of said sleeve into said head slot and thumb opening.

US 6,540,581 B2

7

4. The method of claim **3**, including the step of attaching rigid wire supports to said simulated arms for manipulation by the second hand of the operator.

5. A kit of components for making a personalized hand operated puppet, said kit comprising:

 a) a generally rectangular block of sculptable material defined by front and rear faces, a pair of long sides and a pair of short sides, with a thickness greater than the breadth of the operator's hand;

 b) a template pattern having a flat bottom edge, parallel edges, and an upper Z-shaped edge to define first and second portions connected by a foldable thin wall section;

 c) an ink marker to trace said template pattern onto said front face, and for tracing facial features onto said sculptable material;

 d) a pair of eye balls to simulate the eyes of the puppet; and

 e) a generally rectangular piece of fabric of a dimension equal to said block thickness and said long side.

6. The kit of components of claim **5**, further comprising a fabric sleeve having a pair of simulated arms extending therefrom, a pair of simulated hands, and a pair of rigid wire members for attaching to said simulated arms for manipulating same.

7. A method of fabricating a personalized, hands operated puppet, said method comprising the steps of:

 a) selecting a generally rectangular block of a flexible foam, where said block has front and rear faces, each defined by a pair of parallel long sides, a pair of parallel short sides, and a thickness greater than the breadth of the operator's hand;

 b) tracing a Z-shaped pattern on said front face from a said short side to the opposite said short side, where a first trace is angled upwardly from a first said side toward a midpoint in proximity to a first said long side, a second trace downwardly from said midpoint to an internal location in proximity to said second long side, and a third trace upwardly from said internal location to a midpoint along said second side wall;

 c) cutting through said block along said traces to provide essentially two mirror image pieces of foam

 d) undercutting said block from said internal location parallel to said long walls and in a direction toward said first side wall;

 e) folding the block portion defined by the third trace upon said second long side, to define the lower jaw and head portions for the puppet;

 f) cutting a slot in said head portion as an extension of said undercutting, where said slot is of a size to receive the operator's fingers;

 g) cutting an opening in said lower jaw portion to receive the operator's thumb, whereby engagement and movement of said fingers and thumb will simulate the opening and closing of said lower jaw;

 h) tracing facial features along exposed faces of said head portion;

 i) personalizing the character of the head and jaw portions by removing excess foam about said facial features to reveal a shaped head;

 j) applying a sheet of fabric to said block portion that defines the mouth to simulate the inside of the mouth of said puppet;

 k) adhering a fabric sleeve member to said head portion, where said sleeve member includes a pair of extensions to simulate arms, each said arm terminating in hand and wrist; and,

8

 l) attaching a rigid wire member to said wrist, whereby said wire members may be used to manipulate said arms.

8. The method of claim **7**, including the further step of applying a lighter and smaller piece of fabric to said mouth fabric to simulate the tongue of the puppet.

9. A kit of components for making a personalized hand operated puppet, said kit comprising:

 a) a generally rectangular block of sculptable material defined by front and rear faces, a pair of long sides and a pair of short sides, with a thickness greater than the breadth of the operator's hand;

 b) a template pattern having a flat bottom edge, parallel side edges, and an upper Z-shaped edge to define first and second portions connected by a foldable thin wall section;

 c) a pair of eye balls to simulate the eyes of the puppet; and,

 d) a piece of fabric.

10. The kit of components of claim **5**, further comprising a fabric sleeve having a pair of simulated arms extending therefrom, a pair of simulated hands, and a pair of rigid wire members for attaching to said simulated arms for manipulating same.

11. A kit of components for making a personalized hand operated puppet, said kit comprising:

 a) a generally rectangular block of sculptable material defined by front and rear faces, a pair of long sides and a pair of short sides, with a thickness greater than the breadth of the operator's hand;

 b) a template pattern having a flat bottom edge, parallel side edges, and an upper Z-shaped edge to define first and second portions connected by a foldable thin wall section;

 c) an ink marker to trace said template pattern onto said front face, and for tracing facial features onto said sculptable material; and,

 d) a piece of fabric.

12. The kit of components of claim **5**, further comprising a fabric sleeve having a pair of simulated arms extending therefrom, a pair of simulated hands, and a pair of rigid wire members for attaching to said simulated arms for manipulating same.

13. A kit of components for making a personalized hand operated puppet, said kit comprising:

 a) a generally rectangular block of sculptable material defined by front and rear faces, a pair of long sides and a pair of short sides, with a thickness greater than the breadth of the operator's hand;

 b) a template pattern having a flat bottom edge, parallel side edges, and an upper Z-shaped edge to define first and second portions connected by a foldable thin wall section;

 c) an ink marker to trace said template pattern onto said front face, and for tracing facial features onto said sculptable material; and,

 d) a pair of eye balls to simulate the eyes of the puppet.

14. The kit of components of claim **5**, further comprising a fabric sleeve having a pair of simulated arms extending therefrom, a pair of simulated hands, and a pair of rigid wire members for attaching to said simulated arms for manipulating same.

15. A personalized, hand operated puppet constructed by a method, comprising the steps of:

 a) selecting a block of a sculptable material, where said block has front and rear faces, each defined by a pair of

US 6,540,581 B2

9 | 10

parallel long sides, a pair of parallel short sides, and a thickness greater than the breadth of the operator's hand;

b) cutting a Z-shaped pattern from a said short side to the opposite said short side, where a first cut is made angled upwardly from a first said side toward a midpoint in proximity to a first said long side, a second cut is made downwardly from said midpoint to an internal location in proximity to said second long side, and a third cut is made upwardly from said internal location to a midpoint along said second side wall, so as to provide two pieces of sculptable material;

c) undercutting said block from said internal location parallel to said long walls and in a direction toward said first side wall;

d) folding the block portion defined by the third cut upon said second long side, to define the lower jaw and head portions for the puppet;

e) cutting a slot in said head second portion as an extension of said undercutting, where said slot is generally of a size to receive the operator's fingers;

f) cutting an opening in said lower jaw portion to receive the operator's thumb, whereby movement of the fingers and thumb will simulate the opening and closing of said lower jaw;

g) personalizing the character of the head and jaw portions by removing excess sculptable material from said block; and,

h) applying a sheet of fabric to said block portion that defines the mouth to simulate the inside of the mouth of said puppet.

16. The puppet of claim 15, further including a step i) providing a pair of sockets for receiving eyes.

17. The method of claim 16, including a step j) selecting a fabric sleeve to receive the operator's arm, said sleeve adjacent one end being provided with a pair of elongated extensions to simulate the arms of the puppet, and gluing the end of said sleeve into said head slot and thumb opening.

18. The method of claim 17, further including a step k) attaching rigid wire supports to said simulated arms for manipulation by the second hand of the operator.

* * * * *

Ergonomic Mouse

Patent agent and author Jack Lo (he coauthored Nolo's *How to Make Patent Drawings*) came up with an improvement on the computer mouse that eliminates the forearm twisting required by ordinary mice. Lo's Evoluent Verticalmouse allows the user to position the hand and forearm in a neutral, relaxed handshake position, thereby improving comfort, especially for those who move their mice over prolonged periods for surfing, graphic manipulation, and sound editing. The device has received endorsements from *PC World*, *Tech TV*, and *The Wall Street Journal*. For more information check out www.evoluent.biz. Below, we provide a sample PPA of Lo's mouse invention, followed by the patent.

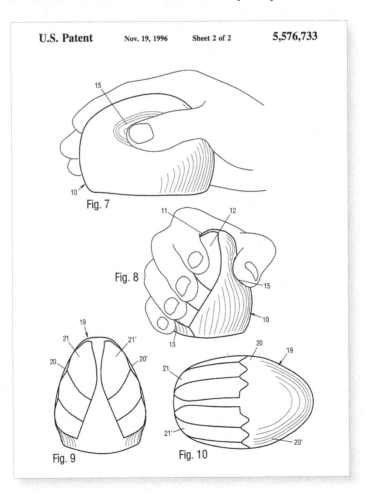

U.S. Patent   Nov. 19, 1996   Sheet 2 of 2   **5,576,733**

Fig. 7

Fig. 8

Fig. 9

Fig. 10

Provisional Patent Application

Ergonomic Mouse

I, Jack Lo, have invented an ergonomic mouse.

Objects:

   The primary object of the present invention is to provide an ergonomic computer mouse which is shaped to allow a hand holding it to remain in a natural, untwisted, and relaxed position. Another object is to provide an ergonomic computer mouse which minimizes or eliminates fatigue, discomfort, and pain even after prolonged and continuous use. Other objects and advantages will become apparent from a consideration of the drawings and ensuing description in this application.

   My ergonomic computer mouse has an upright finger-supporting surface for supporting a hand in a natural, untwisted, and upright position to minimize or eliminate fatigue and discomfort even after prolonged use. It also includes a thumb-supporting surface, one or more buttons arranged on the upright finger-supporting surface, and a motion sensor on a bottom side.

Relevant prior art includes:

US Pat. D302426	Jul., 1989	Bradley et al. D14/114.
US Pat. D328597	Aug., 1992	Clouss D14/114.
US Pat. 2498105	Feb., 1950	Dolan 401/48.
US Pat. 3972628	Aug., 1976	Stevers 401/48.
US Pat. 4780707	Oct., 1988	Selker 345/163.
US Pat. 4862165	Aug., 1989	Gart 341/20.
US Pat. 4917517	Apr., 1990	Ertz 401/6.
US Pat. 5137384	Aug., 1992	Spencer et al. 400/489.
US Pat. 5157381	Oct., 1992	Cheng 345/163.
US Pat. 5160919	Nov., 1992	Mohler et al. 340/711.
US Pat. 5287090	Feb., 1994	Grant 345/163.
US Pat. 5296871	Mar., 1994	Paley 345/163.
US Pat. 5355147	Oct., 1994	Lear 345/163.

Foreign Patent Documents

413606	Feb., 1991	EP 345/179.
41435	May, 1908	CH 15/437.
2237160	Apr., 1991	GB 273/148.
2244546	Dec., 1991	GB.

Other References

Appoint Flashpoint, Guide to Operations, p. 2; *Computer Shopper Magazine*, May 1994, p. 548; describing operation and showing photo of mouse pen, respectively.

Cadence Magazine, May 1994, p. 74, showing photo of mouse pen.

Microsoft Mouse User's Guide, pp. 2, 22, and 23, showing drawings of the mouse being held by a hand.

Advantages:

One advantage of the invention is that it does not require the user to force the hand, wrist, and forearm to be twisted 80 to 90 degrees out of their natural and relaxed positions, or require constant muscular force to be applied by the hand, wrist, and forearm to maintain their positions.

Another advantage of the invention is that it eliminates the discomfort that the user of a traditional computer mouse experiences over a prolonged and continuous period of use—including fatigue, discomfort, and even pain in the hand and wrist.

Another advantage of the invention is that it supports the user's hand in the most natural and relaxed position for a hand placed on a desk by a seated person—the upright position. The little-finger side of the hand rests on the desk, and the fingers and palm generally define a vertical plane.

Drawings—Figures:

FIG. 1 - is a right-side view of an ergonomic computer mouse in accordance with a first embodiment of the invention.

FIG. 10 – is a top view of the ergonomic computer mouse of FIG. 9.

FIG. 2 - is a left-side view of the ergonomic computer mouse of FIG. 1.

FIG. 3 – is a front view of the ergonomic computer mouse of FIG. 1.

FIG. 4 - is a rear view of the ergonomic computer mouse of FIG. 1.

FIG. 5 - is a top view of the ergonomic computer mouse of FIG. 1.

FIG. 6 - is a bottom view of the ergonomic computer mouse of FIG. 1.

FIG. 7 - is a left-side view of the ergonomic computer mouse of FIG. 1 held by a right hand.

FIG. 8 - is a front view of the ergonomic computer mouse of FIG. 1 held by a right hand.

FIG. 9 - is a front view of an ergonomic computer mouse in accordance with a second embodiment of the invention.

Drawings—Reference Numerals:

10 - housing

11 - finger-supporting surface

12 - three buttons

13 - shallow undercut portion

14 - flat bottom side

15 - concave thumb-supporting surface

16 - feet

17 - feet

18 - motion sensor

19 - housing

20 - right side

21 - right-side buttons

F - front

Description:

As shown in the right-side view in FIG. 1, a computer mouse includes an ergonomically shaped, upright housing 10 having an upright, finger-supporting surface 11 on its right side serving as the primary supporting surface of the mouse. Finger-supporting surface 11 includes three buttons 12 arranged in a generally vertical column on its front portion, although more or fewer buttons can be provided. The lowest button is spaced apart from the bottom edge of housing 10 by a shallow undercut portion 13 that extends from the front F of housing 10 to about its midpoint.

Housing 10 is generally rounded, except for a flat bottom side 14 for stably resting on and sliding over a flat, stationary surface, such as a desk or mouse pad (not shown).

As shown in the left-side view of the ergonomic computer mouse in FIG. 2, housing 10 includes a concave, thumb-supporting surface 15 located on the upper half of its left side.

Unlike prior art mice, which have a generally horizontal primary supporting surface, the ergonomic computer mouse has a generally upright, primary finger-supporting surface 11, as shown in the front and rear views in FIGS. 3 and 4, respectively. Finger-supporting surface 11 can be slightly more or less vertical than the example shown. FIG. 5 shows a top view of the ergonomic computer mouse.

As shown in the bottom view of the ergonomic computer mouse in FIG. 6, flat bottom side 14 includes feet 16 and 17 made of a conventional low-friction material, such as Teflon™ PTFE, and a motion sensor 18 for sensing the movement of the mouse over the stationary surface or desk.

Unlike prior-art mice, which are held with a horizontal hand generally parallel to a desk, the ergonomic computer mouse is held with the hand generally upright, as shown in the left-side and front views in FIGS. 7 and 8, respectively. Finger-supporting surface 11 is long and tall enough (FIG. 1) to support the four fingers (those other than the thumb) of a right hand in extended, but slightly bent, positions and in a generally upright stack. Concave thumb-supporting surface 15 on the right side supports the thumb. In one embodiment, the mouse is 67 mm high, 95 mm long, and 62 mm wide.

When held in this manner, the mouse can be moved a great distance by moving the hand and arm together, or it can be precisely and finely maneuvered by just flexing the fingers and the thumb. The little finger engages undercut portion 13 so that the mouse can be lifted without slipping. Unlike prior art mice, which are held with a horizontal hand that is supported on the desk by a small area of the wrist on the little finger side, a hand holding the ergonomic mouse has its weight distributed along an entire lower edge.

Although the example shown is a right-handed mouse, a left-handed version can easily be made by simply providing a mirror image of it.

A second embodiment is shown in the front and top views in FIGS. 9 and 10, respectively. Here an ergonomic computer mouse includes a housing 19 having symmetrical right and left sides 20 and 20', respectively. When the mouse is held by a right hand, right side 20 serves as a finger-supporting surface to support the fingers that will operate right-side buttons 21, while left side 20' serves as a thumb-supporting surface to support the thumb; when the mouse is held by a left hand, the opposite sides and buttons are used. Therefore the second embodiment of the ergonomic mouse can be used by either left- or right-handed users.

Operation:

The upright shape of the ergonomic computer mouse, in either embodiment, allows the hand holding it to remain in a relaxed and naturally upright position. It eliminates the substantial twisting of the hand, wrist, and forearm that are common to users of prior-art mice. The upright hand distributes its weight along its entire lower edge (FIG. 7), which eliminates the pressure sores on the wrist that prior-art mice can cause. As a result, fatigue, discomfort, and pain are minimized or eliminated even after a long period of continuous use.

Alternative Embodiments:

Alternatively, the finger-supporting surface can be somewhat more or less vertical; fewer or more buttons can be provided; and the thumb-supporting surface can be flush with the side of the housing instead of being concave.

Also, the mouse can be easily adapted for use with a digitizing tablet by providing it with a cross-hair and suitable electronics well known in the art. The undercut portion can be made taller for engaging both the little finger and the ring or third finger.

The overall dimensions of the mouse can also be changed for accommodating different hands.

Also, in the example shown, motion sensor 18 is a conventional ball-type device well known in the art. Other types of suitable motion sensors can also be used.

Patent

US005576733A

United States Patent [19]

Lo

[11] **Patent Number:** **5,576,733**

[45] **Date of Patent:** **Nov. 19, 1996**

[54] **ERGONOMIC COMPUTER MOUSE**

[76] Inventor: **Jack Lo**, 1415 Eddington La., Daly City, Calif. 94014

[21] Appl. No.: **248,737**

[22] Filed: **May 25, 1994**

[51] **Int. Cl.⁶** G09G 3/02

[52] **U.S. Cl.** **345/163**; D14/114

[58] **Field of Search** .... 345/163, 164, 345/165, 166, 168, 160, 179, 157; 74/471 XY; 341/20, 22; 400/489, 715; 248/918; 361/680; 401/6–8, 48; 15/436, 435, 438, 443, 444; D14/114, 107

[56] **References Cited**

U.S. PATENT DOCUMENTS

D. 302,426	7/1989	Bradley et al.	D14/114
D. 328,597	8/1992	Clouss	D14/114
2,498,105	2/1950	Dolan	401/48
3,972,628	8/1976	Stevers	401/48
4,780,707	10/1988	Selker	345/163
4,862,165	8/1989	Gart	341/20
4,917,517	4/1990	Ertz	401/6
5,137,384	8/1992	Spencer et al.	400/489
5,157,381	10/1992	Cheng	345/163
5,160,919	11/1992	Mohler et al.	340/711
5,287,090	2/1994	Grant	345/163
5,296,871	3/1994	Paley	345/163
5,355,147	10/1994	Lear	345/163

FOREIGN PATENT DOCUMENTS

413606	2/1991	European Pat. Off.	345/179
41435	5/1908	Switzerland	15/437
2237160	4/1991	United Kingdom	273/148 B
2244546	12/1991	United Kingdom .	

OTHER PUBLICATIONS

Appoint Flashpoint, Guide to Operations, p. 2; Computer Shopper Magazine, May 1994, p. 548; describing operation and showing photo of mouse pen, respectively.

Cadence Magazine, May 1994, p. 74, showing photo of mouse pen.

Microsoft Mouse User's Guide, pp. 2, 22, and 23, showing drawings of the mouse being held by a hand.

Primary Examiner—Richard Hjerpe
Assistant Examiner—Lun-Yi Lao
Attorney, Agent, or Firm—Jack Lo

[57] **ABSTRACT**

An ergonomic computer mouse includes an upright, primary finger-supporting surface for supporting all of the fingers of an upright hand in straight positions and in an upright stack. It also includes an opposite thumb-supporting surface for supporting the thumb. A hand holding the ergonomic computer mouse will be in a naturally upright and relaxed position, without requiring twisting of the hand, wrist, or forearm. As a result, fatigue, discomfort, and pain are minimized or eliminated even after a long period of continuous use.

17 Claims, 2 Drawing Sheets

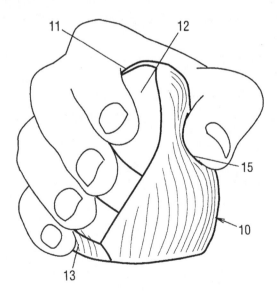

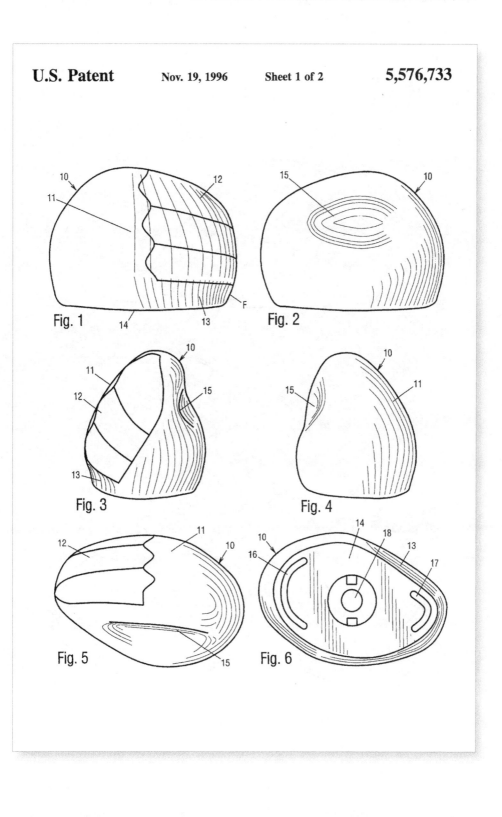

Fig. 1

Fig. 2

Fig. 3

Fig. 4

Fig. 5

Fig. 6

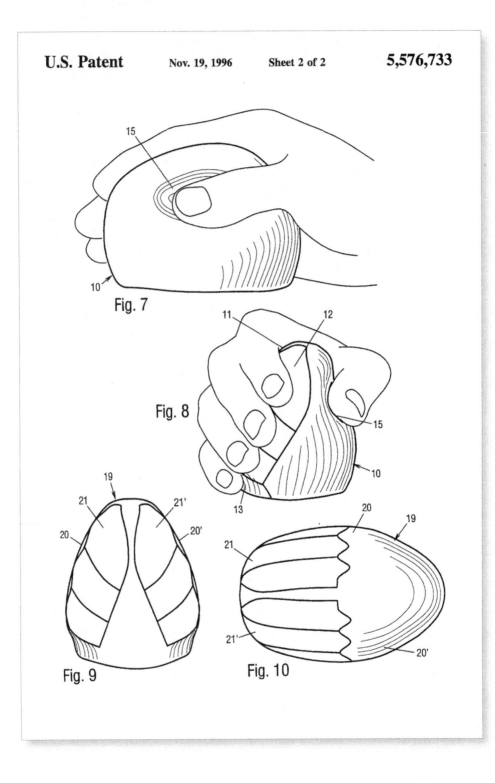

Fig. 7

Fig. 8

Fig. 9

Fig. 10

5,576,733

1

ERGONOMIC COMPUTER MOUSE

BACKGROUND OF THE INVENTION

1. Field of the Invention

This invention relates generally to computer peripherals, specifically to an ergonomically shaped computer mouse.

2. Prior Art

Many software programs use movable cursors for selecting data and objects or drawing on a display monitor. The cursors are generally controlled by a manually manipulated pointing device connected to a computer. Common pointing devices include the mouse, trackball, touch pad, and digitizing tablet.

The mouse is the most popular pointing device. It includes a housing that is slidably moved about on a flat, stationary surface. The housing contains a motion sensor on its bottom side for tracking its movement, one to three buttons on its front edge, and electronic circuitry for communicating with an attached computer. When the mouse is moved about, the cursor moves in corresponding directions; and when the buttons are pressed, certain actions can be performed, depending on the software application using the mouse. The internal parts, and electrical and software operations of computer mice are well known in the art.

Most mice, such as the one shown in U.S. Pat. No. D302,426 to Bradley et al., are substantially wider than they are tall, and have generally symmetrical sides so that they can be used by either the right or the left hand. Some mice are specially shaped for providing an optimal fit for a user's right hand. The mouse shown in U.S. Pat. No. D328,597 to Clouss, and sold under the trademark "MouseMan" by Logitech Inc. in Fremont, Calif., has a slightly angled but generally horizontal top surface for supporting the fingers and palm of a right hand. The Microsoft Mouse, Version 2, sold by Microsoft Corporation in Redmond, Wash., includes a concave left side for closely engaging the base of the thumb and palm of a right hand. The mouse shown in U.S. Pat. No. 4,862,165 to Gart includes a surface for supporting some fingers in substantially curled positions. Some ergonomic mice, including the Logitech MouseMan™, are also made in left-handed versions.

All prior art mice have a generally horizontal, primary supporting surface for supporting a hand in a horizontal position, as exemplified by the drawing figures of U.S. Pat. No. 5,157,381 to Cheng, and the drawings in the user's manual of the Microsoft Mouse. However, the most natural and relaxed position for a hand—when placed on a desk by a sitting person—is an upright position: the little finger side of the hand rests on the desk, and the fingers and palm generally define a vertical plane. Therefore prior art mice force the hand, wrist, and forearm to be twisted 80 to 90 degrees out of their natural and relaxed positions, and require constant muscular force to be applied to the hand, wrist, and forearm to maintain their positions. For a three-button mouse, the fore, middle, and ring fingers must be kept in constant tension to prevent them from resting too heavily on the buttons and depressing them inadvertently. A horizontal hand holding a prior art mouse is supported on the desk by only a small area at the wrist on the little finger side, so that a pressure sore may develop thereon. The total effort and discomfort may not seem great at first, but when these mice are used over a prolonged and continuous period of time, users may experience fatigue, discomfort, and even pain in the hand and wrist.

2

OBJECTS AND SUMMARY OF THE INVENTION

Accordingly the primary object of the present invention is to provide an ergonomic computer mouse which is shaped to allow a hand holding it to remain in a natural, untwisted, and relaxed position. Another object of the invention is to provide an ergonomic computer mouse which minimizes or eliminates fatigue, discomfort, and pain even after prolonged and continuous use. Further objects and advantages of the invention will become apparent from a consideration of the drawings and ensuing description. These and other objects are achieved with an ergonomic computer mouse having an upright finger-supporting surface for supporting a hand in a natural, untwisted, and upright position to minimize or eliminate fatigue and discomfort even after prolonged use. It also includes a thumb-supporting surface for supporting the thumb, one or more buttons arranged on the upright finger-supporting surface, and a motion sensor on a bottom side.

BRIEF DESCRIPTION OF THE DRAWINGS

FIG. 1 is a right side view of an ergonomic computer mouse in accordance with a first embodiment of the invention.

FIG. 2 is a left side view of the ergonomic computer mouse of FIG. 1.

FIG. 3 is a front view of the ergonomic computer mouse of FIG. 1.

FIG. 4 is a rear view of the ergonomic computer mouse of FIG. 1.

FIG. 5 is a top view of the ergonomic computer mouse of FIG. 1.

FIG. 6 is a bottom view of the ergonomic computer mouse of FIG. 1.

FIG. 7 is a left side view of the ergonomic computer mouse of FIG. 1 held by a right hand.

FIG. 8 is a front view of the ergonomic computer mouse of FIG. 1 held by a right hand.

FIG. 9 is a front view of an ergonomic computer mouse in accordance with a second embodiment of the invention.

FIG. 10 is a top view of the ergonomic computer mouse of FIG. 9.

DESCRIPTION OF THE INVENTION

In accordance with a first embodiment of the invention shown in the right side view in FIG. 1, a computer mouse includes an ergonomically shaped, upright housing **10** having a generally upright, finger-supporting surface **11** on its right side serving as the primary supporting surface of the mouse. Finger-supporting surface **11** includes three buttons **12** arranged in a generally vertical column on its front portion; although more or fewer buttons can be provided. The lowest button is spaced apart from the bottom edge of housing **10** by a shallow undercut portion **13** that extends from the front F of housing **10** to about its midpoint. Housing **10** is generally rounded, except for a flat bottom side **14** for stably resting on mad sliding over a flat, stationary surface, such as a desk or mouse pad (not shown).

As shown in the left side view of the ergonomic computer mouse in FIG. 2, housing **10** includes a concave, thumb-supporting surface **15** located on the upper half of its left side.

5,576,733

3

Unlike prior art mice, which have a generally horizontal primary supporting surface, the ergonomic computer mouse has a generally upright, primary finger-supporting surface 11, as shown in the front and rear views in FIGS. 3 and 4, respectively. Finger-supporting surface 11 can be slightly more or less vertical than the example shown. FIG. 5 shows a top view of the ergonomic computer mouse.

As shown in the bottom view of the ergonomic computer mouse in FIG. 6, flat bottom side 14 includes feet 16 and 17 made of a conventional low-friction material, such as Teflon™, and a motion sensor 18 for sensing the movement of the mouse over the stationary surface or desk. In the example shown, motion sensor 18 is a conventional ball-type device well known in the art, although other types of suitable motion sensors can also be used.

Unlike prior art mice, which are held with a horizontal hand generally parallel to a desk, the ergonomic computer mouse is held with the hand generally upright, as shown in the left side and front views in FIGS. 7 and 8, respectively. Finger-supporting surface 11 is long and tall enough (FIG. 1) to support the four fingers (those other than the thumb) of a right hand in extended, but slightly bent, positions and in a generally upright stack. Concave thumb-supporting surface 15 on the right side supports the thumb. In one embodiment, the mouse is 67 mm high, 95 mm long, and 62 mm wide.

When held in this manner, the mouse can be moved a great distance by moving the hand and arm together, or it can be precisely and finely maneuvered by just flexing the fingers and the thumb. The little finger engages undercut portion 13 so that the mouse can be lifted without slipping. Unlike prior art mice, which are held with a horizontal hand that is supported on the desk by a small area of the wrist on the little finger side, a hand holding the ergonomic mouse has its weight distributed along an entire lower edge thereof. Although the example shown is a right-handed mouse, a left-handed version can be easily made by simply providing a mirror image of it.

In accordance with a second embodiment of the invention shown in the front and top views in FIGS. 9 and 10, respectively, an ergonomic computer mouse includes a housing 19 having symmetrical right and left sides 20 and 20', respectively. When the mouse is held by a right hand, right side 20 serves as a finger-supporting surface to support the fingers that will operate right side buttons 21, while left side 20' serves as a thumb-supporting surface to support the thumb; when the mouse is held by a left hand, the opposite sides and buttons are used. Therefore the second embodiment of the ergonomic mouse can be used by either left or right handed users.

Accordingly the upright shape of the ergonomic computer mouse, in either embodiment, allows the hand holding it to remain in a relaxed and naturally upright position. It eliminates the substantial twisting of the hand, wrist, and forearm that are common to users of prior art mice. The upright hand distributes its weight along its entire lower edge (FIG. 7), which eliminates the pressure sores on the wrist that prior art mice can cause. As a result, fatigue, discomfort, and pain are minimized or eliminated even after a long period of continuous use.

The present invention only relates to the ergonomic aspects of a computer mouse. It can employ any electronic communication and motion sensing technologies well known in the art, or any that may arise in the future.

Although the above descriptions are specific, they should not be considered as limitations on the scope of the invention, but only as examples of the embodiments shown. Many

4

other ramifications and variations are possible within the teachings of the invention. For example, the finger-supporting surface can be somewhat more or less vertical; fewer or more buttons can be provided; and the thumb-supporting surface can be flush with the side of the housing instead of being concave. The mouse can be easily adapted for use with a digitizing tablet by providing it with a cross-hair and suitable electronics well known in the art. The undercut portion can be made taller for engaging both the little finger and the ring or third finger. The overall dimensions of the mouse can be changed for accommodating different hands. Therefore, the scope of the invention should not be determined by the examples given, but only by the appended claims and their legal equivalents.

I claim:

1. An ergonomic computer mouse for translation over a horizontal stationary surface, comprising:

a generally horizontal bottom surface for stably and translatably positioning said mouse over said stationary surface;

a housing attached on top of said bottom surface, said housing having a forward end, a rear end, and opposite sides extending continuously between said forward end and said rear end;

one of said sides being a generally vertical finger-supporting surface for supporting the fingers of a generally upright hand in a generally vertical stack, so that the little finger is at the bottom thereof and the index finger is at the top thereof, said finger-supporting surface being generally elongated in a horizontal direction for supporting the fingers in generally straight positions; and

another one of said sides being a thumb-supporting surface for supporting the thumb of said hand, so that said mouse is securely gripped between the thumb and the fingers, and is easily maneuvered by flexing the straight fingers and the thumb, and the hand is in a relaxed, untwisted, and naturally upright position.

2. The computer mouse of claim 1 wherein said finger-supporting surface has a predetermined height for supporting all four fingers in said vertical stack.

3. The computer mouse of claim 1 wherein said finger-supporting surface includes an undercut portion extending along a bottom edge thereof for engaging one of the fingers, so that said mouse can be lifted without slipping.

4. The computer mouse of claim 1, further including a plurality of low-friction feet attached to said bottom surface for allowing said mouse to be easily translated over said stationary surface.

5. The computer mouse of claim 1, further including a button disposed adjacent a front portion of said finger-supporting surface.

6. The computer mouse of claim 1, further including a plurality of buttons disposed in a generally vertical column adjacent a front portion of said finger-supporting surface.

7. The computer mouse of claim 1 wherein said thumb-supporting surface is a mirror image of said finger-supporting surface for forming symmetrical left and right sides, respectively, of said mouse, whereby said mouse can be comfortably held by either a left hand or a right hand.

8. The computer mouse of claim 7, further including a button disposed on each of the sides.

9. An ergonomic computer mouse for translation over a horizontal stationary surface, comprising:

a generally horizontal bottom surface for stably and translatably positioning said mouse over said stationary surface;

5,576,733

<table>
<tr><td>5</td><td>6</td></tr>
</table>

a generally vertical finger-supporting surface connected to said bottom surface for supporting the fingers of a generally upright hand in a generally vertical stack, so that the little finger is at the bottom thereof and the index finger is at the top thereof, said finger-supporting surface being generally elongated in a horizontal direction for supporting the fingers in generally straight positions; and

a thumb-supporting surface for supporting the thumb of said hand, said thumb-supporting surface being generally parallel to and laterally spaced from said finger-supporting surface, said thumb-supporting surface being positioned no higher than an upper portion of said finger-supporting surface for supporting the thumb no higher than the index finger, so that said mouse is securely gripped between the thumb and the fingers, and is easily maneuvered by flexing the straight fingers and the thumb, and said hand is in a relaxed, untwisted, and naturally upright position.

10. The computer mouse of claim **9** wherein said finger-supporting surface has a predetermined height for supporting all four fingers in said vertical stack.

11. The computer mouse of claim **9** wherein said finger-supporting surface includes an undercut portion extending along a bottom edge thereof for engaging one of the fingers, so that said mouse can be lifted without slipping.

12. The computer mouse of claim **9** wherein said thumb-supporting surface includes a concave portion for generally fitting the contour of said thumb.

13. The computer mouse of claim 9, further including a button disposed adjacent a front portion of said finger-supporting surface.

14. The computer mouse of claim **9**, further including a plurality of buttons disposed in a generally vertical column adjacent a front portion of said finger-supporting surface.

15. The computer mouse of claim **9** wherein said thumb-supporting surface is a mirror image of said finger-supporting surface for forming symmetrical left and right sides, respectively, of said mouse, whereby said mouse can be comfortably held by either a left hand or a right hand.

16. The computer mouse of claim **15**, further including a button disposed on each of the sides.

17. An ergonomic computer mouse for translation over a horizontal stationary surface, comprising:

a generally horizontal bottom surface for stably and translatably positioning said mouse over said stationary surface;

a generally vertical finger-supporting surface connected to said bottom surface for supporting the fingers of a generally upright hand in a generally vertical stack, so that the little finger is at the bottom thereof and the index finger is at the top thereof, said finger-supporting surface being generally elongated in a horizontal direction for supporting the fingers in generally straight positions; and

a thumb-supporting surface laterally spaced from said finger-supporting surface for supporting the thumb of said hand, said thumb-supporting surface including a concave portion for generally fitting the contour of said thumb, so that said mouse is securely gripped between the thumb and the fingers, and is easily maneuvered by flexing the straight fingers and the thumb, and the hand is in a relaxed, untwisted, and naturally upright position.

* * * * *

Talking Stick Horse

In D.H. Lawrence's short story, "The Rocking Horse Winner," a young boy develops an obsession with a toy rocking horse. Only when riding the toy horse can the child hear the name of winning race horses. With the help of a handyman, he uses this information to bet, giving his winnings to his greedy mother. Although the invention shown below cannot whisper winners to potential riders, it can provide some audible responses. By combining the popular riding horse toy with our fascination with talking animals—for example, Mr. Ed—the inventors have created an interactive children's toy, "Talking stick horse."

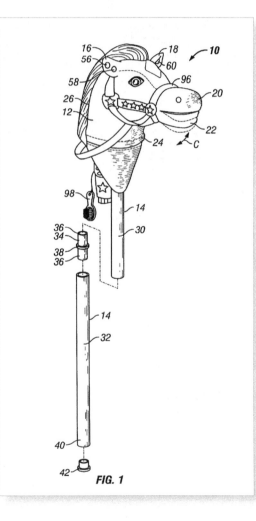

FIG. 1

Provisional Patent Application

Talking Stick Horse

We, Jack Horchler, Damian Mucaro, and Kevin Lai, have invented an interactive ride-on toy, having a stuffed toy horse's head which includes ears, a movable mouth and is connected to a stick. One or more buttons, each with an icon depicting an image, is positioned on one or both ears of the horse's head. An electronically programmed chip responds to activation of the button to operate a speaker and a mechanism for moving the horse's mouth, the speaker playing sounds relating to the image depicted on each button.

Objects. One object of our invention is to provide a stick horse or similar ride-on toy that can interact with a child to encourage creative play.

Another object of our invention is to provide a stick horse or similar ride-on toy that can add teaching value to the toy.

Advantages. Ride-on toys, such as stick horses, are well known and allow the child to pretend that he or she is riding an actual horse. Stick horses typically comprise a toy resembling a horse's head connected to one end of a rigid stick. The child "rides" the stick horse by straddling the stick while holding the head portion. In addition to enhancing a child's motor skills, and developing the child's imagination, our toy has an advantage over similar ride-on stick horses because it not essentially static and encourages creative play.

Prior Art.

U.S. Patent Documents

U.S. Pat. 3201117	Aug., 1965	Gursha.
U.S. Pat. 4808142	Feb., 1989	Berliner.
U.S. Pat. 5074820	Dec., 1991	Nakayama.
U.S. Pat. 5100362	Mar., 1992	Fogarty et al.
U.S. Pat. 5145447	Sep., 1992	Goldfarb.
U.S. Pat. 5279514	Jan., 1994	Lacombe et al.
U.S. Pat. 5316515	May, 1994	Hyman et al.
U.S. Pat. 5823847	Oct., 1998	Gellman.
U.S. Pat. 5944533	Aug., 1999	Wood.
U.S. Pat. 6315631	Nov., 2001	Bechman et al.

Drawings.

FIG. 1 is an exploded front perspective view of one embodiment of the present invention.

FIG. 2 is a partial rear perspective view of the head portion of the embodiment of FIG. 1, showing the battery compartment and battery.

FIG. 3 is a side section view of the head portion of the embodiment of FIG. 1, schematically showing the electrical and mechanical parts.

FIG. 4 is a section view taken along lines 4—4 of FIG. 3.

FIG. 5 is a side section view of the mouth operating mechanism of the embodiment of FIG. 1.

FIG. 6 is a top section view of the mechanism shown in FIG. 5.

FIG. 7 is a circuit diagram of the control system of the embodiment of FIG. 1.

Reference Numerals

10 stick horse or pony

12 horse's head

14 stick

16, 18 left and right ears

20, 22 upper and lower mouth portions

24 rigid base

26 mane

28 closure

28 closure

30 short upper tube

32 longer lower tube

34 connector

36 pair of sleeves

38 spacer

40 bottom end of lower tube 32

42 friction fit cap

44 cylindrical collar

46 top end of upper tube 30

46 top end of upper tube 30

48, 50 complementary openings in top end of upper tube 30 and in collar 44, respectively

52 rivets

54 end

56, 58, 60 buttons

56a, 58a, 60a switches concealed within the ears

62 speaker

64 gear box

66 housing

68 motor

70, 72, 74 gears

76 arm

78 pivot

80 end

82 plate

84 opposite end of arm 76

86 push rod

88 pivot

90 pivot

91 control system

92 programmed chip

94 battery compartment

Detailed Description. An interactive stick horse or pony 10 comprises a toy resembling a horse's head 12 that is connected to a riding member, such as a stick 14. FIG. 1 shows a horse's stuffed toy head 12, with left and right ears 16, 18, a movable mouth with upper and lower mouth portions 20, 22, and a rigid base 24. FIG. 2 shows a mane 26 that conceals a closure 28 for accessing the interior of horse's head 12. In a preferred embodiment, closure 28 is a strip of a hook-and-loop fastener.

Stick 14 is a two-piece hollow cylinder comprising a short upper tube 30 and a longer lower tube 32. To facilitate packaging of stick horse 10, lower tube 22 has roughly the same length as height of upper tube 20 plus horse's head 12. Stick 14 is assembled from upper and lower tubes 30, 32 of by means of a connector 34, which consists of a pair of sleeves 36 positioned on either side of a spacer 38. Sleeves 36 are sized and shaped to fit within the inner circumference of upper and lower tubes 30, 32, and hold the two tubes together by friction.

As shown in FIG. 1, the bottom end 40 of lower tube 32 has a friction fit cap 42. The top end 46 of upper tube 30 is connected to base 24 of horse's head 12. Base 24 is provided with a cylindrical collar 44 that has an inner circumference sized and shaped to receive top end 46 of upper tube 30. To secure upper tube 30 to collar 44, complementary openings 48, 50 are provided in top end 46 of upper tube 30 and in collar 44, respectively. Rivets 52 are inserted through both openings 48, 50 to fasten upper tube 30 to collar 44. As shown in FIG. 1, a decorative scarf 54 is attached to the base of horse's head 12 to conceal the connection between upper tube 30 and base 24.

We prefer to construct stick 14 and base 24 of a durable, lightweight material, such as plastic. As shown in FIG. 4, rivets 52 are similarly made of plastic and are provided with slotted, tapered ends 54, that may be compressed to permit rivets 52 to be inserted through openings 48, 50. Once end 54 passes completely through openings 48, 50, end 54 expands to its original shape to hold rivet 52 in place and lock upper tube 30 to collar 44.

As shown in FIG. 1, left and right ears 16, 18 have buttons 56, 58, 60, which mark the position of switches 56a, 58a, 60a (shown in FIG. 7) concealed within the ears. Depressing or squeezing buttons 56, 58, 60 activates the corresponding switches 56a, 58a, 60a, which causes a speaker 62 concealed within horse's head 12 to play a song, speak a phrase or make other sounds. In a preferred embodiment, buttons 56, 58, 60 are cloth patches embroidered with different icons depicting various images, such as a horse, a musical note or other design that relates to the sounds produced by activating that button.

For example, button 56 may have an icon depicting a horse's head and may be activated to play a short phrase, such as "let's go for a ride." Activating button 56 a second time may produce an alternate phrase, such as "I like it when you brush me." Button 58 may have an icon depicting a whole horse and may be activated to play the sound of a horse's neigh or galloping sounds. Button 60 may have an icon depicting a musical note and may be activated to play a song.

In addition to playing sounds, the activation of buttons 56, 58, 60 also causes the horse's mouth to move while the sounds are being played. As shown in FIGS. 3, 5 and 6, horse's head 12 contains a gear box 64, that controls the up and down movement of lower mouth portion 22. Gear box 64 comprises a housing 66, which contains a motor 68 that drives a series of gears 70, 72, 74. An arm 76 is pivotally connected to gear box 64 at pivot 78. End 80 of arm 76 extends beyond gear box 64 and is connected to a plate 82, which is sized and shaped to fit within lower mouth portion 22. Opposite end 84 of arm 76 is connected to gear 74 through a push rod 86, which is pivotally connected to gear 74 at pivot 88 and arm 76 at pivot 90.

As shown in FIG. 5, the operation of motor 68 causes the rotation of gear 74, which raises and lowers push rod 86. The movement of push rod 86 raises and lowers end 84 of arm 76, causing arm 76 to rotate on pivot 78 through a short arc A. The rotation of arm 76 causes the up and down movement of plate 82 through an arc B, which results in the opening and closing movement of lower mouth portion 22 as shown by arrow C in FIGS. 1 and 3.

FIG. 7 depicts a general circuit diagram of the control system 91 of the present invention. The operation of the speaker 62 and gear box 64 is controlled by an electronically programmed chip 92 contained within horse's head 12, such as a W583 speech synthesizer chip (Winbond Electronics Corp., Taiwan). Depressing or squeezing buttons 56, 58, 60 actuates switches 56a, 58a, 60a, which send a signal to the corresponding trigger inputs 56b, 58b, 60b, directing chip 92 to actuate speaker 62 to play a preprogrammed sound or operate gear box motor 68 to move lower mouth portion 22.

A power supply of 4.5 V, 3 AA sized batteries is required for operation of chip 92, speaker 62 and motor 68. As shown in FIG. 2, the batteries are stored in a battery compartment 94 concealed beneath mane 26 of horse's head 12, such that battery compartment 94 is readily accessible through closure 28, which may be a hook-and-loop fastener, snaps, a zipper, or other suitable fastening closure means.

To summarize, our invention comprises a stuffed toy animal's head connected to a riding member, such as a stick. The head includes a movable mouth, a nose, eyes and ears. At least one button is positioned on at least one ear, the button having an icon depicting an image. In a preferred embodiment, one ear contains two buttons and the other ear contains a single button. An electronically programmed chip responds to activation of the ear button(s) to operate a speaker to produce sounds relating to the image and to operate a mechanism for moving the mouth. Electrical power is supplied by a battery located in a compartment provided, e.g., in the back of the head, such as within the mane of the horse or pony. Where the riding member is a stick, it may comprise two or more parts to facilitate packaging. Where the animal is a play horse or pony, a mane of simulated horse hair is provided, together with a comb for combing the horse's or pony's mane.

Alternative Embodiments. It will be apparent to those skilled in the art that changes and modifications may be made in the embodiments illustrated, without departing from the spirit and the scope of the invention. Thus, the invention is not to be limited to the particular forms herein shown and described except insofar as indicated by the scope of the appended claims.

Although we prefer that horse's head 12 be a stuffed toy, it may also be made of a rigid material, such as wood or plastic, having a hollow interior to accommodate the speaker, gear box, control system and batteries described above. Stick horse 10 may also have various accessories to enhance interactive play, such as a bridle 96 and brush 98 (FIG. 1).

In addition to the stick horse 10 described above, the present invention is readily applied to rocking horses, spring horses, and other ride-on toys.

Patent

US006524156B1

(12) **United States Patent**
Horchler et al.

(10) **Patent No.:** **US 6,524,156 B1**
(45) **Date of Patent:** **Feb. 25, 2003**

(54) **TALKING STICK HORSE**

(75) Inventors: **Jack Horchler**, Mokena, IL (US);
Damian Mucaro, Wayne, NJ (US);
Kevin Lai, Kowloon Bay (HK)

(73) Assignee: **Tek Nek Toys International Inc.**,
Mokena, IL (US)

(*) Notice: Subject to any disclaimer, the term of this
patent is extended or adjusted under 35
U.S.C. 154(b) by 0 days.

(21) Appl. No.: **09/968,069**

(22) Filed: **Oct. 1, 2001**

(51) Int. Cl.[7] A63H 33/00
(52) U.S. Cl. **446/29**; 472/98; 446/301
(58) Field of Search 446/29, 330, 313,
446/331, 369, 397, 408, 411, 301; 434/322;
280/1.13, 1.14; 472/95–98

(56) **References Cited**

U.S. PATENT DOCUMENTS

3,201,117 A * 8/1965 Gursha

4,808,142 A	*	2/1989	Berliner 446/301
5,074,820 A	*	12/1991	Nakayama 446/29
5,100,362 A	*	3/1992	Fogarty et al. 446/272
5,145,447 A	*	9/1992	Goldfarb 446/408
5,279,514 A	*	1/1994	Lacombe et al. 446/297
5,316,515 A	*	5/1994	Hyman et al. 446/28
5,823,847 A	*	10/1998	Gellman 446/301
5,944,533 A	*	8/1999	Wood 434/322
6,315,631 B1	*	11/2001	Bechman et al. 446/297

* cited by examiner

Primary Examiner—Derris H. Banks
Assistant Examiner—Jamila Williams
(74) *Attorney, Agent, or Firm*—Michael Best & Friedrich
LLC

(57) **ABSTRACT**

An interactive ride-on toy, having a stuffed toy horse's head
which includes ears, a movable mouth and is connected to
a stick. One or more buttons, each with an icon depicting an
image, is positioned on one or both ears of the horse's head.
An electronically programmed chip responds to activation of
the button to operate a speaker and a mechanism for moving
the horse's mouth, the speaker playing sounds relating to the
image depicted on each button.

26 Claims, 5 Drawing Sheets

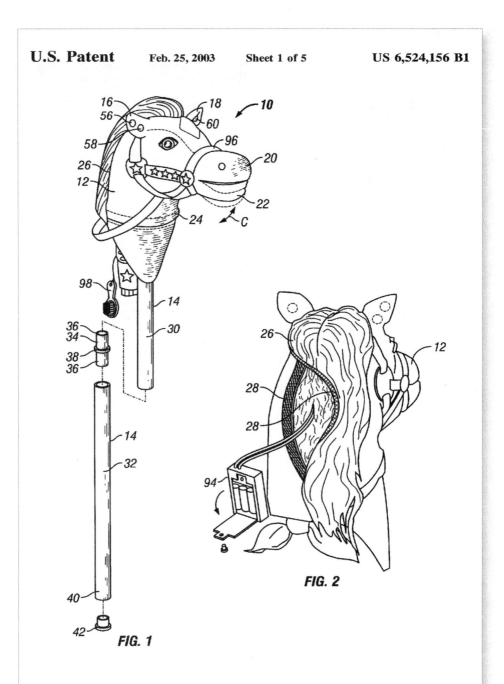

FIG. 1

FIG. 2

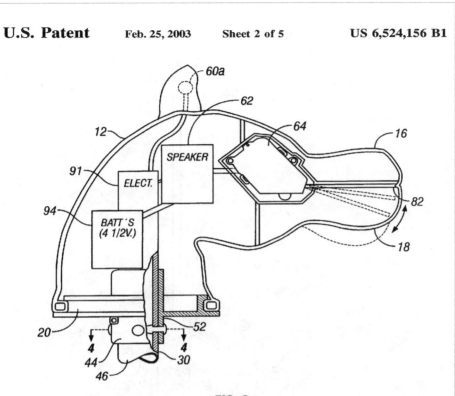

FIG. 3

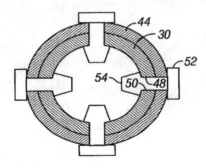

FIG. 4

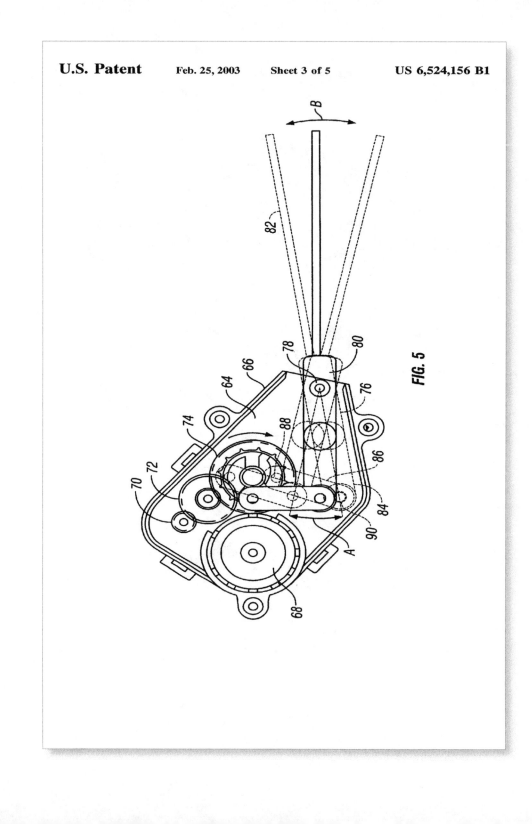

FIG. 5

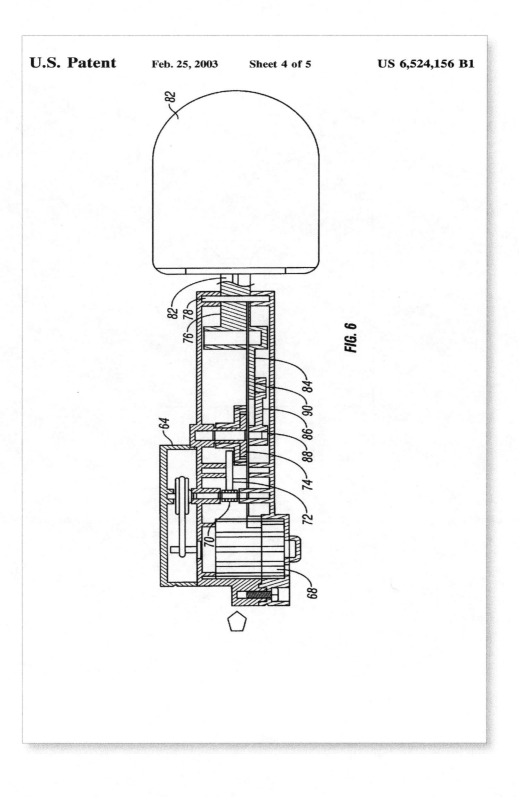

FIG. 6

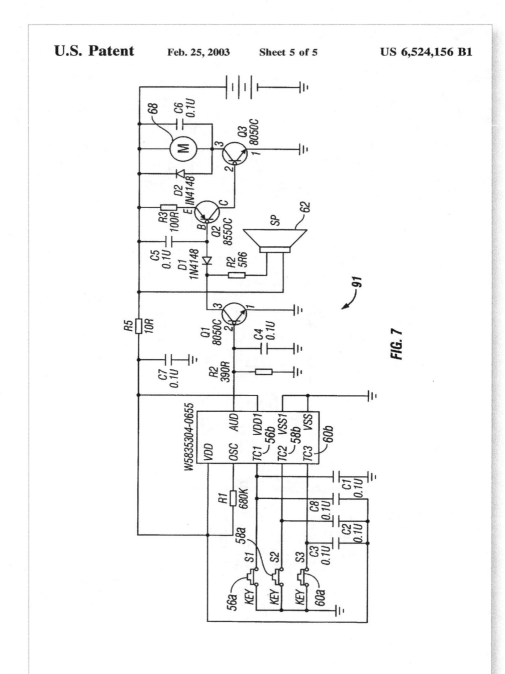

FIG. 7

US 6,524,156 B1

1

TALKING STICK HORSE

FIELD OF THE INVENTION

The present invention relates to interactive toys for children that talk and sing, and in particular, to interactive ride-on toys such as stick horses.

BACKGROUND OF THE INVENTION

Ride-on toys, such as stick horses, are well known in the art and allow the child to pretend that he or she is riding an actual horse. Stick horses typically comprise a toy resembling a horse's head connected to one end of a rigid stick. The child "rides" the stick horse by straddling the stick while holding the head portion.

Stick horses and similar toys are useful for enhancing a child's motor skills, and developing the child's imagination. However, such toys have limited play value because they are essentially static. Thus, there is a need for stick horse or similar ride-on toy that can interact with a child to encourage creative play and add teaching value to the toy.

SUMMARY OF THE INVENTION

These needs and other needs are satisfied by the interactive ride-on toy of the present invention, comprising a stuffed toy animal's head connected to a riding member, such as a stick. The head includes a movable mouth, a nose, eyes and ears. At least one button is positioned on at least one ear, the button having an icon depicting an image. In a preferred embodiment, one ear contains two buttons and the other ear contains a single button. An electronically programmed chip responds to activation of the ear button(s) to operate a speaker to produce sounds relating to the image and to operate a mechanism for moving the mouth. Electrical power is supplied by a battery located in a compartment provided, e.g., in the back of the head, such as within the mane of the horse or pony. Where the riding member is a stick, it may comprise two or more parts to facilitate packaging. Where the animal is a play horse or pony, a mane of simulated horse hair is provided, together with a comb for combing the horse's or pony's mane.

BRIEF DESCRIPTION OF THE DRAWINGS

FIG. 1 is an exploded front perspective view of one embodiment of the present invention.

FIG. 2 is a partial rear perspective view of the head portion of the embodiment of FIG. 1, showing the battery compartment and battery.

FIG. 3 is a side section view of the head portion of the embodiment of FIG. 1, schematically showing the electrical and mechanical parts.

FIG. 4 is a section view taken along lines 4—4 of FIG. 3.

FIG. 5 is a side section view of the mouth operating mechanism of the embodiment of FIG. 1.

FIG. 6 is a top section view of the mechanism shown in FIG. 5.

FIG. 7 is a circuit diagram of the control system of the embodiment of FIG. 1.

DETAILED DESCRIPTION OF THE INVENTION

In accordance with the present invention, an interactive stick horse or pony 10 is described, comprising a toy

2

resembling a horse's head 12 that is connected to a riding member, such as a stick 14. As shown in FIG. 1, horse's head 12 is a stuffed toy, with left and right ears 16, 18, a movable mouth with upper and lower mouth portions 20, 22, and a rigid base 24. As shown in FIG. 2, a mane 26 conceals a closure 28 for accessing the interior of horse's head 12. In a preferred embodiment, closure 28 is a velcro strip.

Stick 14 is a two-piece hollow cylinder comprised of a short upper tube 30 and a longer lower tube 32. To facilitate packaging of stick horse 10, lower tube 22 has roughly the same length as height of upper tube 20 plus horse's head 12. Stick 14 is assembled from upper and lower tubes 30, 32 of by means of a connector 34, which consists of a pair of sleeves 36 positioned on either side of a spacer 38. Sleeves 36 are sized and shaped to fit within the inner circumference of upper and lower tubes 30, 32, and hold the two tubes together by friction.

As shown in FIG. 1, the bottom end 40 of lower tube 32 is provided with a friction fit cap 42. The top end 46 of upper tube 30 is connected to base 24 of horse's head 12. Base 24 is provided with a cylindrical collar 44 that has an inner circumference sized and shaped to receive top end 46 of upper tube 30. To secure upper tube 30 to collar 44, complementary openings 48, 50 are provided in top end 46 of upper tube 30 and in collar 44, respectively. Rivets 52 are inserted through both openings 48, 50 to fasten upper tube 30 to collar 44. As shown in FIG. 1, a decorative scarf 54 is attached to the base of horse's head 12 to conceal the connection between upper tube 30 and base 24.

It is preferred to construct stick 14 and base 24 of a durable, lightweight material, such as plastic. As shown in FIG. 4, rivets 52 are similarly made of plastic and are provided with slotted, tapered ends 54, that may be compressed to permit rivets 52 to inserted through openings 48, 50. Once end 54 passes completely through openings 48, 50, end 54 expands to its original shape to hold rivet 52 in place and lock upper tube 30 to collar 44.

As shown in FIG. 1, left and right ears 16, 18 are provided with buttons 56, 58, 60, which mark the position of switches 56a, 58a, 60a (shown in FIG. 7) concealed within the ears. Depressing or squeezing buttons 56, 58, 60 activates the corresponding switches 56a, 58a, 60a, which causes a speaker 62 concealed within horse's head 12 to play a song, speak a phrase or make other sounds. In a preferred embodiment, buttons 56, 58, 60 are cloth patches embroidered with different icons depicting various images, such as a horse, a musical note or other design that relates to the sounds produced by activating that button.

For example, button 56 may have an icon depicting a horse's head and may be activated to play a short phrase, such as "let's go for a ride." Activating button 56 a second time may produce an alternate phrase, such as "I like it when you brush me." Button 58 may have an icon depicting a whole horse and may be activated to play the sound of a horse's neigh or galloping sounds. Button 60 may have an icon depicting a musical note and may be activated to play a song.

In addition to playing sounds, the activation of buttons 56, 58, 60 also causes the horse's mouth to move while the sounds are being played. As shown in FIGS. 3, 5 and 6, horse's head 12 contains a gear box 64, that controls the up and down movement of lower mouth portion 22. Gear box 64 comprises a housing 66, which contains a motor 68 that drives a series of gears 70, 72, 74. An arm 76 is pivotally connected to gear box 64 at pivot 78. End 80 of arm 76 extends beyond gear box 64 and is connected to a plate 82,

US 6,524,156 B1

3

which is sized and shaped to fit within lower mouth portion **22**. Opposite end **84** of arm **76** is connected to gear **74** through a push rod **86**, which is pivotally connected to gear **74** at pivot **88** and arm **76** at pivot **90**.

As shown in FIG. **5**, the operation of motor **68** causes the rotation of gear **74**, which raises and lowers push rod **86**. The movement of push rod **86** raises and lowers end **84** of arm **76**, causing arm **76** to rotate on pivot **78** through a short arc A. The rotation of arm **76** causes the up and down movement of plate **82** through an arc B, which results in the opening and closing movement of lower mouth portion **22** as shown by arrow C in FIGS. **1** and **3**.

FIG. **7** depicts a general circuit diagram of the control system **91** of the present invention. The operation of the speaker **62** and gear box **64** is controlled by an electronically programmed chip **92** contained within horse's head **12**, such as a W583 speech synthesizer chip (Winbond Electronics Corp., Taiwan). Depressing or squeezing buttons **56**, **58**, **60** actuates switches **56a**, **58a**, **60a**, which send a signal to the corresponding trigger inputs **56b**, **58b**, **60b**, directing chip **92** to actuate speaker **62** to play a preprogrammed sound or operate gear box motor **68** to move lower mouth portion **22**.

A power supply of 4.5 V, 3 AA sized batteries, is required for operation of chip **92**, speaker **62** and motor **68**. As shown in FIG. **2**, the batteries are stored in a battery compartment **94** concealed beneath mane **26** of horse's head **12**, such that battery compartment **94** is readily accessible through closure **28**, which may be a hook and loop fastener (such as Velcro), snaps, a zipper, or other suitable fastening closure means.

Although it is preferred that horse's head **12** is a stuffed toy, it will be understood by those of skill in the art that horse's head **12** may also be made of a rigid material, such as wood or plastic, having a hollow interior to accommodate the speaker, gear box, control system and batteries described above. The stick horse **10** may also be provided with various accessories to enhance interactive play, such as a bridle **96** and brush **98** (FIG. **1**).

In addition to the stick horse **10** described above, the present invention is readily applied to rocking horses, spring horses, and other ride-on toys.

It will be apparent to those skilled in the art that changes and modifications may be made in the embodiments illustrated herein, without departing from the spirit and the scope of the invention. Thus, the invention is not to be limited to the particular forms herein shown and described except insofar as indicated by the scope of the appended claims.

What is claimed is:

1. An interactive ride-on toy, comprising:
   a toy animal's head, having a movable mouth;
   a riding member connected to said head;
   at least one button on said head;
   an electronically programmed chip for responding to activation of the button; and
   a speaker and a mechanism for moving said mouth located within the head, wherein the chip is programmed to operate both the speaker and the mechanism in response to activation of the button.

2. An interactive ride-on toy, comprising:
   a toy animal's head, having a movable mouth;
   a stick connected to said head;
   at least one button on said head;
   an electronically programmed chip for responding to activation of the button; and
   a speaker and a mechanism for moving said mouth located within the head, wherein the chip is pro-

4

grammed to operate both the speaker and the mechanism in response to activation of the button.

3. The interactive toy of claim **2**, wherein the stick comprises two pieces adapted to interconnect, whereby packaging of the toy is facilitated.

4. The interactive toy of claim **2**, wherein said head is a stuffed toy.

5. An interactive ride-on toy, comprising:
   a toy animal's head, having a movable mouth and at least one ear;
   is a riding member connected to said head;
   at least one button on said ear;
   an electronically programmed chip for responding to activation of the button; and
   a speaker and a mechanism for moving said mouth located within the head, wherein the chip is programmed to operate both the speaker and the mechanism in response to activation of the button.

6. An interactive ride-on toy, comprising:
   a toy animal's head, having a movable mouth;
   a riding member connected to said head;
   at least one button on said head, wherein said button has an icon depicting an image;
   an electronically programmed chip for responding to activation of the button; and
   a speaker and a mechanism for moving said mouth located within the head, wherein the chip is programmed to operate both the speaker and the mechanism in response to activation of the button, wherein the speaker produces sounds relating to said image.

7. The interactive toy of claim **6**, wherein said image is a musical note and said chip is programmed to operate said speaker to play a song.

8. The interactive toy of claim **6**, wherein said image is a horse and said chip is programmed to operate said speaker to play a horse's neigh.

9. The interactive toy of claim **6**, wherein said image is a horse and said chip is programmed to operate said speaker to play galloping sounds.

10. The interactive toy of claim **6**, wherein said image is a horse's head and said chip is programmed to operate said speaker to play a phrase.

11. An interactive ride-on toy, comprising:
   a toy animal's head, having a movable mouth and two ears, wherein each ear has at least one button and each button has an icon depicting a different image;
   a riding member connected to said head;
   an electronically programmed chip for responding to activation of the button; and
   a speaker and a mechanism for moving said mouth located within the head, wherein the chip is programmed to operate both the speaker and the mechanism in response to activation of the button, wherein the speaker produces different sounds corresponding to each different image.

12. An interactive stick horse, comprising:
   a head depicting a horse's head;
   a movable mouth located on the head, the mouth comprising upper and lower members;
   a stick connected to said head;
   at least one button on said head, said button having an icon depicting an image;
   an electronically programmed chip for responding to activation of said button; and

US 6,524,156 B1

5

a speaker and a mechanism for moving said mouth, said chip programmed to operate said speaker to produce sounds relating to said image and to operate said mechanism to move at least one member of said mouth in response to activation of said button.

13. The stick horse of claim **12**, wherein the head has two ears, each ear has at least one button, each button having an icon thereon depicting an image, and the chip is programmed to operate the speaker to produce sounds relating to each image.

14. The stick horse of claim **13**, wherein the head includes a compartment, and at least one battery located therein for generating electrical power to activate the chip and the mechanism for moving the mouth.

15. The stick horse of claim **14**, wherein the mechanism for moving the mouth includes an electric motor, a series of gears driven by the motor, and a pivoting arm driven by the gears and connected to one of the upper and lower members of the mouth, causing that member to move in relation to the other.

16. The stick horse of claim **15** wherein the head is provided with a mane of simulated hair.

17. The interactive stick horse of claim **16**, wherein said head is a stuffed toy, and the compartment is located within the mane and contains a closure having a hook and loop fastener that conceals the battery within the compartment.

18. The interactive stick horse of claim **17**, wherein at least one image is a musical note and said chip is programmed to operate said speaker to play a song.

19. The interactive stick horse of claim **17**, wherein at least one image is a horse and said chip is programmed to operate said speaker to play a horse's neigh.

6

20. The interactive stick horse of claim **17**, wherein at least one image is a horse and said chip is programmed to operate said speaker to play galloping sounds.

21. The interactive stick horse of claim **17**, wherein at least one image is a horse's head and said chip is programmed to operate said speaker to play a phrase.

22. The interactive stick horse of claim **17**, wherein the stick has at least two parts adapted to fit together, whereby packaging of the stick horse is facilitated.

23. An interactive ride-on toy, comprising:

a toy figure having a movable mouth;

a stick connected to said figure;

at least one button on said figure, said button having an icon depicting an image;

an electronically programmed chip for responding to activation of said button; and

a speaker and a mechanism for moving said mouth, said chip programmed to operate said speaker to produce sounds relating to said image and to operate said mechanism to move said mouth in response to activation of said button.

24. The interactive ride-on toy of claim **23**, wherein the stick comprises two pieces adapted to interconnect.

25. The interactive ride-on toy of claim **23**, wherein said figure has at least two buttons, each button having an icon depicting a different image, and said chip is programmed to operate the speaker to produce different sounds corresponding to each different image.

26. The interactive ride-on toy of claim **23**, wherein said image is a musical note and said chip is programmed to operate said speaker to play a song.

* * * * *

Agreements

n this appendix, we've provided four invention-related agreements including:

- **Nondisclosure Agreement.** Use this if you're showing your invention to someone—for example, a potential licensee, manufacturer, or colleague—and you want to maintain your invention as a secret.
- **Joint Ownership Agreement.** Use this agreement if you co-own your invention with someone else—for example, a business partner or another inventor—and you want to preserve ownership rights, obligations, and revenues.
- **Model Maker/Artist Agreement.** Use this if you're hiring someone to create drawings or a prototype of your invention.
- **Assignment.** Use this if you are transferring all or part of your invention rights to someone—for example, you are transferring your invention to your corporation or to a partnership.

> **CAUTION**
>
> **Question authority.** Before you enter into an agreement, make sure the person signing has authority to do so and that his or her signature will legally bind the entity on whose behalf he or she is signing. If you have doubts as to whether someone has authority to sign an agreement, ask for written proof. Don't proceed until you're satisfied—otherwise, you could well end up with an agreement that is worthless.

Nondisclosure Agreement

Here, we've included a standard nondisclosure agreement (NDA) that you can photocopy and use with clients, customers, or prospective business partners. We provide an explanation for each provision of the nondisclosure agreement. You can also use these explanations if you must review a nondisclosure agreement someone else furnishes to you.

> **RESOURCE**
>
> **For a collection of free nondisclosure agreements and an explanation of trade secret law,** visit NDAs for Free (www.ndasforfree.com).

Signing Instructions

No matter what type of agreement you use, you must make sure to sign it in the proper format—and on behalf of the proper business entity.

Sole Proprietorship. If one of the people entering the agreement is acting as a sole proprietorship—that is, a business solely owned by one person—that person signs using his or her own name. (An independent inventor often operates as a sole proprietorship.) If the sole proprietorship uses a fictitious business name (sometimes known as a *dba*), list the name of the business above the signature line.

> **EXAMPLE:** Tina Molina is an inventor who calls her sole proprietorship business "TM Visions." She would sign as follows:
>
> TM Visions By: _____
>
> Tina Molina, sole proprietor

Partnership. When a partnership enters into an agreement, one of the general partners (or someone who has written authority from a general partner in the form of a partnership resolution) must sign the agreement. The name of the partnership must be placed above the signature line. Otherwise, the partnership will not be bound—only the person signing the agreement.

> **EXAMPLE:** Cindy Peacock is a general partner in Speculative Ventures Partnership. She would sign as follows:
>
> Speculative Ventures Partnership
>
> By: _____
>
> Cindy Peacock, general partner

Corporation or LLC. If either a corporation or limited liability company (LLC) enters into an agreement, an authorized officer—usually the president or chief executive officer (CEO)—must sign the agreement. (If someone's signing authority is in doubt, ask for written proof—usually in the form of a corporate resolution.) You must indicate the name of the corporation above the signature line.

> **EXAMPLE:** Matthew Polazzo is CEO of Sunday Marketing. He would sign as follows:
>
> Sunday Marketing, Inc., a New York corporation
>
> By: _____
>
> Matthew Polazzo, CEO

Essential Provisions of an NDA

A nondisclosure agreement should:
- define the trade secrets
- state what is not protected as a trade secret
- establish a duty to keep the confidential information secret, and
- state the length of time the agreement will be in force.

Who Is Disclosing? Who Is Receiving?

In the sample agreement, the "Disclosing Party" is the person disclosing secrets (most likely you, the inventor), and the "Receiving Party" is the person or company who receives the confidential information and is obligated to keep it secret. The terms are capitalized to indicate that they are defined within the agreement. The sample agreement is a "one-way" (or in legalese, "unilateral") agreement—that is, we're anticipating that only one party (you) will disclose secrets.

Defining the Trade Secrets

Every nondisclosure agreement defines its trade secrets, often referred to as "confidential information." In our agreement, you must mark any document that you furnish as "Confidential" in order for it to qualify as confidential information. Therefore, you must make sure to (a) label all drawings or documents with a CONFIDENTIAL legend, (b) follow up any oral disclosures with a written confirmation that the information disclosed was confidential, and (c) make sure you preserve all confidential information under the trade secret principles discussed below in "Agreement for Creation of Prototype or Patent Drawings."

> **Because he had heavily invested in DC machines, Thomas Edison opposed the use of alternating current as a standard for electricity in the United States.**

Excluding Information That Is Not Confidential

You cannot prohibit the receiving party from disclosing information that is publicly known, legitimately acquired from another source, or developed by the receiving party before meeting you. Similarly, it is not unlawful for the receiving party to disclose your secret with your permission. These legal exceptions exist with or without an agreement, but they are commonly included in a contract to make it clear to everyone that such information is not considered a trade secret.

Duty to Keep Information Secret

The heart of a nondisclosure agreement is a statement establishing a confidential relationship between the parties. The statement sets out the duty of the Receiving Party to maintain the information in confidence and to limit its use. Often, this duty is established by one sentence: "The Receiving Party shall hold and maintain the Confidential Information of the other party in strictest confidence for the sole and exclusive benefit of the Disclosing Party." In our agreement, the provision is more detailed (in order to provide maximum protection for your invention) and includes an obligation to return any confidential documents.

> E.H. Armstrong, the brilliant inventor of high fidelity FM radio, leapt to his death in 1953 primarily from woes over a patent lawsuit against RCA. (His estate was eventually victorious in the lawsuit.)

Duration of the Agreement

How long does the duty of confidentiality last? The sample agreement requires that the duty last for an indefinite period that terminates when the information is no longer a trade secret.

Miscellaneous Provisions

The sample NDA includes four miscellaneous provisions. These standard provisions (sometimes known as "boilerplate") are included at the end of most contracts:

- **Relationships.** To avoid liability, most agreements include a provision like this one, disclaiming any relationship other than that defined in the agreement.
- **Severability.** The severability clause provides that if you wind up in a lawsuit over the agreement and a court rules that one part of the agreement is invalid, that part can be cut out and the rest of the agreement will remain in effect.
- **Integration.** In the process of negotiation and contract drafting, you and the other party may make many oral or written statements.

Some of these statements make it into the final agreement. Others don't. The integration provision verifies that the version you are signing is the final version, and that neither of you can rely on statements made in the past.

- **Waiver.** This provision states that even if you don't promptly complain about a violation of the NDA, you still have the right to raise the issue later.

Clarence Birdseye worked as a naturalist and fur trader before he patented a method of freezing foods.

Signatures

The parties don't have to be in the same room when they sign the agreement. It's even fine if the dates are a few days apart. Each party should sign two copies. This way, both parties can have an original signed agreement for their records.

> **CAUTION**
>
> **You must protect your confidential information.** Although a nondisclosure agreement assures your right to sue and demonstrates your diligence in protecting secrets, it will not guarantee your success in court. You can never rely solely on an agreement as a basis for protecting confidential information. You must also be able to prove that you took reasonable steps to protect your secret and that the secret has not become known to the public.

Percy Shaw, inventor of road reflectors, enjoyed being chauffeured in his Rolls Royce while eating fish and chips in the back seat.

Basic Nondisclosure Agreement

Basic Nondisclosure Agreement

This Nondisclosure Agreement (the "Agreement") is entered into by and between ＿＿＿＿＿＿＿, located at ＿＿＿＿＿＿＿, ("Disclosing Party") and ＿＿＿＿＿＿＿, located at ＿＿＿＿＿＿＿, ("Receiving Party") for the purpose of preventing the unauthorized disclosure of Confidential Information as defined below. The parties agree to enter into a confidential relationship with respect to the disclosure of certain proprietary and confidential information ("Confidential Information").

1. **Definition of Confidential Information.** For purposes of this Agreement, "Confidential Information" shall include all information or material that has or could have commercial value or other utility in the business in which Disclosing Party is engaged. If Confidential Information is in written form, the Disclosing Party shall label or stamp the materials with the word "Confidential" or some similar warning. If Confidential Information is transmitted orally, the Disclosing Party shall promptly provide a writing indicating that such oral communication constituted Confidential Information.

2. **Exclusions From Confidential Information.** Receiving Party's obligations under this Agreement do not extend to information that is: (a) publicly known at the time of disclosure or subsequently becomes publicly known through no fault of the Receiving Party; (b) discovered or created by the Receiving Party before disclosure by Disclosing Party; (c) learned by the Receiving Party through legitimate means other than from the Disclosing Party or Disclosing Party's representatives; or (d) disclosed by Receiving Party with Disclosing Party's prior written approval.

3. **Obligations of Receiving Party.** Receiving Party shall hold and maintain the Confidential Information in strictest confidence for the sole and exclusive benefit of the Disclosing Party. Receiving Party shall carefully restrict access to Confidential Information to employees, contractors, and third parties as is reasonably required and shall require those persons to sign nondisclosure restrictions at least as protective as those in this Agreement. Receiving Party shall not, without prior written approval of Disclosing Party, use for Receiving Party's own benefit, publish, copy, or otherwise disclose to others or permit the use by others for their benefit

or to the detriment of Disclosing Party, any Confidential Information. Receiving Party shall return to Disclosing Party any and all records, notes, and other written, printed, or tangible materials in its possession pertaining to Confidential Information immediately if Disclosing Party requests it in writing.

4. **Time Periods.** The nondisclosure provisions of this Agreement shall survive the termination of this Agreement and Receiving Party's duty to hold Confidential Information in confidence shall remain in effect until the Confidential Information no longer qualifies as a trade secret or until Disclosing Party sends Receiving Party written notice releasing Receiving Party from this Agreement, whichever occurs first.

5. **Relationships.** Nothing contained in this Agreement shall be deemed to constitute either party a partner, joint venturer, or employee of the other party for any purpose.

6. **Severability.** If a court finds any provision of this Agreement invalid or unenforceable, the remainder of this Agreement shall be interpreted so as best to effect the intent of the parties.

7. **Integration.** This Agreement expresses the complete understanding of the parties with respect to the subject matter and supersedes all prior proposals, agreements, representations, and understandings. This Agreement may not be amended except in a writing signed by both parties.

8. **Waiver.** The failure to exercise any right provided in this Agreement shall not be a waiver of prior or subsequent rights.

This Agreement and each party's obligations shall be binding on the representatives, assigns, and successors of such party. Each party has signed this Agreement through its authorized representative.

Signature: _____

Typed or Printed Name: _____

Date: _____

Signature: _____

Typed or Printed Name:_____

Date: _____

Joint Ownership Agreement for Inventors

Disagreements and problems are all too common when several people share ownership rights to an invention. For example, owners may question which owners can make deals about the invention and how much each owner earns when the invention generates revenue. These issues can be resolved by the use of a Joint Owners' Agreement (JOA). If the sample agreement does not meet your requirements, ask an intellectual property attorney to help you come up with a suitable contract.

Essential JOA Provisions

A typical JOA:

- **Prohibits any joint owner from exploiting the invention** (or resulting patent) without the other joint owners' consent. However, if the joint owners cannot reach an agreement after discussing the issue, a majority of owners can take action despite the objections of a dissenter.
- **Provides a method of resolving disputes.** For example, in case of a split vote, the parties can select an arbiter, whose decision shall break the tie.
- **Provides that the joint owners shall share profits proportionately—** usually according to their interests in expenditures and income. For example, if one owner does not agree to an expenditure, the others can advance the amount in question and will be entitled to an increased reimbursement (often double the expenditure) from any resulting income.
- **Requires an owner who wants to manufacture or sell the invention to pay a reasonable royalty to all other owners.**

The contract we supply includes the following provisions.

Introduction

Insert the names of the joint owners. If any of the owners are corporations or partnerships, indicate the correct business form (for example, The Techno Consortium, a New Jersey general partnership). Insert a brief description of your invention at the end of the introductory paragraph.

You probably do not have a patent yet, but we have included several options just in case you decide to use this agreement after a patent issues. Choose the correct option—patent, patent application, or no patent. If you have two patents or a patent and a provisional patent application, we recommend that you make a separate agreement for each invention.

Ownership Percentage Interests

This provision sets forth each owner's percentage interest and proportionate share of revenues, expenses, and liabilities. The owners must agree on the percentage each of them will receive (for example, each partner receives one-half of the revenue). The total of all of the owner percentages must equal 100%.

Decision Making

Joint owners must decide many potentially contentious issues, including whether to:

- enter into agreements with other parties to make, license, use, distribute, or sell the invention
- permit any party to make, use, distribute, or sell the invention
- file foreign patent applications
- file a lawsuit to stop infringement of the invention, or
- hire someone to help prepare and file the patent application or help file an infringement lawsuit.

The joint ownership agreement can establish which issues require unanimous or majority approval. For at least one issue—assignment of ownership rights—the owners should insist on a unanimous vote. In our agreement, we have chosen majority vote for most decisions. You can also establish a method of breaking a tie. In the sample agreement, we suggest the use of mediation and arbitration.

Rights to Manufacture and Sell

The agreement can specify who is authorized to negotiate deals. It can also permit an individual owner to make, use, or sell the invention. The provision in the sample agreement, for example, permits any joint owner to sell the invention, as long as the owner sells it on the same terms as deals made with third parties. In other words, an owner doesn't get more favorable terms than a nonowner.

Improvements, Revisions

The provision in the sample agreement permits all co-owners to share in improvements of the invention, provided that the owners have made themselves available to assist in such improvements. For example, if the relationship between the owners becomes hostile and they can no longer work together to improve the invention, then the revenues from improvements will be divided according to the contribution each has made. This can be a touchy subject. For example, what if the improvement is minor? Should the owners who made this improvement be entitled to all of the revenue from it? Some co-owners use a sliding scale, such as splitting one quarter of the revenue from an improvement among those who contributed to it, then dividing the rest according to the original agreement. The percentages can change as more improvements are made.

Disputes

The agreement provides for discussion, mediation, and, if necessary, arbitration to resolve disputes among owners. Some people, however, do not like arbitration—and if you and/or your co-owners are among them, you may need to remove the sentences dealing with arbitration from the agreement.

Miscellaneous

"Miscellaneous Provisions" under "Nondisclosure Agreement," above explains the boilerplate provisions at the end of the agreement.

Signature

Most joint owners are individuals acting as sole proprietors, which means they can simply sign the agreement in their own name. However, if any joint owner is signing as a general partner representing a partnership or on behalf of a corporation, that person must have the authority to sign the agreement and bind the company to its terms.

Sample Joint Ownership Agreement

1. **Introduction.**
   This Agreement (the "Agreement") is made between
   [*insert name, address, and business form of owner #1*]
   [*insert name, address, and business form of owner #2*]
   [*insert name, address, and business form of owner #3*]
   [*insert name, address, and business form of owner #4*]
   (the "Parties") as of [*insert date agreement is to be effective*]. The Parties
   wish to set forth their respective rights to and obligations for the invention
   tentatively named [*insert the name of invention*] (the "Invention") and more
   accurately described below. The ownership rights to the Invention include
   all patent rights, copyrights, trade secrets, and trademark rights comprising,
   associated with, or derived from the Invention.

2. **Invention Status.** [*select one*]

   Provisional patent application filed
   ☐ The Invention as described in the provisional patent application filed on
   _____ (a copy of the provisional patent application is attached)

   Regular patent application pending
   ☐ The Invention as described in the regular application for United States
   patent
   (U.S. Patent Office Application Serial No. _____)

   Patent issued
   ☐ The Invention as described in the United States patent number
   _____ , dated _____

   No patent issued or application filed
   ☐ Description of Invention: _____

3. **Ownership Percentage Interests.** The Parties to this Agreement are the
   owners of all legal rights in the Invention described above. The percentage
   ownership interests of the Parties are as set forth below. Unless otherwise
   agreed: (a) all income derived from exploiting the Invention shall be
   apportioned according to the percentage interests set forth below; and
   (b) any costs, expenses, or liabilities relating to the Invention and agreed
   to by the Parties under this Agreement shall also be apportioned by the

same percentage interests. In the event any Party is unable to contribute a proportionate share for any cost or expense, the other Parties may contribute the noncontributing Party's share and shall be entitled to reimbursement from subsequent revenues related to the cost or expense. Reimbursement shall include interest at 1.5% per month or the maximum rate permitted by law, whichever is less.

Name	Percentage Interest
_____	_____
_____	_____
_____	_____
_____	_____

4. **Decision Making.** Each Party shall have the right to participate in decisions regarding the Invention, including decisions regarding exploitation, protection, and enforcement of legal rights associated with Invention. All decisions require a majority vote except for an assignment of all rights to the Invention which requires the unanimous consent of all owners. If there are equal votes in a case where a majority decision is required, the issue shall be resolved through the procedures set forth in the Dispute Resolution section, below.

5. **Decision-Making Process/Time Limits.** All decisions shall be made promptly and with the cooperation of all Parties, acting fairly and in good faith. If a decision requires some time to contemplate (for example, an offer to license or a decision by one Party to manufacture), the Parties may agree to postpone a decision for a period of up to 30 days.

6. **Rights to Manufacture and Sell.** Any Party may make, sell, or use any product embodying the Invention (or any portion of the Invention) as long as the Parties have approved such action by a vote as required under this Agreement. In the event that any Party desires and is approved to license, manufacture, sell, or distribute the Invention, the terms of such arrangement shall be the same as those available to third parties in similar transactions. That is, a Party to this Agreement will have to pay a competitive royalty to the joint owners after deduction of reasonable manufacturing and overhead expenses.

7. **Improvements, Revisions.** Each Party to this Agreement shall share, according to the proportions set forth in this Agreement, in any revenue derived from improvements or revisions of this Invention as long as each Party made a good-faith attempt to consult, contribute, or otherwise make themselves available for services on such improvements or revisions of the Invention. If any Party refuses to participate in any work resulting in an improvement or revision of the Invention, revenues derived from such improvements or revisions shall be distributed on a pro rata basis among the contributing Parties.

8. **Disputes.** The Parties agree that they will attempt to resolve disputes or differences between them arising under this Agreement, including a failure to reach a decision as described in Section 4 of this Agreement, by meeting and conferring in a good-faith manner. If the Parties cannot resolve their dispute after conferring, any Party may require the other Parties to submit the matter to nonbinding mediation, utilizing the services of an impartial professional mediator approved by all Parties. If the Parties cannot come to an agreement following mediation, the Parties agree to submit the matter to binding arbitration at a location mutually agreeable to the Parties. The arbitration shall be conducted on a confidential basis pursuant to the Commercial Arbitration Rules of the American Arbitration Association. Any decision or award resulting from any such arbitration proceeding shall include the assessment of costs, expenses, and reasonable attorneys' fees and shall include a written record of the proceedings and a written determination of the arbitrators. Absent an agreement to the contrary, any such arbitration shall be conducted by an arbitrator experienced in intellectual property law. The Parties reserve the right to object to any individual who is employed by or affiliated with a competing organization or entity. In the event of any such dispute or difference, either Party may give the other notice requiring that the matter be settled by arbitration. An award of arbitration shall be final and binding on the Parties and may be confirmed in a court of competent jurisdiction.

9. **Severability.** If a court finds any provision of this Agreement invalid or unenforceable, the remainder of this Agreement shall be interpreted so as best to effect the intent of the parties.

10. **Integration.** This Agreement expresses the complete understanding of the parties with respect to the subject matter and supersedes all prior proposals, agreements, representations, and understandings. This Agreement may not be amended except in a writing signed by all parties.

11. **Waiver.** The failure to exercise any right provided in this Agreement shall not be a waiver of prior or subsequent rights.

12. **Governing Law and Attorneys' Fees.** This Agreement shall be governed by the laws of the state of [*insert state name*]. In the event of any dispute arising under this Agreement, the prevailing Party shall be entitled to its reasonable attorneys' fees.

This Agreement and each party's obligations shall be binding on the representatives, assigns, and successors of such party. Each party has signed this Agreement through its authorized representative.

MY SIGNATURE BELOW INDICATES THAT I HAVE READ AND UNDERSTOOD THIS AGREEMENT.

Signature _____ Dated: _____

Signature _____ Dated: _____

Signature _____ Dated: _____

Signature _____ Dated: _____

Agreement for Creation of Prototype or Patent Drawings

In this agreement, the model maker or artist assigns to you all rights in the work he or she creates—the drawings or prototype of your invention. Because the model maker/artist assigns all rights to you, the grant section is as broad as possible. The model maker/artist will not retain any rights after the job is done.

Because you are disclosing secrets about your invention, we've included a lengthy nondisclosure provision that tracks the language from the NDA at the beginning of this appendix. This agreement is self-explanatory and you won't need much help completing it. The miscellaneous provisions (6–9) are explained under "Nondisclosure Agreement," above.

Besides inventing a magnetic memory device that was the precursor of the modern hard drive, Jacob Rabinow also invented a new kind of venetian blind, the self-regulating clock, and a method of hanging pictures that didn't damage walls.

Artist/Model Maker Agreement

1. **Parties.** This Agreement (the "Agreement") is entered into by and between
   _____ , ("Inventor") and _____ , ("Contractor") for
   the purpose of preparing drawings, renderings, models, prototypes, or similar
   visual representations (the "Work") of Inventor's creation (the "Invention").

2. **Services.** In consideration of the payments provided in this Agreement,
   Contractor agrees to perform the following services:

   _____

3. **Payment.** Inventor agrees to pay Contractor as follows:

   _____

   _____

4. **Assignment of Intellectual Property Rights.** To the extent that any Work
   commissioned pursuant to this Agreement is protectable under copyright,
   patent, trade secret, or trademark law, Contractor agrees to assign such
   rights to Inventor. Contractor agrees to sign and deliver to Inventor, either
   during or after the term of this Agreement, such other documents as
   Inventor considers desirable to evidence the assignment of all such rights.

5. **Confidential Information.** Contractor agrees to prevent the unauthorized
   disclosure of certain proprietary and confidential information related to
   the Invention ("Confidential Information"). Confidential Information shall
   also include all information or material, written or oral, that has or could
   have commercial value or other utility in the business in which Inventor is
   engaged.

   In the event that Inventor furnishes physical or tangible copies of any of
   the Confidential Information to Contractor, Contractor acknowledges and
   agrees that these materials are furnished under the following conditions: (a)
   These materials are loaned to Contractor solely for purposes of evaluation
   and review; (b) these materials shall be treated consistent with the
   Contractor's obligation for Confidential Information under this Agreement;
   (c) Contractor may not copy or otherwise duplicate these materials; and
   (d) Contractor shall return to Inventor any and all material pertaining to

Confidential Information, including but not limited to records, notes, and other written, printed, or tangible materials, immediately if Inventor requests it in writing.

Contractor's obligations under this Agreement do not extend to information that is: (a) publicly known at the time of disclosure or subsequently becomes publicly known through no fault of the Contractor; (b) discovered or created by the Contractor before disclosure by Inventor; (c) learned by the Contractor through legitimate means other than from the Inventor or Inventor's representatives; or (d) disclosed by Contractor with Inventor's prior written approval.

Contractor shall hold and maintain the Confidential Information in strictest confidence for the sole and exclusive benefit of the Inventor. Contractor shall carefully restrict access to Confidential Information to employees, contractors, and third parties as is reasonably required and shall require those persons to sign nondisclosure restrictions at least as protective as those in this Agreement. Contractor shall not, without prior written approval of Inventor, use for Contractor's own benefit, publish, copy, or otherwise disclose to others, or permit the use by others for their benefit or to the detriment of Inventor, any Confidential Information. The nondisclosure provisions of this Agreement shall survive the termination of this Agreement and Contractor's duty to hold Confidential Information in confidence shall remain in effect until the Confidential Information no longer qualifies as a trade secret or until Inventor sends Contractor written notice releasing Contractor from this Agreement, whichever occurs first.

6. **Relationships.** Nothing contained in this Agreement shall be deemed to constitute either party a partner, joint venturer, or employee of the other party for any purpose.

7. **Severability.** If a court finds any provision of this Agreement invalid or unenforceable, the remainder of this Agreement shall be interpreted so as best to effect the intent of the parties.

8. **Integration.** This Agreement expresses the complete understanding of the parties with respect to the subject matter and supersedes all prior proposals,

agreements, representations, and understandings. This Agreement may not be amended except in a writing signed by both parties.

9. **Waiver.** The failure to exercise any right provided in this Agreement shall not be a waiver of prior or subsequent rights.

This Agreement and each party's obligations shall be binding on the representatives, assigns, and successors of such party. Each party has signed this Agreement through its authorized representative.

Inventor: _____

Signature: _____

Typed or printed name _____

Date: _____

Contractor _____

Signature _____

Typed or printed name _____

Date: _____

Invention Assignment

An assignment permanently transfers all or part of your ownership of your invention. You can use this document to transfer ownership to your company or to a partnership, a corporation, or another third party. Because this is a permanent transfer of rights, you should weigh your decision very carefully. If you're not sure whether to assign rights, consult with an attorney specializing in intellectual property law.

In the document, the owner of invention rights is "the Assignor" and the person acquiring rights is "the Assignee." In the second paragraph insert the percentage of interest that you are assigning. You can assign less than 100% if, for example, you want to split the ownership with a business partner. (You cannot assign more than 100%.)

Charles Goodyear invented vulcanized rubber when he accidentally dropped rubber mixed with sulfur on a hot stove. His patented vulcanizing process transformed the rubber industry but he never earned any money because he couldn't afford to sue numerous infringers. He was sent to debtor's prison in 1855 when his company went out of business.

Assignment of Invention Rights
Provisional Patent Application Filed

[*Insert name of person or company assigning rights*] ("Assignor") is owner of [*insert name of invention*] as described in the U.S. Provisional Patent Application signed by Assignor on _____ , filed [*insert filing date*], (the "Provisional Patent Application"). [*Insert name of person or company to whom rights will be assigned*], ("Assignee") desires to acquire rights in and to the invention described in the Provisional Patent Application and to the patent (and any reissues or extensions), if any, that may be granted based on the Provisional Patent Application.

Therefore, for valuable consideration, the receipt of which is acknowledged, Assignor assigns to Assignee _____% of his or her right, title, and interest in the invention, the above Provisional Patent Application, and all priority rights of such Provisional Patent Application to Assignee. This assignment shall last for the entire term of any issued patent resulting from the Provisional Patent Application and any reissues or extensions that may be granted and for the entire terms of any and all foreign patents that may issue from foreign applications (as well as divisions, continuations in whole or part, or substitute applications) filed claiming the benefit of the Provisional Patent Application.

Assignor authorizes the United States Patent and Trademark Office to issue any patents claiming benefit from the Provisional Patent Application to Assignee according to the percentage interest indicated in this assignment. The right, title, and interest is to be held and enjoyed by Assignee and Assignee's successors and assigns as fully and exclusively as it would have been held and enjoyed by Assignor had this assignment not been made.

Assignor further agrees to: (a) cooperate with Assignee in the prosecution of the Application and foreign counterparts; (b) execute, verify, acknowledge, and deliver all such further papers, including patent applications and instruments of transfer; and (c) perform such other acts as Assignee lawfully may request to obtain or maintain the patent for the invention in any and all countries.

Date: _____

Assignor: _____

Signature _____

Typed or printed name _____

Glossaries

T he first section contains a glossary of words used to describe parts and functions of inventions. The second section contains a glossary of patent terms and their definitions as used in patent law.

Glossary of Useful Technical Terms

This glossary provides a list of useful words to describe the hardware, parts, and functions of your invention in the specification and claims. The most esoteric of these words are briefly defined. While some definitions are similar, this is due to space limitations; all words have nuances in meaning.

If you're looking for a word to describe a certain part, look through the list for a likely prospect and then check a dictionary for its precise meaning. If you can't find the right word here, look in your search patents, in *What's What* or another visual dictionary, or in a thesaurus. If you can't find an appropriate word, you'll probably be able to get away with "member" or "means-plus-a-function" language. Also, for new fields, you may invent words, preferably using Latin or Greek roots, as Farnsworth did with "television," or by extending the meaning of words from analogous devices (e.g., "base" for a part of a transistor). Very technical or specialized fields have their own vocabulary (e.g., "catamenial" in medicine, "syzygy" in astronomy); look in appropriate tutorial texts for these. The words are grouped loosely by the following functions:

1. Structure
2. Mounting & Fastening
3. Springs
4. Numbers
5. Placement (Relation)
6. Voids
7. Shape
8. Materials & Properties
9. Optics
10. Fluid Flow
11. Electronics
12. Movement
13. Rotation/Machine

Kekule von Stradonitz reportedly conceived of the benzene ring while dreaming of serpents eating their own tails.

Structure

annulus (ring)
apron
apse (dome)
arbor (shaft)
arm
bail (arch wire)
band
barrel
bascale (seesaw)
base
beam
 —cantilever
 —simple
belt
bib
billet (ingot or bar)
blade
blower
board
bob (hanging weight)
body
bollard (thick post)
boom
boss (projection)
bougie (body-insertion member)
boule (pear-shaped)
branch
breech (back part)
bunker
caisson
canard (front wing)
carriage
case
channel

charger (shallow dish)
chase
chord
cincture (encircling band)
clew (sail part)
column
configuration
container
conveyor
cornice (horiz. top of structure)
cover
crenation (rounded edge)
cupola (projection)
cylinder
dasher (plunger, churn)
derrick
detent
device
dibble (pointed tool)
die
disparate (dissimilar)
diversion
doctor blade (scraper)
dog (holder)
drum
echelon (staggered line)
element
enclosure
fence (stop on tool)
felly (rim of spoked wheel)
fillet (narrow strip)
fin
finger
finial (ornament)
flabellate (fan-shaped)

flange

fluke (triangular part)

flute (groove on shaft)

frame

fret

frit (vitreous substance)

frustrum (cut-off area)

furcate (branch)

futtock (curved ship timber)

gaff (hook, spar)

gauge

generatrix (path traced)

gnomon (sundial upright)

graticulate (squares)

grommet

groove

gusset (triangular insert)

handle

head

header (base, support conduit)

homologous

horn

housing

hub

jacket

jaw

jib (crane arm)

knocker (clapper)

lagging (support)

ledger (horizonal support)

leg

lip

list (margin strip)

lobe

magazine

mandrel (tapered axle)

manifold

marge (edge)

marginate (w/margin)

medium

member

mullion (dividing strip)

nacelle (pod)

napiform (turnip-shaped)

neck

obcordate (heart-shaped)

object

outcrop

panel

parietal (wall)

particle

partition

piece

piston

placket (slit in garment)

platform

plug

plunger

pontoon

portion

post

pounce (fine powder)

projection

purlin (horiz. rafter support)

putlog (horiz. support above ledger)

race

raceway

rank (row, series, range)

reticulum (netlike)

rib

riddle (sieve)
riffles (obstructions)
ring
rod
sash (frame)
screed (guide strip)
scroll
sear (catch)
shell
shoe
shoulder
skeleton
sleeve
sluice (channel)
snare
snorkel
spar (pole, support)
spline (projection on shaft)
spoke
sprag (spoke stop)
spur
stanchion
station
stay
stem
stent (stretcher)
step
stepped
stile (dividing strip)
stop
strake (ship plank)
strip
strut
tang (shank, tool)
tare (net weight)

tine
tip
tittle (a tiny bit)
tongue
trace (pivoted rod)
tracery (scrolling)
track
trave (crossbar)
truss
tuft
turret
tuyere (air pipe)
upright
vang (guy)
volar (palm, sole)
wall
ward (ridge or notch)
warp
woof (weft)
ziggurat (pyramid with terraces)

Mounting & Fastening

attach
billet (tip of belt)
bolt
bonnet
braze
busing
cable
camber
caster
clamp
cleat (reinforcer)
clevis (U-shaped pin)
colligate (bound together)

connection
couple
coupling
cribbing (support)
demountably
docking
dowel
engage
fay (join tightly)
ferrule (barrel)
ferruminate (attach, solder)
fix
funicular (ropelike)
gib (holding member)
gland (sliding holder)
guy wire
harp (lamp shade support)
hold
holder
hook
imbricate (regular overlap)
joint
—universal
keeper
key
latch
lock
lug
matrix
mount
nail
nut
pin
plinth (base)
pricket (holding spike)

pylon (support)
ribband (holds ribs)
rivet
scarf (notched joint)
screw
seam
seat
secure
set
sheathed
sliding
snare/loop
solder
spike
spline (projection or groove on a shaft)
springably
support
toe-in
thill (horse joinder stake)
thrust
weld

Springs

air
bias
—element
coil
compressed
elastic
expanded
helical
—compression
—tension

leaf
press
relaxed
resilient
springably
torsional
urge

Numbers

argument
caboodle (collection, bunch)
compound
congeries (collection, aggregation)
difference
dividend
divisor
equation
formula
index
lemma
minuend
modulo
multiplicand
multiplicity
multiplier
plurality
power
product
quotient
remainder
sheaf
subtrahend
variable

Placement (Relation)

adjacent
aft
aligned
angle
aposition (facing)
array
attached
axial
bottom
close
complementary
concentric
contiguous
contracted
course
crest
disposed
distal
divided
edge
engaged
equitant (overlap in two ranks)
evert (inside out)
extended
external
face
fiducial (reference)
film
fore
horizontal
imbricate (overlapping series)
incline
integral
intermediate

internal
interposed
juxtaposed
layer
located
lower
mating
meshing
mesial (between)
normal
oblique
obtuse
offset
open
opposed
overlapping
parallel
perpendicular
pitched
positioned
projecting
prolapsed (out of place)
proximal
proximate
raked (pitched)
reference
removable
resting
rim
row
sandwich
section
slant
spacer
staggered

superimposed
supported
surface
surrounding
symmetrical
tilt
top
ubiety (located in a place)
vernier (9:10 gauge)
vertical

Voids

aperture
bore
cavity
chamber
concavity
cutout
dimple
duct
embrasure (slant opening)
engraved
erose (irregular notch)
filister (groove)
foramen (opening)
fossa (depression)
furrow (groove)
gain (notch)
gap
groove
hole
hollow
infold
intaglinated (engraved)
invaginate (enclosed, turned in)

lumen (bore of tube)
lunette (crescent opening)
mortise (cutout)
nock (notch on arrow)
notch
opening
orifice
passage
placket (garment slit)
polled (dehorned)
rabbet (groove)
raceway
recess
rifling (spiral groove)
separation
slit
slot
spandrel (triangular gap above arch
  side)
sulcus (groove)
ullage (lost liquid)
via (path)
void
wicket (small door or gate)

Shape

acclivity (slope)
acicular (needle-shaped)
agonic (no angle)
annular
anticline (peak)
applanation
arch
arcuate
barrel

bevel
bifurcated (2 branches)
bight (bend)
botryoidal (like a bunch of grapes)
bucket
buckled
chamfer (beveled)
channel
circular
coin
concave
congruent (same shape)
conical
convex
convoluted (curled in)
corner (inside, outside)
corrugated
crest
crimp
crispate (curled)
cup
cusp (projection)
cylinder
depression
dihedral (two-faced)
direction
disc
dome
draw (depression)
drawing (pulling out)
elliptical
fairing (streamlined)
fin
flange
fold

fork

fossa (groove)

fundus (base)

furcate (branched)

goffer (ridges or pleats)

helical

hook

incurvate (curved in)

invaginate (sheathed, folded in)

line

lobe

lozenge (diamond-shaped)

lune (crescent)

mammilated (nipple-shaped)

navicular (boat-shaped)

notch

oblate (flattened)

oblong

ogive (pointed arch)

orb (globe)

oval

parabolic

parallelogram

plane

prolate (cigar-shaped)

rectangular

reticulated (gridlike)

rhomboid (nonequal adjacent sides)

rhombus (equal adjacent sides)

rick-rock

rill (long narrow valley)

round

salient (standing out)

serrated

setaceous (bristlelike)

sheet

shelf

sinusoidal

skive (shaven)

slab

spall (broken chips)

spherical

spica (overlapping reverse spirals)

square

stamped

striated (grooved or ridged)

swaged (flattened)

swale (depression)

syncline (V-shaped)

taper terminus (end)

tesselated (tiled)

topology (unchangeable geometry)

tortuous (twisting)

tram (on wheels)

trefoil (three-leaved)

triangular

trihedral (3-sided)

trough

tubular

tumescence (detumescence)

turbinate (top/spiral shaped)

twist

upset (distorted)

vermiculate (worm-eaten)

volute (spiral)

wafer

web

wedge

whorl (spiral)

xyresic (razor-sharp)

Materials & Properties

adhesive
alluvial (sand or clay deposited by
  water)
concrete
cork
dappled (spotted)
denier (gauge)
dense
elastic
enlarged
fabric
fiber
flexible
foraminous
frit (fused glass)
haptic (sense of touch)
humectant (moistener)
insulation
intenerate (soften)
liquid
material
metal
nappy
opaque
pied (splotched)
placer (glacial deposit)
plastic
porous
prill
refractory
resilient
rigid
rubber
sand
screen
shirred (gathered)
smectic (cleaning)
stratified (layered)
strong
sturdy
translucent
transparent
wood
xerotic (dry)

Optics

aniseikonic (unequal sizes)
astigmatic
bezel
bulb
  —fluorescent
  —incandescent
fresnel
lamp
light
  —beam
  —ray
opaque
parallax (change in direction)
pellicle
pellucid (clear)
reflection
refraction
schlieren (streaks)
translucent
transmission
transparent
window

Fluid Flow

accumulator

afferent (to center)

aspirator

bellows

bibb (valve)

bung (hole or stopper)

cock (valve)

conduit

confluent (flow together)

connector

convection

cylinder

—piston

—rod

dashpot

diaphragm

discharge

dispenser

efferent (away from center)

filter

fitting

flue

gasket

hose

hydraulic

medium

navicular (like boat)

nozzle

obturator (blocker)

outlet

pipe

plunger

poppet (axial valve)

port

—inlet

—outlet

pump

—centrifugal

—gear

—piston

—reservoir

—seal

—siphon

—tank

—vane

sparge (spray)

spud (short connecting pipe)

sprue (vent tube)

suctorial (sucking)

sufflate (inflate)

swash (channel barrier)

tube

valve

—ball

—check

—control

—gate

—shutoff

wattle (intertwined wall)

weir (dam)

wicket (gate or door)

Electronics

adder

amplifier

astable

capacitance

clipping

conductor

contact
control element
demodulator
diode
electrode
electromagnet
filament
flip flop
gate (AND, OR, etc.)
impedance
inductance
insulator
integrated circuit
laser
lead
light-emitting diode
line cord
liquid crystal
maser
memory
motor
multiplier
multivibrator
oscillator
pixel (CRT spot)
power supply
raster
read-and-write memory
read-only memory
resistance
sampling
Schmitt trigger
shift register
Schottky diode
socket

solenoid
switch
terminal
thermistor
transformer
transistor
triode
valve
varistor
wire
Zener diode

Movement

alternate
articulate (jointed)
avulsion (tear away)
cam
compression
cyclic
detent (click)
downward
draft (pull)
drag
drift pin
drill
eccentric
emergent
epicyclic (on circle)
equilibrate (bring into equilibrium)
escapement
extensible
extrude
grinding
impact
inclined plane

inertia
interval
lag
lead
lever
linkage
  —parallel
longitudinal
machine
meeting
nutate (to and fro)
pressing
propelling
pulverize
sagging
sequacious (regular)
severing
shuttle (to & fro member)
skive (peel)
slidable
snub (stop)
straight line
  —motion
terminating
toggle
torque
traction
transverse
traversing
triturate (grind to powder)
trochoid (roll on circle)
urging
vibrating
wedge

Rotation/Machine

antifriction
  —ball
  —needle
  —roller
  —tapered
arbor (shaft)
bell crank
brake
  —band
  —disk
  —shoe
bushing
cam
chain
clevis (circular holder)
clutch
  —centrifugal
  —one-way
  —sprag (stop)
  —toothed
cog (tooth)
connecting rod
crank arm
drive
  —belt
  —pulley
  —sheave
  —toothed
flexible coupling
friction
fulcrum
gear
  —bevel
  —crown

—internal
—noncircular
—pinion
—right-angle
—spur
—wheel
—worm
gin (hoist, pile driver, pump)
guide
gudgeon (axle)
intermittent
—escapement
—geneva
—pawl
—pendulum
—ratchet
jack
journal
mandrel
orbit

pinion (small wheel)
pintle (axle)
pivot
pulley
radial
radius bar
screw
seal
sheave (pulley)
spindle
sprocket
swash (wobble) plate
tappet (valve cam)
trunnion
variable speed
vertiginous (turning)
ward (ridge or notch)
winch
yoke

Glossary of Patent Terms

Abstract. A concise, one-paragraph summary of the patent. It details the structure, nature, and purpose of the invention. The abstract is used by the PTO and the public to quickly determine the gist of what is being disclosed.

Actual damages (also known as compensatory damages). In a lawsuit, money awarded to one party to cover actual injury or economic loss. Actual damages are intended to put the injured party in the position he or she was in prior to the injury.

Answer. A written response to a complaint (the opening papers in a lawsuit) in which the defendant admits or denies the allegations and may provide a list of defenses.

Best mode. The inventor's principal and preferred method of embodying the invention.

Board of Appeals and Patent Interferences (BAPI). A tribunal of judges at the PTO that hears appeals from final Office Actions.

Cease and desist letter. Correspondence from the owner of a proprietary work that requests the cessation of all infringing activity.

Clear and convincing proof. Evidence that is highly probable and free from serious doubt.

Complaint. Papers filed with a court clerk by the plaintiff to initiate a lawsuit by setting out facts and legal claims (usually called causes of action).

Compositions of matter. Items such as chemical compositions, conglomerates, aggregates, or other chemically significant substances that are usually supplied in bulk (solid or particulate), liquid, or gaseous form.

Confidentiality agreement (also known as a nondisclosure agreement). A contract in which one or both parties agree not to disclose certain information.

Continuation application. A new patent application that allows the applicant to re-present an invention and get a second or third bite at the apple. The applicant can file a new application (known as a "continuation") while the original (or "parent") application is still pending. A continuation application consists of the same invention, cross-referenced to the parent application, and a new set of claims. The applicant retains the filing date of the parent application for purposes of determining the relevancy of prior art.

Continuation in Part (CIP). Less common than a continuation application, this form of extension application is used when a portion or all of an earlier patent application is continued and new matter (not disclosed in the earlier application) is included. CIP applications are used when an applicant wants to present an improvement but is prevented from adding a pending application to it because of the prohibition against adding "new matter."

Contributory infringement. An infringement that occurs when a material component of a patented invention is sold with knowledge that the component is designed for an unauthorized use. This type of infringement cannot occur unless there is a direct infringement. In other words, it is not enough to sell infringing parts; those parts must be used in an infringing invention.

Copyright. The legal right to exclude others, for a limited time, from copying, selling, performing, displaying, or making derivative versions of a work of authorship such as a writing, music, or artwork.

Counterclaim. A legal claim usually asserted by the defendant against an opposing party, usually the plaintiff.

Court of Appeals for the Federal Circuit (CAFC). The federal appeals court that specializes in patent appeals. If the Board of Appeals and Patent Interferences rejects an application appeal, an applicant can further appeal to the CAFC within 60 days of the decision. If the CAFC upholds the USPTO, the applicant can ask the United States Supreme Court to hear the case (although the Supreme Court rarely hears patent appeals).

Date of invention. The earliest of the following dates: (a) the date an inventor filed the patent application (provisional or regular), (b) the date an inventor can prove that the invention was built and tested in the United States or a country that is a member of the North American Free Trade Association (NAFTA) or the World Trade Organization (WTO), or (c) the date an inventor can prove that the invention was conceived in a NAFTA or WTO country, provided the inventor can also prove diligence in building and testing it or filing a patent application on it. The date of invention generally became irrelevant after March 16, 2013, when the United States adopted a first-to-file patent system.

Declaratory relief. A request that the court sort out the rights and legal obligations of the parties in the midst of an actual controversy.

Deposit date. The date the PTO receives a patent application.

Deposition. Oral or written testimony by a party or witness, given under oath.

Design patent. A patent that covers the unique, ornamental, or visible shape or design of a nonnatural object.

Divisional application. A patent application used when an applicant wants to protect several inventions claimed in the original application. The official definition is "a later application for a distinct or independent invention, carved out of a pending application and disclosing and claiming only subject matter disclosed in the earlier or parent application" (MPEP 201.06). A divisional application is entitled to the filing date of the parent for purposes of overcoming prior art. The divisional application must be filed while the parent is pending. A divisional application can be filed as a CPA.

Doctrine of Equivalents (DoE). A form of patent infringement that occurs when an invention performs substantially the same function in substantially the same manner and obtains the same result as the patented invention. A court analyzes each element of the patented invention separately. Under a recent Supreme Court decision, the DoE must be applied on an element-by-element basis to the claims.

Double patenting. When an applicant has obtained a patent and has filed a second application containing the same invention, the second application will be rejected. If the second application resulted in a patent, that patent will be invalidated. Two applications contain the same invention when the two inventions are literally the same or the second invention is an obvious modification of the first invention.

Enhanced damages (treble damages). In exceptional infringement cases, financial damages may be increased, at the discretion of the court, up to triple the award for actual damages.

Exclusive jurisdiction. The sole authority of a court to hear a certain type of case.

Exhaustion. (See "first sale doctrine.")

Ex parte (Latin: one party only). Refers to legal proceedings where only one party is present or represented.

File wrapper estoppel (or prosecution history estoppel). Affirmative defense used in patent infringement litigation that precludes the patent owner from asserting rights that were disclaimed during the patent application process. The term is derived from the fact that the official file in which a patent is contained at the Patent and Trademark Office is known as a "file wrapper." All statements, admissions, correspondence, or documentation relating to the invention are placed in the file wrapper. Estoppel means that a party is prevented from acting contrary to a former statement or action when someone else has relied to his or her detriment on the prior statement or action.

Final Office Action. The examiner's response to the applicant's first amendment, the final Office Action is supposed to end the prosecution stage but a "final action" is rarely final.

First Office Action (sometimes called an "official letter" or "OA"). Response from the patent examiner after the initial examination of the application. It is very rare that an application is allowed in the first Office Action. More often, the examiner rejects some or all of the claims.

First sale doctrine (also known as the exhaustion doctrine). Once a patented product (or product resulting from a patented process) is sold or licensed, the patent owner's rights are exhausted and the owner has no further rights as to the resale of that particular article.

Generic (genus). An entire group or class, or a group of related items or species.

Grace period. A period in which an action may be taken even though the normal period for taking action has passed.

Indirect infringement. Occurs either when someone is persuaded to make, use, or sell a patented invention without authorization (inducing infringement); or when a material component of a patented invention is sold with knowledge that the component is designed for an unauthorized use (contributory infringement). An indirect infringement cannot occur unless there is a direct infringement. In other words, it is not enough to sell infringing parts; those parts must be used in an infringing invention.

Infringement. An invention is infringing if it is a literal copy of a patented invention or if it performs substantially the same function in substantially the same manner and obtains the same result as the patented invention (see "Doctrine of Equivalents").

Injunction. A court order requiring that a party halt a particular activity. In the case of patent infringement, a court can order that all infringing activity be halted at the end of a trial (a permanent injunction) or the patent owner can attempt to halt the infringing activity immediately, rather than wait for a trial (a preliminary injunction). A court uses two factors to determine whether to grant a preliminary injunction: (1) Is the plaintiff likely to succeed in the lawsuit and (2) will the plaintiff suffer irreparable harm if the injunction is not granted? The patent owner may seek relief for a very short injunction known as a temporary restraining order, or TRO, which usually only lasts a few days or weeks. A temporary restraining order may be granted without notice to the infringer if it appears that immediate damage will result—for example, that evidence will be destroyed.

Interference. A costly, complex USPTO proceeding that determines who will get a patent when two or more applicants are claiming the same invention. It is basically a method of sorting out priority of inventorship. Occasionally an interference may involve a patent that has been in force for less than one year.

Inter partes (Latin: between parties). Refers to legal proceedings where all parties to the action are represented.

Interrogatories. Written questions that a party to a lawsuit must answer under oath.

Invention. Any new article, machine, composition, or process or new use developed by a human.

Jury instructions. Explanations of the legal rules that the jury must use in reaching a verdict.

Lab notebook. A system of documenting an invention that usually includes descriptions of the invention and novel features; procedures used in the building and testing of the invention; drawings, photos, or sketches of the invention; test results and conclusions; discussions of any known prior-art references; and additional documentation such as correspondence and purchase receipts.

Literal infringement. This type of infringement occurs if a defendant makes, sells, or uses the invention defined in the plaintiff's patent claim. In other words, the infringing product includes each and every component, part, or step in the patented invention. It is a literal infringement because the defendant's device is actually the *same* invention as in the patent claim.

Machine. A device or things used for accomplishing a task; usually involves some activity or motion performed by working parts.

Magistrate. An officer of the court, who may exercise some of the authority of a federal district court judge, including the authority to conduct a jury or nonjury trial.

Manufactures (sometimes termed "articles of manufacture"). Items that have been made by human hands or by machines; may have working or moving parts as prime features.

Means-plus-function clause (or means-for clause). A provision in a patent claim in which the applicant does not specifically describe the structure of one of the items in the patent and instead describes the function of the item. Term is derived from the fact that the clause usually starts with the word "means."

Micro entity. Established under the America Invents Act, micro-entity status is a subcategory of small-entity status. To qualify as a micro entity, the filer must be a small entity and must meet the following criteria: (1) The applicant has not been named as the inventor on a total of more than four utility patents (regular utility patents, not provisional patent applications), design patents or plant patents. This also does not include certain international PCT applications and applications owned by a previous employer. In addition, the applicant had to have had a gross income in the previous year of less than three times the median household income reported by the Bureau of the Census. (The median household income has been hovering around $50,000 for the past two years.) In the event that the patent application has been assigned, the assignee had to have a gross (not net) income of less than three times the U.S. median household income; or (2) the majority of the patent filer's employment income is from an institution of higher learning, or the applicant has assigned, or is obliged to assign the patent to an institution of higher learning. An institution of higher learning is a public or nonprofit accredited institution that admits post-secondary students for programs of not less than two years.

New matter. Any technical information, including dimensions, materials, and so on, that was not present in the patent application as originally filed. An applicant can never add new matter to an application (PTO Rule 118).

New-use invention. A new and unobvious process or method for using an old and known invention.

Nonobviousness. A standard of patentability that requires that an invention produce "unusual and surprising results." In 1966, the U.S. Supreme Court established the steps for determining unobviousness in the case of *Graham v. John Deere*, 383 U.S. 1 (1966).

Notice of Allowance. A document issued when the examiner is convinced that the application meets the requirements of patentability. An issue fee is due within three months.

Objects and advantages. A phrase used to explain "what the invention accomplishes." Usually, the objects are also the invention's advantages, since those aspects are intended to be superior to prior art.

Office Action (OA, also known as Official Letter or Examiner's Action). Correspondence (usually including forms and a letter) from a patent examiner that describes what is wrong with the application and why it cannot be allowed. Generally, an OA will reject claims, list defects in the specification or drawings, raise objections, or cite and enclose copies of relevant prior art demonstrating a lack of novelty or nonobviousness.

Patent. A grant from a government that gives an inventor the right to exclude others from making, using, selling, importing, or offering an invention for sale for a fixed period of time.

Patent application. A set of papers that describes an invention and that is suitable for filing in a patent office in order to apply for a patent on the invention.

Patent Application Declaration (PAD). A declaration that identifies the inventor or joint inventors and provides an attestation by the applicant that the inventor understands the contents of the claims and specification and has fully disclosed all material information. The PTO provides a form for the PAD.

Patent misuse. A defense in patent infringement that prevents a patent owner who has abused patent law from enforcing patent rights. Common examples of misuse are violation of the antitrust laws or unethical business practices.

Patent pending (also known as the "pendency period"). Time between filing a patent application (or PPA) and issuance of the patent. The inventor has no patent rights during this period. However, when and if the patent later issues, the inventor will obtain the right to prevent the continuation of any infringing activity that started during the pendency period. If the application has been published by the USPTO during the pendency period and the infringer had notice, the applicant may later seek royalties for these infringements during the pendency period. It's a criminal offense to use the words "patent applied for" or "patent pending" (they mean the same thing) in any advertising if there's no active, applicable regular or provisional patent application on file.

Patent prosecution. The process of shepherding a patent application through the Patent and Trademark Office.

Patent Rules of Practice. Administrative regulations located in Volume 37 of the Code of Federal Regulations (37 C.F.R. § 1).

Pendency period. (See patent pending.)

Permanent injunction. A durable injunction issued after a final judgment on the merits of the case; permanently restrains the defendant from engaging in the infringing activity.

Petition to Make Special. An applicant can, under certain circumstances, have an application examined sooner than the normal course of USPTO examination (one to three years). This is accomplished by filing a "Petition to Make Special" (PTMS), together with a supporting declaration.

Plant patent. Covers plants that can be reproduced through the use of grafts and cuttings (asexual reproduction).

Power of attorney. A document that gives another person legal authority to act on your behalf. If an attorney is preparing an application on behalf of an inventor, a power of attorney should be executed to authorize the patent attorney or agent to act on behalf of the inventor. The power of attorney form may be combined with the PAD.

Prima facie (Latin: on its face). At first sight, obvious.

Prior art. The state of knowledge existing or publicly available prior to the patent application date.

Process (sometimes referred to as a "method"). A way of doing or making things that involves more than purely mental manipulations.

Provisional patent application (PPA). An interim document that clearly explains how to make and use the invention. The PPA is equivalent to a reduction to practice (see below). If a regular patent application is filed within one year of filing the PPA, the inventor can use the PPA's filing date for the purpose of deciding whether a reference is prior art. In addition to an early filing date, an inventor may claim patent pending status for the one-year period following the filing of the PPA.

Reissue application. An application used to correct information in a patent. It is usually filed when a patent owner believes the claims are not broad enough, the claims are too broad (the applicant discovered a new reference), or there are significant errors in the specification. In these cases, the applicant seeks to correct the patent by filing an application to get the applicant's original patent reissued at any time during its term. The reissue patent will take the place of the applicant's original patent and expire at the same time as the original patent would have expired. If the applicant wants to broaden the claims of the patent through a reissue application, the applicant must do so within two years from the date the original patent issued. There is a risk in filing a reissue application because all of the claims of the original patent will be examined and can be rejected.

Repair doctrine. Affirmative defense based on the right of an authorized licensor of a patented device to repair and replace unpatented components. It also includes the right to sell materials used to repair or replace a patented invention. The defense does not apply for completely rebuilt inventions, unauthorized inventions, or items that are made or sold without authorization of the patent owner.

Request for admission. Request to a party to a lawsuit to admit the truthfulness of a statement.

Request for Continued Examination (RCE). A paper filed when a patent applicant wishes to continue prosecuting an application that has received a final Office Action. Filing the RCE with another filing fee effectively removes the final action so that the applicant can submit further amendments, for example, new claims, new arguments, a new declaration, or new references.

Request for production of documents. A request by one party to a lawsuit for documents or other physical evidence in the possession of the other side.

Reverse doctrine of equivalents (or negative doctrine of equivalents). A rarely used affirmative defense to patent infringement in which, even if there is a literal infringement, the court will excuse the defendant's conduct if the infringing device has a different function or result than the patented invention. The doctrine is applied when the allegedly infringing device performs the same function in a substantially different way.

Sequence listing. An attachment to a patent application used if a biotech invention includes a sequence listing of a nucleotide or amino acid sequence. The applicant attaches this information on separate sheets of paper and refers to the sequence listing in the application (see PTO Rule 77). If there is no sequence listing, the applicant states "Nonapplicable."

Small entity. A status that enables small businesses, independent inventors, and nonprofit companies to pay a reduced application fee. There are three types of small entities: (1) independent inventors, (2) nonprofit companies, and (3) small businesses. To qualify, an independent inventor must either own all rights, or have transferred—or be obligated to transfer—rights to a small business or nonprofit organization. Nonprofit organizations are defined and listed in the Code of Federal Regulations and usually are educational institutions or charitable organizations. A small-entity business is one with fewer than 500 employees. The number of employees is computed by averaging the number of full- and part-time employees during a fiscal year.

Species. One of a group of related individual items collectively subordinate to a genus.

Specification. A patent application disclosure made by the inventor and drafted so that an individual skilled in the art to which the invention pertains could, when reading the patent, make and use the invention without needing further experiment. A specification is constructed of several sections. Collectively, these sections form a narrative that describes and distinguishes the invention. If it can later be proved that the inventor knew of a better way (or "best mode") and failed to disclose it, that failure could result in the loss of patent rights.

Statute of limitations. The legally prescribed time limit in which a lawsuit must be filed. In patent law, there is no time limit (statute of limitations)

for filing a patent infringement lawsuit, but monetary damages can only
be recovered for infringements committed during the six years prior
to the filing the lawsuit. For example, if a patent owner sues after ten
years of infringement, the owner cannot recover monetary damages for
the first four years of infringement. Despite the fact that there is no law
setting a time limit, courts will not permit a patent owner to sue for
infringement if the owner has waited an unreasonable time to file the
lawsuit ("laches").

Statutory Invention Registration (SIR). A document that allows an applicant
who abandons an application to prevent anyone else from getting a valid
patent on the same invention. This is accomplished by converting the
patent application to a SIR.

Statutory subject matter. An invention that falls into one of the five
statutory classes: process (method), machine, article of manufacture,
composition, or a "new use" of one of the first four.

Substitute application. Essentially a duplicate of an abandoned patent
application (see MPEP § 201.09). The disadvantage of a substitute
application is that the applicant doesn't get the benefit of the filing date
of the previously abandoned patent application, which could be useful,
because any prior art occurring after the filing date of the earlier case
can be used against the substitute case. If the applicant's substitute
application issues into a patent, the patent will expire 20 years from the
filing date of the substitute.

Successor liability. Responsibility for infringement that is borne by
a company that has purchased another company that is liable for
infringements. In order for successor liability to occur, there must be an
agreement between the companies to assume liability, the companies
must have merged, or the purchaser must be a "continuation" of the
purchased business. If the sale is made to escape liability and lacks any of
the foregoing characteristics, the successor will still be liable.

Summons. A document served with the complaint that tells the defendant
he or she has been sued, has a certain time limit in which to respond,
and must appear in court on a stated date.

Temporary restraining order (TRO). A court order that tells one party to
do or stop doing something—for example, to stop infringing. A TRO is

issued after the aggrieved party appears before a judge. Once the TRO is issued, the court holds a second hearing where the other side can tell his or her story and the court can decide whether to make the TRO permanent by issuing an injunction. The TRO is often granted *ex parte* (without allowing the other side to respond). For that reason, it is short in duration and only remains in effect until the court has an opportunity to schedule a hearing for the preliminary injunction.

Traverse. To argue against.

Tying. A form of patent misuse in which, as a condition of a transaction, the buyer of a patented device must also purchase an additional product. For example, in one case, a company had a patent on a machine that deposited salt tablets in canned food. Purchasers of the machine were also required to buy salt tablets from the patent owner. A party that commits patent misuse may have its patent invalidated, may have to pay monetary damages, or both.

Utility patent. The most common type of patent, which covers inventions that function in a unique manner to produce a utilitarian result.

Verified statement. A statement made under oath or a declaration. A false verified statement is punishable as perjury.

Vicarious liability. Legal responsibility that results when a business such as a corporation or partnership is liable for infringements committed by employees or agents. This liability attaches when the agent acts under the authority or direction of the business, an employee acts within the scope of employment, or the business benefits from, adopts, or approves the infringing activity.

Voir dire (Latin: speak the truth). Process by which attorneys and judges question potential jurors in order to determine whether they may be fair and impartial.

The Inventor's Notebook

The most reliable and useful way to document an invention is to use a permanently bound notebook with consecutively numbered pages, usually known as a lab notebook. Engineering and laboratory supply stores sell these notebooks—they usually include lines at the bottom of each page for the inventor and the witnesses to sign and date. A standard crackle-finish school notebook is also suitable, as long as the inventor numbers all of the pages consecutively and has each page or each invention description dated, signed, and witnessed.

The lab notebook usually includes:

- descriptions of the invention and its novel features
- procedures used in the building and testing of the invention
- drawings, photos, or sketches of the invention
- test results and conclusions
- discussions of any known prior-art references, and
- additional documentation, such as correspondence and purchase receipts.

Your entries should be handwritten and should accurately describe how events occurred. All entries should be dated on the date the entry is made or include an explanation for any delays in making an entry. The inventor should sign every entry. Computer printouts or other items that can't be entered directly in the notebook can be signed, dated, and witnessed, then pasted or affixed in the notebook in chronological order. Photos or other entries that can't be signed should be pasted in the notebook with a permanent adhesive and referenced by legends (descriptive words, such as "photo taken of machine in operation") written directly in the notebook, preferably with lead lines that extend from the notebook page over onto the photo—this will help you defeat a charge that the photos were substituted later. These pages should be signed, dated, and witnessed in the usual manner. An item covering an entire page should be referred to on an adjacent page. A sketch drawn in pencil should be photocopied and affixed in the inventor's notebook in order to preserve a permanent copy.

Notebook entries must be witnessed because your own testimony, even if supported by a properly completed notebook, might not be enough to prove an entry date.

The witnesses do more than verify your signature; they must actually read or view and understand the technical subject material in the notebook, including the actual tests of your invention, if they are witnessing the building and testing. For this reason, you must choose witnesses who have the ability or background to understand the invention. If your invention is a very simple mechanical device, practically anyone will have the technical qualifications to be a witness. But if it involves advanced chemical or electronic concepts, find witnesses with adequate background in the field. If called upon later, the witnesses must be able to testify to their own knowledge that the facts of the entry are correct.

General Electric rejected Raymond Damadian's ideas regarding magnetic resonance imaging (MRI) in the 1970s. Twenty years later, the Supreme Court ordered GE to pay Damadian $128.7 million for infringement of his MRI patents.

While one witness may be sufficient, two are preferred—this enhances the likelihood that at least one of them will be available to testify at a later date. If both are available, your case will be very strong.

Some notebooks already contain, on each page, a line for the inventor's signature and date, together with the words "Witnessed and Understood" with lines for two signatures and dates. If the inventor's notebook doesn't already contain these words and signature lines, write them in.

We have included sample notebook pages at the end of this section. To preserve the trade secret status of your invention, modify the end statement to read "The witness agrees to maintain the above confidential information and it is witnessed and understood."

TIP
You can purchase lab notebooks through Eureka Lab Book, Inc. (www.eurekalabbook.com) or Scientific Notebook Company (www.snco.com/index.htm).

Record of Conception of Invention

Title of invention:

"Orange Peeling Knife" or "knife that can score oranges through skin without cutting pulp."

Circumstances of conception:

On March 2 or 3 of this year, when visiting my sister Shirley Goldberger in Lancaster, PA, I decided to eat an orange just before we all went shopping. When I tried to score through the orange's skin to peel it, I cut too deeply, and the juice dripped onto my lap. It stained my new pants and embarrassed me in front of Shirley, my wife, and my mother. I had to change my pants, delaying everyone in the process.

After we eventually got in the car, I remarked that there must be a better way to score and peel oranges. The problem preoccupied me so much that I didn't go shopping; instead, I came up with a solution while waiting in my car for my family. I remember telling them, on the way back, "Why not make a knife with an adjustable blade stop so that the depth of the cut could be controlled? That way you wouldn't cut into the orange's pulp, it would be easier to peel, and it wouldn't drip."

I didn't make any record of the invention at that time since I didn't know I should until I read this book yesterday.

Purpose or problem solved:

To peel oranges (or grapefruits or pomelos), it is desirable to score them first, preferably with two encircling cuts that cross at the blossom and stem ends so that the skin can be neatly peeled off in quarters. However, this is difficult with an ordinary knife because one inevitably cuts past the skin into the pulp, making the orange drip and the peel difficult to remove without removing some of the pulp with it. The problem is compounded because the thickness of orange peels varies among varieties. A tool that could neatly score oranges with peels of various thicknesses without cutting into the pulp would solve the problem.

Invented by: _Edward R. Furman_   Date: _July 23, 20xx_

Invented by: _____ Date: _____

The above confidential information is witnessed and understood by:

Ruben Santiago   Date: _July 23, 20xx_

Date: _____

Record of Conception of Invention

Description and operation:

My knife will have a handle and blade similar to those on a conventional paring knife. Attached to each side of the blade, however, will be a strip of plastic or wood that will serve as a stop or fence to control the depth of cuts that can be made with the knife. These fences will be movable, allowing the depth of the cut to be varied by adjustments made to a thumbscrew that will be attached to the two fences. For thin-skinned oranges, the fences will be adjusted to permit a shallow cut, and for thick-skinned oranges, the fences will be adjusted to allow a deeper cut. In either case, the knife will be easily used to score through the skin completely around the orange without cutting deeper than the distance from the edge of the blade to the fences, and thus without cutting its pulp.

Invented by: _Edward R. Furman_   Date: _July 23, 20xx_

Invented by: _____   Date: _____

The above confidential information is witnessed and understood by:

Ruben Santiago   Date: _July 23, 20xx_

_____   Date: _____

Record of Conception of Invention

Drawing:

Invented by: _Edward R. Furman_____ Date: _July 23, 20xx_

Invented by: _____ Date: _____

The above confidential information is witnessed and understood by:

_Ruben Santiago_____ Date: _July 23, 20xx_

_____ Date: _____

Record of Conception of Invention

Ramifications:

Instead of adjustable stop strips on both sides of the blade, a fixed stop strip, on one
or both sides, can be used. This fixed stop strip can be mounted parallel to the edge,
or it can even be included on the edge so that the depth of cut can be controlled by
changing the longitudinal part of the blade that contacts the orange.

Novel features:

I have never seen or heard of any knife with a depth-of-cut controlling stop strip, much
less an adjustable one.

Closest known prior art:

I have seen orange peelers comprising a curved knife and a curved metal rod that is
inserted under the peel to move it around and free the peel from the pulp; and, of
course, conventional paring knives.

Advantages of my invention:

My knife is the only one that can cut through an orange's peel to any desired depth.
It makes peeling an orange neater, safer, and faster. All one has to do is score around
the skin with two encircling cuts and then peel off the four quarter peels, leaving a
peeled orange that is ready to segment and eat. The messy and difficult-to-use prior-
art methods, which involve cutting the orange in quarters and peeling off the pulp, are
tools that require skill to use and are not nearly as fast, neat, and easy to use as mine.

Invented by: _Edward R. Furman_ Date: _July 23, 20xx_

Invented by: _____ Date: _____

The above confidential information is witnessed and understood by:

Ruben Santiago Date: _July 23, 20xx_

Date: _____

Attorneys

nventor Maurice Kanbar had a strong 35-year relationship with his patent attorney, Mike Ebert. In his book, *Secrets from an Inventor's Notebook* (Council Oak), Kanbar wrote, "Most basically, you need to be able to communicate with your attorney. I can call Mike on the phone, describe my idea and detail its mechanics, and Mike will 'get it' instantly and start writing it up. If an attorney has a different understanding of your invention, or if he or she doesn't quickly get your drift, go elsewhere."

Finding an Attorney

There are two groups of attorneys for inventors: those licensed to practice before the USPTO (patent attorneys) and those who are not. You should consult a patent attorney for assistance performing patent searching, drafting a provisional or regular patent application, responding to patent examiners, and dealing with the USPTO. An attorney does not have to be licensed to practice before the USPTO in order to enforce your patent in a court case. We recommend that you use a patent attorney to prepare or analyze patent-related agreements on your behalf—for example, to prepare invention assignments, license agreements, or coinventorship agreements.

The best way to get a referral to a good patent lawyer is to talk to other people who have actually used a particular lawyer's services. The worst is to comb through advertisements or unscreened lists of lawyers provided by a local bar association or the phone company.

Local bar associations often maintain and advertise lawyer referral services. However, a lawyer can usually get on this list simply by volunteering. Very little (if any) screening is done to find out whether the lawyers are any good. Similarly, advertisements in the yellow pages, in newspapers, on television, or online say nothing meaningful about a lawyer's skills or manner—just that he or she could afford to pay for the ad. In many states, lawyers can advertise any specialization they choose— even if they have never handled a case in that area of law.

Leo Baekeland was seeking an artificial substitute for shellac but the durable resin that resulted from his research—a substance called Bakelite—became the first commercially successful plastic.

If you are having difficulty locating an attorney knowledgeable about inventions and patent law, check out the American Intellectual Property

Law Association (AIPLA) (www.aipla.org) or the Intellectual Property Law Association of the American Bar Association (www.abanet.org). The USPTO website (www.uspto.gov) also maintains a list of attorneys and patent agents licensed to practice before the USPTO.

Keeping Fees Down

Patent and intellectual property attorneys generally charge $250 to $500 per hour, and a full-blown patent lawsuit can run to hundreds or even thousands of hours' work, before it even goes to trial.

> U.S. citizens sent 300 million emails a day in 1995. Seven years later they sent 8 billion emails a day.

To save yourself a lot of money and grief, follow these tips.

Keep it short. If you are paying your attorney on an hourly basis, keep your conversations short—the meter is always running. Avoid making several calls a day; instead, consolidate your questions and ask them all in one conversation.

Get a fee agreement. Always get a written fee agreement when dealing with an attorney. Read it and make sure you can understand it. Your fee agreement should give you the right to an itemized billing statement that details the work done and time spent. Some state statutes and bar associations require a written fee agreement—for example, California requires that attorneys provide a written agreement when the fee will exceed $1,000.

Review billings carefully. Your lawyer's bill should be clear. Do not accept summary billings, such as the single phrase "litigation work," to explain a block of time for which you are billed a great deal of money.

Watch out for hidden expenses. Find out what expenses you will have to pay. Don't let your attorney bill you for services such as word processing or administrative services. This means you will be paying the secretary's salary. Also beware of fax and copying charges. Some firms charge clients per page for incoming and outgoing faxes.

Remember, you can always fire your lawyer. (You're still obligated to pay outstanding bills, though.) If you don't respect and trust your attorney's professional abilities, you should find a new attorney. But switching attorneys is a nuisance, and you may lose time and money.

Resources

Inventor Resources

The following Internet links provide information and assistance to independent inventors:

- **Intellectual Property Owners (IPO)** (www.ipo.org). An association that serves owners of patents, trademarks, copyrights, and trade secrets. It is the sponsor of the National Inventor of the Year Award.
- **Invention Convention** (www.inventionconvention.com). The National Congress of Inventor Organizations (NCIO) and its executive director, Stephen Paul Gnass, maintain this invention website that includes links, trade show information, and advice for inventors.
- **InventNet Forum** (www.inventnet.com). Provides an online forum and mailing list if you wish to contact other inventors.
- **Inventor's Digest Online** (www.inventorsdigest.com). Publishes online information and a print publication for independent inventors ($36/year U.S./$60/year international). Includes articles on new inventions, licensing and marketing, and advertisements from reputable inventor promotion companies.
- **Minnesota Inventors Congress** (www.invent1.org). One of the oldest and most respected inventor organizations.
- **National Technology Transfer Center (NTTC)** (www.nttc.edu) at Wheeling Jesuit University. Helps entrepreneurs and companies looking to access federally funded research and development activity at U.S. universities.
- *Patents and Business* (www.intellectualpropertylawfirms.com). Sponsored by Nolo, this site provides essential information for anyone in the invention business.
- **USPTO Independent Inventor Resources** (www.uspto.gov). Click "Patents" on the left side, then click "Main" and then click "Inventor Resources" under "eBusiness." In 1999, the PTO established a new office aimed at providing services and support to independent inventors. The PTO expects to eventually offer seminars and expanded educational opportunities for inventors.
- **Ronald J. Riley's Inventor Resources** (www.inventored.org). Comprehensive links and advice for inventors.

- **Software Patent Institute** (www.spi.org). Maintains and catalogs a software prior-art database.
- **United Inventors Association (UIA)** (www.uiausa.org). A national inventors' organization.

Internet Patent-Searching Resources

In addition to the resources in Chapter 3, check out these Internet sites:

- **Delphion** (www.delphion.com) provides fee-based services. Delphion's searchable database of U.S. patents goes back to 1971 (versus 1976 at the USPTO); you can also search the front pages of European patents and other internationally published patent applications. Delphion delivers U.S. patents and permits you to search text of international patents.
- **International patents** can be located on the Internet. Try Espacenet. com (www.espacenet.com), where you can access a worldwide database available to the European Patent Office examiners (63 countries are covered).
- **LexPat** (www.lexis-nexis.com) is a commercial database of U.S. patents searchable from 1971 to the present. In addition, the LEXPAT library offers extensive prior-art searching capability through its collection of technical journals and magazines.
- **Micropatent** (www.micropatent.com) provides a commercial database of U.S. patents allegedly searchable from 1836 to the present. (Be warned—the U.S. patents before 1971 have been entered into the database by optical character recognition and are packed with errors.) The site also includes Japanese and International PCT patent applications from 1983, European patents from 1988, and the *Official Gazette (Patents)*.
- **Patent Fetcher** (www.patentfetcher.com) is a website that allows you to download a PDF of a U.S. patent or published patent application.
- **Patent Hunter** (www.patenthunter.com) is a software program from Patent Wizard that downloads patents from the USPTO website and places them on your computer in an easy-to-use listing. It can also perform searches of the USPTO patent database.

- **QPAT** (www.qpat.com) and Questel/Orbit (www.questel.orbit.com) provide access to the QPAT database that includes U.S. patents searchable from 1974 to the present and full-text European A (1987–present) and B (1991–present) patents.
- **Software Patent Institute** (www.spi.org) provides a comprehensive database of prior-art references for software, such as computer manuals and older textbooks, journal articles, conference proceedings, computer science theses, and other such materials.
- **Thesaurus Resource.** You can speed the process of finding search terms by using a thesaurus or a flip dictionary. Online, try Merriam-Webster.com (www.m-w.com), Dictionary.com (www.dictionary.com), or YourDictionary.com (www.yourdictionary.com).
- **Thomas Register.** The Thomas Register (www.thomasregister.com) can enhance your prior-art searching by providing you with images from thousands of company catalogs as well as providing websites, CAD imagery (computer-assisted drawings), and other product information.

Assessing Foreign Patent Potential

Consult the following resources when deciding whether to pursue foreign patent rights:

- **EUBusiness** (www.eubusiness.com) is a reliable source of information for facts and statistics on EU economy and specific industries.
- **European Patent Office** (www.epo.org) provides links to patent-licensing exchanges, mailing lists, patent information providers, registered European patent agents, law offices, and patent offices for member states.
- **The Federation of International Trade Associations** (FITA) (www.fita.org/webindex/index.html) has many international business and trade links, leads, statistics, and other helpful information.
- **The U.S. Department of Commerce** (DOC) (www.doc.gov) and the **U.S. Small Business Administration** (SBA) (www.sbaonline.sba.gov) are interested in helping the sales of U.S. goods overseas. If an inventor has a good track record and the possibility of actually placing a product in the market (or already has a product and is seeking to market it overseas), the DOC and SBA offer assistance.

Index

A

Abstract, 71, 73

Acknowledgment receipt, 145–146

Advantages of invention, 72, 76–77, 120–122

Advertising system for airport
  patent for, 298, 304–309
  provisional patent application, 299–303

Agreements, invention-related, 384
  assignment, 384, 402–403
  assignment, preinvention, 35, 36–37
  attorney's help with, 440
  authority to sign, 384
  joint ownership agreement, 384, 391–397
  model maker/artist agreement, 384, 398–401
  nondisclosure agreement, 10, 85, 384–390
  signing instructions for, 385

Alternative embodiments, 130–131. *See also* Improvements to invention; Ramifications of invention

Application Data Sheet, 141–143, 151

Application number, 145

Articles of manufacture, 41

Artist
  hired to create drawings, 98, 106
  written agreement with, 384, 385, 398–401

Art projectors, 103–104

Assignee
  listed in online filing, 142
  micro entity fees and, 144, 152

Assignment, 384, 402–403
  preinvention, 35, 36–37
  signing, 384, 385

Attorneys. *See* Patent attorneys

B

Baby Tears. *See* Doll with LED-simulated tears

Bag of parts analysis, 29

Beer, pasteurization of
  patent for, 14–15, 40, 169, 171–173
  provisional patent application, 14, 17, 170

Best mode, 130
  of software inventions, 111

Board game, pre-Monopoly
  patent for, 289, 293–297
  provisional patent application, 290–292

Bulleted lists, 131–132

Credit Card Payment Form, 146,
153, 154
Cross-licensing, 49
Crying doll. *See* Doll with LED-
simulated tears
Customer number, 142, 143, 145, 151

D
Date of invention, 10
Decision whether to file PPA, 24–26
classes of utility patents and,
39–42
employed inventor and, 35–38
inventor's identity and, 32–35
marketability and. *See* Commercial
potential
nonobviousness and, 44–45
novelty and, 43
after preliminary search, 83
toy inventor's consideration of,
45–46
usefulness and, 38–39
Dependent claims, 74–75
Description, 71–72. *See also*
Specification of PPA
Design patents, 6, 39
classification of, 58
PPA not available for, 16
Dictionaries, 124, 446
visual, 107
Disclosure. *See* Public disclosure of
invention
Docket number, 142, 143
Documentation in notebook, 34–35,
433–438
record of searches in, 55

Dogpile.com, 80
Doll with LED-simulated tears
drawings of, 112–114
filing PPA, 165
initial problems, 21–22
patent hurdles, 45–46
patent searching, 86–87
Draftsperson, 106. *See also* Artist
Drawings
basic principles of, 92–96
figure numbers on, 95
filing by mail, 147, 151, 155
filing online, 141, 142, 144
flowcharts, 97, 99, 108–111
found in patent search, 56
of inventor who can draw, 98,
103–104
of inventor who can't draw, 98,
99–103, 105–107
of inventor without prototype, 98,
105–107
of inventor with prototype, 98,
99–104
paper for, 94
photographs used for, 98, 99–103
planning of, 96–99
in preparing specification, 72, 92,
117, 122–123, 124–128
reference numbers on, 95–96, 124,
125–128
requirements for, 91
schematics, 99, 108–109
sheet numbers on, 95
usually necessary, 91
views in, 92–94, 96–98, 122–123
Drawing sheets, 94, 95

⚖ NOLO *Online Legal Forms*

Nolo offers a large library of legal solutions and forms, created by Nolo's in-house legal staff. These reliable documents can be prepared in minutes.

Create a Document

- **Incorporation.** Incorporate your business in any state.
- **LLC Formations.** Gain asset protection and pass-through tax status in any state.
- **Wills.** Nolo has helped people make over 2 million wills. Is it time to make or revise yours?
- **Living Trust (avoid probate).** Plan now to save your family the cost, delays, and hassle of probate.
- **Trademark.** Protect the name of your business or product.
- **Provisional Patent.** Preserve your rights under patent law and claim "patent pending" status.

Download a Legal Form

Nolo.com has hundreds of top quality legal forms available for download—bills of sale, promissory notes, nondisclosure agreements, LLC operating agreements, corporate minutes, commercial lease and sublease, motor vehicle bill of sale, consignment agreements and many more.

Review Your Documents

Many lawyers in Nolo's consumer-friendly lawyer directory will review Nolo documents for a very reasonable fee. Check their detailed profiles at **Nolo.com/lawyers**.

On Nolo.com you'll also find:

Books & Software

Nolo publishes hundreds of great books and software programs for consumers and business owners. Order a copy, or download an ebook version instantly, at Nolo.com.

Online Legal Documents

You can quickly and easily make a will or living trust, form an LLC or corporation, apply for a trademark or provisional patent, or make hundreds of other forms—online.

Free Legal Information

Thousands of articles answer common questions about everyday legal issues including wills, bankruptcy, small business formation, divorce, patents, employment, and much more.

Plain-English Legal Dictionary

Stumped by jargon? Look it up in America's most up-to-date source for definitions of legal terms, free at nolo.com.

Lawyer Directory

Nolo's consumer-friendly lawyer directory provides in-depth profiles of lawyers all over America. You'll find all the information you need to choose the right lawyer.

PEND7